GOVERNED BY OPINION

INTERNATIONAL LIBRARY OF
HISTORICAL STUDIES

SERIES ISBN 1 86064 079 6

Governed by Opinion

*Politics, Religion and the
Dynamics of Communication
in Stuart London
1637–1645*

by

Dagmar Freist

Tauris Academic Studies
I.B.Tauris Publishers
LONDON · NEW YORK

Published in 1997 by Tauris Academic Studies
an imprint of I.B.Tauris & Co. Ltd
Victoria House, Bloomsbury Square, London WC1B 4DZ
175 Fifth Avenue, New York, NY 10010

In the United States and Canada distributed by
St Martin's Press, 175 Fifth Avenue, New York, NY 10010

A full CIP record for this book is available
from the British Library

A full CIP record for this book is available
from the Library of Congress

ISBN 1 86064 110 5

Set in Original Garamond BT by Thomas Adolph, Freiburg (Germany)
Printed and bound in Great Britain by WBC Ltd, Bridgend, Mid Glamorgan

CONTENTS

For my Parents
Bernhard and Hannelore

Acknowledgements

Many people have helped me write this book, and I would like to thank them all.

Most of the original research was conducted while writing my PhD, *The Formation of Opinion and the Communication Network in London 1637 to c. 1645*, which I submitted to Cambridge University in January 1992. For the book I have undertaken new research, and I have entirely rewritten and restructured the manuscript, adding new chapters that have not previously appeared.

I acknowledge with gratitude the support I have received from various scholarships while undertaking my original research: the Evangelische Studienwerk Villigst e.V.; the German Historical Institute in London; the Prince Consort and Thirlwall Fund; and the Archbishop Cranmer Fund.

The staff of the various record offices, archives and libraries I visited deserve a special mention for their assistance: the Bodleian Library, Oxford; Worcester College Library, Oxford; the University Library, Cambridge; the British Museum and the British Library, London; the University Library, Freiburg; the Corporation of London Record Office; the Greater London Record Office; the Guildhall; and the Public Record Office, London.

Very special thanks go to Bob Scribner and John Morrill for their encouragement to write this book, and for their support, inspiration, critical comments and suggestions. Both were always there when I needed advice, and I am most grateful for this. Amy Erickson, Ann Hughes, John Morrill, and Bob Scribner I thank most warmly for reading the manuscript and making perceptive comments. A big thank you goes to Angela Davies who read the final draft of the manuscript. In the I.B. Tauris editorial team, I am grateful to Lester Crook and the anonymous reader of my manuscript for their encouraging support. I would also like to thank Thomas Adolph, who prepared the camera-ready copy for this book.

At different stages of my research, various people and friends inspired me in many discussions, and I would like to thank Amy

Erickson, Tim Harris, Don McKenzie, John Morrill, Lyndal Roper, Ulinka Rublack, Ernst Schulin, Bob Scribner, Tim Stretton and Helen Weinstein. Finally, I cannot adequately thank my husband Thomas Held and our children Jonas and Rahel for their support, curiosity, and patience.

List of Abbreviations

Arber, Transcript	*A Transcript of the Company of Stationers of London 1554-1640 ed. E. Arber (5 vols., London, 1875-94)*
Ashm	*Ashmole, volume of verses ballads, carols, libels etc. in Manuscript in the Bodleian Library, Oxford*
BL	*British Library*
BM	*British Museum*
CJ	*Journals of the House of Commons*
C.L.R.O.	*Corporation London Record Office*
Douce	*Francis Douce collection of prints and drawings in the Bodleian Library, Oxford*
DNB	*Dictionary of National Biography*
Firth	*Firth collection of ballads in the Bodleian Library, Oxford*
G.L.R.O.	*Greater London Record Office*
EHR	*English Historical Review*
Harl.	*Harleian Manuscripts*
H.L.M.P.	*House of Lords Main Papers*
Jeaffreson	*Middlesex County Records ed. John Cordy Jeaffreson (Old Series), III, 1622-1667 Greater London Council (London, 1974)*
KB	*King's Bench*
LJ	*Journals of the House of Lords*
MJ/GDB	*Gaol Delivery Books, Middlesex*
MJ/GDR	*Gaol Delivery Rolls, Middlesex*
MJ/SPB	*Sessions of the Peace and Oyer and Terminer Books, Middlesex*
MJ/SPR	*Sessions of the Peace Rolls, Middlesex*
PRO	*Public Record Office, London*
Prob.	*Probate*
Rep. of the Aldermen	*Repertories of the Aldermen*
SP West R.	*Session of the Peace Rolls, Westminster*
SP	*State Papers*

Stat. Court Book C.	*Stationers' Hall, Court Books*
Surrey Assi	*Surrey Assize Records*
TRHS	*Transactions of the Royal Historical Society*
Wood	*Anthony Wood Collection of Ballads in the Bodleian Library, Oxford*

Note: *In quoting from seventeenth-century sources I have retained the original spelling although I have extended contemporary contractions and occasionally supplied punctuation necessary to the sense of the passage. Dates are given with the year regarded as beginning on 1 January.*

List of Illustrations

1 · Introduction

> In the meane space (amongst mutable and contentious spirits) Reli-
> gion is made a Hotch-porch, and as it were tost in a Blanquet, and
> too many places of England too much Amsterdamnified by severall
> opinions; Religion is now become the common discourse and Table-
> talke in every Taverne and Ale-house, where a man shall hardly find
> five together in one minde, and yet one presumes he is in the right.[1]

Among the various reasons given by contemporaries in mid-
seventeenth-century England why the 'world [was] turned upside down' was the freedom with which people expressed their
opinions on political and religious issues. The main charge in
various criticisms of public opinion was that of meddling with
things above one's calling, thus breaking rules of proper conduct, and spreading false news and lies. In 1641, a pamphleteer
argued that 'the dissenting and disagreeing in matter of opinion
together with the sundry sorts of Sects, now raving and reigning,
being the maine causes of the disturbance and hinderance of
the Common-wealth ... It is easier to reckon up all the Species
and kinds of nature, than to describe all the Sects, Divisions,
and opinions in Religion that is now in London'.[2] Another
claimed '(Be)cause one Opinion many doth devise And propa-
gate till infinite they bee ... Opinions found in everie house and

1   John Taylor, *Religion's Enemies* (1641), BL E.176.7.
2   *The dolefull Lamentation of Cheapside-Crosse: Or old England sick of the Stag-
      gers* (1641), BL E.134.9.

streete'.³ A third was convinced that the disagreement on opinions was the main reason for social unrest and disorder.⁴ In support of the Jesuits, the devil in one pamphlet proposed: 'Ile scat-
ter strange Hereticall opinions, In every corner of the Lands
Dominions.'⁵ In 1648, *Mercurius Pacificus* wrote 'Divided as far
as Hounds and Hares in antipathizing disaffection: Heads divided in opinions, like those of the Serpent Amphibena, one fighting with another, hearts divided, like fire and water, tongues divided, as still in Babel's confusion, hands divided'.⁶

Public opinion was usually held to be the opposite of truth
and justice, a conception which might account for the immense
concern caused by the spread of opinions down the social scale,
which, in this reading, implied the spread of lies, and the undermining of morality: 'Truth is made the object of every contentious fancy, and so becomes opinion.'⁷ The eyes of Justice, one
of the cardinal virtues, are blurred; she can neither see nor hear
properly, and thus 'Superstitious Ielousies' are framed that 'breed
distaste twixt Subjects and the King ... They scarcely shall beleeve,
or trust each other'.⁸ This theme is further developed in a broadside entitled *The World Is Ruled And Governed by Opinion*.⁹
Here, the author expresses his criticism of public opinion through
a gendered political symbolism which employed the well-known
negative connotations of women's talk. The broadside featured
a woodcut presenting Opinion as a female figure 'majestically'

3   Henry Peacham with an engraving by Wenceslaus Hollar, *The World is Ruled
     and Governed by Opinion* (1641), British Museum, Department of Prints and
     Drawings BM 272. See book jacket.
4   *Lucifer's Lucky Or, The Devil's new Creature* (1641), BL E.180.3.
5   John Taylor, *A Delicate, Dainty, Damnable Dialogue Between the Devill and a
     Jesuite* (1642), BL E.142.8.
6   Cit. in Sharon Achinstein, 'The Politics of Babel in the English Revolution', in
     Pamphlet Wars. Prose in the English Revolution, ed. James Holstun (London,
     1992), pp 14–44, p 19.
7   *The dolefull Lamentation*.
8   *A Delicate Dialogue*.
9   *The World Is Ruled*. See also Achinstein, 'Politics', p 20–2.

seated in a tree. At first sight she resembles Iustitia, but a closer look reveals that it is an inversion. Her eyes are blinded, the tower of Babel decorates her head, and a chameleon sits on her arm. Each of these tokens symbolizes a different aspect of confusion: the inability to see what is just and right, the unintelligibility of what is said, and opinions changing according to fashion, not truth. The text confirms that Opinion 'cannot as cleare judgement see' or tell the truth because of pride, self-conceit and folly. In her lap rests the globe, which she rules with a long stick, and from the tree fall numerous well-known pamphlets of the period. A fool waters the tree, nourishing the production of more false news and opinions.

Similarly, the woodcut on the title page of a pamphlet called *Square Caps Turned Into Roundheads* personifies Opinion as a woman who turns the wheel of fortune.[10] On top of the wheel are five Roundheads (a derogatory term for the Puritans), and below are five hats symbolizing the bishops. Through the influence of Opinion they were transformed into nonconformists, that is 'Roundheads'. In the ensuing dialogue between Time and Opinion, the former defends the good deeds of the bishops and presses Opinion to reconsider her views and to turn the wheel again to move the bishops back to the top – something Opinion refuses to do. In one of the many printed assaults on the 'water-poet' John Taylor for his alleged royalist sympathies, Henry Walker accused him of being the help-mate of 'Satan'. A woodcut shows the water-poet lying flat on his back in a boat with a winged she-devil with long dangling bosoms sitting on top of him.[11] Taylor grabs her tail, while the monster 'squirts' into his mouth. The symbolism here is almost a conglomerate of all possible negative connotations: the devil, its female naked shape and

---

10 *Square Caps Turned Into Roundheads, Or the Bishops Vindication, And the Brownists Conviction. Being a Dialogue between Time, and Opinion* (1642), BL E. 149.1. See picture section.
11 Henry Walker, *Taylors Physicke has Purged the Divel* (1641), BL E. 163.9.

scatological elements. Taylor's poetry was the result not merely of the devil's influence, but of the 'squirt' of a female devil who shamelessly displays her nakedness. Walker further exploits the imagery of base talk with its female and sexual connotations when comparing Taylor's language with that of 'any scould or fishwoman at Billingsgate'.

The negative female personification of 'opinion' in the 1640s was influenced by the familiar image of women as 'scolds', 'shrews' and 'gossips', who violated the social order with their loathing, lust and lies. Throughout early seventeenth-century England, negative images of women time and again furnish political symbolism equating opponents with women's vices and sexuality, a phenomenon which will be discussed in subsequent chapters at greater length. Public opinion thus threatened to turn society upside down, to leave it bereft of its traditional hierarchies and rules. Accordingly, a people 'governed by opinion' lacked any sense of truth, justice, deference, order, and morality. Hand in hand with these conceptions of 'opinion' went the belief that the common people were more interested in rumours, sensational gossip, and false news than in truth. Authors and printers were accused of catering for these tastes, and the discourse against the press gained momentum by comparing the protagonists of the booktrade with stereotypes of female vices, too.

Official concern at the effects of news circulation and the spread of opinions is not a seventeenth-century invention. It can be traced back, in fact, to the first *Statute of Westminster* in 1275 which ruled that 'from henceforth none be so hardy to tell or publish any false News or Tales, whereby discord ... may grow between the King and his People, or the Great Men of the Realm'.[12] Subsequent statutes followed the same pattern of outlawing the publication and spread of false news, which was

---

12   3 Edw. I Stat. Westm. prim. c. 34 A.D. 1275.

thought to cause discord, subversion and, ultimately, rebellion.[13] However, there were differences in meaning and significance. Legislation dealing, broadly speaking, with what people had said was occupied with 'seditious words' and with the assessment of the truth of what had been said or published and its degree of subversion. Hence the description in statutes of unruly popular 'utterances' as 'false, horrible, malicious, vile, unseemely, heynous, phantasticall, lies, seditious and slanderous'.[14] Furthermore, the emphasis was laid on individual instances of misconduct that had to be dealt with.

In contrast, the discourse on public opinion that became so predominant in the seventeenth century dealt with the cultural phenomenon of communication processes and their impact on society and politics. It thus marked a great historical shift away from the concern with individual or group misbehaviour and rebellion to a growing awareness of a new social force, the emergence of the public sphere. The voicing of opinions by ordinary men and women on state affairs threatened the monopoly of secular and divine authority as the sole interpreter of politics. In fact, as Habermas has righly argued, it is in the very nature of public opinion to pose a potential challenge to authority.[15] At the same

---

13 2 Ric. II. 1. c. 5. A.D. 1378; 1 & 2 Phil. & Mar. c. 3. A.D. 1554–1555; 23 Eliz. c. 2. A.D. 1580–81. Throughout, the statutes become increasingly specific about the ways news was spread, namely by means of speaking, carving, writing, printing, or simply by dispersion. Statutes thus tend to reflect the complexity of communication in the early modern period.

14 Compare the respective statutes of the realm as quoted above. On the problem of the truth value of what had been said or published and its legal implications see Philip Hamburger, 'The Development of the Law of Seditious Libel and the Control of the Press', *Stanford Law Review*, 37 (1984–1985), pp 661–765.

15 Jürgen Habermas, *The Structural Transformation of the Public Sphere*, tr. Thomas Burger and Frederick Lawrence (Cambridge, Mass., 1989), first published in Germany as *Strukturwandel der Öffentlichkeit* (Darmstadt, 1962). Also Andreas Würgler, *Unruhen und Öffentlichkeit. Städtische und ländliche Protestbewegungen im 18. Jahrhundert*, Frühneuzeitforschungen, 1 (Tübingen, 1995), p 41.

time public opinion divided those in power. John Bond observed in 1642 that 'the inumerable multitude of pamphlets ... highly incensed' the Parliament against the King.[16] It was this characteristic which was recognized by contemporaries and reflected in the negative discourse on the public sphere. The tension public opinion created between ruler and ruled, and the implicit emancipation of the people was unprecedented in history. Throughout the crisis-ridden seventeenth century, politics spilled over into everyday life, and people readily discussed the issues they were confronted with.

Contemporary theories of the state in the seventeenth century were modelled on the ideal of the patriarchal family which implied the authority of the father and the submission of children and women.[17] Social equilibrium was seen to depend on the unquestioned authority of a (divine) ruler, the 'family patriarch', and the submission of subjects, like women and children in the family. Read in this context, it is not surprising to find an equation of opinion with women and female vices. Seventeenth-century conduct books and marriage manuals and, on a more popular scale, proverbs and ballads, throughout emphasized silence as the 'best ornament of women'.[18] Women were to refrain from any 'discourse of state matters' or 'high points of divinity' since not understanding them 'they would intangle others of equall understanding to themselves'.[19] Speech in public, especially with strangers, was not appropriate for women, whose voice was no less to be dreaded than their nakedness.[20] The negative represen-

16   John Bond, *The Poet's Recantation having suffered in the Pillorie* (London, 1642).
17   One of the most prolific writers was Sir Robert Filmer. See Peter Laslett (ed.), *Patriarcha and Other Political Works by Sir Robert Filmer* (Oxford, 1949).
18   *A Collection of English Proverbs* (Cambridge, 1670), p 24. See also Ruth Kelso, *Doctrine for the Lady of the Renaissance* (Urbana, 1956), p 50.
19   Richard Braithwait, *The English Gentlewoman, Drawne out to the Full Body: Expressing what Habilliments do Best Attire her, What Ornaments Do best Adorn her, What Complements Do Best Accomplish her* (London, 1631).
20   Kelso, *Doctrine*, p 101.

tations of women's speech with their subtexts of social disorder which flourished in the seventeenth century thus became a metaphor for a major political and cultural transition within the social hierarchy through the emergence of the public sphere, which also affected gender relations.

This shift is not without its history, and it is closely linked with the rise of the printing press, and with the professionalization of the news trade in the early seventeenth century, which made news items available to a broader section of society. Furthermore, the growing emphasis put upon conflicting cases of 'private conscience and public duty', which greatly influenced social and gender relations in the seventeenth century, played a central part in the formation of independent political and religious judgements by ordinary men and women.[21] 'The generally accepted view was that any person unlucky enough to be caught in a dilemma which made it difficult to know how to act should follow the dictates of his or her conscience.'[22] In the majority of these cases religious beliefs played a vital role and influenced political judgement. Especially the question of whether or not personal religious convictions could justify fighting the King weighed heavily on people's minds and frequently cropped up in conversation and popular prints. Likewise, problems arose from conflicting duties owed to divine authority and to God. Quite often, women were caught between 'wifely duties' and 'religious duties'. Since obedience to God came first, different views on religion could strain marital relations. The growing emphasis on private con-

---

21 See the essays in John Morrill, Paul Slack and Daniel Woolf (eds.), *Public Duty and Private Conscience in Seventeenth-Century England. Essays Presented to Gerald E. Aylmer* (Oxford, 1993).

22 Keith Thomas, 'Cases of Conscience in Seventeenth-Century England', in *Public Duty*, ed. Morrill et al, pp 29–56, p 30. For a different approach see Kaspar von Greyerz, *Vorsehungsglaube und Kosmologie*, Publications of the German Historical Institute, 25 (Göttingen/Zurich, 1990). Greyerz emphasizes the individual relationship with God in the pursuit of salvation throughout the seventeenth century in England.

science granted women some independence in religious issues.[23] These 'cases of conscience' strongly influenced people's ability and willingness to form their own individual opinions and codes of behaviour, an attitude which informed everyday discussions of politics and religion.

Important factors that stimulated the whole printing and publishing profession in England anew were, firstly, the foundation of the news syndicate in 1622, which regulated the production of the first newsbooks on a popular scale. These early newsbooks were, however, restricted to printing foreign news only, by a Star Chamber ban on domestic reporting, which was in force until 1641.[24] Secondly, the professionalization of news circulation through private entrepreneurs played a vital role in making news accessible outside the closed circles at court and among the nobility, who had been always well informed by newsletters and other means of communication.[25]

Ben Jonson was one of the first distinct commentators on these developments. In 1620, he scored a major success with his masque *Newes from the New World*, which was a parody of the circulation and fabrication of news.[26] Five years later, increasingly fearful of popular influences on government, Jonson vilified the commercialization of the news trade and the economic

---

23 Patricia Crawford, 'Public Duty, Conscience, and Women in Early Modern England', in *Public Duty*, ed. John Morrill et al, pp 57–76.

24 Joseph Frank, *The Beginning of the English Newspaper* (Cambridge, Mass., 1961); Frank S. Siebert, *Freedom of the Press in England, 1476–1776* (Urbana, 1952).

25 Richard Cust, 'News and Politics in Early Seventeenth Century England', *Past and Present*, 52 (1985), pp 60–90; Michael Frearson, *The English Corantos of the 1620s* (Cambridge University PhD, 1993); J. Crofts, *Packhorse, Waggon and Post. Land Carriage and Communications under the Tudors and Stuarts* (London, 1967). For the spread of news among the learned see F. J. Levy, 'How Information Spread among the Gentry, 1550–1640', *Journal of British Studies*, xxi (1982), pp 20–4.

26 Ben Jonson, *Newes from the New World* (1620), reprinted in *The Complete Masques*, ed. Stephen Orgel (New Haven and London, 1969), pp 292–305.

exploitation of language in his play *The Staple of News*.[27] Echoing widely felt worries, he characterized the press as a symbol of mass ignorance exploiting people's curiosity by feeding them with dazzling rumours, sensational gossip, and exciting lies rather than educating them in morality and virtue as the dramatic poet had done on the stage. The contrast Jonson

> draws is not between a responsible and an irresponsible press, but between poets and news-vendors, ideal truth and that literal falsehood or competing fantasy of news made like "the times Newes, (a weekly cheat to draw money) and [it] could not be fitter reprehended, then in raising this ridiculous Office of the Staple, wherein the age may see her own folly, or hunger and thirst after [not righteousness, but] publish'd pamphlets of Newes, set out every Saturday, but made all at home, & no syllable of truth in them".[28]

In his critique of *The Staple of News*, McKenzie has pointed to Jonson's deep conservatism blinding him to the chance inherent in the development of a communication network which comprised the whole of society and laid the foundations for 'a new language of conscience and independent political judgement'.[29] He argues that '*The Staple of News* marks the end of the theatre as the only secular mass medium, the end of the playhouse as the principal forum of public debate, the end of the actors' popular function as the abstracts and brief chronicles of the time. The dramatic poet, as rhetor in the truest sense, had lost his vocation to a journalist'.[30]

In word and in image, the Tower of Babel was a strong metaphor for the disquieting effects of public opinion. Throughout,

---

27 *The Staple of News* (1625), ed. Anthony Parr (Manchester and New York, 1988).

28 Don F. McKenzie, '"The Staple of News" and the late Plays of Ben Jonson', in *A Celebration of Ben Jonson*, Papers presented at the University of Toronto in October 1972, ed. William Blissett, J. Patrick and Richard W. van Fossen (Toronto, 1973), pp 83–128, p 124.

29 Ibid., p 107.

30 Ibid., p 126.

'the metaphor of Babel was used in Royalist Civil War pamphlets to register horror at the fact of political disagreement [and the] participation of many different voices in political debate'.[31] Mutual understanding was lost 'at the tower of Babel', wrote Hobbes in 1651, 'when by the hand of God, every man was stricken for his rebellion, with an oblivion of his former language'.[32] 'Seditious doctrines', such as 'that every private man is Judge of Good and Evill', were poisoning the commonwealth, so Hobbes thought.[33] Consequently, men were disposed 'to debate with themselves, and dispute the commands of the Common-wealth; and afterwards to obey, or disobey them, as in their private judgements they shall think fit'.[34] In contrast, John Milton envisaged an emancipated people which would be able to appropriate and judge opinions independent of any authoritarian guideline. In his controversial *Areopagitica*, Milton, who himself had just become the victim of censorship, wrote:

> Truth and understanding are not such wares as to be monopoliz'd and traded in by tickets and statutes, and standards. Nor is it to the common people lesse then a reproach; for if we be so jealous over them, as that we dare not trust them with an English pamphlet, what doe we but censure them for a giddy, vitious, and ungrounded people; in such a sick and weak estate of faith and discretion, as to be able to take nothing down but through the pipe of a licenser.[35]

Similarly, John Lilburne believed that a free press implied a free public. He argued that those who would restrict the press sought to 'supress every thing which hath any true Declaration of the

---

31   Achinstein, 'Politics', p 17–8.
32   Thomas Hobbes, 'Of Speech', in *Leviathan* (London, 1651), ed. Crawford B. Macpherson (1951, repr. 1984), p 101.
33   Hobbes, 'Of things that Weaken, or tend to the Dissolution of a Commonwealth' in *Leviathan*, p 365.
34   Ibid. For an excellent reinterpretation of Hobbes' *Leviathan* in the light of the emerging public sphere, see Achinstein, 'Politics', esp. pp 33–7.
35   John Milton, *Areopagitica* (London, 1644). On the impact of Milton on his contemporaries see Sharon Achinstein, *Milton and the Revolutionary Reader* (Princeton/New Jersey, 1994).

just Rights and Liberties of the free-born people of this Nation, and to brand and traduce all such Writers and Writings with the odious terms of Sedition, Conspiracy and Treason'.[36] Samuel Hartlib's detailed plan for the foundation of an 'Office of Publicke Addresse For Accommodation' also reflected on communication and its role for the advancement of the 'Happinesse of this Nation'.[37] A surviving manuscript version of this project dates from 1648, entitled *A Further Discoverie Of the Office of Publicke Addresse*.[38] There are references to an earlier proposal 'before we fell into these last fears and troubles'. The author proposed to 'designate' a 'certain place whereunto it shall be free for every one to make his Addresse upon all occasions, as well to offer unto others, as to receive from them, the commodities which are desirable, and the informations of things profitable to be taken notice of in a private or publick way'. An officer and 'certain men under him' were to be employed to keep registers, make extracts and furnish customers with the desired information. Especially the poor, who suffered mainly 'for want of employment' because 'they cannot find Masters... or their abilities and fitnesse to do service are not known to such as might employ them', would greatly benefit from the Office. Special provisions were also to be made for women who desired to publish their writings or submit a memorial to the government. They were, however, to be kept well in their allocated place under male supervision within a patriarchal society:

> As for the Female Kind their memorials are to be brought into the Office by some Men whom they should employ to that Effect; and the Office shall have some Grave and Pious Matrons to be employed about the Direction of all Addresses in that Nature; to whom the

---

36 John Lilburne, *England's Birth-Right* (1645), cit. in Achinstein, 'Politics', p 10.
37 See also Kevin Dunn, 'Milton among the monopolists: *Areopagitica*, intellectual property and the Hartlib circle', in *Samuel Hartlib and Universal Reformation, Studies in intellectual communication*, ed. Mark Greengrass, Michael Leslie and Timothy Raylor (Cambridge, 1995), pp 177–236.
38 Ashm 1639:15. Also Samuel Hartlib, *A briefe discourse concerning the accomplishment of our reformation* (London, 1647).

Cases of Women (as well as the Inspection of the affaires of the Poore,
as the accommodation of others in their lawful desires and offers)
may be referred.

Plans for the promotion of a communication network from which
all members of society would benefit were also developed for
the English postal service which had hitherto been limited to the
King's business and those of government officials. In the 1630s
various proposals were made for a service 'that would be more
rapid and that would, for the first time, attempt a systematic
carriage of the letters of the people'.[39] The plans fell through,
however, because of the growing crisis between England and Scotland. Anything that could further the spread of seditious ideas
and treasonable plots was to be undermined, and the carriage of
letters was restricted to official correspondence again. As before,
people had to rely on common carriers and friends for the transport of their letters. Under the Long Parliament a bitter strife
between the Lords and Commons began for the control of the
postal service.[40] At the same time, independent carriers made
determined efforts to provide postal services free from government control. While opposing monopolies and fixed rates, 'the
Undertakers' of a private postal service argued in favour of free
communication for both economic and idealistic reasons:

> The very light of Nature shews, that originally to a community of
> free men linked together as a commonwealth, and by civil commerce
> and Intercourse aiming at temporal weal, a right of liberty to com-
> municate their intents and mindes, by all lawfull ways, and therefore
> by this way of postage, as well as by any other, is innate and inher-
> ent, as that without which free commerce cannot consist. Why should
> they give up their liberty to communicate their affairs by this way of
> common postage, more then by any other way? To restrain all ways
> of free Communication is downright to destroy Society.[41]

---

39   Howard Robinson, *The British Post Office. A History* (Princeton, 1948), p 33.
40   Ibid., p 37ff.
41   *The Case of the Undertakers For reducing Postage of inland Letters to just and
     moderate rates, Stated. And therein, the Liberty of a Commonwealth...and the*

Clearly, by the first half of the seventeenth century new forms of *communication* and their impact on the formation of people's opinions as political subjects were recognized in a phenomenon worthy of serious attention. Whereas some commentators could only envisage the overthrow of the existing social order by politically immature men unable to interpret news independently, others welcomed the free communication of all subjects, half-heartedly including women, for the promotion of the 'common weal', and a third group discovered a new field for economic enterprise.

Our modern conception of the 'public sphere' has been strongly influenced by the well-known study by Jürgen Habermas, *The Structural Transformation of the Public Sphere*. Habermas characterized the emergence of the public sphere as a phenomenon of the eighteenth century which was inseparably linked with the rise of the 'Bürgertum' (middle classes) and its values of equality and freedom of mind. Its governing principle was reason and the self-perception of the middle classes as capable of understanding and challenging political processes and those in power. According to Habermas, the formation of public opinion depended on newspapers and journals as well as on 'public' debate in clubs, salons and societies, all flourishing in the eighteenth century. One of his central claims is that these forms of 'public reasoning' over politics are unprecedented in history and thus differed significantly from other types of the public sphere which he mentions only in passing, namely the hellenic public sphere, the medieval and early modern plebeian public and the 'representative public sphere' of the seventeenth century. Modern historiography on communication, literacy, and the emergence of the public sphere has been highly influenced by Habermas.[42] However, research on popular or plebeian opinions has started to challenge his con-

---

birthright of every free-man vindicated from Monopolizing restraints, and mercenary Farming of Publicke Offices [1646]. Harl. MS 5954.6/7.

42   His study was also translated into French in 1978.

ception. Most recently, Andreas Würgler has convincingly demonstrated the interrelation of unrest and the public sphere in
eighteenth century rural and municipal regions in southern Germany and Switzerland. Based on his empirical findings, he re-
jects Habermas' conception of the public sphere as a middle class
hegemony and offers, instead, a typology of the public sphere
which combines popular, communal and elite elements.[43] In England, the interest Habermas has attracted among scholars has
most recently been demonstrated by the bulky collection of articles on *Habermas and the Public Sphere*, edited by Craig
Calhourn.[44]

All critical assessments of Habermas have in common that
they continue to concentrate on the eighteenth century. Popular
political participation in the sixteenth and seventeenth century
has been viewed until recently in terms of popular unrest and
crowd behaviour with little analysis of the political awareness of
the common people and their impact on politics through public
opinion. Early modernists so far have been more interested in
forms of popular political culture, analysing the ways in which
people expressed their discontent with politics, or voiced their
criticism of social misconduct. Through a number of influential
works by scholars such as Natalie Zemon Davis, Carlo Ginzburg,
Keith Thomas, Peter Burke, Martin Ingram, David Underdown,
Robert Scribner and others, we are now quite familiar with the
meaning of 'women on top', charivari, carnivalesque inversion,
processions and festivals, rituals and cross-dressing in early modern Europe. Another important approach to the study of popu-

---

43   Würgler, *Unruhen.* For his critical discussion of Habermas, including a survey
     of most recent studies on Habermas published in Germany, see esp. pp 21–41.
     See also Andreas Gestrich, *Absolutismus und Öffentlichkeit. Politische
     Kommunikation in Deutschland zu Beginn des 18. Jahrhunderts*, Kritische
     Studien zur Geschichtswissenschaft, 103 (Göttingen, 1994). It is reviewed by
     Timothy C. W. Blanning in *Bulletin of the German Historical Institute London*,
     Vol. XVIII, No. 1 (February, 1996), pp 32–5.
44   Craig Calhourn (ed.), *Habermas and the Public Sphere* (Boston, 1992).

lar political behaviour is research on riots, protests, and rebellion in early modern Europe.[45]

In his work on the diffusion of Reformation ideas among the 'simple folk' in sixteenth-century Germany, and his interest in how oral forms of communication influenced the nature of 'Reformation public opinion', Robert Scribner was one of the first to look at the emergence of 'public opinion' and the public sphere.[46] Similarly, Rainer Wohlfeil argued in favour of a Reformation public, which comprised all social groups. He, however, interpreted it as an isolated historical phenomenon which was in force only between 1517 and 1525 and had no further impact on

---

45   See for instance John Walter, 'Grain Riots and Popular Attitudes to the Law: Maldon and the Crisis of 1629' in *An Ungovernable People*, ed. John Brewer and John Styles (London, 1980), pp 47–84; Keith J. Lindley, 'Riot Prevention and Control in Early Stuart London', *TRHS*, 5th ser., 33 (1983), pp 109–26; David Underdown, *Revel, Riot and Rebellion. Popular Politics and Culture in England 1603–1660* (Oxford, 1985, pb. 1987); John Morrill and John D. Walter, 'Order and Disorder in the English Revolution', in *Order and Disorder in Early Modern England*, ed. Anthony Fletcher and John Stevenson (Cambridge, 1985), pp 137–65; Clive Holmes, 'Drainers and Fenmen: the Problem of Popular Political Consciousness in the Seventeenth Century', in ibid., pp 166–95; John Stevenson, '"Moral Economy" of the English Crowd: Myth and Reality', in ibid., pp 218–38; Buchanan Sharp, 'Popular Protest in Seventeenth-Century England', in *Popular Culture in Seventeenth-Century England*, ed. Barry Reay (1985, repr. London, 1988); Tim Harris, *London Crowds in the Reign of Charles II*, Cambridge Studies in Early Modern British History (Cambridge, 1987); Rudolf M. Dekker, 'Women in Revolt. Popular Protest and Its Social Basis in Holland in the Seventeenth and Eighteenth Century', *Theory and Society*, 16 (1987), pp 337–62; in Germany and Switzerland the study of unrest and rebellion has formed a field of research in its own right since the 1970s. For a discussion of the most recent literature see Würgler, *Unruhen*, esp. pp 23–9.

46   Robert W. Scribner, 'Oral Culture and the Diffusion of Reformation Ideas', in *Popular Culture and Popular Movements in Reformation Germany* (London, 1987), pp 49–69, p 50 and id., 'Mündliche Kommunikation und Strategien der Macht in Deutschland am Anfang des 16. Jahrhunderts', in *Kommunikation und Alltag im Spätmittelalter und in der frühen Neuzeit*, Österreichische Akademie der Wissenschaften, Phil.-hist. Klasse, Sitzungsberichte Bd. 596 (Vienna, 1992), pp 183–98.

later developments.[47] More recently, Günter Berghaus has argued
that seventeenth-century Germany saw the emergence of a so-
phisticated middle-class public sphere due to the revolution-
ization of the newspaper trade which was closely linked to the
professionalization of the postal service.[48] Yet he challenges only
Habermas' chronology, while reiterating his argument on the link
between the middle classes and the rise of the public sphere. In
England, the study of popular opinion and its impact on the Civil
War owes much to the work of Christopher Hill, although he
concentrates mainly on radical ideas, popular protest, and written and printed expressions of popular political discontent.[49] Only
a few studies have taken up the issue of public opinion and political consciousness of the people by looking at a wider range of
sources. This shift of interest is often revealed in the choice of
title. There is Richard Cust's pioneering work on 'News and
Politics in Early Seventeenth-Century England'. He discusses a
range of genres central for the spread of news, such as the 'pure
newsletter', 'separates', verses, ballads and 'oral news', suggest-
ing that, in spite of his doubts about the extent to which the
'alehouse audience was familiar with national politics', developments in news circulation 'were coming to affect a broader social
spectrum'. Foreshadowing recent discussions about the political
significance of sexual imagery, Cust argued that scatological and
pornographic imagery was employed to 'fit political figures into
popular stereotypes'.[50] Pauline Croft, for instance, analyses the

---

47   Rainer Wohlfeil, 'Reformatorische Öffentlichkeit', in *Literatur und Laien-*
      bildung im Spätmittelalter und in der Frühen Neuzeit, Symposium Wolfenbüttel
      1981, Germanistische-Symposien Berichtsbände, 5, ed. Ludger Grenzmann
      and Karl Stackmann (Stuttgart, 1984), pp 41–52.
48   Günter Berghaus, *Die Aufnahme der englischen Revolution in Deutschland 1640–*
      1669, vol. 1., Studien zur politischen Literatur und Publizistik im 17. Jahrhun-
      dert mit einer Bibliographie der Flugschriften (Wiesbaden, 1989).
49   See the introduction and the select bibliography in Donald Pennington and
      Keith Thomas (eds.), *Puritans and Revolutionaries. Essays in Seventeenth-Cen-*
      tury History presented to Christopher Hill (1978, repr. pb. 1989).
50   Cust, *'News'*, pp 68–9.

politico-religious significance of what appear at first to be merely scandalous allegations in her essay 'The Reputation of Robert Cecil: Libels, Political Opinions and Popular Awareness in the early Seventeenth Century'.[51] Although showing little awareness of the complex meanings of figurative everyday language, Buchanan Sharp was innovative in looking at indictments for seditious words and related offences in order to analyse how people verbalized popular discontent with politics.[52] In his study of *London Crowds under Charles II*, Tim Harris persuasively demonstrates that the masses were widely informed and concerned about the political issues of their day.[53] Mark Knights seeks to analyse developments in public opinion by concentrating on newsletters and the press in *Politics and Opinion in Crisis 1678–1681*.[54] In a fascinating study of the 'Politics of Babel', Sharon Achinstein sees the growing interest in universal language schemes and the dispute over the use of language between 1640 and 1670 implicated in 'the rise of the public sphere'.[55]

Whereas some of these studies include a ritual obeisance to Habermas in their introduction, none of them offer an alternative concept of the public sphere, nor discuss the dynamics of communication that were characteristic for the seventeenth century with regard to their impact on politics and religion. Furthermore, the role of women in the formation of political opinions in this period has received little attention. Nevertheless, fas-

---

51 Pauline Croft, 'The Reputation of Robert Cecil: Libels, Political Opinions and Popular Awareness in the early Seventeenth Century', *TRHS*, 6th ser., 1 (1991), pp 43–69. See also Adam P. Fox, *Aspects of Oral Culture and its Development in Early Modern England* (Cambridge University PhD, December 1992). Fox devotes one chapter to popular attitudes towards church, state, and society, and one of his sub-sections deals with 'the anatomy of popular opinion'.

52 Buchanan Sharp, 'Popular Political Opinion in England 1660–1685', *History of European Ideas*, 10 (1989), pp 13–29.

53 Harris, *London Crowds*.

54 Mark Knights, *Politics and Opinion in Crisis 1678–1681* (Cambridge, 1994).

55 Achinstein, 'Politics', p 16.

cinating work has been done on the diffusion of ideas across
social groups, the interfaces of orality and literacy, and the appropriation of meaning, to which this present study is highly
indebted. While many scholars viewed the rise of the printing
press as an 'agent of change', the first studies of popular opinions tended to analyse pamphlets, broadsides, and woodcuts.
These were based on well known early modern collections such
as the *Thomason Tracts*, or the Pepys Library in England, the
modern editions of German 'Flugschriften' by Wolfgang Harms,
Roger Paas, and Hans-Joachim Köhler, and the 'Bibliothèque
bleue' in France.[56] The methodological problems inherent in the
equation of pamphlets with popular opinions were recognized
in the early 1980s, when Robert Scribner argued that 'indeed,
study of printed sources may even tell us very little about how
the literate received their information about the Reformation,
telling us more about their authors than about the response of
their readers'.[57] In consequence, he set out to analyse the diffusion of ideas, questions of literacy and heterodoxy, and public
opinion and the strategies of power by focusing on visual forms,
participational forms, and above all oral forms of communication in the context of the German Reformation and the state.[58]
In his influential work on the cultural uses of print in France,
Roger Chartier has emphasized the individual and subjective appropriation of texts which 'created uses and representations not
necessarily in accordance with the desires of those who produced
the discourses and fashioned the norms'.[59] It became clear that,

---

56   See Elisabeth L. Eisenstein, *The printing press as an agent of change*, vol. 2 (Cam-
     bridge, 1979), esp. chap. 4.
57   Scribner, 'Oral Culture', p 50.
58   See the new introduction to the paperback edition of Robert W. Scribner, *For
     the Sake of Simple Folk – Popular Propaganda for the German Reformation* (Lon-
     don, 1994); id., 'Mündliche Kommunikation'; and id., 'Heterodoxy, Literacy
     and Print in the German Reformation', in *Literacy and Heresy 1000–1530*, ed.
     Peter Biller and Ann Hudson (Cambridge, 1994), pp 255–78.
59   Roger Chartier, *The Cultural Uses of Print in Early Modern France*, tr. Lydia
     G. Cochrane (Princeton, 1987), p 7.

given that the majority of society possessed only moderate literacy skills, symbolic action, the power of images, rituals, processions, political songs, and the spread of news by word of mouth were still all part of popular communication even in the seventeenth century. Especially in England there followed a number of studies on literacy, the costs of 'cheap print', the circulation of popular literature, the availability of 'small books and pleasant histories' to the semi-literate even in rural areas, and the variety of media involved in the spread of news and opinions, namely songs, pictures, the spoken and the written word, libels, printed matter, and performances.[60]

The emergence of the public sphere as a new social and political force in the early seventeenth century must be understood as part of these communication patterns. Society was still largely immersed in verbal communication which was influenced by tales and folklore despite growing literacy skills. In the process of news presentation and the formation of public opinion residues of oral culture and the characteristics of a literate culture began to merge. Robert Scribner has aptly compared this process with a musical score in which different voices, sounds, tempi, and moods resonate to form a new whole.[61] Reading was a social event rather than an individual pastime, and printed papers were generally read aloud to a group of friends or bystanders (often of different social backgrounds and both sexes), and immediately sparked

---

60 David Cressy, *Literacy and the Social Order. Reading and Writing in Tudor and Stuart England* (Cambridge, 1980); and a critical reassessment by Keith Thomas, 'The meaning of Literacy in Early Modern England', in *The Written Word. Literacy in Transition*, ed. Gerd Baumann (Oxford, 1986), pp 97–131; Margaret Spufford, *Small Books and Pleasant Histories. Popular Fiction and its Readership in Seventeenth-Century England* (Cambridge, 1981); Tessa Watt, *Cheap Print and Popular Piety* (Cambridge, 1991, pb. 1994). See also the publications in the series *Cambridge Studies in Oral and Literate Culture*, ed. Peter Burke and Roy Porter.

61 Robert W. Scribner, 'Flugblatt und Analphabetentum. Wie kam der gemeine Mann zu reformatorischen Ideen?', in *Flugschriften als Massenmedium der Reformationszeit*, ed. Joachim Köhler (Stuttgart, 1981), pp 65–76, p 75.

off comments. Pictures, too, provoked particular interpretation, adjusting their meaning to explain current political and religious phenomena. Likewise, songs and ballads carried political messages across the country. These were often passed on by word of mouth, or in manuscript form. The stage provided opportunities to vent popular criticism. Even after the closure of the theatres under the Long Parliament in 1642, *ad hoc* performances abounding in political allusions seem to have continued in alehouses and taverns.

Central for the diffusion of abstract political and religious issues was their adjustment to the mental frame of mind of ordinary men and women, and to their habits of communication. The analysis of the spoken and printed language used in seventeenth-century England for the spread of news and opinions demonstrates the extent to which the still vivid oral culture with its images and moral values penetrated public debate, and vice versa. Similar to the political and religious satires of the period, which were largely written in rhymes, imaginative narratives and fictitious dialogues, and employed a range of rhetorical persuasive techniques and sexual imagery, oral comments on political and religious events of the time were characterized by a highly figurative language which abounded in social types, personifications, symbols, and sexual insult. The resort to familiar stories and images corresponded to the mental world of the illiterate or semi-literate to the extent that realities outside their immediate personal experience could be understood. Both popular and learned political criticism drew on a shared social memory, couching arguments in exemplary stories and tales, or comparing present conflicts with past events. Popular criticism of Parliament, for instance, was expressed by comparing its members with popular leaders of revolt and with folk heroes who threatened the existing social order: 'The Parliament was nothing but a Company of Robin Hoods and Little Jacks'.[62] Furthermore, the figu-

---

62   CJ III.17 (1643).

rative political language of seventeenth-century England had its roots in the language and symbolism of everyday life and culture, and comments often sprang directly from everyday occurrences. Frequently, popular political verdicts were spelled out in the everyday language of defamation and sexual slander. In spite of these forms of reasoning, which were influenced by traditional images and oral culture, popular discourse on politics was informed by factual news, and it drew on a political symbolism that mirrored the order and values of seventeenth-century England and changes in them. Popular political debate was characterized by the ability, and the willingness, of an increasing number of men and women to comprehend and judge issues that lay outside their immediate everyday context.

The emerging public sphere of the seventeenth century was characterized by spontaneous and well-informed debate. In its spontaneity, it differed from more structured forms of reasoning in a specific time and space, for example, the literary clubs of the eighteenth century. In its independence of argument based on knowledge other than tradition and touching on issues outside the immediate locality, it greatly differed from earlier forms of verbalizing popular discontent. 'Public opinion' in the seventeenth century must be understood as a process which was sparked off the moment politics spilled over into everyday life and challenged people's opinions and private consciences. Public opinion 'happened' when men and women moved from ordinary discourse and the habitual exchange of news to discussing politics. In a variety of informal everyday settings, people embarked on discussions of the political and religious issues of their time: at home, during dinner, at work, when travelling, in alehouses and coffee shops, after church or during visits with neighbours, even at the entirely women's gathering of child birth, politics entered private lives through the passing on of information and opinions. Vice versa, private debate time and again became public through the issues discussed and the genres of talk. Being a part of public opinion, rumours and gossip thrived even more at moments of crisis throughout the seventeenth century, and gossip, which is usually associated with private talk and women, became politicized. In the guise of a seemingly trivial story, political gossip about the King and his family, for instance, could signal personal and collective disapproval of his religious and political sympathies.

Throughout this study it will be shown that in the formation of public opinion and the dynamics of communication in the seventeenth century, there was no rigid division between the public and private, although a clear conceptual public/private distinction was obviously defined as that which occurred in the household. Both realms interacted and boundaries were fluid.[63] Thus, a narrow definition of the political as the politics of official institutions misses out an essential part of the participatory political culture of this period.[64] Similarly, politics is traditionally seen as a male domain, and the few female rulers are considered an exception to the rule. Consequently, the question of women and politics in early modern Europe has been neglected. In the light of women's engagement with politics through private and public debate, women's conduct and gossip must be brought into consideration of the political.

Politics, religion and communication in the seventeenth century cannot be understood without considering the issue of 'popular' and 'elite' participation, the growing importance of a 'private conscience', and the interaction of oral and print culture. Taking these various elements into account it can be argued that in seventeenth-century England political culture underwent a process of 'inner modernization', which involved a change of

---

63   See Scribner, 'Kommunikation', p 184. For a most recent collection of essays on the public and private sphere see *Prose Studies* 18 No. 3. Special Issue: 'The Intersections of the Public and Private in early modern England', ed. Paula A. Backscheider and Timothy Dykstal (December, 1995).

64   See Tim Harris' argument in favour of a participatory model instead of a polarized model for understanding the social and political relations of people in the reign of Charles II. Harris, *Crowds*, p 17. Patrick Collinson, *De Republica Anglorum. Or, History with the Politics Put Back* (Inaugural Lecture, Cambridge, 1990).

meaning and function in various forms of popular protest and language.[65] In contrast to, for instance, early modern Germany, where these changes are attributed to the eighteenth century, English politics in the seventeenth century is centrally connected to communication, information, and public opinion. During the English revolution, the belief in the divine authority of the King was finally shattered among all social groups (though not all people), and the legitimacy of the monarch was judged by his or her deeds, not by divine authority. Throughout the rest of the century, politics, the church, and the monarchy remained issues of public debate. Those in power had to reckon with popular protest that was based on a critical assessment of political and religious affairs. Ordinary men and women showed great concern with the conduct of politicians, the rights and freedom of the people, and the balance of power between King and Parliament. The old, seemingly static hierarchy between ruler and ruled had become a field of continuous negotiations between divine and secular authorities and the people under the impact of the public sphere. Apart from long-term factors of changes in communication patterns, the outbreak of the Civil War revolutionized public debate. The political and religious conflicts were on everyone's mind and, informed by an unprecedented number of politico-religious pamphlets, men and women discussed the whole range of issues: the Scottish war; Charles I's religious policy; the influence of his Catholic wife, Henrietta Maria; the designs of his 'evil councillors'; the alleged Catholic affiliation of Archbishop William Laud; plots and riots in London; or the question of whether or not 'religion can be a lawfull cause for subjects to take Armes against their Prince'.[66] Thus, the peak of political

---

65   See Wolfgang Kaschuba, 'Ritual und Fest. Das Volk auf der Straße. Figurationen und Funktionen populärer Öffentlichkeit zwischen Frühneuzeit und Moderne', in *Dynamik der Tradition. Studien zur historischen Kulturforschung*, ed. Richard van Dülmen (Frankfurt, 1992), pp 240–67.

66   SP 16/457.129–30.

crisis in the early 1640s and the intensity of communication processes is vital for understanding the emergence of the public sphere,
which increasingly involved the provinces, too.

In this study I will look at these crucial years, choosing the
period 1637 to 1645, in order to recreate as complex a picture as
possible of the dynamics of communication and its impact on
politics and religion. Although there will be frequent references
to communication and the spread of news outside the capital,
thus acknowledging the importance of the provinces in the formation of public opinion, I will focus mainly on London which
will allow me to trace the spread of opinions in much detail. Furthermore due to the laws regulating printing, London remained
the main market and monopoly for the 'production' and spread
of news. Bearing in mind one of the main characteristics of public opinion – the contest between ruler and ruled and among those
in power – I will look in Chapter Two at the politics of censorship at a time of upheaval of divine and secular authorities. Between 1637 and 1645, we witness a period changing from tight
rules of censorship under church and crown authorities to fierce
attempts by Parliament to set up a new framework of censorship
after the abolition of the Star Chamber and the High Commission, to renewed control of the presses by the new authorities in
power. During this power vacuum, when King and Parliament
were fighting over the control of printing and the validity of
proclamations, ordinary men and women were drawn into these
disputes at a local level when forced to make up their minds independently about which side they wanted to support. Central
for the formation of public opinion was the communication network providing and distributing news items. Thus, in Chapter
Three I will analyse the London news trade, looking at the location of presses and shops, the production and distribution of
news in both official and subversive ways, and the access to information such as through leaks from Parliament for payment.
The choice of media and the language used were vital for the
diffusion of news to a broad social spectrum. Amongst the most
popular genres were ballads and satires, which will be analysed in

Chapter Four. Apart from carrying political and religious messages, these genres met a number of important conditions. They
could be easily shared in a communal setting – ballads could be
performed and sung, and satirical dialogues could be acted out
easily. They were often funny, drawing people together in laughter, and they were generally provocative, which sparked off comments by their audience. Finally, they abounded in vivid imagery
familiar to people from other cultural sources. Central for understanding not only what people were confronted with but essentially how they appropriated news individually are the ways
in which men and women discussed politics. How did they gain
their information about the political and religious issues of their
time and on what grounds did they defend their personal opinions? Furthermore, in view of women's engagement in political
debate, how did men and women interact in their exchange of
opinion? Were there any gender specific modes of communication? And how did women view their own political engagement
against the backdrop of contemporary pressure on women to be
silent, or the abuse of women's talk in the political symbolism of
the period? These questions will be tackled in Chapters Five and
Six through an analysis of court records on sedition. In Chapter
Five I will analyse the genres of talk, namely gossip and rumour,
and the language and imagery used to express opinions about
political and religious issues. Chapter Six will be devoted, firstly,
to the study of the interfaces of orality and literacy, and, secondly, to the study of 'people in communication', looking for
instance at the way men and women discussed the political opinions they were reading together in a ballad, or the importance of
story-telling in order to pass on a personal viewpoint about the
religious conflicts of the period. And finally, I will discuss gender relations with regard to gender stereotypes and the self-perception of men and women, as these issues emerge from the dynamics of communication.

2 · Opinions under Scrutiny: The Politics of Censorship

Censorship in mid-seventeenth-century England was not an abstract policy, which concerned only its administrators and offenders against it. It concerned society at all levels and constituted the legal, political and moral framework *within* and *against* which communication processes and the formation of opinions took place. In contrast to our post-modern societies at the end of the twentieth century, early modern society appears to have been held together by a strict order of things. Often, these rules were not visible because people had internalized certain viewpoints as part of society's shared cultural assumptions such as religious beliefs, moral values, deference, and gender roles. Thus, without necessarily inhibiting people's freedom, the guidelines laid down by state and church authorities greatly influenced men and women in their behaviour and thinking. Furthermore, people tended – as they do today – to enter into a cultural bargain with the holders of power in pursuit of security and success, and authors willingly accepted that their works were altered to conform to established opinion. In their everyday encounters, however, people's communication was characterized by conflict rather than consensus. This is apparent in the wide range of conflicting viewpoints on political and religious issues in the various news genres of the time. On a different scale, it is manifest in the widely recognized cases of neighbourly disputes about a person's honour, chastity, and conduct which were brought before the local justices in the first half of the seventeenth century.

Censorship in early modern England was arbitrary, and it mirrored the political and religious disputes of the period. Censorship always implied interpretation on the part of the holders of power, of licensers, authors and readers, and interpretation in turn implied a struggle for meaning which, by its nature, resisted any codification that could ensure just control.[1] This was especially difficult during a period where we find 'a system of communication in which ambiguity becomes a creative and necessary instrument' for authors in order to express their opinions publicly without provoking the authorities.[2] One of the most popular genres for the spread of political and religious opinions in the 1640s were satires which were full of illusions and images, and often resorted to wordplay and fantastic stories, perhaps with an underlying meaning. There was always scope for interpretation.[3] Quite often, writers invited people to 'Turn over and Read, and after Reading Censure'. They encouraged others to 'Buy, Read and Judge' and to 'reade it over, and the Lord give thee grace to make the best use of it'.[4] At the same time, authors were very concerned not to be misinterpreted and added wordy prefaces to their texts to explain their intentions – or they opted for anonymity. Censorship thus created a fragile relationship between authors, readers or listeners, and the holders of power. The maintenance of this relationship entered a new phase with the expan-

---

1   See Annabel Patterson, *Censorship and Interpretation. The Conditions of Writing and Reading in Early Modern England* (Madison, 1984).
2   Patterson, *Censorship*, p 11.
3   For the rare surviving evidence of subjective interpretation of pamphlets see *The Diary of John Rous*, ed. Mary A. Everett Green (Camden Society, 1861). Rous copied many pamphlets into his diary and commented on them.
4   BL E.130.14. *The Poet's Blind mans bough* (1641), BL E.172.6. *A Discovery of 29 Sects here in London* (1641), BL E.168.7.

sion of communication networks and the availability of often contradictory news to large sections of society in the seventeenth century. Whereas official pronouncements were characterized by a consensual rhetoric, news reports which tended to concentrate on conflict or were in themselves controversial, helped to erode the impression of a harmonious society. Furthermore, as a result of the Reformation, individuals were increasingly encouraged to decide for themselves on the meaning of texts, a skill that, once developed in reading the Bible, could be easily applied to other things, too. This time and again created 'cases of conscience' when men and women were compelled by statutes and proclamations under threat of punishment to report seditious words or publications to the next local official who then had to pass these reports on to the secretary of state.[5]

In the politicized everyday talk of the 1640s, opinions were continuously censored by ordinary men and women participating in or overhearing a 'discourse': if they considered something to be seditious they said so, and often denounced the speaker. Likewise, the content of printed and written papers was critically viewed, and whatever was considered seditious was passed on to official representatives of state and church. However, ordinary men and women were far from any consensus in their definition of 'sedition'. People's arguments for or against particular opinions reflected the conflicting politico-religious views of the time. In order to lend their views more weight, men and women often referred to proclamations and hearsay about court cases, which voiced the authorities' views on what was politically acceptable. During a discussion with her fellow servant Thomas Poulter in June 1638 about the Gunpowder Plot and the examination of Samuel Pickering before the Star Chamber, Mary Cole, a Catholic widow from Camden Hall in Essex, angrily exclaimed: 'If shee wear as the Queene shee would quickly make away with the king Charles for dealing so hardly with that Reli-

---

5   For instance, *Statutes of the Realm* 1 Eliz.c.5, 6. A.D. 1558–59.

gion.' Hearing this, her son-in-law, Roger Hepthrow, a labourer from a neighbouring village, was greatly troubled and warned her: 'Oh mother, take heed what you say. I have known one hanged for a less word.' Whereupon Mary Cole quickly corrected her words: 'As Christ save me, I meant the Keeper. I pray God bless me, and sweet Jesus bless the King.'[6]

During the upheaval of secular and divine authorities in the early 1640s, the common folk were confronted with a unique situation: the Parliament, itself divided over the issue of censorship, and the King were struggling to gain the upper hand in establishing new rules for censorship even before the demolition of the chief courts that dealt with sedition, riot, and religious nonconformity in the summer of 1641 (the secular Star Chamber Court, and the ecclesiastical High Commission Court).[7] What has been widely accepted by scholars as the 'collapse of censorship' was in fact not collapse of censorship and definitely not a deliberate freedom of the press, but a competition for control among those in power, which, as long as it lasted, forced the population 'to choose' between the rules of the two competitors.[8] Henry Parker described the situation in his *Observations* in 1642:

> The King says; the Parliament denies; the King commands, the Parliament forbids: The King says the Parliament is seduced by a traitorous faction; the Parliament says the King is seduced by a Malignant Party: The King says the parliament tramples upon his crown; the Parliament says the King intends War upon them: to whether now is the Subject to adhere?[9]

---

6   SP 16/392.61 and SP 16/393.24i. (1638).
7   For a brief introduction to these courts see John P. Kenyon, *The Stuart Constitution 1603–1688. Documents and Commentary* (Cambridge, 1966).
8   For studies arguing for the collapse of censorship see Christopher Hill, 'Society and Literature in 17th century England', *Collected Essays of Christopher Hill; I: Writing and Revolution* (Brighton, 1985), p 39–40; Handover, *Printing*, p 60; Siebert, *Freedom*.
9   Henry Parker, 'Observations', in *Revolutionary Prose of the English Civil War*, ed. Howard Erskine-Hill and Graham Storey (Cambridge, 1983), p 50. See

Men and women found themselves in an unfamiliar situation where they had to take sides and make up their minds, no matter if they were prepared to do so or not. Those with strong opinions defended their personal convictions. Some expressed sympathies for the King and others for the Parliament. Disagreement regularly arose about religious views and people readily defended their support of the established church, of Catholicism or Puritanism or other nonconformist groups regardless of any attempts to impose a consistent censorship from above. But even they justified their views by appealing to the authority they supported, no matter if it was still (or already) in power: the King or the Parliament. Thus, it can be argued that without being suppressed by censorship to the extent of growing silent, men and women in the 1640s were acutely aware of the rules laid down by censors, the competition among them, and the mechanisms of censorship, which they reproduced in their everyday communicative encounters.

The period 1637 to 1645 provides unusually complex insights into the politics of censorship. There is the growing severity in the execution of censorship in the 1630s. Especially the Star Chamber became notorious for its harsh sentences.[10] Corporal punishment, particularly the cropping of ears, was imposed by the court nineteen times between 1630 and 1641. Another cruel form was the branding iron, which stigmatized the convict for life as a seditious libeller – s.l.[11] Then there was a phase of competition over censorship which created a power vacuum and put pressure on the people to decide for themselves, for instance, when they were confronted at a local level with contradictory

---

also Nigel Smith, *Literature and Revolution in England, 1640–1660* (New Haven and London, 1994), p 98.

10 Henry E. I. Phillips, 'The Last Years of the Court of Star Chamber, 1630–1641', *TRHS*, 4th ser., xxi (1939); pp 103–31 and Thomas G. Barnes, 'Due Process and Slow Process in the late Tudor and early Stuart Star Chamber', *American Journal of Legal History*, 6 (1962).

11 Kenyon, *Constitution*, p 118.

proclamations issued by the King and by the Parliament. And finally, censorship hardened at the end of the period when Parliament gained the upper hand.

Throughout this period we witness the redefinition of meaning and of what was considered 'seditious', a process which engaged writers and the holders of power just as much as ordinary people. In a society which had suffered greatly from forced deportation and half-voluntary emigration on the grounds of untolerated religious beliefs, and in which people had to endure painful bodily harm and isolated imprisonment for their opinions, the impact changes in censorship must have made on many people seems to have been underestimated. Censorship could not only uproot or destroy whole families, it was also a physical presence through various forms of public punishment ranging from book burning to repentance in the pillory. Often, acts of censorship re-entered the public sphere through the publication of recantations, or in the form of mockery like the famous play *Canterbury His Change of Diot* [Diet].[12] This play does not only comment on the punishment of the Puritans William Prynne, Henry Burton and John Bastwick in 1637, but it underlines the whole iconography of censorship, in this case the cropping of Prynne's ears. One of the woodcuts in the text shows Archbishop Laud sitting at a dining-table with a lawyer, a 'doctor of physicke', and a divine. Prynne stands nearby dressing his wounds, and Laud is about to eat one of his ears which have been served on a plate. In the course of the play he is made so ill by the aftermath of his politics that he vomits everything up again. This iconographic representation of censorship appeared in pamphlets, too. The King's jester, 'Archy', who was expelled from court by 'Canterbury's malice', replied when asked what plans he had for

---

12   *A new Play called Canterburie His Change of Diot. Which sheweth variety of wit and mirth: privately acted neare the Palace-yard at Westminster* (1641), BL E.177.8. See picture section.

his sons: ' He would gladly make Schollers of them, but that he feared the Arch-Bishop would cut their eares.'[13]

Whereas some people suffered under censorship, others obviously thrived as long as they belonged to the right side. Thus, far reaching changes in censorship also turned opponents upside down, with Puritans getting on top in the 1640s. This turn has been nicely captured in a woodcut where a female Opinion (instead of Fortuna) is turning the wheel of fortune, catapulting 'roundheads' to the top and 'square heads' to the bottom.[14] Furthermore, it is well exemplified by Prynne and Laud, partly because their case was so spectacular and is thus well documented. In 1643, when Laud was already imprisoned, Prynne seized his personal diary, documents, and books and used them for his account of Laud's religious policy. The book was called *Canterburies doom* and first appeared in 1646, one year after the execution of the archbishop.[15]

The following sections will analyse the politics of censorship by concentrating on printing and publishing mainly in London. The first section will look at the way censorship affected individuals and how it operated in the streets of London where ordinary men and women, common informers, and holders of power seemed to co-operate – within limits. The second will consist of a discussion of change and continuity in censorship under the Long Parliament and the role of the Stationers' Company as a pressure group for control based on their economic interests. The final section will take up the question of competing censors – the King, the Parliament and the people. In subsequent chapters, issues of censorship will come up again when looking more closely at communication networks and the ways in which people discussed their political and religious opinions.

---

13   *Archy's Dream, Sometimes Jester to his Maiestie* (1641), BL E.173.5.
14   See the Introduction.
15   William Prynne, *Canterburies doome. or the first part of a compleat history of the commitment, charge, tryall, condemnation and execution of W. Laud late Archbishop of Canterbury* (London, 1646).

The Practice and Impact of Censorship
in the Streets of London

> But now to make you a little acquainted how it faires with me sence
> you parted with mee. It is this I had some books which were not of
> the Lordly prelates liking And an honest man being in some trouble
> about them did betray me & my Brother with divers others (in hope
> to free himselfe) that we were had up into the Starre Chamber Cort
> which is a very ch[a]rgable Cort and it cost me a grat dele of mony &
> lose of time with much greefe annd Sorrow and could not be fred
> out of the Cort but yet God hath turned it that all hath worked to
> the best.[16]

When Nehemiah Wallington wrote this letter to his friend James
Cole in New England in 1642, the incident referred to lay four
years back, but it still weighed heavily on Wallington's mind. On
Shrove Tuesday, 5 February 1638, he had been called before the
Star Chamber straight from his place of work on London Bridge
and was charged with the possession of forbidden books. In his
own words he remembered:

> there were great matters laid to our charge containing xxxv sheets of
> paper and we were infected in the same bill with Mr Burton, Mr
> Prynne and Doctor Bastwicke (and divers other godly men) how we
> had long [m]aligned the King's happie government and did vilifie
> and devolved libellous books with other hanious crimes, which wee
> did Answere wee ware cleare off them all.[17]

Wallington's account mirrors the typical pattern of censorship
and its surrounding rhetoric as it was practised in the streets of
London during this period. Usually inquiries started on the basis
of information against suspects, which common informers or
private persons presented to secular or divine authorities. When
Henry Burton was summoned to the High Commission follow-

---

16   Sloane MSS 922.196 (1642).
17   Guildhall MS 204/468.

ing his sermon on Guy Fawkes Day in November 1636, his anger was aimed at official searchers:

> The while the Prelates Pursuivants, those Barking Beagles ceased not night nor day to watch, and rap, and ring at my doores, to have surprised me in that my castle, nor yet, to search and hunt all the Printing houses about London, to have prevented the coming forth of my Book, which they heard to be at the Presses.[18]

The motivation for private persons to inform on suspects and their social and politico-religious background and gender differed from case to case and is not always clear. In spite of the legal pressure on everyone to inform about sedition, the majority of people were unlikely to report anything without some kind of personal interest unless they felt the matter was too hot to be kept to themselves. Nehemiah Wallington, for instance, was betrayed – in his own words – by 'an honest man' who was himself involved in the same affair and seems to have acted out of necessity in hope 'to free himself'. Loyalty to the King and state, and to the Parliament, sometimes combined with the hope of reward, often moved people to convey information. However, it is very difficult to establish today exactly what 'loyalty' meant for a small office-holder in seventeenth-century England. Was it a feeling of duty, thus some kind of external pressure, or can it also be understood as a personal conviction and thus an inner motivation to behave in certain ways? One John Smith introduced his report on seditious words which he sent to Secretary Windebank in 1638 as follows: 'Now I being a nere Stranger in the Countrie, and never hereing of this before out of my fidelity love obedience and true subiection to his majesty did forthwith hereupon send to informe you of it.'[19] In 1639 one Timothey Tournew sent

---

18   Steven Foster, *Notes from the Caroline Underground. Alexander Leighton, the Puritan Triumvirate, and the Laudian Reaction to Nonconformity* (London, 1978), p 51.
19   SP 16/404.64 (1638).

'according to my duty' a letter to Sir John Coke, secretary of state, in which he enclosed a rhyme against the bishops written on a portion of a fly-leaf of a letter to one Thomas Jones in Shrewbury. This letter had been found by 'the wife of an alehouse keeper in the commons', and Tournew assured Coke that he would try his best to discover the actor.[20] John Wellch, overseer to the workhouse in Newport, justified his message to the King and the enclosed list of 'certain pernicious books which are now spread abroad in support of Romish articles against the Church, and the Supremacy of our Sovereign' with his personal conviction: 'I hold it treason against the State for me to keep silence in such a case for so it goes in our Oath (of allegiance).'[21] On 4 June 1640, Judith, the wife of William Gerrard, clerk to the 'Petty Pag', brought a 'fictitious letter' to Sir Francis Windebank, secretary of state, which gave detailed instructions about how to blow up London. This letter had been found the night before by a maidservant in Gray's Inn Field.[22]

Many people, in most cases local office-holders, reported on suspects and sent in seditious material in direct response to proclamations and their threat of punishment in case of disobedience. Charles I, like his predecessor, frequently expressed his distaste at the prospect of popular discussion of political affairs.[23] On 11 August 1639, the King published a proclamation against a 'scandalous Paper' which presented the peace treaty of Berwick with Scotland in a false light: 'which Paper being in most parts full of falsehood, dishonour, and scandall to His Majesties proceedings in the late pacification given (...) to His Subjects of Scotland'. It was ordered

> that no person or persons hereafter, of what degree or condition soever, presume to keep any Copy thereof, but that within ten dayes

---

20   SP 16/420.48 (1639).
21   SP 16/450.123–23i.
22   SP 16/455.42 (1640).
23   See Cust, 'News', p 81.

after the said Proclamation published, every such person and persons shal deliver to the next Justice of Peace adjoyning to his or ther dwelling, all and every Copy and Copies thereof, the same to be by the said Justice of peace immediately sent or brought to one of his Majesties principall Secretaries, upon perill of incurring the uttermost of such punishments and penalties as by the Laws of this Realme are to be inflicted upon those that keep such scandalous and seditious Papers.[24]

The mayor of Chester, Robert Sproston, sent to Secretary Windebank part of the 'forbidden Scottish Version' of the King's peace treaty 'in obeying the King's proclamation',[25] as did William Lord Maynard, who had found transcripts of the false proclamation.[26] On 21 August 1640, a Cambridge justice of the peace, Richard Foxton, sent a letter to Secretary Windebank on behalf of one Robert Ibbot of Cambridge, chandler: 'May it please you to be informed that Robert Ibbot (...) did on the 19th present required me, according to the King's proclamation at Whitehall the 31 March last against Seditious pamphlets sent from Scotland to receive from him and send you certain printed pamphlets concerning the intentions of the Scotch army.'[27]

The same kind of obedience was given to orders of the Parliament after the King had attempted to impeach five members of the Commons in January 1642, and subsequently left London.[28] However, in the intermediary process, old and new alliances clashed. The following case demonstrates how this affected printing. On 16 March 1642, Peter Lord of the parish of Welby, and John James of Barten, Northamptonshire, gave evidence before the House of Commons that the high sheriff of Northamptonshire, Sir William Willmer, had sent them a warrant 'for Publishing of a Book containing all Petitions and Messages from the

---

24   *Stuart Royal Proclamations*, 2 vols., (Oxford, 1973), ed. James F. Larkin and P. L. Hughes, ii, pp 688–90.
25   SP 16/427.14 and SP 16/429.39.
26   SP 16/427.93.
27   SP 16/464.57.

Parliament, and his Majesty's several and respective Answers to the same, concerning the Militia'. They had queried the warrant with the sheriff and refused to publish the book 'without the consent of Parliament'. Peter Lord related his dispute with the sheriff:

> I came to know his Mind about it: Said he, Have you not published it? I will send you to the Gaol: You are to publish it in the Church, and to every one of the Inhabitants of the Town: Have not you the Book; the King's Hand, Charles Rex; and my Hand, William Wilmore, High Sheriff: This is to hinder the Militia, That is the End of it. You go contrary to all Men; and think yourself wiser than others. The King must be obeyed for all the Parliament. Then I told him I durst not publish it without Consent of Parliament. He said, I must do it.[29]

Sir William Willmer was sent for as delinquent, and both witnesses were 'thanked for refusing to publish anything that concerned passages in the House, and given 5 (...) each to defray the expenses of their journey'.

Mostly not for reasons of sedition but for economic reasons, there was a great deal of spying and betrayal amongst the members of the book trade. This was either motivated by the need to protect one's own privileges and shares, or by personal animosities.[30] Often, licensing authorities were called for help to punish delinquents. Likewise, the master and wardens of the Stationers' Company were continuously ordered to watch over the imple-

---

28   Still the most detailed account of the events surrounding the outbreak of the Civil War is Anthony Fletcher, *The Outbreak of the English Civil War* (London, 1981). For the King's attempt to impeach the five members see id., *Outbreak*, ch. 5.

29   CJ II.480, 482. For further references to disputes over the militia see: *The Petition of Alderman Wollaston and other citizens of London*. LJ IV.651–52, LJ V.78 and LJ V.151.

30   Handover, *Printing*, p 45–98; Cyprian Bladgen, 'The Stationers' Company in the Civil War Period', *The Library*, 5th ser., XIII, 1 (1958), pp 2–17; Robin Myers, *The Stationers Company Archive 1554–1984*, St Paul's Bibliography (London, 1990).

mentation of laws and orders on printing. Extremely painful for many printers was the Star Chamber decree in 1637, which reduced the number of printers in London to twenty. Many printers petitioned Archbishop Laud to be allowed to continue printing. They stressed their experience, their family tradition in the trade, their loyalty to the state, and the large families they had to provide for.[31] Out of necessity, many printers continued their trade in small printing houses in the suburbs, which were more difficult to control. Ideally, the whole newstrade was thus kept under surveillance by its own members, by common informers, and by loyal individuals. Not all delinquents caught within the trade had to answer for sedition. Printers and publishers could break the law by working without a licence, by reproducing something which was the privilege of another, or by printing something before it had been licensed. Thus, there needs to be a distinction between the violation of rights and procedures, and the violation of tolerated opinions. The journals of the two Houses of Parliament, the House of Lords' main papers, and the state papers, on which the following sections are mainly based, give much detail about the practice of censorship. Unfortunately, they are not always precise about the kind of offence involved, namely illicit printing or the printing of seditious pamphlets, and further research is necessary to explore individual cases to the full by establishing more bibliographical detail about the items mentioned and the authors and printers involved. Here I am concerned with the practice of censorship.

Once suspicion was created, definite steps were taken. Depending on the case and circumstances, a warrant was issued either to 'search and seize' unlicensed or seditious papers and printing presses, or to 'send for' the delinquent to attend one of the appointed courts. 'Search and seize' was conducted in close co-

---

31 See Henry Plomer, 'Some Petitions for Appointment as Master Printers called forth by the Star Chamber Decree of 1637', *The Library*, 3rd ser., X , 39 (1919), p 101–16 and id., 'More Petitions to Archbishop Laud', ibid., p 129–38.

operation with the Stationers' Company and often must have caused friction amongst its members. In August 1641, Nicholas Bourne, one of the wardens of the Company of Stationers, searched for the 'scandalous pamphlet *The Anatomy of the Etcetera*' by virtue of an order of the House of Commons.[32] He found it printed in the House of Richard Herne and tried to seize it. 'Herne told him whosoever laid their Hands upon his Goods, he would be the death of him: He reported these words twice, and bound it with an oath. He farther said, that he would do somewhat else, and justify it, too. It likewise appeared, that Herne would have wrested the Order of the House of Commons out of Bourne's Hands.'[33] Eventually, Herne and others involved were sent for and examined. In February 1644, Peter Cole confessed before the Stationers' Court that he had behaved in a way that was unloyal to the Company: 'Whereas I Peter Cole Staconer did disobediently carry myselfe in resistance to the Warden of my Company (& those that assisted him) in a search & taking downe a presse in the house of Gregory Dexter, wherewith was unlawfully printed divers bookes Contrary to a late ordinance of Parliament Concerning Printing. I the said Peter Cole according to the Comand of the honourable Comittee of Examinacons, doe hereby acknowledge my disobedience & Error craveing pardon for the same.'[34] The order to search and seize was aimed at people and goods. The author, printer, publisher, distributor or any other person involved in the production of an unlicensed paper had to be found and, likewise, all copies of a 'scandalous and seditious' imprint had to be discovered and handed in. Such orders were either very general in the form of statutes of the realm, proclamations, or the recurrent warrants

---

32   This pamphlet is a reference to the 'etcetera' oath introduced with the controversial church canons of 1640. For the content and administration of the oath see William Laud, *Constitutions and Canons Ecclesiastical, Treated upon by the Archbishop of Canterbury and York* (1640).

33   CJ II.269.

34   Stat. Court Book C. 197.

to search for papists, recusants, and popish books, or they were aimed at a particular offence. On 2 July 1640, for instance, a warrant was issued

> from the High Commission Court signed by Archbishop Laud and John Warner, Bishop of Rochester, to Thomas Thrasher, messenger to the Chamber, and to all justices of peace, mayors, sheriffs, and others to aid him in searching all places where Jesuits, popish priests, or other dangerous persons, or Popish and heretical books or any kind of seditious writings or printing presses employed in the printing of any such as are suspected to be, and to apprehend and search every such person found, as also all person procuring or permitting mass to be said ... and also all makers and sellers of superstitious relics or monuments of popery and those known or suspected to carry those from place to place or bring them from foreign places.[35]

The diligence and expenditure taken in some cases appear to have been out of all proportion to the possible outcome. In December 1642, the House of Commons ordered that the serjeant send one of his men with Mr Temple (messenger), to seize the books entitled *A Complaint to the House of Commons*, in a house in White Lyon Court, in Fleet Street, 'where there are divers of the said books, as Mr Temple informed the House'.[36] Two days later, on Monday 2 January 1643, John Wright (stationer) was ordered to be committed to the Compter in Woodstreet 'for publishing a scandalous Book against the Parliament, intituled *A Complaint to the House of Commons*'. The said books were to be 'burnt by the hand of the hangman in the pallace at Westminster and in Smithfield under the careful supervision of the sheriffs of London'. Furthermore, the serjeant's men were ordered 'to go and search the Shops, in and about Westminster, or elsewhere, for the Book, intituled *A Complaint to* (etc.): And in case they find any, or Suspicion that any hath them, that the Serjeant's

---

35   SP 16/459.15. For an order to search for popish books imported from abroad see PC.2.52.561.

36   CJ II.910.

Men take him or her into safe Custody; and him or her to keep, till this House hath taken Order to the contrary'.[37] Pictures, too, could provoke the authorities, and search orders were issued. By order of the House of Commons, Friday, 10 June 1642, 'this scandalous Picture of Sir John Hotham on Horseback upon the Walls of Hull, his Majesty on Foot before the Walls, shall be burnt by the Hands of the common Hangman, presently, in the Palace yard'. The selling or further publishing of them was strictly forbidden, and the matter was referred to the committee for printing to inquire 'who was the Inventor, and who the Printer and Publisher that they may be brought to condign Punishment'. The members of Parliament were strictly charged to deliver all pictures they had for burning, and the serjeant was ordered 'to seize all the Pictures he can meet with in Westminster-hall: And that the Master and Wardens of the Company of Stationers be required to seize, in all Places, all such Pictures as they shall meet with; and bring them to the Bailiff of Westminster to be immediately burnt.'[38]

How ineffective these search activities must have been in the numerous, often cramped bookshops and stalls in London, with piles of paper and bundles everywhere, becomes evident in the order for a large-scale search, issued by the House of Commons on Thursday, 9 March 1643.[39] Under the surveillance of the committee for examinations everyone possible, including hired informants, justices of the peace, captains, officers, constables and the Company of Stationers, was mobilized to search 'in any House or Place, where there is just Cause or Suspicion that Presses are kept, and employed in the Printing of scandalous and lying pamphlets'. They were empowered to demolish presses, to take away 'scandalous pamphlets', and to apprehend suspects. Searches were not always peaceful: frequently doors were blocked, the

37   CJ II.910–11.
38   CJ II.617.
39   CJ II.996–97.

authenticity of warrants questioned, angry words exchanged, and even violence practised.

The production, distribution, and possession/hiding of offensive papers cut across all social boundaries and gender, and offenders were not necessarily members of the booktrade. Once a suspect was discovered, he or she was 'sent for' and ordered to appear before a court together with witnesses. Nehemiah Wallington's notes about his examination in the Star Chamber Court in 1638 provide a rare insight into the ways the court operated. Since Wallington found it too expensive to buy a copy of his interrogation, which would have cost him 'three pounds a peece', he wrote down the whole procedure from memory immediately after the hearing was over. As a unique and immediate description of the impact of censorship on ordinary people, the whole document is reproduced here:

> These be the questions and my answeres in order as well as I can remember:

> *Question*   Where doe you dwell and what trade are you.
> *Answer*   In little Escheap a turner
> *Question*   Have you had the divine tragedy and the newes of epsich.
> *Answer*   Yes
> *Question*   What bookes eles have you had
> *Answer*   The apologie and appeale to the King
> *Question*   Where did you see these Books first or in whose hands did you see them first
> *Answer*   I read them first in my one house
> *Question*   Hade you the lettany
> *Answer*   I know not what that Book is
> *Question*   How long agoe is it sence you had them
> *Answer*   About a yeere a goe
> *Question*   Of whome had you y divine tragedie
> *Answer*   Of my brother Wallington
> *Question*   Of whom had you the Apologie and appeale to the King
> *Answer*   Of an unknown party that brought them to my doore
> *Question*   Of whom had you the newes of epsech
> *Answer*   I know not of whom, whither of my brother or the other man

Question	You must answer directly of whom you had it
Answer	I doe thinke I had it of the other man for I doe not remember I did se my brother have any
Question	To whom have you dispersed any
Answer	I did let one Edward Brown see one of them but I sold him non: but being something timorous I had it of him againe and have burnt it
Question	Where does he dwell and what trade is hee
Answer	He did dwell in little Eschheap a turner, hee was my neighbour
Question	Have you any coppies of them at home
Answer	No
Question	Doe you know who selleth any of them
Answer	No
Question	Do you know who printed them and what they cost printing
Answer	No I cannot tell that is out of my element
Question	Have you sent any of those bookes into the Country
Answer	No
Question	Have you had any letters out of the country for any
Answer	No for I thinke ther was non in the country did know I had any of them.[40]

This is a unique testimony which speaks for itself. It encapsulates the whole range of issues the holders of power were concerned with in respect of censorship. Although the fact that this was written from memory might cast doubt on the full authenticity of these questions and answers, the central concern of the examiners, which is so apparent here, can also be detected in numerous other contemporary documents including statutes and orders for search: it was the authorities' preoccupation with the possible network and the scale of distribution which might lie behind the delinquent and his or her seditious opinions and conduct.

---

40   Guildhall MS 204/470. On his neighbour see Paul S. Seaver, *Wallington's World: A Puritan Artisan in Seventeenth-Century London* (Stanford, 1985), p 100.

There are numerous examples from the practice of censorship. During his examination before the High Commission, the bookseller John Bartlett was pressed by Sir John Lambe, dean of the arches, to give away the name of the man who had brought him the *Scottish News*.[41] Francis Grove, prisoner in the Fleet for printing a 'scandalous' ballad was ordered to be released after the burning of the ballads to assist in the search for the author of the ballad.[42] Abigail Dexter, printer, was committed to the King's Bench in September 1642 because 'she would not clearly confess who the author of the book called *King James' his Judgement of a King, and of a tyrant* was', which had been printed by her directions.[43] It was common practice that a seized pamphlet or a book was read by a designated state officer, and a catalogue of offensive phrases was compiled, which was then to be discussed in one of the appointed courts.[44]

The final element in the chain of control over right and wrong opinions – and illicit printing – was the iconography of punishment which was designed to deter others: the public burning of books in busy places in London – the Exchange, Cheapside Cross, West Smithfield near the market, and at the new Palace in Westminster – explicit orders for exemplary punishment, corporal punishment, public recantations and confessions which were often published afterwards, and branding as a seditious libeller. In the majority of cases the kind of punishment is not explicitly stated. The usual phrase was to 'receive condign (or exemplary) punishment to deter others'. In February 1642, for instance, the Commons' committee for printing was directed 'to think of some

---

41   SP 16/374.25.
42   LJ IV.382–83.
43   LJ V.385–86.
44   See *A Breefe of M. Foxleys papers, for so much as is questioneable in the H. Commission* SP 16/422.127. Sir John Lambe's statement in the High Commission 'That Bartlet was articled against in twoe particulars', SP 16/374. 13i., the House of Lords' list of offensive phrases in two of Dr Pocklington's books, LJ IV.160–61, 180.

way how, by making an example of some notorious delinquents',
others might be 'deterred from this inordinate and insufferable
Licentiousness of Printing'.[45] Printers and publishers were usually punished by the burning or confiscation of the books in
question, the destruction of their printing presses, imprisonment
and a fine. The authors (and licensers) of seditious books and
pamphlets were punished more severely, since they were considered the source of sedition. One of the more lenient forms was a
public recantation. In March 1642, John Bond confessed, that
he, 'being a poor scholar and having nothing else to live upon',
had composed a letter from the Queen in Holland to the King at
York, which had greatly disturbed the Parliament.[46] With the case
manifestly clear, Bond was ordered to suffer exemplary punishment: he had to stand in the pillory at Westminster Hall from 10
to 11 o'clock on the following Friday, 1 April, with a paper on
his head declaring him to be 'A Contriver of false and scandalous
libels', and again at Cheapside the next morning. Furthermore,
the letters were to be called in and burned near him while he
stood in the pillory.[47] In his published recantation Bond expressed
his hope that 'the apprehensive eye of the world will not mis-
interpretate what I have don'.[48] Religious offenders were regularly forced to make humiliating public confessions in church,
usually dressed in a white cloth of repentance.[49] Corporal punishment was still exercised in the early 1640s, or it was at least an
option. On the very day the judgement was to be passed against
Sir Matthew Mennes for writing a seditious book, the King ordered the lord chief justice that 'it is his pleasure that the giving
Mennes his book and burning his hand be suspended until his
Majesty's further pleasure shall be known'.[50] In March 1642, the

---

45   CJ II.441.
46   LJ IV.680.
47   LJ IV.681.
48   Bond, *The Poet's Recantation*.
49   For the survival of some of these confessions see Prynne, *Canterburies doome*.
50   SP 16/456.53.

Commons ordered the committee for printing to inflict 'corporal punishment' on the printer and author of the pamphlet *A Declaration of Sir Phelim Oneil*.[51]

These practices of censorship remained in effect throughout the whole period from 1637 and to 1645. The policy of censorship, however, and the definition of 'right and wrong' changed once the Puritans 'were on top' and tried to impose their views on public opinion.

Change and Continuity of Censorship under the Long Parliament

With the abolition of the High Commission and Star Chamber Court on 1 August 1641, both the House of Commons and the House of Lords set out independently to familiarize themselves with licensing practices, the rights and customs of the Stationers' Company, and the London bookmarket in order to create their own infrastructure for the control of the printing presses. The *Ordinance for Regulating the Abuses in Printing* of 14 June 1643, which provoked Milton's *Areopagitica*, did not revoke a formerly liberal policy, but was the logical consequence of a gradual development. Milton's powerful plea for the freedom of the press has often been over-emphasized by scholars as marking the watershed in Parliament's attitude towards printing. In fact, Milton published his treatise not as a direct response to the ordinance, but under the impact of his own examination before the House of Commons.[52]

It is true that there was a *lapse* of censorship in the early 1640s, which was due, firstly, to a power vacuum and overlapping responsibilities. The last two Laudian licensers, for instance, were entered in the register of the Stationers' Company on 17 No-

---

51   CJ II.472.
52   CJ III.606.

vember 1642 and 8 April 1643 respectively, alongside those newly appointed by the Parliament.[53] Secondly, inefficiencies resulted from division within and between the two Houses of Parliament on key issues, and thirdly, from the half-hearted measures and lack of co-ordination in the execution of censorship. It is common knowledge that 'from the opening of the Long Parliament, the knowledge that the courts of High Commission and Star Chamber had been rendered harmless led to the publication of pamphlets on religious and political topics in a quantity and variety quite unknown before'.[54] Furthermore, the printers 'must have been encouraged by the Commons' known hostility to monopolists and their willingness to accept complaints against Laud's licensing practices'.[55] In March 1641, for instance, various ministers complained about 'the licensing of bad Books, and suppressing the license of orthodox Books'.[56] Their petition was referred to the committee for religion and the ministers were told to attend it, bringing instances with them.

However, to interpret the rapid increase of publication in the 1640s as the welcome consequence of a freedom of the press intended by Parliament ignores the struggle behind the scenes. Christopher Hill's list of unpublishable books which could appear after 1640 needs to be supplemented with a list of books and pamphlets which were seized and ordered to be burnt under the Parliament before 1643.[57] Likewise, Sheila Lambert's important studies on printing for Parliament, with her analysis of authorized and unauthorized publications of parliamentary procedures, do not go beyond this genre to probe the bias of the

---

53   William W. Greg, 'Licensers for the Press * to 1640', *The Bibliographical Society*, n.s., 41 (Oxford, 1962), p 105–6. Cit. in Sheila Lambert, 'The Beginning of Printing for the House of Commons, 1640–1642', *The Library*, 6th ser., III, 1 (March, 1981), pp 43–61, p 47.

54   Lambert, 'Beginning', p. 43.

55   Ibid.

56   LJ IV.182.

57   Hill, 'Society'.

two Houses towards various other genres, such as ballads or plays, or the publications of Anglican authors.[58] She does show, however, that Parliament, especially the House of Commons, took an active interest in printing for its own ends, that it had a 'thorough grasp of the importance of printed propaganda, and rapidly became expert in its use'.[59] Alan Cromartie takes a different view. In his essay on the printing of parliamentary speeches he concludes from the 'history of fabrications' that 'the House of Commons lacked both the ability and the will to control the printers', and that 'neither house of parliament bothered either to condemn, or to regulate, a practice of which every member must have been aware'.[60] Yet on the other hand he suggests that Parliament did exercise control by pointing out that the very production of fabrications supported the cause of the Parliament, and that published speeches 'presupposed a substantial consensus about political and religious ends, and truly controversial speeches were not printed, there are almost no royalist printed speeches'. A speech which 'defied that consensus, paid the penalty'. These observations and the fact that both Houses *did* each set up a special committee as early as 1641 to deal with the publication of speeches, unlicensed printing and sedition demonstrate first steps in censorship on the part of the Parliament prior to 1643.

The foundations for the control of printing and the redefinition of the politics of censorship were laid right at the beginning of the Long Parliament. In the House of Commons on 26 November 1640 Sir Edward Dering proposed forming a sub-com-

---

58   Lambert, 'Beginning'. Sheila Lambert, 'Printing for Parliament 1641–1700', *List and Index Society*, Special Series (1984). In a more recent essay Lambert argued that even in the 1630s there was little enforcement of censorship. Sheila Lambert, 'Richard Montague, Arminianism and Censorship', *Past & Present*, 124 (1989), p 36–68, 68.

59   Lambert, 'Beginning', p 44–5.

60   Alan D. T. Cromartie, 'The Printing of Parliamentary Speeches November 1640 – July 1642', *The Historical Journal*, 33 (1990), pp 23–44, p 35.

mittee of the grand committee for religion. The grand committee was concerned with 'abuses in licensing and printing of books',
and the new committee was to 'examine the printers, what books,
by bad licenses, have been corruptly issued forth; and what good
books have been, like good ministers, silenced, clipped or
cropped'.[61] The task of this new sub-committee found public
support in the Root and Branch Petition which was presented to
the House of Commons on 11 December 1640 by 'the militant
Puritans of the City'.[62] Among the 'manifold evils practiced and
occasioned by the prelates' and their dependants the petition listed
'the hindering of godly books to be printed, the blotting out or
perverting those which they suffer, all or most of that which
strikes at Popery or Arminianism; The adding of what or where
pleaseth them, and the restraint of reprinting books formerly
licensed, without relicensing'.[63] The complaints about the constraints on printing were complemented by attacks on 'the swarming of lascivious, idle, and unprofitable books and pamphlets,
play-books and ballads', and 'the publishing and venting of popish, Arminian, and other dangerous books and tenets'. Some of
the offensive books were named: Ovid's *Fits of Love*, *The Parliament of Women*, Barn's *Poems*, and Parker's *Ballads*. The publication of these books was 'in disgrace of religion, to the increase
of all vice, and withdrawing of people from reading, studying,
and hearing the Word of God, and other good books'. Offence
was taken especially at some opinions spread in Arminian and
popish books, namely, 'That the Church of Rome is a true

---

61 CJ II.84. *Cobbett's Parliamentary History of England from the Norman Con-
    quest in 1066 to the Year 1803*, 2 vols. (London, 1807), ed. Richard Bagshaw, ii,
    p 67. Cit. in Helen A. Long, *Appearance into Public Light: Aspects of the Con-
    trol and Use of Print in London in the 1640s* (unpubl. D. Phil. dissertation,
    University of La Trobe, Melbourne, 1984), p 84. For the structure of commit-
    tee work in general during this period see Sheila Lambert, 'Procedure in the
    House of Commons in the Early Stuart Period', *EHR*, 95 (1980), pp 753–81.
62 *The Constitutional Documents of the Puritan Revolution 1625–1660*, ed. Samuel
    R. Gardiner (Oxford, 1979), pp 137–44. See also Fletcher, *Outbreak*, ch. 3.
63 Gardiner, *Constitutional*, p 139.

Church, and in the worst times never erred in fundamentals, that the subjects have no propriety in their estates, but that the King may take from them as he pleaseth, that all is the King's, and that he is bound by no law'.

The committees worked slowly but steadily. On 21 January 1641, the House of Commons ordered that a warrant should be issued requiring the registrar of the High Commission Court to deliver into the custody of the clerk of the Commons 'all such Bibles and other Books, as are remaining and detained in his Hand by colour of a Warrant from the High Commission Court'.[64] This move encouraged a number of people to petition for the return of their books, and on 5 February a special 'committee for the Lord Canterbury' was set up to deal with these petitions, and to examine 'by what Power the inhibiting the Printing of divers orthodox and good Books of late hath been granted'.[65] However, not much actually happened. In June the registrar of the High Commission approached the House of Lords, asking how he should dispose of the 'diverse Cart-loads of Books' put into his custody on the order of the Archbishop of Canterbury. The Lords ordered the Bishops of Durham, Lincoln, Exeter, Carlisle, Ely, Bristol, and Rochester, and the assistants of their choosing, to peruse the books and report back to the House.[66]

Furthermore, the High Commissioners were confronted with a number of questions which they had to answer before the committee 'appointed to examine their jurisdiction':

> (1) By what authority they authorise their messengers to search for and seize any man's books or goods, or to break open any house or houses, for any of those purposes.

---

64   CJ II.71.
65   CJ II.79.
66   LJ IV. 295. The bishops were appointed from a mixed group of Laudian and anti-Laudian men, probably reflecting the opinions in the House of Lords. Whereas the Bishops of Durham, Lincoln, Exeter, and Carlisle (Thomas Moreton, John Williams, George Hall, Barnaby Potter) were anti-Laudian, the other three (Matthew Wren, Robert Skinner, John Warner) were pro-Laudian.

(2) By what authority they send forth general warrants, or warrants dormant for apprehension of persons supposed to be schismatic, separatists, etc without naming any certainty, and to search and seize the books of such persons at the discretion of the messenger.

(3) By what authority they hold plea ... concerning books offensive to the State, printing, uttering, and publishing books concerning decrees and orders made in Star Chamber touching the disorders in printing or uttering books, or the execution thereof.[67]

There are no written accounts of the answers, yet an undated paper with notes by John Lambe survives for this period, in which he lists several points that were generally inquired into by the High Commission Court. Among them were the publishing of false rumours, seditious books and libels; the search for seditious popish books and libels or portraitures; and the breach of Star Chamber Orders in printing.[68] It is possible that Lambe's private notes were written in reaction to the inquiries launched by the House of Commons.

While these first inquiries were under way, books and pamphlets continued to be licensed, forbidden, searched and burnt, and delinquents punished by the old authorities. Against the backdrop of the Scottish war, pamphlets touching on this conflict made up the bulk of cases. A pamphlet called *The Intentions of the Armie of the Kingdome of Scotland* was 'swarming all over London', and it was secretly dispersed in the army.[69] Under the impact of growing tension in the City, popish books or any books, pamphlets, and manuscripts tending to sedition seemed increasingly to disturb those in power. Decrees and proclamations were published to control unlicensed printing, and towards the second half of 1640 search warrants were issued for private houses of named individuals, many of them craftsmen, or of 'any other

---

67   SP 16/477.14.
68   SP 16/474.71.
69   SP 16/465.231–237 (copy with notes written in the margin), SP 16/465.12, SP 16/465.43.

person whatever suspected of having Popish or seditious books (printing or in manuscripts), which are to be brought away'.[70]

On 13 February 1641, the sub-committee on licensing was converted into a select committee to examine 'all abuses in printing, licensing, importing and suppressing of books of all sorts; and in denying license to some books, and expurging several passages out of other books'.[71] Furthermore, the committee had power 'to send for Parties, Witnesses, Papers, Records, Bookes printed or Manuscripts, conducing to this Service'. Dering was appointed chairman of the new-born committee, which was consequently referred to as the committee for printing. Complaints of the fabrication of speeches and the printing of parliamentary procedures without license induced the Commons to set up an additional committee in May 1641 'to consider of the Printing of the Speeches of the Members of this House'.[72] It was added to the committee for printing 'to have the like Power joined, as either of them had, severed'.[73] In June 1641, even prior to the abolition of the Star Chamber and the High Commission Court, the House of Commons started to prepare a bill for printing.[74] A month later the newly founded and enlarged committee for print-

---

70   SP 16/467.92–5, PC 2.52.739.

71   CJ II.84. Lambert, 'Beginning', p 43.

72   CJ II.146. The members named were 'Mr Glyn, Mr Maynard, Mr Corbett, Sir John Colpeper, Sir Edward Deeringe, Sir John Evelyn, Mr Richard Moore, Mr Nicholls'. For a committee report on the printing of Lord Digby's speech concerning the *Bill of Attainder of the Earl of Strafford*, see *Sir John Evelyn his Report*, BL E.163.6 and CJ II.208, 209.

73   CJ II.148. In January 1642 the committee for printing was again enlarged and appointed to consider the 'Bill of Printing', CJ II.402. The House of Commons seemed to have a number of different committees in addition to the committee for printing engaged in inquiring into unlicensed and 'scandalous' printing: the committee of information, the committee of examination; the committee to consider the best way of putting public orders and votes of the House into execution, CJ II.604, and the committee to 'consider of some way of preventing the publishing of any declaration (...) concerning the Parliament', CJ II.611.

74   CJ II.181.

ing and the 'committee for examination and printing of books' merged, 'and both committees so joined were to consider that Bill (for printing)'.[75] In August 1641, the House of Commons was enjoined by the lord chamberlain to prevent inordinate printing until the bill was passed.[76] Consequently, the committee for printing ordered that the master and wardens of the Stationers' Company were to be authorized to take the best course they could to suppress and hinder 'this Licence of Printing: And to inform this House, upon all Occasions, what Books, Pamphlets, and Speeches, are printed; and to use the best Means they can for the Preventing and Suppressing of them'.[77] On the same day, the Stationers' Company accused Thomas Harper of 'printing the proceedings at the trial of Strafford's defence'. With reference to the Commons' order, the House was further informed that there was a volume of speeches allegedly by members of the House 'in the presse'.[78]

The Stationers' Company gladly embraced these new orders for stricter censorship. It had, in fact, already started its own campaign for stricter censorship in March, when the master and wardens of the Stationers' Company, worried about its privileges, presented a petition to the House of Lords, desiring the execution of stricter censorship.[79] They also sent a paper which listed some unlicensed books recently printed, with the names of the printers. In their petition the stationers announced that they were preparing 'a Bill for these and other things concerning Bookes and printing', which they 'intend shortly and humbly to present to your Lordships'.[80] Already incensed at the publication of the

---

75 SP 16/483.4.

76 CJ II.266. See also CJ II.267; 268; 402

77 CJ II.168.

78 SC A f.132.

79 For a recent study of the 'old partnership of the state and the Stationers' between 1640 and 1643, see Michael Mendle, 'De Facto Freedom, De Facto Authority: Press and Parliament, 1640–43', in *Historical Journal* 38 (1995), pp 307–32.

80 LJ IV.175. H.L.M.P. 4 March 1640–41.

articles of charge against Thomas Wentworth, first Earl of Strafford, the House of Lords responded with the appointment of a 'Committee to examine the whole business concerning the printing and selling of unlicensed Books and Pamphlets'.[81] The new committee devoted several meetings to the stationers' complaint about the breakdown of licensing procedures: a resolution against the sale of unlicensed books and in favour of exemplary punishment for 'greatest offenders that others may be deterred' was drafted,[82] and the Charter of the Stationers' Company was carefully studied in order for the House to become familiar with licensing procedures and the right of search and seizure.[83] Furthermore, delinquents were sent for and examined, and because there were so many, three people were ordered to receive exemplary punishment, whereas the others were sent home after having been admonished for the future. Special offence was taken at Henry Walker's *The Prelates Pride*, and his *Verses on the Wren and Finch*. However, the accused Walker and John Wells were released from the Fleet Street prison five days later, and the third person, Stephen Buckley, escaped imprisonment altogether for lack of proof. Finally, 'it was ordered that the house doe require the Master and Wardens of the Company of Stationers of London to execute such ordinances as they have made concerning printing, according to law'.[84]

The lenient punishment of delinquents suggests that at this stage the Lords were not terribly interested in enforcing stricter licensing procedures and merely redressed the grievances of the Stationers' Company. Again in reaction to a complaint made to the House of the 'great Abuse in printing and publishing of Pam-

---

81   LJ IV.175. The committee members were: 'the Earl of Bath, the Earl of Clare, the Earl of Monmouth, Lord Viscount Saye and Seale, Lord Bishop of Lincoln, Lord Bishop of Sarum, Lord Bishop of Exeter, Lord Bishop of Ely, Lord Bishop of Chester, Ds Howard de Charl.'

82   H.L.M.P. 10 March 1640–41.

83   H.L.M.P. 12 March 1640–41.

84   H.L.M.P. 12 March 1640–41, LJ IV.180, 82.

phlets and unlicensed Books', the committee was enlarged by
five members and explicitly ordered 'to consider how the Press
may be regulated and ordered, that so the Printing of such Books
may be suppressed'.[85] Renewed pressure to pass a bill for the regulation of printing came from the Stationers' Company after the
abolition of the Star Chamber and the High Commission Court,
because it feared great financial losses through the breach of licence and privilege. In September 1641 it presented its *Reasons
to induce the passing of the Bill touching Printing*.[86] In order to
guarantee strict licencing procedures, property and copyright,
and to prevent the importation of books from abroad, they advocated a mixture of control and punishment. Licensers were to
be appointed, and 'for the better and further suppressing such
bookes sharpe punishments and censures are to bee enacted and
declared against all that shall publish disperse or sell such books
as shall seeme fitt to the wisdome of the state to establish in this
case'. In an attempt to cloud over their explicit economic interests, the stationers emphasized their concern for the common
good and reiterated contemporary concern about the impact of
public opinion on the stability of the state:

> If printing in England be not under good rule and government every
> libelling speritt will have libertie to traduce the proceedinge of the
> state, every malicious spirit may then revile whensoever he pleaseth

85 LJ IV.396. The new members named were 'the Earl of Sarum, Lord Viscount
    Conway, Ds Pagett, Ds Kymbolton, Ds Brooke'. On 9 December 1641 the
    following were added: 'The Lord Privy Seal, the Lord Wharton, and the Lord
    Bruce.' LJ IV.468. Time and again members of the House of Lords were ap-
    pointed *ad hoc*, independently of the committee, to inquire into special cases
    such as the printing of the book *Certain Grievances or Errors of the Service
    Book*, LJ IV.478.
86 SP 16/484.121. For the period from 1604 to 1637, Sheila Lambert has demon-
    strated that the provisions of the Star Chamber decrees of 1586 and 1637 were
    prescribed 'at the desire of the Stationers' Company, rather than being im-
    posed by government'. Sheila Lambert, 'The Printers and the Government,
    1604–1637', in *Aspects of Printing from 1600*, ed. Michael Harris and Robin
    Myers (Oxford, 1987), pp 1–29, p 2.

to accompt his adversary, yea every pernitious hereticke may have opportunity to poyson the minds of good mynded men of wicked errors and deplorable distractions which at this present doe soemuch blemish and offend the glorious light of the reformed Religion hapily established amongst us will be fomented by every ignorant person that takes advantage of a loose presse may publish the fancies of every idle braine as so manyfestly appeareth by the swarmes of scandalous and irksome pamphletts that are cryed about the streetes to the great dyshonor of the state and government.

In August 1642, a first *Ordinance for restraining the Licence of Printing* was read in the House of Commons and referred back to a committee of 'White, Rigby, Rous, Gourdon, and Sir Simonds D'Ewes who withdrew immediately about it'.[87] This ordinance reflected the urgency and impatience which characterized the attempts of Parliament to bring the London printing presses under its control. After complaining about the 'late great Disorders and Abuses by irregular Printing', it explicitly stated that 'a Bill is in Preparation for the Redress of those Mischiefs'. Only the 'present Distractions' prevented the bill from being 'so speedily perfected and passed as is desired'. In order to cope with the grievous situation in the meantime, it was ordered that 'no Person or Persons shall print, publish, or utter any Book or Pamphlet, false or scandalous to the Proceedings of the Houses of Parliament, or either of them'. Without special order from either of the two Houses, nothing about the proceedings of the Parliament was allowed to be published. Once permission was given, the printed document had to be 'entered in the Register' of the Stationers' Company, 'according to the ancient Custom'. The master and wardens of the Stationers' Company, the serjeant of the Black Rod, and the serjeant of the House of Commons and his deputies were given far reaching powers to search and confiscate unlicensed printing presses and 'other Printing Materials'. On request 'all his Majesty's Officers shall … aid and assist to

---

87   CJ II.734, BL E.114.32, CJ II.739, LJ V.322.

apprehend the Offenders in the Premises, and to bring them'
before either of the two Houses or the 'Committees appointed
for Printing; upon whose Report of the Fact, such Course shall
be taken with the said Offenders as shall be just'. On 18 October
1642, the select committee appointed to deal with printing was
ordered to sit daily.[88]

Although both Houses seemed preoccupied with the preparation of an ordinance and a bill for censorship and the administration of daily grievances concerning illicit and seditious printing, the inquiry into old licensing practices and censorship started
the moment the Long Parliament opened.[89] Both Houses started
to reconsider what was a politically acceptable publication, and
what needed redefinition. On 22 March 1641, a warrant was issued by the 'committee for preparation of the charge against
William Laud, Archbishop of Canterbury' requiring him 'to bring
before the committee all books of accounts or other notes in
writing which have been made by you, or any of your servants in
the last 13 years, of the names and number of all books seized by
you or them within that time as forfeited goods'.[90] On 1 December 1641, the committee reported back to the House of Lords:

These books were found to be of three types:

(1) good and vendible books that were fit to be returned to their
owners and sold by stationers, such as *The holy table, name and thing*;
Mr Walker's *Treatise of the sabbath*; *A French commentary on the Rev-*

---

88   CJ II.812.
89   Interesting details on the licensing practices of the four licensers responsible
      in the 1630s (William Heywood, William Bray, Samuel Baker, and Thomas
      Weekes) can be found in Prynne, *Canterburies Doome*. Prynne lists whole pas-
      sages which had been expurgated by these licensers. See Anthony Milton, *The
      Laudians and the Church of Rome c.1625–1640* (PhD dissertation, University
      of Cambridge, 1989), pp 128–31, and id., *Catholic and Reformed: Roman and
      Protestant Churches in English Protestant Thought, 1600–1640*, Cambridge Stud-
      ies in Early Modern British History (Cambridge, 1996).
90   SP 16/478.54.

elation; Dr Burges his *Rejoinder for ceremonies*, and some old books of controversies.

(2) books that were fit to be sold to choice persons only such as Caussin's *4th tome (sic) of Holy Court*; Thomas de Kempis *Of the following of Christ*; and *The life of Sir Thomas Moore*.

(3) superstitious tablets and books, fit only to be burnt, such as missals, primers, *Offices of Our Ladie* etc.[91]

The House of Lords declared that the first group of books were approved 'by this House and are to be delivered to the Owners, and be sold by the Stationers'. The second set had to be delivered into 'safe Hands, to be sold to Noblemen, Gentlemen, and Scholars, but not to Women'. And the last group of books was to be burnt by the sheriffs of London in Smithfield.[92]

There are also individual instances where earlier judgements were reversed. On 23 January 1641, Heily presented a petition about a book of his father's 'compiling', which had been taken by the Archbishop of Canterbury. Two days later the book was ordered to be restored to Heily.[93] The apprentice William Flower had been imprisoned for possessing Prynne's book *News from Ipswich*.[94] The Commons resolved on 26 May 1641 that his imprisonment was 'illegal and that reparation should be made'.[95] The revision of earlier judgements also worked the other way round and books formerly licensed under Laud were now banned. On 10 May 1641, the House of Lords ordered that two books by John Pocklington called *Sunday no Sabbath* and *Altare*

91   LJ IV.45, SP 16/486.6–7. The report had been presented to the Lords by the Bishop of Exeter, a member of the committee appointed by the House of Lords to deal with printing.

92   LJ IV.457.

93   LJ IV.141, 143.

94   For some of the objections voiced against this 'pamphlet or libel' during the Star Chamber trial against Prynne, Burton, and Bastwick see the (copy of the) information filed in the Star Chamber against them. SP 16/354.380–388.

95   CJ II.158.

Christianum, licensed on 24 February 1636 and 7 March 1637, were to be burnt in the City of London and in both Universities.[96] The decision was based on a number of passages in both books which made his doctrine 'appear to be most seditious and dangerous' and to spread 'judaical and corrupt ideas'. He was accused that in *Sunday no Sabbath* he 'maliciously inveigeth against the Sabbath-day Lectures and Preaching, calling it the dull Invention of a foggy Brain, and many other such unfitting Laws and Constitutions established in the Church of England. And lastly, he terms the Martyrs and other Learned Men of our Church, to be no better than Hereticks, and Rebels, and other such like vile and ignominious Appellations'.[97] The licenser of the two books, William Bray, was called for, and he confessed that 'he had read them over, but not so cautiously as he should have done', for which he was heartily sorry, and he was 'now of another Opinion than he was when he licensed and approved those two books'. Bray's case demonstrates the inconsistency and limitations of the work of censors, an issue which is worth looking at in further depth. Obviously, a licenser's signature did not necessarily imply a careful judgement. In fact, a close analysis of editing processes, as Anthony Milton has demonstrated in a recent paper for the first half of the seventeenth century, further undermines the notion of a monolithic state control of censorship in support of the notion of 'interpretation' as part of censorship. 'What posed a threat was what people thought would pose a threat.'[98] Bray was ordered to make a recantation over 'His Licensing and Approbation' in a sermon at St Margarets, Westminster, which was afterwards ordered to be published and printed. Finally he was forbidden to license further books.[99] Holdsworth, who apparently continued to license for the press

---

96   LJ IV. 180. See also Greg, 'Licensers', pp 12-3.
97   LJ IV.160, 161.
98   Paper given at the conference of the Anglo-American Society in July 1996.
99   LJ IV.183 and LJ IV.219.

at the University of Cambridge until 1643, finally aroused the displeasure of the House of Commons. In October 1643 he was committed to the Tower for 'licensing books to be printed to the prejudice and scandal of Parliament'.[100] In the course of Laud's trial on 13 March 1644 evidence was put forward that the archbishop had 'procured the publication of various sermons and books containing in them matter contrary to Parliament's right and the fundamental laws and government of the kingdom'.

Special concern was caused by John Cowell's *The Interpreter*. Under the heading 'King' it said 'that the King was above the law by his absolute power'; under the title 'Parliament' we read 'And of these two one must needs bee true that either the king is above the Parliament ... the positive Lawes of the kingdome or that hee is not an Absolute King...yet simply to binde the Prince to or by these Lawes were repugnant to the nature and constitution of an absolute Monarchy'; and under the heading of 'Prerogative', that he had a prerogative above the law.[101] This book had been condemned by a judgement of Parliament and called in by a proclamation of 1610. It was ordered that none should be sold or published.[102] At that time, the book was brought to the attention of the House of Commons and described by Sir Edwin Sandys as 'very inadvised and indiscreet, tending to the disreputation of the House and the power of the common law'. James I himself had read *The Interpreter*, which he believed had been 'too bold with the Common Law of the land holding it a great presumption in any subject to speak or write against those under which he must live'.[103] Notwithstanding this order, the

100 CJ III. 124. CJ III. 265. See also the reference in CJ II. 951 to a report on the information given against Holdsworth for licensing Dr Fearne's *The Resolving of the Conscience*.

101 SP 16/499 262. LJ VI.468. For the complete list of the offending passages see SP16/499.262–263.

102 R. Steele, *Bibliotheca Lindesiana. A Bibliography of Royal Proclamations of the Tudor and Stuart Sovereigns* (Oxford, 1910), p 128.

103 Leona Rostenberg, *The Minority Press and the English Crown: A Study in Repression, 1558–1625* (Nieukoop, 1971), p 85.

book was reprinted several times. In July 1638, the Stationers'
Company informed Archbishop Laud that they had discovered
that 'a great part of a Book called *The Interpreter* was secretly
kept in a victualling house neere Turnebulstreet, where a private
printing press had been set up'.[104] Laud ordered that 'the delinquents were to be attached' and they had to appear before the
High Commission Court 'the first Court day of ye next Terme'.
Hunscott and Walley, who had discovered the illicit printing activities, deposed in 1638:

> Richard Hodgkinson Being brought Before the Lorde of Canter-
> bury for printing of A Booke caled Cowels interpreter forbiden on
> order of parlament and A proclamasion for no to keepe it not to
> bring them to the preese/and the Bishope Refered the matter to Sir
> John Lambe who testified the booke asking what herte was in it/we
> tolde him it was prohibited by the king and parlament and shoed
> him the proclamasion and/Hodgkinson took it up and floung it
> downe againe saing in A scornefole maner/this came forth in a sedicios
> scandolos parlament time. Hodgkinson printed it for Sadlor in Ducke
> lane and our company often compleyned to the Bishop of Canter-
> bury but could not get it stoped.[105]

On 25 March 1640, the proclamation was affirmed, prohibiting
'the uttering' of John Cowell's book *The Interpreter*, and requir-

---

104 Plomer, 'More Petitions', pp 136–38.
105 SP16/499.260 (the paper is headed 'About the midle of July 1638'). Earlier
that year the master and wardens of the Company of Stationers had already
petitioned Laud that a book called *Cowell's Interpreter* was printed contrary to
the decree of the Star Chamber, SP 16/400.37. During Laud's trial in 1644, the
case was reviewed: 'The said Book was re-printed in Duck Lane, at a private
House, by one Hodskins, Printer, to the said Archbishhop Laud, without any
Order of Licence; and upon complaint thereof to the Archbishop by Joseph
Hunscott and [?] Walley, he put them off to Sir John Lambe, and he to the
printer, who said: "The Proclamation was made in a schismatical and scandalous Parliament Time." And the Archbishop told the said Hunscott, when he
came to him about it, "That if he would not go his way, he would trounce
him". Hunscot and Walley deposed this on oath.' LJ VI. 468. For other cases
see SP 16/374.24–7, SP 16/499.255, SP 16/501.18, LJ IV.469.

ing all who had copies of it to bring them in.[106] In 1643, a broadside was printed in Oxford 'for William Web' entitled *The Interpreter*. It was a 'mock-interpreter' consisting of questions and answers with the latter ridiculing the phenomena inquired into:

Question: The Common Prayer Booke?
Answer: A Messe of Pottage, the Masse in English.
Question: Brownisme and Anabaptisme?
Answer: Protestant Religion, reformed, refined.[107]

However, the old licensing authorities were not the sole cause of grievances. Parliament also had to take steps against its critics. In July 1642, the House of Lords ordered 'Dutton to be committed forthwith to the Gatehouse for behaving scornfully to the House and for seeking to justify "the foulest and most scandalous pamphlet that ever was raised or published against the Parliament", to remain there at its pleasure'.[108] The pamphlet in question was *The Declaration or Resolution of the County of Hereford*, which accused the Parliament of driving the country to utter ruin.[109] Dutton's 'scornful behaviour' was witnessed in a Stationer's shop:

> Maddison gave evidence that on reading this pamphlet in a stationer's shop, he called it "a foul scandal" upon the Parliament and said the author deserved to be whipped. Sir William Boteler told him he deserved to be whipped for saying so and that he would justify every word in it, and threatened to slash him. Dutton, a minister, joined in, saying likewise, that Maddison deserved to be whipped for speaking nonsense and calling the pamphlet a libel.[110]

Boteler was out on bail, and had to appear the same day before the Lords for examination. Little evidence survives of authors who complained about the licensing practices or censorship policies of the two Houses. In a letter to Dering, Richard Ward pro-

---

106 SP 16/501.19.
107 William Clark Collection. G.3.13.
108 LJ V.192.
109 Fletcher, *Outbreak*, pp 305f.
110 LJ V.192.

tested at the treatment his book on St Matthew had received in
the Commons' committee for printing. He called England's
Imprimatur worse than Italy's *Index Expurgatorius* and demanded
satisfaction 'from Dr Weeks (licenser already under Laud) for
the wrong received through the sides of my book by his means'.[111]
In February 1642, the Parliament itself became dissatisfied with
Dering. He was 'expelled the House and sent to the Tower for
publishing a collection of speeches which indicated his tendency
to uphold the existing order in church and state. The vote passed
by 85 to 61 and this was the largest majority recorded in any of
the twelve divisions which took place during February and March
1642'.[112] On 7 February 1642, Dering was ordered to deliver to
the House of Commons 'the writings, books, etc., in his custody as chairman of the Committee for Printing'.[113] He was succeeded by John White.

Obviously, the most spectacular reversal of former judgement
by the Parliament was Prynne's, Bastwick's and Burton's release
from prison by order of Parliament in December 1640. Clarendon
commented on this event that 'this time the license of preaching
and printing increased to that degree that all pulpits were freely
delivered to the schismatical and silenced preachers, who till then
had lurked in corners or lived in New England; and the presses
(were) at liberty for the publishing the most invective, seditious
and scurrilous pamphlets that their wit and malice could invent.'[114]
Others welcomed these changes. On 24 November 1640, Thomas Knyvett wrote home to a friend in Norfolk: 'Now reformation goes on again as hot as toast'. And he added, 'If thou didst
hear what sermons are preached to the Parliament men, thou
wouldst bless thyself'.[115]

---

111 SP 16/479.11.
112 Lambert, 'Beginning', p 55.
113 CJ II.419.
114 Edward H. Clarendon, *History of the Rebellion and Civil Wars in England*, ed.
William D. Macray, 6 vols. (Oxford, 1888), i, p 269.
115 Paul S. Seaver, *The Puritan Lectureship. The Politics of Religious Dissent 1560–
1662* (Stanford, 1970), p 268. Another crucial step was the closure of London

Competing Censors: The King and the Parliament

With the growing friction between the King and the Parliament, the latter became increasingly concerned with checking publications that might favour the King's side of the story. Nevertheless, delinquents were usually accused of undermining both the authority of the Parliament *and* of the King, a regulation which was true for all proceedings of Parliament during this period. Furthermore, Parliament's attitude towards the King's authority over and interest in censorship was ambivalent and only gradually took shape, as evident, for instance, in the *Notes on the prerogative power of the Crown regulating printing*.[116] As a victim of censorship, John Bond claimed that the only reason for his severe punishment was that the Parliament wanted 'to give plenary satisfaction as well to the whole kingdome in generall, as also to his Majestie in particular' for the 'inumerable multitude of Pamphlets, which have beene surreptitiously inserted above this twelve months and halfe to the ignominious scandall of the State'. They 'did not only exasperate his Majesties just indignation against them, but also highly incensed his Parliament against the same'.[117] Earlier that month, on 9 March 1642, the King had, in fact, complained in general of seditious pamphlets, which caused Parliament to start the proceedings against Bond.[118] Not much else happened. Relations between the King and the Parliament were strained by 'the late strange and unheard-of Breach of our Laws, in the Accusation of the Lord Kymbolton and the Five Members', and both Houses rather reluctantly answered to the King's concerns about printing: 'As for Your Majesty's Fears and Doubts, the Ground whereof is from seditious Pamphlets and Sermons,

---

theatres on 31 August 1642, and the order to burn the *Book of Sports*, BL 669.f.7.12. See picture section.
116 SP 16/378.24.
117 Bond, *Recantation*.
118 Lambert, 'Beginning', p 56.

we shall be as careful to endeavour the Removal as soon as we shall understand what Pamphlets and Sermons are by Your Majesty intended.'[119] The King sent a frosty reply within a fortnight: 'If it should be asked of Us to name any, the mentioning of *The Protestation Protested, The Prentices Protestation, To your Tents O Israel*, or any other, would bee too great an Excuse for the rest: If you think them not worthy the Enquiry, We have done.'[120] In a 'second message', the King became more explicit and demanded the exemplary punishment of the author and publisher of a paper entitled *A Question answered, how Laws are to be understood, and Obedience yielded*. He objected that the pamphlet's message – 'human Laws do not bind the Conscience' – would, if it were believed, disturb the 'Civil Government and Peace of the Kingdom'.[121] The two Houses instructed their committees to take seriously the King's complaints about seditious pamphlets and ordered them 'to make some speedy progress in these businesses'. Yet not much was actually done.[122] When the lord chief justice informed the Lords that Henry Walker, the author of the pamphlet *To your Tents O Israel* had been found and committed to the Tower, they left it to the King's council to proceed against him according to law. But before his trial actually began, Walker managed to escape.[123]

The two Houses became increasingly reluctant to comply with the King's wishes. In March 1642, the King went to York where he set up his own press, operated by the King's printer, Robert Barker. The conflict between the King and Parliament broke out openly in May 1642, when Parliament noticed the output of Robert Barker's press in York. In their eyes, this was another indication of the power the malignant party had over Charles I.

---

119 LJ IV.661.
120 LJ IV.686.
121 LJ V. 14.
122 Lambert, 'Beginning', pp 55–7; Long, *Appearance*, pp 97–102.
123 LJ V. 160.

It seemed clear that the King had turned against Parliament, 'which the more speedily to effect, they have caused a press to be transported to York from whence several Papers and Writings of that kind are conveyed to all parts of the kingdom, without the authority of the great seal, in an unusual and illegal manner, and without the advice of his majesty's privy council'.[124] The King countercharged that it was Parliament which had ignored established custom in failing to control the presses. In numerous declarations and orders Parliament now attempted to give its publications priority over those of the King. In June 1642, an order was presented for publishing the orders and declarations of the House of Commons to provide every county with a sufficient number of them, and to guarantee their 'true and well printing'.[125] An officer was especially appointed to monitor the financial side of this large scale of publication.[126] A month later the Lords and Commons declared and ordered:

> That no Sheriff, Mayor, Bayliff, Parson, Vicar, Curate, or other Officer, shall from henceforth publish or proclaim, or cause to be proclaimed or published, any such Proclamations, Declarations or Papers which are or shall be contrary to any Order, Ordinance, or Declarations of the said Houses of Parliament, or tending to the scandall or derogation of their proceedings, but shall use all lawfull wayes to hinder the proclaiming and publishing thereof.[127]

In August, both Houses became more explicit and ordered that neither the King's printer nor any other printers were to print the following proclamations:

(1) A Proclamation concerning the present Rebellion.

(2) A Proclamation requiring the Aid and Assistance of all his Subjects on the North Side of Trent, and within Twenty Miles

---

124 *Cobbett's Parliamentary History of England from the Norman Conquest in 1066 to the year 1803*, 2 vols. (London, 1807), ed. Richard Bagshaw, ii, p 1250.
125 CJ II.604, 609.
126 CJ II.611.
127 BL 669.f.5.54, CJ II.647.

Southward thereof, for the Suppressing of Rebels now marching against us.

(3) His Majesty's Message to the House of Commons dated 13 August 1642.

(4) The Declaration of the Lords and Commons, with his Majesty's Answer to the Declaration, now brought from the King by warrant to be printed.[128]

At this point the universally accepted story of the 'King's evil councillors' was still shared by the Parliament. When they received a letter from the King with a printed paper entitled *A Proclamation for the suppressing of the present Rebellion*, the Lords and Commons declared and published that 'the Matter of this libelous and scandalous Paper is the Venom of those traiterous counsellors about His Majesty'.[129] One of the biggest problems for the Parliament was that the publication of royalist pamphlets 'could not be prevented in London so long as the King's Printer's patent was being operated there according to the King's order'.[130] A first step towards resolving the dilemma was taken on 13 August 1642, when the House of Commons ordered that the King's Printer 'be injoined from this House, not to print anything by Warrant from his Majesty that concerns the Parliament without the consent of both or either House of Parliament'.[131] The Commons' committee for printing was further requested to find out what was being printed at the King's printing house that concerned the Parliament.

In the execution of these orders a number of conflicts arose at a local level, which reflect conflicting loyalties to the King and Parliament. Since the early summer of 1642, people had already

---

128   CJ II.724, SC A.f.136.
129   LJ V.288.
130   Lambert, 'Beginning', p 57. SP 16/378.24.
131   CJ II.719.

been pressed to declare their allegiance to one side or the other under the impact of Parliament's militia ordinance and the King's ordinance for the commission of array. Both competed to win over the militia of the various counties, and to muster and train them.[132]

In June 1642, the sheriff of Essex drew the attention of the House of Commons to various proclamations concerning the proceedings of Parliament which had appeared in his county. He was urged to refuse to publish any of them and to obey and publish instead the orders of the House.[133] On 26 July 1642, the churchwardens of Cople (county unknown) provided the House of Commons with information against Guyn, the vicar of Cople. According to their story Guyn had received two declarations from Parliament and one from the King, with a note on the back of one of those from Parliament that he should not publish the King's declaration. Guyn demanded whether he was to obey God or man and said: 'By God's word I am commanded to obey the King; I find no such Command for the Parliament.' And then, he 'scornfully threw the Declaration from the Parliament to be published by the officious churchwardens, as he said'. They also declared that he was a man of 'a debauched, lewd, and contentious Disposition, and very averse to all Proceedings of Parliament, and that he had spoken divers opprobious and scandalous words against the House and in particular against Pym.'[134] A month later, Edward Walker and 'two other inhabitants of Greenwich' were called before the House of Commons where they gave the following testimony: 'The previous Sunday they had been present when Lake, the curate of the Church in Greenwich, read out the *Kentish Petition* and *Instructions* presented lately to the King at York, which the House had caused to be suppressed as it was being printed.'[135]

132 See Fletcher, *Outbreak*, pp 347–68.
133 CJ II.622.
134 Ibid.
135 CJ II.735.

Orders continued to be published forbidding the publication
of the King's proclamations, and the King's printer was summoned to attend the House of Commons for printing a proclamation of the King 'without first acquainting the House there-
with'.[136] But attempts to suppress the King's printing press were
not very successful, and the Parliament enforced stricter con-
trols by the end of the year: the serjeants from the Lords delivered to the Commons some papers from the King to his printer
which had been intercepted.[137] Furthermore, on 23 December
1642, the Commons authorized five of the justices of the peace
to search for and seize scandalous pamphlets and to inquire after
the authors, printers and publishers.[138] They were empowered to
'send for any person, as they should think fit, who could give
them information concerning this business, and were to report
the same to the House'. In January 1643, the clerk of Parliament
was ordered to provide a printer to print what Parliament should
appoint, and the printer was 'to provide a letter only' for such
printing.[139] Finally, in March 1643, the Commons granted to the
committee for examinations (part of the committee for printing) extensive rights to search and seize illicit prints, to destroy
printing presses, and to send for and examine suspects. The order was to be executed by those persons they should appoint and
think fit.[140] So far search orders had been executed in coopera-
tion between the master and wardens of the Stationers' Company and 'the nearest Justice of the Peace'.[141] As early as September 1641, the stationers had argued for the necessity of a 'standing power' to control printing, declaring that the use of justices
of the peace was not very effective, and the new order was inter-

---

136 CJ II.835.
137 CJ II.857.
138 CJ II.900. (The justices were: George Longe, George Garrett, John Hooker,
     John Herne, and Robert Dixon).
139 LJ V.554.
140 CJ II.996–97.
141 LJ IV.232 and LJ IV. 398.

preted as an encroachment on the Company's ancient right of
'search and seize'.[142] The Stationers' Company reacted by re-
monstrating to both Houses of Parliament.[143]

Perhaps under this pressure and the increasing problems, the
two Houses of Parliament decided to publish yet another ordinance for the regulation of printing. It was published on 14 June
1643 since the 'Bill in preparation for redresse of the said disorders hath hitherto bin retarded through the present distractions'.[144] The ordinance refers to the 'divers good Orders' that
had been issued without success for 'suppressing the great late
abuses and frequent disorders in Printing many, false forged scandalous, libellous, and unlicensed Papers, Pamphlets, and Books
to the great defamation of Religion and government. Which orders (notwithstanding the diligence of the Company of Stationers to put them in full execution) have taken little or no effect.'[145]
The order reiterated the sole right of the two Houses to print
and publish the proceedings of Parliament. Strict licensing procedures and the registration of licensed books were to be enforced 'according to the Ancient Custom'. The property and
copyright of the Stationers' Company was guaranteed, and the
importation of books formerly printed in England was forbidden. Finally, a number of different bodies were installed with far-
reaching powers to search for and seize illicit prints, deface
presses, and send for delinquents: the master and wardens of the
Stationers' Company, the gentleman usher of the House of Peers,
and the sergeant of the House of Commons together with the
persons formerly appointed by the committee for examinations.
The two Houses and the committee for examinations reserved
for themselves the right to examine delinquents and to dispose

---

142 Long, *Appearance*, p 106.
143 Arber, *Transcript*, i, pp 584–88.
144 BL E.106.15, LJ VI. 96–97, SP 16/497.172. The Commons presented the ordi-
       nance to the Lords to seek their approval, which was granted. CJ III. 129 and
       LJ VI. 95.
145 BL E.106.15, p 3.

of the seized goods. All justices of the peace, captains, constables and other officers were required to assist the aforenamed persons in the execution of this order. In case of opposition, doors and locks were to be opened by force. In a separate order the licensers, who were appointed by the House of Commons and the House of Lords were named:

> Licensers for Books of Divinity: Mr Tho: Gattaker, Mr John Downham, Dr. Callibut Downing, Dr. Tho: Temple, Mr. Joseph Carrell, Mr Edmund Callamy, Mr Carter of Yorkshire, Mr Charles Herle, Mr James Cranford, Mr Obadiah Sedgwick, Mr Batchelour, Mr John Ellis jn. For law books: Sir John Bramston, Mr Serjeant Rolle, Mr Serjeant Phesant, Mr Serjeant Jermine. For Physick and Chirurgie Books: The president and four sensories for the time being. For Civil and Canon Law Books: Sir Nathaniel Brent, or by any three of the Doctors of the Civil Law. For Books of Heraldry, Titles, Honor and Arms: One of the tree Heralds. Kings of Arms. For Books of Philosophy, History, Poetry, Morality, and Arts: Sir Nathaniel Brent, Mr Langley, the schoolmaster of Pauls, Mr Farnaby. For Declarations, Ordinances, Fast-Sermons, and other things agreed on by Order of one or both Houses of Parliament: By Order of either House of Parliament, or Committee for Printing; under their or either of their hands in writing. For small Pamphlets, Portraitures, Pictures and the like: The Clerk of the companie of Stationers for the time being. For the Mathematicks, Almanacks and Prognostications: The Reader for the time being of Gresham College or Mr John Booker.[146]

In this ordinance, the Parliament finally managed to lay the foundations for a closer control of printing, which would enable it to impress its own views more firmly on public opinion.

The politics of censorship between 1640 and 1643 were characterized by inexperience and external distractions, as well as by a determination on the part of Parliament to redefine censorship

---

146   BL E.55.9. For further references to licensers see CJ III.131, 138, 139 and 332, CJ III. 457–58.

in its own terms as early as the end of 1640. On the basis of day-to-day survival, the two Houses attempted to satisfy grievances concerning licensing practices, or the breach of licence and privilege. Regular complaints obviously came from the Stationers' Company, which worried about the future of its monopoly at the sight of a rapidly growing printing trade. However, grievances were also put forward by people who had suffered under the Star Chamber and the High Commission Court and now hoped that Parliament would sympathize with their opinions. Thus as early as 1641, special committees re-evaluated the politics of censorship of the 1630s and literally re-established books and authors that had been condemned by the old licensing bodies during those years. Furthermore, Parliament developed a strong sense of the impact of publications on public opinion and effectively used the press for its own ends. First of all, Parliament tried to ensure that parliamentary procedures and speeches were only published with its consent and under its authority. Similarly, Parliament struggled to suppress publications in support of the King which undermined its politics, or favoured the doctrine of the Anglican High Church. Both Houses reacted strongly to any abuse of their members, of the King and the royal family, or of foreign diplomats in print. They grudgingly dealt with the King's complaints about seditious pamphlets and libels. However, in view of escalating conflicts in 1642, Parliament became increasingly determined to overrule the King's proclamations, and to prevent the King from printing and spreading royal orders. The Parliament went as far as sending messages to local officials alongside its proclamations, ordering them not to publish incoming proclamations from the King. The biggest step in this direction was taken on 19 November 1643, when the House of Commons ordered:

> That all such Stationers, or others, that shall from henceforth sell or vend any Pamphlet, printed at Oxford, or elsewhere, or print the same, which is scandalous to the Parliament, or the Proceedings thereof, shall have their Estates sequestered: And the Committee for Sequestration is required to take care to sequester such Persons Es-

tates as shall be found so offending as aforesaid: And Mr Whittacre is to bring in an ordinance to this Purpose.[147]

In 1647, another ordinance for the regulation of printing was put in effect. Finally, on 20 September 1649, the Parliament passed an *Act against Unlicensed and Scandalous Books and Pamphlets, and for better regulating of Printing*.[148] The written response to this Act was immediate and diverse. Parliamentary newsbooks mainly confined their response to detailed reports about the provisions of the Act. Anti-Parliamentary comments were 'consistently virulent in tone'.[149] The newsbook *Mercurius Elencticus* asked:

> Doe they thinke the Printers and Stationers so cowardly and cold in their affections to the kings service that this Paper-squib can deterre them: Will the Founders and smiths be so silly and so undervalue their Persons and callings, as to acquaint the Master and Wardens with all they cast or forge that are no waies concerned in it?[150]

In its comment the newsbook pointed to the central and possibly weakest link in the enforcement of censorship: authors, printers, and publishers. They were vital for the dissemination of news and opinions, and they were largely responsible for the professionalization of communication networks in London and across the country. If they did not conform to the politics of censorship laid down by the holders of power, they were, as demonstrated, liable to harsh punishment. However, the upsurge in the number of pamphlets printed in the early 1640s, and the frequency of anonymous publications, seems to suggest that there were ways and means to escape control. Time and again the Par-

---

147 CJ III.315. For further references see CJ III.394, 398, 612. SC C.f.211, 214.
148 *Acts and Ordinances of the Interregnum 1642–1660*, 3 vols. (London, 1911), ed. Charles H. Firth and R. S. Rait, ii, pp 245–54.
149 Long, *Appearance*, p 148.
150 Long, *Appearance*, p 153.

liament during this period complained about the publication of its procedures. How did details about parliamentary debates reach the printing presses? Scandalous and seditious pamphlets represented a further grievance of the time. How, and especially where, were they produced? Who co-operated in the dissemination of such material?

Behind what looks like individual instances of censorship lies a vivid and professionalized 'trade in opinions' that defied control and thus competed with official statements about the political and religious issues of the time. Often with astonishing speed, proceedings, news, rumours, and 'general views of the time' – opinions – appeared in print and were disseminated in both official and subversive ways. In the capital and across the country there seems to have been a secret understanding about how and where to obtain the most recent news, and men and women who were not officially connected to the publishing trade co-operated in the dissemination of pamphlets, newsletters, and the like. A political culture with its own dynamics and laws developed and greatly influenced the perception of national politics by the common people. In a way, printing and publishing in the 1640s can be seen as the outcome of a 'negotiated' censorship. The holders of power had to give up their monopoly over the definition of 'meaning' to a busy market which prospered from diversity of opinions. Authors and printers tended to please the authorities less than their readership. From the 1640s, those in power had to be more inventive in ways to gain public support. The mere publication of ordinances and the display of authority was no longer enough, because they were open to public scrutiny, comments and competition. In the next chapter I will take up these issues by looking at the ways in which the communication network in London operated.

3 · Opinions *En Vogue*:
The London Pamphlet Market

Authors, printers and publishers were a common target of criticism and satire in mid-seventeenth-century England. They were accused of writing and producing simply to satisfy the tastes of the vulgar, and of lacking any interest in truth. Everyone, it seemed to contemporaries, aspired to be a writer, and the whole profession came under attack for the spread of lies and for bad conduct. Many of these pamphlets directed against members of the trade acted in the way of censors, warning the public of false news, and even providing lists of offensive authors and pamphlets. In effect, they asked people to be critical of what they heard, and to make up their own minds. Martin Parker invites his readers to 'Buy, Reade, and Iudge'.[1] Like a censor, the anonymous author of *The Poets' Knavery Discovered* gives a list of offensive authors and pamphlets, telling his readers that it is 'well worth the reading and knowing of every one, that they may learn how to distinguish betwixt the Lies and real Books'.[2]

These criticisms were part of the general concern in the seventeenth century with the rise of public opinion, and there was

---

1   Martin Parker, *The Poet's Blind mans bough* (1641), BL E.172.6.
2   *The Poets' Knavery Discovered, in all their lying Pamphlets.* Written by J. B. [1641?], reprinted in *Harleian Miscellany*, 12 vols. (London, 1808–1811), ed. Thomas Parker, 9, p. 199–201.

an interesting shift of perspective in the continuous attacks on minor writers throughout the early modern period. In the late sixteenth and early seventeenth centuries complaints about printing seemed to concentrate on the problem of 'hack-writers' and their corrupt behaviour. In *Pierce Penniless*, Thomas Nashe, for instance, complained about hackwriters in his epistle to the printer. About the same time, Thomas Dekker gave an amusing account of the tricks some of 'these falconers' played on others in *Lanthorne and Candle-Light*.[3] Accusations against the whole publishing trade in the seventeenth century of lying and deceiving, of aspiring to a higher status, and of meddling with things above one's calling were inspired by fears that the trade in news and opinions would undermine the loyalty to state and church of broad sections of society. The interpretation of 'writing' as an act of violating the social order was applied especially to women's writing, which was said to contradict proper rules of conduct – as did women's speech in public.[4] Thus, it is not surpris-

---

3   *Pierce Penniless* (1592), reprinted in Thomas Nashe, *Works*, 5 vols. (London, 1904–10), v, ed. Ronald McKerrow. *Lanthorne and Candle-Light* (1609), reprinted in *The Non-Dramatic Works of Thomas Dekker*, 5 vols. (New York, 1963), iii, ed. Alexander B. Grosart. See also E. H. Miller, *The Professional Writer in Elizabethan England* (Cambridge/Mass., 1959).

4   Since the mid-seventeenth century, women in England had increasingly published their works in spite of moral and gender arguments against female speech and writing in public. For a detailed discussion of women's writing and the obstacles and prejudices women had to overcome during the second half of the seventeenth century, see Elain Hobby, *Virtue of Necessity. English Women's Writing 1649–88* (London, 1988) and *Her Own Life. Autobiographical writings by seventeenth-century Englishwomen* (London/New York, 1989), ed. Elspeth Graham, Hilary Hinds, Elain Hobby and Helen Wilcox. For a survey of women writers during this period see *Women and the Literature of the Seventeenth Century, An annotated Bibliography based on* Wing's *Short-title Catalogue*, ed. Hilda L. Smith and S. Cardinale, (London, 1990); *A Bibliographical Dictionary of English Women Writers 1580-1720*, ed. Maureen Bell, George Parfitt, and Simon Sheperd, (New York, 1990); and Patricia Crawford, 'Women's published writings 1600-1700', in *Women in English Society 1500-1800*, ed. Mary Prior, (London/New York, 1985), pp 211–31, with an appendix by Crawford and Richard Bell, pp 232–82.

ing that criticism of writers, printers and publishers was often expressed through a gendered political symbolism which employed the well-known negative connotations of women's speaking and writing, as will be demonstrated below. In the light of the emergence of public opinion, the dispute over 'writing' and publication became a question of social status and deference in general. Now the whole of society was in focus as potential authors, and as the source of public opinion. Drawing on the discourse on women, speech, and writing – and, in fact, the negative female image of Opinion – it was now argued that the common folk were interfering with great matters of state and church that they had little knowledge of, which inevitably led to unrest.

In his letter to Sir John Pennington in January 1642, Thomas Wiseman complained that the 'liberty of the press, the liberty of factious preaching of ill-affected ministers ... and the liberty that tumultuous persons have taken to themselves and their unlawfull meetings in the City, has poisoned the obedience of too many of his Majesty's subjects'.[5] In 1648 a contemporary onlooker observed:

> Among the many causes which have cherished and heightened our late and present distempers, there is none have been more powerfull then the audacious liberty, and carelesse permission of printed Pamphlets, which seeming inconsiderable, have better familiarity with the vulgar, and being fraught with reasons fit for their capacity, do not onely confirm those malignant whom they finde so; but by their tart aspersions laid on the best Persons, and their bold misinterpretations put upon the sincerest actions, corrupt and poyson many times the best and purest integrities; while they of the adverse Party laugh in their sleeves to see so many good names sullied, and so little opposition to be made against them.[6]

Contemporaries were well aware of the interdependence of professional communication networks, the spread of news and opin-

---

5   SP 16/488.57.
6   *A Parallel Between the Proceedings of this Present King and this Present Parliament* (1648). Cit. in Smith, *Literature*, pp 30-1.

ions, and the formation of a popular political consciousness that increasingly challenged the holders of power.

In the following sections I will look, firstly, at the perception and self-perception of the London pamphlet world. The negative discourse on authors, printers, publishers and hawkers is in itself a vivid testimony to the disquieting effects of the spread of news and opinions during this period. Furthermore, it provides fascinating insights into the development of a political symbolism which borrowed from gender-specific rules of conduct and their violation to emphasize the political dangers inherent in news circulation and public opinion. Secondly, I will look at the network of authors, printers, and publishers, their access to information, and the dissemination of news and opinions. In view of the impact of communication networks on the formation of public opinion it will be interesting to see whether any political or religious alliances between printers, publishers and authors can be discovered in this early phase of the emergence of the public sphere.

Critical Voices of 'Male-Female' Authors, Printers, Booksellers and Hawkers

> The Presse is overprest and (iustly) grones
> Under the burthen of these heavie tones
> Of Scritch-oule musick, threatening death and hell,
> One striving all in malice to excell;
> And he who can best rayle, scoffe, and invent,
> The greatest lyes, shall give the most content:
> In this the age that doth most truth professe,
> Are these the dayes of zeale and righteousnesse ...
> Why then, O why are lyes and falsehoods spread,
> Shall men by lying earne their daily bread?[7]

---

7   Parker, *The Poet's Blind mans bough.*

Many of the satirical pamphlets of the 1640s on the booktrade and the spread of news were preoccupied with 'the vanity of the Authors, who for a small gaine will endeavour with opprobrious lines to abuse God and Man'.[8] Throughout, pamphleteers were accused of lying and of fabricating news, even of feigning 'false Orders and Proceedings from the Parliament with many fictitious Speeches'.[9] Authors were said to resort to special stylistic devices and genres, such as 'Letters to Friends', in order 'to put a fairer glosse upon their forgeries'.[10] So 'that they who heare it may conjecture that It may be true; but these men care not what They write, be't contradictory or not, So they can get the silver by the plot'.[11] The author of *The Poets' Knavery Discovered* compiled a list of 'every lying Libel that was Printed last Year, and the Authors who made them; being above three hundred'.[12] According to him, by the year 1641, 'the temporizing poets have broached such impudent scurrility, and ementitious pamphlets, out of the inexhaust mintage of their roving fancies, that the whole city is embroidered with nothing but incredible lies'. An anonymous pamphlet of the same year, entitled *The Liar*, gives a broader definition of 'lye', which was not seen as the opposite of truth alone, but as fiction and wonder stories interwoven with facts: 'He [a lying traveller] told, too, that the very same day that my Lord Archbishop of Canterbury was committed to the Tower, there was a child born in the county of Somerset with a Miter on its head, a marke on his breast like a crucifix, and many other strange things which were there seene'.[13]

---

8   *No Pamphlet But A Detestation Against all such Pamphlets As are Printed Concerning the Irish Rebellion* (1642), BL E.134.3.
9   *The Poet's Knavery.*
10   *No Pamphlet.* On the loss of privacy of letters in early modern England and the formation of a new genre see Patterson, *Censorship*, pp 203–18.
11   Parker, *The Poet's Blind mans bough.* The phrase 'to get the silver by the plot' refers to the regulation that people who conveyed a plot received money for a reward.
12   *The Poets' Knavery.*
13   *The Liar* (1641), BL E.169.8. This pamphlet appeared in 1641 without reference to the author, John Taylor.

The poor poetic quality and the baseness of pamphlets were other popular targets of criticism. Most likely with reference to the popular ballad writer Martin Parker, the anonymous author of *A True Description Of The Pot-Companion Poet* writes: 'His verses are like his cloaths, miserable Centos and Patches ... his frequent works go out in single sheets, and are formed in every part of the City, and then chanted from Market to market, to a vile tune, and a worse throat'.[14] Just as base as these pamphlets were their authors: 'frothy brains, temporizing pamphlet-mongers, pot-companion, male-female, poetical needy brains, pecurious pennyless wits, brain sick fancies, hellish brains', most of whom published, so it was said, anonymously and without licence. Their creativity was allegedly at its best after they had 'fill'd the Pan so full of Liquor, that they drown'd their wits and ... betook themselves to fabulous invention'.[15] The verses of the nameless pot-companion poet 'run like the Tap, and his inventions as the Barrell, ebbs and flowes at the mercy of the Spiggot, in Thin drink he aspires not above a Ballad, but a cup of Sack inflames him, and sets his muse and nose a fire together'.[16]

'Everyman', so was the common belief, suddenly aspired to making verses, driven either by profit, sack, or the madness of the times:

Ci: How long have you been a poet?

Gl: As long as you have beene a convert, you see this age
    is full of changes, but indeed this whimsie tooke me
    at the first discovery of the black cloudes that have
    bred all these Tempests, when I saw distraction in
    the face of the Kingdom, I could no longer contain my
    selfe, but grew mad, too, and fel to making verses.[17]

---

14 *A True Description Of The Pot-Companion Poet* (1642), BL E.143.6.
15 *A Presse Full Of Pamphlets* (1642), BL E.142.9.
16 *A True Description.*
17 *The Cities Warning-Peece, in the Malignants description and Conversion* (1642), BL E.246.28.

Opinions were voiced and spread everywhere, and people – 'the rabble' – meddled increasingly with things 'above their calling' – writing, for instance. A penitent 'book-maker', Edward Browne observed in a letter to his brother:

> And what ever others thinke to be the reason of these distractions, my weake judgement is, that it is chiefly for our pride and selfe conceit, though I will not exclude other sins; for we are so glutted with the heavenly *Manna* of Divine Doctrine, that now every boy or ignorant tradesman, that can reade his hornebooke or write a scribbling character, assumes to himselfe a spirit of *Revelation* far greater then the Apostles of our blessed Saviour, not that I doe disapprove of any man woman or child, even the meanest capacities, to reade, and search the Scripture, for I acknowledge my selfe to be no Scholer, Therefore let them be warned by me to take heed how they meddle with things above their capacities, lest they receive a worser punishment then I have for Booke-making.[18]

For his many losses – time, 'my precious love', money, the 'goodwill of my friends' – Edward Browne remorsefully blamed his aspirations to higher things in spite of his happy prospects in life as clerk to a justice of the peace. Furthermore, he made his individual fate exemplary of a universal imperative of his time: those who climb too high are doomed to fall as low.

> In these my Bookes of fruitlesse prose and rime,
> You may behold a picture of this time
> Wherein we live, for first from low degree
> My Masters favour had exalted me,
> But my aspiring minde did higher fly
> To things above my reach presumptuously
> (...) for I assure thee all,
> That thinke by pride, selfe-love, and vaine conceite,
> To make themselves most famous and most great,
> Shall be defeated in their enterprise
> As tis apparent in all peoples' eyes

---

18 *Sir James Cambels Clarks Disaster, By Making Books* (1642), BL E.122.22.
19 *Sir James*, p 17.

> By Strafford, Bishops, *and* Gentility
> Whose falls as low as they aspired high.
> And my selfe have had a woefull fall,
> In Credit, profit, yea and Bookes and all.[19]

John Bond, who had suffered exemplary punishment by the House of Lords in 1642 for feigning a letter from the Queen to the King, expressed a similar view in his mock-recantation. Bond, however, stressed not so much the act of writing as above his station, but the theme he had chosen, which was an even more serious offence than expressing heretical views:

> Now I perceive the Cause, hence doth distill
> That I have beene too sawcy in my Quill
> Tis not expedient that a Vulgar eye,
> Should gaze upon superior Maiestie (...)
> T'was not for periurie, that I have beene
> Thy Captive, Pillorie, nor was there seene
> Hereticke thoughts in me.[20]

For the quick dissemination of their works, authors made use of – and increasingly depended on – the network of the London booktrade: publishers, printers, booksellers and hawkers. The dependency was evidently mutual. In the 1640s, printers and booksellers were increasingly seen as collaborators of 'lying authors', helping them to spread sedition and discord. Edward Browne claimed that his volume *Labours of Love* had been rejected by the Stationers' Company because it was too learned. People demanded sensational news and pamphlets should be market-oriented:

> But no executioner I meane a Stationer or Printer had the heart to undertake the worke, and in excuse thereof told mee, That such a book as that of thirty or forty sheets of paper is not like to sell in this age were the matter never so good, but if it had beene a lying and scandalous pamphlet of a sheete of paper that could produce a Scripture text, or some reviling tearmes against Monarchy, and Hierarchy

---

20   Bond, *Recantation*.

to uphold an Anarchy, they would have embraced my profer, for it is
like such would have proved vendable ware, if I could obtain an *Order* or a *Vote* upon it.[21]

Edward Browne was not alone in making this accusation. In 1643,
the stationer A.W. exhorted his fellow stationers to 'beware of
intemperance and excesse', since they were already 'more profane, and wicked, then such as are of many other callings'.[22] A
contemporary joke ran: 'Printers (saies one) are the most lawlesse
men in a kingdome, for they commit faults *cum privilegio*.'[23] The
fullest account of this satirical contemporary perception of the
London booktrade is provided by a surreptitious pamphlet dated
1641, and entitled *The Downfall of Temporizing Poets, unlicenst
Printers, upstart Booksellers, trotting Mercuries, and bawling Hawkers*.[24] This 'very pleasant Dialogue' between Light-foot, the
Mercurie, Suck-bottle, the Hawker, and Red-nose, the Poet,
promised to lay bare 'all their corruptions'. Without doubt, the
pamphlet was drafted for a small street-theatre performance, giving, for instance, stage directions such as 'Enter Poet'. This suggests that the theme was highly popular, and it is known that
even after the closure of the theatres, plays or interludes continued to be staged in side streets, and puppet performances were
still permitted.[25]

Packed with allusions to well-known people, circumstances,
and cliches, this pamphlet has three protagonists who highlight
various facets of the London (underground) pamphlet world:
some (would-be) members of the book trade were notorious for
their partiality for drink – an accusation which accounted for the

---

21   *Sir James*, p 7–8.
22   *The Young-Mans Second Warning-peece* (1643), BL E.78.7, pp 7–8.
23   *Conceits, Clinches, Flashes and Whimzies; a jest-book of the 17th century, hith-
     erto unknown to bibliographers, repr. from the unique copy of 1639*, ed. James O.
     Halliwell (London, 1860), p 48.
24   *The Downfall of Temporizing Poets, unlicenst Printers, upstart Booksellers, trot-
     ting Mercuries, and bawling Hawkers* (1641), BL E.165.5.
25   *The Actors Remonstrance Or Complaint* (1643), B.L. E.86.8, p 5.

poor quality of their work and their vagrant life – and the Stationers' Company was called the 'Bacchanalian Society of the most reverend wandering Stationers'. Common hawkers who specialized in book-selling were called 'wandering booksellers or Stationers', who cried out the latest news and new books on offer. They were seen to compete with mercuries in the vending of 'new books' rather than good books. Among these mercuries were many women, and both male and female alike were famous for their scolding. As a result of this confusion of gender specific characteristics, mercuries were called 'male-females', an offence that was increasingly common during the early seventeenth century when contemporaries complained that men were dressing and behaving in an effeminate manner and women were assuming masculine dress and conduct.[26]

The central role of sexuality and gender in these accusations becomes apparent when trade members are compared to Adamites, a sect that was accused of immorality and sexual looseness, and of having domineering women.[27] Direct allusions to women's sexuality and unruliness – 'her tippet standing up' and 'her tongue being almost weary with Billingsgate worke' – further discredited the trade. The tongue of a woman was said to be her strongest weapon, made of iron or other strong metals, and a number of tracts evoke the parallel between the female tongue and the male penis.[28]

Another sector involved in the 'news trade' was the ballad society – 'an indifferent strong Corporation of 23 writers and Martin Parker'. The fiddlers, however, who used to perform ballads now 'go a begging' since hawkers have taken over with 'tearing throats' and a 'voyce made of cannon proofe'. Censorship

---

26   See *Hic Mulier; or, The Man-Woman* (1620), and *Haec Vir; or, The Womanish Man* (1620).

27   See, for instance, *A Sermon Preached* (1643); *A New Sect of Religion Descryed, Called Adamites* (1641); and *The Adamites Sermon* (1641).

28   Lisa Jardine, *Still Harping on Daughters. Women and Drama in the Age of Shakespeare* (Brighton, 1983), p 121.

and continuous breach of the law also cropped up in the dialogue. The 'Wandering Stationer', so the argument went, was totally impoverished and criminalized, and became a homeless lodger in hedges and prisons. Furthermore, the poets with their 'Strangullian Poetry' and frequent character assassination were bound to be imprisoned if they could not trust their legs. Ultimately, we witness the downfall of all three, because fortune was against them: the poet could not sell his book because it was not 'licenseable', the hawker had nothing to sell for there were no 'new books', and the mercury fell mad at the sight of such 'sadness'. It has already been mentioned that these attacks on the news trade must be read as a nervous reaction to the rise of public opinion. A closer look at the communication network ridiculed here demonstrates its central role in the dissemination of news and opinions, and its political impact.

The Politics of Printing and the Distribution Network of the London Pamphlet Market

There is no agreement amongst researchers on the early modern period about the political involvement of those (subversively) producing and dealing in political pamphlets, broadsides, and newsbooks. The two extreme positions are probably best exemplified by the works of Robert Darnton and Elisabeth Eisenstein. Whereas Darnton emphasizes the commercial motivation behind foreign and clandestine printing and suggests the well-known thesis of the growing proletarianization of writers, Eisenstein makes a strong case for the close involvement of publishers and printers with the ideas they handled, and argues that a number of writers were successful.[29] As so often, the truth probably lies

---

29 Robert Darnton, *The literary underground of the Old Regime* (Cambridge/Mass., 1982); id., *Edition et sédition: L'univers de la littérature clandestine au xviii siècle* (Paris, 1991); Elisabeth Eisenstein, *Grub Street Abroad. Aspects of the French Cosmopolitan Press from the Age of Louis XIV to the French Revolution* (Ox-

somewhere in the middle. Certainly in the case of seventeenth-century England it is possible to show that there were a number of printers and publishers who specialized in working for a specific clientele only, whereas others were ready to print a variety of things for commercial reasons.[30] In fact, a survey I have made of the wills and inventories of printers and publishers shows great differences in the wealth of individual members of the trade: poorer members tended to live in the suburbs, and wealthier stationers in the City or the west.[31] These sources also provide glimpses of the kinds of friendships people had formed, however biased they are towards better-off and male trade members. A survey of stationers' wills between 1640 and 1650 shows that printers and booksellers formed close friendships with men and women who were directly connected with their trade, or who worked in trade-related occupations: scriveners, bookbinders, chapmen, apprentices, stationers, and stationers' wives. Some also mentioned their function within their parish, for instance, Thomas Cotes who was parish clerk in St Gyles without Cripplegate, or Christopher Meredith, who was governor of Christ's Hospital.[32] Friendships also existed outside the profession. Among sta-

---

ford, 1992); and id., *Printing*. See also Natalie Zemon Davis, 'Printing and the People', in ead., *Society and Culture in Early Modern France* (Stanford, 1975), pp 189–226.

30   Timothy Christ, *Francis Smith and the Opposition Press in England, 1660-1688* (unpublished PhD dissertation, University of Cambridge, 1977) and John S. T. Hetet, *A Literary Underground in Restoration England: Printers and Dissenters in the Context of Constraints 1660-1689* (unpublished PhD dissertation, University of Cambridge, 1987).

31   This observation is based on my survey of inventories surviving for the second half of the 17th century in the C.L.R.O., Orphans' Court Inventories, Sergeant's Book vols. 2 and 4, the Orphans' Court Inventories Miscellany, and a few inventories scattered through the Archdeaconry Original Wills in the Guildhall. Unfortunately, the great majority of the surviving inventories date from the 1660s onwards. This means, however, that the deceased lived during the period under discussion.

32   PRO Prob. 11/186.288–289, 20 June 1641, Thomas Cotes, parish of St Gyles without Cripplegate. PRO Prob. 11/229.93–96. 24 January 1652. Christopher Meredith, parish of St Faith.

tioners' friends whose status was specified were 'loveinge neighbours', both men and single women, a salter, a clothmaker, several ministers, nurses, maids, and servants. Family ties were
strongly expressed by all testators and went beyond the nuclear
family, mentioning brothers and sisters and their families, cous-
ins, uncles, and grandchildren. Those stationers who were first-
generation Londoners mentioned their relatives in the country,
and they often made small bequests to their home parish.

Finally, some provisions made in wills throw light on the political and religious convictions of the testator. The bookseller
Thomas Whitaker in St Paul's Churchyard explicitly asked his
'worthy and reverend friend', the 'old-fashioned Anglican Divine' Thomas Fuller, to preach his funeral service.[33] In contrast,
John Parker, likewise bookseller in St Paul's Churchyard, ruled
in his will that several books inscribed with 'The Gift of John
Parker, Stationer' were to be distributed on his death to poor
children and poor debtors. Among the books was the famous
Puritan martyrology by John Foxe called *Actes and Monuments*.[34]
Similarly, the printer Michael Sparkes asked in his will that two
particular books with Puritan ideas were to be distributed among
the poor, and to those who came to his funeral: *Crums of Comfort*, and *The groanes of the spirit*.[35] Especially the distribution of
particular books seems to demonstrate a belief in the power of
the word and in the influence literature had on people's opinions
among those dealing in print.

This view finds further support in the fact that nonconformist religious and political groups set up their own printing presses,
often secretly, in order to disseminate their views in the hope of
influencing public opinion. Nicolas Tew, for instance, stationer
and bookseller in Coleman Street, kept a secret printing press in
his house. During his examination by two justices on 17 January

---

33 PRO Prob. 11/209. 1649. See also Seaver, *Lectureship*, p 26.
34 PRO Prob. 11/205. 1647.
35 PRO Prob. 11/236. 1653.

1645, he confessed 'that a printing press was brought to his house in Coleman Street, and was used by Robert Overton, who lodged there, and others, but who, he knows not; also confesses that a letter written by Mr Lilburne to Mr Prynne, and a book of Mr Lilburne were printed there but from whom he received them or how much money he made by them he cannot tell.'[36]

Best known are the Leveller tracts of the late 1640s, which were mainly printed by Richard Overton.[37] Many Puritans published and printed in the Netherlands, and in the politico-religious satires of the period Puritan opinions were often referred to as coming from Amsterdam, being 'Amsterdamnified' or as speaking the language of Amsterdam.[38] Printing activities overseas, mainly in Amsterdam, and the smuggling of books into England, played an important role in the secret printing activities of London. There were close connections between printers in the Netherlands and various sectaries in London, who co-operated quite well in smuggling out manuscripts, printing them on the Continent, and reintroducing them into the kingdom. The printer and publisher Matthew Simmons wrote down the routes this secret booktrade took and his *Note of some things I have observed in the Low Countries* has survived in manuscript.[39] A final example of attempts to influence public opinion is the Quakers' professional printing network which was built up in the 1650s and 1660s.[40]

---

36   Henry Plomer, 'Secret Printing During the Civil War', *The Library*, n.s., V (1966), pp 374–403, p 377.

37   *The Leveller Tracts 1647–1653*, ed. William Haller and Godfrey Davies (Gloucester/Mass., 1964), *The Levellers in the English Revolution*, ed. Gerald E. Aylmer (London, 1975).

38   See, for instance, *Religions Enemies, The Devil Turn'd Round-Head: Or, Pluto became a Brownist* (1642), BL E.136.29 and *Square Caps*.

39   SP 16/387.79. In general, see Foster, *Notes* and Murray Tolmie, *The Triumph of the Saints. The separate churches of London 1616–1649* (Cambridge, 1977).

40   For details see Maureen Bell, 'Mary Westwood, Quaker Publisher', *Publishing History*, 23 (1988), pp 5–66; ead., 'Hannah Allen and the Development of a Puritan Publishing Business, 1646–51', *Publishing History*, 26 (1989),

Distinct political and religious profiles of individual printers, publishers and booksellers sometimes emerge from random references to their beliefs in a number of different sources. The evidence, however, is sketchy, and the following can give only an incomplete impression of possible alliances. A number of printers and booksellers whose shops were in north London, in Newgate near Christchurch, had a record of seditious printing in support of the Puritans in the late 1630s. Among them was Gregory Dexter, who printed some of Prynne's works and cooperated with Richard Oulton in producing a number of tracts and pamphlets 'aimed at upholding the hand of the Parliament in its struggle against Church and King'.[41] He eventually emigrated to Providence, New England. In the choice of the newsbooks he published, Robert White expressed sympathy for the Parliament. Michael Sparkes, well known for his attack on monopolies of the Stationers' Company, published most of Prynne's works, including *Histriomastrix*, for which he was fined 500 pounds and was condemned to stand in the pillory.[42] In contrast, the bookseller Richard Royston was accused in 1645 'of being a factor for scandalous books and papers against the Parliament, and thrown into prison'.[43] Similarly, in 1641, Matthew Simmons, who was largely employed by Independents, and Thomas Paine were accused in an undated memorandum among the main papers of the House of Lords. It was alleged that 'Simons and Payne have continually printed Libells ever since the first setting of this Parlia-

---

pp 5–66; Tom Corns and D. Loewenstein (eds.), 'The Emergence of Quaker writing' *Prose Studies*, 18 (1995); Christ, *Francis Smith*; and Hetet, *Literary*.

41   B.F. Swan, *Gregory Dexter of London and New England 1610-1700* (New York, 1947).

42   Michael Sparkes, *Scintilla or a Light Broken Into Dark Warehouses* (1641). The Stationers' Company convened a special court to discuss Sparkes' paper and appointed a committee to consider the issues raised. SC f.178–178v. Henry Plomer, *A Dictionary of the Booksellers and Printers who were at work in England, Scotland, and Ireland from 1641 to 1667*, The Bibliographical Society (Oxford, 1968), p 169.

43   Historical Manuscript Commission, 6th Report, pp 71–2.

ment. They are known to all the Staconers and theyr Presses in Redcrosse street'.[44] In the same year the printer Walter Wasse had to answer before the justices of the peace for Middlesex for voicing nonconformist ideas. He was accused of saying that 'the Book of Common Prayer was noe divine prayer, and that he had rather heere a sermon under a tree then out of a pulpitt'.[45] Finally, the booksellers Samuel Gellibrand, Edward Brewster and Robert Smith were among the signatories of the Presbyterian petition to Parliament in March 1646.[46]

The following testimony by a member of the Stationers' Company is an exception. It provides a full insight into his beliefs and his attempts to convince others of his opinions. In 1643, the stationer A.W. published the story of his conversion, which ended ten years of sinful life and great misery. Under the influence of the devil, he had suffered long spells of depression, melancholy, and several attempted suicides.[47] His final delivery from Satan's temptations was brought about by a sermon of one Mr Willes, which he heard on the advice of his fellow workman 'at Bartholomew Lane, neere the Exchange'.[48] At the end of his account, A.W. admonished the 'brethren of his society' to learn from his exam-

---

44   H.L.M.P. March 1640-1641.

45   MJ/SPR. 20 July 1641, Jeaffreson, p 174.

46   Michael Mahony, 'Presbyterianism in the City of London, 1645–1647', *Historical Journal*, 22 (1979), pp 93–114, p 103. Mahony argued that the bookshops of St Paul's Churchyard and Fleet Street were a channel for disseminating Presbyterian propaganda.

47   On the general meaning of suicide in early modern England and the role of the devil in luring people into killing themselves see Michael MacDonald and Terence R. Murphy, *Sleepless Souls. Suicide in Early Modern England* (Oxford, 1990).

48   *The Young-Mans Second Warning-peece*. The pattern of A.W.'s conversion story is reminiscent of the martyrologies and lives of the better-known Puritan saints. These abound in stories of remarkable conversions whereby the fortunate, often after long years of painful introspection, suddenly become aware of the gift of saving grace and election. For many of the converts the first awareness of the workings of the Spirit comes during or after hearing the Word plainly but effectually preached. See Seaver, *Lectureship*, p 173.

ple, and not to 'conceive of this relation as a fained or forged thing, for I professe unto you all, it is a most certain truth'. Although members of the Stationers' Company were somewhat privileged since their 'calling is oftener to have to do with good books, then many other callings have', A.W. warned them that 'yet alas brethren, I feare we have beene more proofane, and wicked, then such as are of many other callings: O beware of intemperance and excesse'.[49] A.W. entreated anyone who was not convinced by his story in print, to 'take the opportunity to come to my house in Little-Woodstreete in Bunting Alley, & I will with the Lords helpe give you what satisfaction I am able'.

The majority of printers and publishers had to deal in a variety of works out of economic necessity despite their own political and religious preferences. Even those who operated a secret printing press might have done so for economic reasons. In general, it is almost impossible to infer any pronounced religious or political convictions of booksellers, publishers or printers from their stock (taken from inventories), even if they existed. It seems, instead, that members of the trade actively sought to stimulate the tastes of those in the immediate neighbourhood of their shops. Since their products were not among the basic needs of people, printers and booksellers had to beware of literary preferences in their neighbourhood if they wanted to sell anything. Often, people knew what was in the press and passed it on by word of mouth. When John Oakes was examined in 1637 for printing de Sales' *Introduction to a devout Life* his neighbour and 'intimate' friend, a minister and schoolmaster, testified that Oakes 'assured me yesterday that there is a sermon printing at Mrs Fletcher's house and another divinity book at Mr Harper's'.[50]

The predominance of ballads, plays, and all sorts of ephemeral literature among the stock of booksellers whose shops were in the overcrowded and rather poor northern suburbs as against

---

49   *The Young-Mans Second Warning-peece*, p 8.
50   SP 16/437.55.

the more highbrow literature stocked by booksellers in wealthier areas within the walls and in the west, suggests that dealers in books catered to the tastes of their immediate neighbourhood. This is apparent, too, in the fact that legal works formed the majority of the stock of booksellers near the Inns of Court in the parish of St Dunstan in the west. However, this does not imply that bookshops in the mid-seventeenth century catered exclusively for a specific social class. The social diversity of London society is reflected in the stock of bookshops, which, in addition to catering for the tastes dominant in their neighbourhoods, offered a variety of works including those 'lying pamphlets' that dealt with the political and religious conflicts of their time. The question here is the nature of the network behind the production of such controversial material. Who were the producers and distributors, and what was the context in which they operated?

In the following sections I look at the communication networks of those printers, publishers and booksellers who were involved in 'underground' pamphleteering in the 1640s. I will address the question of secret printing, the evasion of control and censorship, the co-operation between professionals and non-professionals in the 'trade of news', and the subsequent printing and circulation of pamphlets. All names are taken from imprints of politico-religious satires that were published in this period, and from references in parliamentary records and state papers on seditious printing. A total of 156 booksellers, publishers, and printers could be identified.

Only eight women are known to have been examined for seditious printing and selling of pamphlets, five of them not officially entered with the Company, and 52 printers and booksellers were examined several times for seditious printing and bookselling in the early 1640s. However, the number of women estimated to have been in the booktrade and involved in seditious printing is much higher. Since 'women were excluded from position and power within the Company, and it is usually the names of the male members of book trade families which appear in Company records', attempts to trace female booksellers and printers face immense difficulties: 'Only when a man is rendered inactive, temporarily (by flight from London to evade creditors, or by imprisonment), or permanently (by his death) does the woman's name appear.'[51] Women usually inherited the business, and the Stationers' Company conceded a number of valuable rights to them: 'stationers' widows, for example, were allowed to bind apprentices and to hold shares in the Company's copyright monopoly, the English Stock.'[52] Maureen Bell's pioneering work on female printers and booksellers has shown that seventeenth-century women were involved in the booktrade at various levels, and commonly on a day-to-day basis. For the period 1540 to 1730, Bell has so far identified about 300 women as connected with the trade, of whom most were active after 1640.[53] Many other women, however, will probably remain obscure for ever, such as the four women who continued to print and sell seditious prints in the shop of the printer Richard Hearne near West Smithfield after he had been imprisoned for libelling in 1643.[54]

The topographical distribution of these booksellers and printers over London discloses an interesting pattern. Whereas the majority of booksellers are found within the walls, with a high concentration around St Paul's Churchyard, Lombard Street, and the Royal Exchange on Cornhill, the majority of printers had their shops outside the wall around West Smithfield and further north-east in Redcross Street and Grub Street. Several bookshops in St Dunstan Churchyard in Fleet Street and in the Old Bailey, and a number of printing houses near Christ Church in Newgate, were an exception. Furthermore, a few booksellers were found

---

51 Bell *et al* (eds.), *Women Writers*, p 288.
52 Ibid.
53 Maureen Bell, 'A dictionary of women in the London book trade, 1540-1730' (unpublished Master's Dissertation, Loughborough University of Technology, 1983).
54 LJ V.547 and below.

near the residences of the nobility in the Strand and the New Exchange; others had their shops and stalls outside Westminster Hall; one bookseller and printer had his shop in the precinct of the Bedlam Hospital, in north-east London.[55] A final interpretation of this overall pattern will only become possible when the location of all printers and booksellers of this period has been determined. Although occupational clustering is evident – many printers and binders lived and worked in St Botolph Aldersgate – 'most parishes contained a mixture of occupations, even though one or two groups were overrepresented'. In general, seventeenth-century London displays an 'urban scene where occupations and rich and poor are thoroughly jumbled' rather than a pattern of closed occupational and/or wealth zones.[56]

The present topographical picture seems to suggest that the concentration of printers in rougher areas outside the walls was an attempt to escape the regulatory powers of the Stationers' Company over trading and printing, which at the same time assisted the state in its prosecution of seditious printing. But it was not only printers who preferred to set up their businesses outside the walls. Official restraints on production (feltmakers, tallow-chandlers, many types of leatherworker, manufacturers of alum, glass, oil, soap and starch) and the regulatory powers over trading and manufacturing of the City's hundred or so guilds 'helped to boost production' of a number of economic branches outside the walls, where detection was more difficult. It was true for all trades who worked without the wall that 'despite extended areas of search, significant increases in membership, and continued influence upon social and political life within the Walls, guilds were quite unable to control the expanding manufacture outside

---

55 For the location of these shops see the map in Freist, *Formation*.
56 M. J. Power, 'The social topography of Restoration London', in *The Making of the Metropolis. London 1500-1700*, ed. A. L. Beier and Roger Finlay (London, 1986), pp 119–223, 218–19, and 221. See also W. E. Miller, 'Printers and Stationers in the Parish of St. Giles Cripplegate 1561–1640', *Studies in Bibliography* (1966), p 15–38.

them. This was true even of extra-mural parishes immediately adjacent, which were legally not suburban at all'.[57] Especially those printers and publishers who were involved in unlicensed and seditious printing had to hide their work from weekly searches, and in the large and populous suburbs detection was more difficult. According to Henry Plomer, the officials of the Stationers' Company kept a sort of *Black Book*, 'in which they entered the names of all printers, booksellers and publishers, who printed or sold any literature that could by any possibility be called scandalous and seditious, so that when anything more glaring than usual was put on the market, they first of all visited the suspects'.[58]

Secret printing presses were almost exclusively found in the suburbs. Each discovery unmasked interesting alliances between members of the booktrade and people outside the profession who were willing to hide printing instruments and even to defend their owners against searchers or constables. And each discovery turned into a public affair with much noise and sometimes violence. Searchers and constables requested onlookers to assist them in the seizure of books, whereas the delinquents often had their allies, who queried the authenticity of warrants and were ready to employ physical force to stop officials entering the house or taking away anything. In July 1638, a press was found, which had been privately set up in a victualling house near Turnebul Street, in Middlesex. At this press, Lawrence Sadler, bookseller at the Golden Lion in Little Britain, and Richard Hodgkinson, printer in Thames Street near Baynard Castle, secretly printed and published Cowell's forbidden book, *The Interpreter*. When the wardens of the Stationers' Company attempted to seize the said books by virtue of a council warrant, Sadler and Hodgkinson 'violently resisted'. Sadler had especially sent for a constable, William Buston, out of London, who supported them against the said wardens and the neighbouring constables. Buston ar-

---

57 A. L. Beier, 'Engine of manufacture: the trades of London', in *Metropolis*, ed. Beier and Finlay, pp 141–67, p 157.
58 Plomer, 'Secret Printing', p 386.

gued that no books were allowed to be carried away because the
warrant was not sufficient: it did not explicitly name Cowell's
Interpreter. When the Stationers' warden 'willed one' to come
along and seize some of the questionable books 'the said constable, Sadler and Hodgkinson, with much fury, fell upon him &
pulled him by the coller and forced him to lay them down againe,
and ye said Constable taking him by ye Arme threatened to carry
him to Newgate, wherupon your petitioners fearing they might
endanger their lives, departed out of ye house, leaving the said
Bookes behinde them'.[59]

In May 1641, the Stationers' Company reported to the House
of Lords that they had discovered a secret press in a cellar, 'where
Pamphlets and unlicensed Books are printed, but they keep the
doors shut, that they cannot come to view them'. On hearing
this, the House ordered that the nearest justice of the peace should
go with the master and wardens and others of the stationers to
the house near Bunhill in Finsbury Fields. They were to tell the
master of the house of the allegation and insist on checking his
cellar for a private printing press; and if he refused they were to
report back to the Lords.[60] A similar incident happened in October of the same year. A petition from the master and wardens of
the Stationers' Company was read in the House of Lords, which
charged Walkadyn, a packer of cloth, Ashton, a draper, and Thomas Winter with setting up a printing press in an obscure part of
Holborn. Both wardens, Nicholas Bourne and Joseph Hunscott,
who 'had a very keen nose for smelling out secret presses', swore
on oath that the three men had opposed a justice of the peace,
constables, and the wardens of the Company with guns and an
ordinance on the previous Monday.[61] The previous year in Sep-

---

59   Tanner 67.25. Cit. in Henry Plomer, 'More Petitions To Archbishop Laud', in
     The Library, 3rd ser., X, 39 (July, 1919) pp 130-38, pp 136–37.
60   LJ IV.232. There is no further reference to this case.
61   LJ IV. 398. The House referred the matter to the committee for printing and
     ordered the press to be stayed in the meantime. Joseph Hunscott, bookseller
     and for some time printer to the Long Parliament, was employed by the Sta-

tember 1640, Archbishop Laud had received a report by John H[ighlord]

> that Mr Guard and Primacombe have informed me there are 30 in the city joined together to maintain a press to print seditious and libellous books, and in particular one entitled *A Reply to a Relation of the Conference between William Laud and Mr Fisher, the Jesuit,*[62] which Guard had dispersed to the members of the late Parliament, and to divers others of note, and to some of the Lords, and has promised to acquaint me with those that contribute to the press.[63]

Unfortunately, the promised information was never produced, and the location as well as the maintainers of this secret press remain in the dark. However, others could be brought to light. In his article on secret printing during the Civil War, Henry Plomer has traced the different hideouts of a secret press which was operated by several of the Independents. Plomer sums up his detailed account. In 1643,

> Henry Robinson, Robert and Richard Overton, and John Lilburne, aided by William Larner, the bookseller, procured a printing-press which they lodged in Nicholas Tew's (Stationer) house in Coleman Street ... This press being seized, another was obtained, and lodged in premises in Bishopsgate Street, rented by or belonging to William Larner. Finding the hue and cry getting unpleasantly near in July 1645, a new place of hiding was found in Goodman's Fields, where the work was carried on.[64]

Although Goodman's Fields was at that time a lonely district with garden plots and an old farmhouse in the East End of London without Aldgate, the press could not long escape the eager searches of Joseph Hunscott. In a petition to Parliament he dem-

---

tioners' Company to seek out secret printing presses. Plomer, 'Secret Printing' p 386.

62   For an account of this conference see William Laud, *Works*, ed. W. Scott and J. Bliss, 7 vols. (Oxford, 1847–60), ii.

63   SP 467/9.

64   Plomer, 'Secret Printing', pp 393–94.

onstrated his zeal in finding out secret presses and emphasized the difficulties he had had to overcome in this particular case:

> The Petitioner further shewes, That being employed upon a Warrant from the Speaker of the House of Commons, for the seizing of a press in Goodmans Fields, which printed the book called *England's Birthright*: That your Petitioner, with the Master and Wardens of the Company, endeavouring to put in execution the said Warrant, they were kept out by force, untill at last the doores of the house being by authority forced open, those that were at worke, got out at a window with a rope into a garden, and so escaped: But the said Presse was seized upon, which printed that and divers other books, as was at large proved before both Houses of Parliament at Larner's examination by divers honest men.[65]

After this press had been seized, 'a fresh press and type were obtained, and work resumed in the old premises at Bishopsgate'.

We can only guess at the part secret printing played in the tumults of the 1640s. One clue lies in surreptitiously printed pamphlets of this period, and their relation to those items with proper imprimaturs: the name of the licenser and the date of license, and a reference to the printer and bookseller or publisher with the address where it was 'to be sold'.[66] In contrast, surreptitiously printed pamphlets often had fictitious imprints, such as 'Printed for Anti-Dam-mee, in Tell-troth Lane, at the signe of the Holy want, 1643', or 'Printed luckily and may be read happily between hawke and buzzard, 1641'.[67] A survey of

---

65   *The humble petition and information of Joseph Hunscot, stationer* (1646), BL E.340.15.

66   A work is considered surreptitious, a) when it has a fictitious printer's name or imprint, and no location or a false location, b) when it has no printer's name or imprint, and no location or a false location, or c) when it has the actual printer's name fully translated, i.e. Richard Field into Ricardo del Campo, and no location or a false location. See Dennis Woodfield, *Surreptitious Printing in England, 1550-1690* (New York, 1973). For licensing practices in the 1640s see F. Nash, 'English Licenses to Print and Grants of Copyright in the 1640s', *The Library*, 6th ser., IV (1982), pp 174–84.

67   *The Malignants Conventicle* (1643), BL E.245.24; *A Swarme of Sectaries and Schismatiques* (1641), BL E.158.1. It is interesting to note that another pam-

politico-religious satires I have undertaken, based on the *Catalogue of Prints and Drawings in the British Museum*, has shown that between 1640 and 1646, 45.3 % of this collection had been printed with such fictitious imprints, in the year 1640 to 1641 even 67.9 %.[68]

Vital for the financial success of most printing houses and bookshops was the immediate publication of 'sensational news', preferably documents and letters, either feigned or leaked from Parliament, which carried enough authority to sell well. The amount of money publishers and printers were ready to invest in documents like 'letters' or 'speeches' from Parliament men, and the risks they took to get hold of anything that had the touch of authority, suggests that people had a great interest in this kind of immediate and authentic news. Apparently, these short-lived pamphlets were printed in large editions, such as, for instance, the 1,300 copies of 'an original letter from the Lord Falkland to the Earl of Cumberland'.[69] The same impression is gained from satires on pamphleteers, which commented on the people's special liking for anything that had a (feigned) order or signature, and for new books rather than good books. Just as important was the production of polemical and satirical pamphlets on contemporary issues. In order to be successful, printers and booksellers had to outrun their colleagues, and they depended on good contacts with informers, mercuries, servants of Parliament, and authors who were willing to provide, or even 'invent' news, speeches, or letters. The network between sub-suppliers of news and members of the booktrade was quite complex with many

---

phlet, *The Downfall of Temporizing Poets*, bears a very similar fictitious imprint, which might refer to the same printer: Printed merrily, and may be read unhappily, betwixt Hawke and Bussard, 1641. BL E.165.5.

68 *Catalogue of Prints and Drawings in the British Museum*, ed. F.G. Stephens, completed by Dorothy M. George, 7 vols. (London, 1870-1954). This case study is based on those satires that were listed in Stephens' catalogue and dealt exclusively with the politico-religious conflicts of the early 1640s.

69 CJ II.801, 802.

chance 'transactions'. The surviving records provide interesting glimpses of this semi-underworld of the London booktrade.

In 1637, John Oakes printed Francis de Sales' *Introduction to a devout Life*, which Archbishop Laud subsequently ordered to be burned because of popish passages.[70] However, with the summoning of the Parliament, Oakes justified the printing of this book before Dering's committee for printing, and after his death in 1644, his wife Mary Oakes brought the case against Archbishop Laud during his trial. In her statement, she laid open the whole process of licensing, printing, accusation, and punishment:

> Mary widow of John Oakes, attestes that her husband about seven years since printed part of a book enntitled Francis Salis' *Introduction to a Devout Life* licensed by Dr. Heywood, chaplain to Archbishop Laud, for the press. Finding some Popish passages not fit for the press as he conceived, Oakes carried the same to Heywood, who told him to gon and print the same, and he would bear him out therein. When the book was published exceptions were taken to these passages, and the book ordered to be burnt in Smithfield, which was done. Oakes was thereupon sent for and imprisoned about three weeks, and the fault put upon him and the publisher, as if they had put the passages into the licensed copy when Dr Heywood had purged them out, whereas in truth he had summoned the passages to be put in and stand as they were in the copy brought to the press, which was proved before Sir Edward Deering at a Committee this Parliament.[71]

One Nathaniel Tirry, clerk, was summoned before the Privy Council in December 1638 'for publishing a speech in the name of the Duke of Lenox'.[72] Under examination he confessed that 'hee had the same from one Mrs Grawe a Midwife in Towerstreete And that shee hadd itt from one Mrs Kendall dwelling att the signe of the White Rose in Breadstreete'. The council ordered the recorder of the City of London to send for the said women

---

70   SP 16/355.127.
71   SP 16/499.80.
72   PC.2.49.586.

and inquire whether or not they had delivered the speech to Tirry and from whom they had the same. He was to use 'the best meanes and endeavores hee cann for the discoverie of the Author' whilst Tirry remained in the messenger's custody.[73] In May 1640, a flourishing, unprofessional trade with 'popish books imported from forraine parts' came to a sudden end.[74] In the house of one Alexander Lee, 'a popish taylor', dwelling in Bloomesbury in the parish of St Giles in the Field, a trunk of 'new and very handsomely' books in English was discovered: 'Jesus Psalters, Invectives and rimes against Luther and Calvin, Rheims Testaments, Preparative prayers to the Masse, Manuels, and other superstitious prayer bookes and Catechismes.' There were altogether about two hundred books. Under examination, Lee confessed that these books belonged to one Mary Silvester, an English laundry maid 'who hath for these 9 or 10 yeares served in that qualitie in the house of divers succeeding Spanish Embassadors, and at this time so serveth the present Embassador'.[75] Further inquiries brought to light that 'the woman ... driveth a trade in sending for such bookes out of forraine parts, and venting them here to Papists'. Her service in the house of the succeeding ambassadors of Catholic Spain certainly facilitated her secret business. The sheriffs of the City of London were ordered to 'cause all the said Bookes to bee brought into Smithfield and there in the Marketplace betweene ten and eleven of the clock in the morneing on a market day, laid upon a heape, and all publicly burnt by the Hangman'.[76] On 22 August 1640, the bookseller Samuel Gellibrand, dwelling at the sign of the Brazen Serpent, in St Paul's Churchyard, was taken before Sir Henry Spiller, justice of the peace for Middlesex. The issue at stake was the authorship of two manuscripts, *The Queries of the Clergy of the Diocese of London* and *Demands of the Ministers in Kent and Northamptonshire*, which

---

73   There is no further reference to this case.
74   SP 16/455.131.
75   SP 16/455.131.
76   SP 16/453.105 and *Historical Collections*, ed. John Rushworth, iii, p 1180.

had been found in Gellibrand's shop and caused offence to the
authorities. Gellibrand refused to name the author, but he confessed 'that the copy now delivered in, is in his own handwriting,
written out from another copy'. He acknowledged that he had
lent 'the writing' to Dr Potter, of Gray's Inn, who returned it the
next morning, and also to Mr Stevens, a bookseller in St Paul's
Churchyard, who took no copy.[77] Mr Grimston's report from
the committee for printing to the House of Commons in August 1641 about the 'Manner of printing the Copy of the Letter
from the Earl of Holland' documents one of the most complex
transactions between sub-suppliers of information, printers and
booksellers, that has been recorded:

> That Thomas Symonds was the first that printed the Earl of Hol-
> land's Letter: That he had the Copy of the Letter of Francis Cowles
> [Coles] (bookseller at the halfe Bowle in the Old Bailey), who bought
> it of Ambrose Bayly for Two Shillings; and Bayly had it of William
> Harrison, One of the Servants to the Serjeant of this House. They
> examined Harrison how he came by the copy: And he confessed,
> that Sir Edward Payton sent him for it to Sir Anthony Irby; and that
> after he had received it of Sir Anthony Irby he lent it to Bayly before
> he carried it to Sir Edward Payton, who took a copy of it.[78]

In the early 1640s, Bernard Alsop and Thomas Fawcett quickly
gained a reputation for printing 'seditious and scandalous pamphlets', and they were several times sent to be examined before
the Parliament. In March 1641, Alsop had to answer before the
Lords for printing 'several unlawfull books, as Bacon's *Confid:
of the Church*, *Priviledge of Parliament in England*, *Prerogative of
Parliament*, *Englands Joy for banishing of Preists* [priests], and
The blacke box of Rome [opened]'.[79] He confessed that he had
'the copies of these bookes' from the booksellers [William]
Sheares and Nicholas Vavasor.[80] Under examination, Vavasor tes-

---

77   SP 16/464.73.
78   CJ II.268.
79   H.L.M.P. 4 March 1640-41.
80   Ibid.

tified in turn that he sold a book 'called *Smarts Sermons*', which had been printed by Alsop. On the same occasion Thomas Fawcett was charged with printing a number of seditious pamphlets: *The Dreame or newes from Hell* together with Alsop for the booksellers John Hammond and Thomas Bates, and 'at the least' two hundred copies of *The Lord of Canterburies Dreame* which were found in the shop of Henry Walker.

Inquiries into controversial pamphlets did not always go smoothly. When in August 1641, Nicholas Bourne, one of the wardens of the Stationers' Company, attempted by virtue of an order of the House of Commons to seize a 'scandalous pamphlet', *The Anatomy of the Et-cetera*, which he had found in Hearne's printing house near West Smithfield, Hearne fiercely resisted. He tried to wrest the order out of Bourne's hand and told him 'whosoever laid their Hands upon his Goods, he would be the death of him'.[81] Under examination before the committee for printing, Hearne finally 'confesseth that he had this Book of one Richard Harding: And Harding confessed, that he had it of Thomas Bray, an Oxford Scholar, who turned it out of Poetry into Prose'.[82] Matthew Simmons, bookseller and printer, dwelling next door to the Golden Lion in Aldersgate Street, tried to minimize his own role in the printing of *Certain Grievances, or Errors, touching the Book of Common Prayer*, and pleaded ignorance. Under examination before the House of Lords in December 1641, he confessed that he had printed the book, 'but said it was printed many times before by others'. He further informed the House that 'Lewis Hughes, the author, had delivered the copie to him, but he did not know who had licensed it'.[83] Simmons had

---

81 CJ II.269.
82 Both Bray and Hearne were sent for as delinquents, and Hearne was charged with three offences: the printing of *The Anatomy of the Et-cetera*, his contempt for the order of the House of Commons, and his abuse of a warden of the Stationers' Company, when he tried to execute the said order.
83 LJ IV. 462 and 469. A committee was appointed to look into the matter, and Simmons was committed to the Fleet unless he could find bail.

already been examined by 'The printers Committee' of the Lords earlier that year when he confessed 'that he did joyne with Paine in the Printinge of a booke called *The Historicall narracion of that memorable Parliament that wrought wonders*'.[84]

Attempts to discover the author, printer, and promoter of the *Hertfordshire Petition*, which had been put out in the name of the University of Cambridge, produced the following story in January 1642, when suspects were examined before a specially appointed committee of the House of Commons. Martin Eldred of Jesus College, Cambridge, denied authorship of the *Hertfordshire Petition*, but he admitted that Thomas Herbert, formerly of Trinity College, was the author and had sold it to John Greensmith, bookseller in London, for 2s 6d. Greensmith said that Eldred and Herbert had brought the petition to him and that Barnaby [=Bernard Alsop] of Bread Street had printed it. Greensmith further confessed that he had printed various pamphlets composed by the two men, namely, *Good Newes from Ireland*, *Bloody Newes* and the *Cambridge Petition*, and that he received 2s 6d each for them.[85] In the same month, a great stir was caused by a feigned letter from Queen Henrietta Maria in Holland to Charles I in York, which finally resulted – after pressure from the King – in the exemplary punishment of the author, John Bond. Under examination before the House of Lords, the printer John Wilson, dwelling at the Three Foxes in Long Lane near West Smithfield, confessed that he had printed the supposed letter. According to John Bond's statement, which was supported by three witnesses, Wilson was also responsible for its being written in the first place. Allegedly, he had pressed Bond to compose the letter for his printing press. Perhaps hoping to ease his punishment, John Bond produced 'unwanted' information, claim-

---

84   H.L.M.P. 4 March 1640-41.
85   LJ IV. 652, 653. Martin Eldred was committed to prison for composing scandalous pamphlets and selling them to be printed, but just a month later he was discharged. John Greensmith was imprisoned, too, and Alsop and Herbert were sent for as delinquents.

ing that Richard Browne was the author of the scandalous book *The Danes Plot*, and of a feigned letter from the King of France, and of various other scandalous pamphlets, which had been printed by Bernard Alsop in Honey Suckle Court, Grub Street. All suspects and witnesses were brought before the House of Lords for examination, and then the whole case was transferred to the jurisdiction of the chief justice of the King's Bench.[86] While Bernard Alsop was still defending himself before the House of Lords against John Bond's allegations, his partner, Thomas Fawcett, printer in Grub Street, found himself in trouble when it was discovered that the *Kentish Petition for the Commission of Array* had been printed at his house. His 'servant', John Thomas, had brought it for printing, and it had been printed by a woman, who was apparently working at Fawcett's printing house.[87] Despite attempts to hinder the printing and distribution of this petition, it was still printed 'in divers houses' in London, and distributed in 'great bundles' in August 1642.[88]

An almost classic case of the everyday co-operation between sub-suppliers of news, printers, and booksellers emerges from the circumstances that led to the production of the pamphlet *A true Relation of the Proceedings of the Scotts and English Forces in the North of Ireland* in June 1642. Tobias Sedgewick, a barber in the Strand, took a letter which Pike had brought him from someone in Ireland, to the printer Robert White, who lived in Warwick Lane. White took the letter, and walked over into the Old Bailey to the bookshops of Thomas Bates and Francis Coles. He read it to them, and they thereupon hired White to print 3 reams of paper and gave him 18s.[89] Abigail Dexter, who ran a printing

---

86 John Wilson and his father, Thomas Wilson, were put on bail. LJ IV 674–675; 680-81; 699; 708; LJ V 37.
87 CJ II. 514; 516; 518. The name of the woman was not mentioned and her status is unknown.
88 CJ II. 549; CJ II.719; 722; 728.
89 CJ II. 612; 613; 615; 630. All three of them were committed as prisoners to the King's Bench. Bates and Coles faced proceedings as publishers of false

house with her husband, Gregory Dexter, in Newgate Street, was one of the few women printers in the early 1640s whose work – and in this particular case, whose courage – has been recorded. On 12 September 1642, the House of Lords ordered a book entitled *King James his judgement of a King, and of a tyrant* to be burnt, and directed the lord chief justice to examine the printer, publisher and author.[90] When he examined Abigail Dexter, who was one of the suspects, she confessed that the book had been brought to her house to be printed about three weeks before, and that it had been printed by her appointment, after her husband went away.[91] During her first examination, she 'did not deny that she knew who the author was, but for the present refused to name him'.[92] The following day, Abigail Dexter was brought to the bar of the House of Lords, where she was questioned again. When all attempts to get the desired information failed, the House ordered her to be committed to the King's Bench, to remain there at its pleasure, 'because she would not clearly confess who the author was'.[93]

The market value of 'original' documents not only tempted printers and publishers to instigate authors to write feigned letters or speeches, but the former were sometimes also deceived by sub-suppliers of news. Browne, a bookseller near Christ Church, took 'an original letter from the Lord Falkland to the Earl of Cumberland' to John Thomas' printing house in the White Lion in the Strand near the New Exchange. He told Thomas that he had it from the servant of a Parliament man, and Thomas printed some 1,300 copies of it. The pamphlets were then delivered to Browne's bookshop to be sold.[94] However, further in-

---

news, and White was charged with printing and publishing a scandalous libel to the dishonour of the Scots nation. The pamphlet was ordered to be seized and publicly burned.

90   LJ V.345; CJ II.762.
91   For Gregory Dexter see Swan, *Gregory Dexter.*
92   LJ V. 385.
93   LJ V. 386.
94   CJ II.801.

quiry proved that the letter was a falsification put out under Falkland's name, and Robert Shelton, who was suspected of having contrived it, was ordered to be apprehended.[95] Since the whole incident had come to the attention of the House of Commons, the pamphlets were ordered to be burnt in any case, false or original. The pamphlets were ordered to be seized and burnt, half in the Palace Yard, and half near Browne's bookshop in Cheapside. In November 1643, the House of Lords proposed an ordinance regulating 'that all Papers scandalous to any Persons of honour may either be burnt, or publicly put into a speedy way of Examination, whereby the Person may be brought to condign Punishment if guilty'.[96] The majority of such transactions went unnoticed, and had not a rumour unmasked the fraud and stopped people from buying, the deal would have been perfect. The lucky winner was probably the person 'disguised' as the servant of a Parliament man, who made more money by selling an 'original'.

The renewed attachment of Richard Hearne in January 1643 for printing a 'seditious and scandalous pamphlet, and divers other false bookes and pamphlets', incidentally threw light on the organization and staffing of his printing house. Standing at the bar before the House of Lords, Hearne confessed that he printed *His Majesty's Gracious Answer to the Message sent from the Honourable City of London, concerning Peace*, which he had from Glapthorne, a porter, who lived in Fetter Lane.[97] Hearne was committed to the Fleet Prison, but in February he was brought once more to the bar, after Joseph Hunscott and John Wright, stationers, had discovered that pamphlets were still being printed in Hearne's printing house while he was in prison. It turned out that apart from his two apprentices, Joseph Pack and Thomas Turner, Hearne had three servants, William Gall, William Hunt, and Edward Bill. Furthermore, four women, Grace Brown, Eliza-

---

95   CJ II.802.
96   LJ VI.318.
97   LJ V. 547.

beth Hunter, Sarah Wilkinson, and Anne Vines, allegedly printed
and sold pamphlets in Hearne's house, while he was imprisoned.
When Hearne was shown a feigned abstract of the bill against
the bishops and deans and chapters before it had passed the
House, he denied that this paper or any of the other 'scandalous
pamphlets' printed in his house had been produced by his order.
Hunscott and Wright, however, deposed on oath that they had
bought the paper from the women at Hearne's house. And
Hearne's servant William Gall confessed upon oath that 'divers
particular pamphlets had been printed at Hearne's house since
his being in prison'.[98]

A central position within this colourful network was occupied by hawkers and chapmen. They formed, so to speak, a vital
link at the other end of the chain, vending pamphlets and broadsides in the streets of London. These 'wandering Stationers' were
especially welcomed by printers and publishers, who thought it
safer to sell seditious pamphlets or feigned documents through
them than through booksellers in one of the familiar London
bookshops or stalls. But it did not always work. In July 1642,
two men, Evan Lewis and Richard Hubbard, were taken selling
'about the streets a printed paper called *The Resolution of the
County of Hereford*'.[99] The two Houses were already familiar with
this paper, which they considered 'to be full of sedition and scandalous to the proceedings of both Houses', and inquiries were in
full flow.[100] While the Commons debated further steps, a constable, sent by the justices at the Newgate Sessions, brought Lewis
and Hubbard before the House. They confessed that they had
'divulged' copies of the said *Resolution* and revealed that they
had bought them 'of Richard Hammond, a printer in Holborne
over against St Andrewes Church'.[101] Lewis and Hubbard were

---

98   LJ V. 593; 596–598. The *Stationers' Company Apprentices 1641–1700*, ed. Don
      F. McKenzie, The Bibliographical Society (Oxford, 1974), p 77.
99   CJ II. 662.
100   LJ V. 192.
101   CJ II. 662.

committed to Newgate Prison but two weeks later released on their petition,[102] and Hammond was sent for as a delinquent. Katherine Hadley, spinster and 'servant to John Lilborne [sic]', endured seven months of hard imprisonment 'on the mere suspicion' of having 'thrown abroad in Moor Fields' copies of Lilborne's pamphlet *A cry for Justice* in the Whitsun holidays in 1640.[103] In the late 1630s, one William King was imprisoned in Newgate for having bought a parcel of seditious manuscripts of one Richard Gladding. He claimed, however, to have purchased these papers only to pass them on to Secretary Windebank in hope of reward.[104] One Patrick Creely who was carrying 'many small pictures, popish books, and other relics in his portmanteau' was taken by the officers of the customs at Gravesend in May 1640 to be delivered either to Sir Henry Vane, secretary of state, or to Secretary Windebank at Whitehall according to order.[105] In July 1639, 'certain prophesies ... were found and divulged in Ipswich', which had been written by one Mr Ward.[106]

The following case demonstrates how manuscripts which were secretly distributed in obscure places still found an audience. In December 1637, at about six o'clock at night, one Dorothy Lee took up a 'packett of letters', which were lying 'in a window of a starecase in Somersett yard'.[107] According to her testimony, these were 'letters of a madd man, who had used to disperse letters in Somersett yard directed to the Lords of the Privy Councell'. She carried the letters 'immediately to the shop of William Marshall

---

102 CJ II. 683.
103 H.L.M.P. 21 December 1640.
104 SP 16/363.79–i.
105 SP 16/454.52. The trade in these 'popish relics' was not fully forbidden but the authorities apparently tried to control their distribution. In 1639 a privilege was granted to Peter La Dore for a period of fourteen years 'for the glossing of plain and figured saints made in England or imported', SP 16/415.66.
106 PC.2.50.492. The Privy Council ordered all *prophesies* to be collected and the said Mr Ward and one Mr Robert Saltingstall, gentleman, who had brought forth the testimony against Ward, to be examined 'anew'.
107 SP 16/373.61.

in the Strand', informing the people there present about her discovery. Marshall's servant, Walter Baker, 'served him [his mas-
ter] to read', and it turned out that 'there was strange stuffe in
the said letters, and that the kings Majesty was a Catholique'.
Under examination Baker said that the letter read by him 'seemed
to be a letter sensible and composed with great malice and in no
sort to be suspected to be the letter of a madd mann'.[108]

The involvement of hawkers in the booktrade had so increased
in the early 1640s that they not only became subject for satires
on pamphleteers and attracted the attention of engravers,[109] but
actually aroused the anger of the Stationers' Company. In July
1643, they preferred a petition to the lord mayor and Common
Council for an act to suppress hawkers.[110] They were not alone
in complaining. Three years before, the 'Citizens' freemen of
London using the several trades of plateworking, brushmaking
had already presented a similar petition to the Court of Aldermen 'showing that divers ill disposed persons doe daily goe upp
and downe the streetes and lands within this Citty offering and
putting to sale by way of hawking sundry wares and commodities apptayning to the petitioners ... to their great hinderance
and violation of the ancient Customs and act of Common
Councell'.[111] The Court of Aldermen seemed slightly at a loss
and ordered an inquiry into 'what formerly had been done in

---

108 SP 16/373.61i.
109 There are numerous woodcuts and engravings for this period, showing hawk-
     ers and pedlars with their various wares throughout Europe, and illustrating
     their customs. For London in the seventeenth century see, for instance, *The
     Criers and Hawkers of London. Engravings and Drawings by Marcellus Laroon*,
     ed. with an introduction and commentary by Sean Shesgreen (Aldershot, 1990).
     As hawkers were such a familiar sight in the streets of London, pamphleteers
     used their image in woodcuts as an allegory for people selling 'base' and 'cheap'
     stuff. The woodcut from *The devills White Boyes*, for instance, shows the fig-
     ure of a hawker merging with that of *Time* to signify that before long all pop-
     ish items would be carried out of England. BL E.14.11 (1644).
110 Stat. Court Book C. 20 July 1643.
111 Rep. of the Aldermen 1640, p 92 l.

such a case'.[112] The stationers, however, managed to spice their purely economic interests with honourable political motives and thus turned their grievances into an issue of common concern. They succeeded. On 9 October 1643, an *Act of Common Council* was issued 'for the prohibiting of all persons whatsoever, from crying or putting to sale about the streets within this City, and Liberties, any Pamphlets, Bookes, or Papers whatsoever, by way of Hawking, to be sold, and for the punishment of the offenders therein, according to the Custome and Law of this City'.[113] The justification for this act put forward by the Common Council is of great interest – in spite of its biased rhetoric. It completes other evidence, and it supports the general assumption that hawkers were welcome distributors of seditious pamphlets. Furthermore, it gives at least an idea of the social background, gender, and age of hawkers, whose identity generally remains obscure.

> This Common Councell taking into their serious consideration, a complaint made by the Master, Wardens, Assistants, and Commonalty of the Stationers, London, against a multitude of vagrant persons, men, women and children, which after the manner of hawkers, doe openly cry about the streetes, pamphlets, and other bookes, and under colour thereof are found to disperse all sorts of dangerous Libels, to the intolerable dishonour of the Kings Maiesty, and of the high Court of Parliament, and the whole Government of this Realme, and this City in particular.

The act declared further:

> And conceiving it very necessary by all due meanes to suppresse the evils growing by such unlawfull selling of such Pamphlets and Libels, have thought fit, and doe ordaine, that from henceforth the lawes and custome of this City, which make a forfeiture of the goods, that are cryed about the streetes, by way of hawking to be sold. And also the statutes made against Rogues, and Vagabonds, shall be strictly put in execution against such vagrant persons, selling as aforesaid,

---

112 Ibid., p. 92 r.
113 *Act of Common Council*, BL 669.f.7.49.

being petty Chapmen within the said Statutes. And for the more
sure execution of the said Custom and lawes, It is by this Court
further Ordered, that the Officers of the chamber, for the offences
against the Custome and law of hawking, and Marshals of the City,
and the constables of every Precinct within this city, are hereby
streightly charged to doe their utmost duties in their severall places
and offices, in apprehending and bringing before some of his maiesties
Justices of the Peace within this city, all and every such persons which
shal offend in crying, offering, or putting to sale ... pamphlets ...
And that for neglect of the said Officers ... in their duties and places
as aforesaid, informations or indictments, as the case require, shall
be preferred against them, that they may be punished for their neglect therein according to the Law.[114]

Notwithstanding the punishment laid down in the act for hawkers, and for officers who failed to attach them, hawkers and petty
chapmen continued their trade. In February 1644, the Stationers' Company drafted a second petition, which they presented
this time to the Houses of Parliament.[115]

Printers and publishers had their own core of chapmen and
hawkers, whom they could rely on, and who would ensure regular distribution of pamphlets. The bookseller and publisher
Michael Sparke, senior, dwelling in the Old Bailey in Green Ar-
bour Court at the sign of the Blue Bible, named ten chapmen in
his will, to whom he bequeathed a few shillings each if they paid
their debts.[116] Some business connections even turned into friendships. Richard Whitaker, bookseller at the sign of the King's Arms

114 This act was supported by *The articles of the charge of the wardmote Enquest*,
     which ordered amongst other things 'Also, if any be dwelling within this ward,
     which do offer or put to sale any wares or merchandizes in the open streets or
     lanes of this City, or goe from house to house to sell the same commonly
     called hawkers, contrary to the act made in that behalfe', SP 16/473.281–285.
115 Stat. Court Book C. 5 February 1644.
116 PRO Prob. 11/236.49. 20 October 1653. The chapmen were John Hamond,
     Henry Hamond, Thomas Thomas, William [...], Walter Dight, Edward Dight,
     William [...], Richard Price, Richard Ireland, John Jones,

in St Paul's Churchyard, left 'to my good friends and chapmen' 20s each to buy a ring for his remembrance.[117]

The role of chapmen and hawkers was not confined to the distribution of pamphlets. They were ideal informers on most recent events and rumours in the City, since they moved about the streets the whole day. Thus they fulfilled the double function of spreading the printed news up and down the streets among the people, and of bringing the news they found and heard in the streets to the printing presses. A contemporary satire described their fixed route from the Exchange to Westminster, and from Westminster to the Old Bailey, from the Old Bailey to St Paul's Churchyard, and from thence to Westminster again, which allowed them to travel between places of much public interest and the shops and stalls of booksellers and printers.[118] Among the important stops on their tour were the 'Innes, Ordinaries, Hostelries, and other lodgings in, and neere London', where common carriers lodged, who transported goods into the country and back to London according to a fixed timetable and route.[119] Here pamphlets and books could be delivered for further distribution outside London. In August 1640, a young man, 'very well clad', gave a 'pernicious' book enclosed in a cover to a carter, who was loading his cart for his weekly walk between London and Hatfield at the Bell in Saint John's Street.[120] The book was addressed to Mr Tooke, neighbour of William Salisbury, in Hatfield. Tooke informed Salisbury about the book he had received, and the latter ordered the carter 'at his next going to London to use his best means to find him, and should the youth come to inquire after the delivery of the letter to cause him to

---

117 PRO Prob. 11/209.250. 12 October 1649. The chapmen were Mr Hinde, Mr Foster, sen., Mr Foster, jn., Mr London, Mr Swann, Mr Bruns, Mr Swinton, Mr Lethgower, Mr James Harroway, Mr Hill, Mr Modent, Mr Ireland, Mr Forrest, Mr Davies, Mr Joarden, Mr Godwyn.

118 *The Downefall.*

119 John Taylor, *The Carriers Cosmographie* (1637).

120 SP 16/463.90. The address is reconstructed from Taylor's *Cosmographie*.

[be] apprehended'.[121] Powell, a common carrier between London and Cambridge, who lodged at the Black Bull in Bishopsgate Street, received 'from who he knows not' six little books entitled *The Intention of the Scotch Army*, addressed to Robert Ibbot, chandler, in Cambridge.[122] Ibbot, who recalled the King's proclamation forbidding these 'seditious pamphlets', delivered it to the justice of the peace, who sent them with the same common carrier back to London to be delivered to Secretary Windebank. Sometimes explicit book orders were sent from people in the country to relatives in London. Roger Harvey of St. James, sent a letter to his brother Richard Harvey at Mr Endymion Porter's house, over against Durham House, in the Strand asking: 'I pray you procure for me in London a bible of the great Genevy Character, with the large annotations with francis Junius upon the Revelation ... I have two of the small print but cannot use either.'[123]

An informant's report to Archbishop Laud gives a colourful picture of two petty chapmen on their walk:

> And this is he that dispersed the scotch pamphlets which this relator told sir John Lambe of and lurks about Gray's Inn in a satin doublet, with his man Primacombe following him with a cloak bag full of books and has his cloak laced with a great broad gold lace.[124]

The immediate neighbourhood of bookshops and printing houses with its specific atmosphere and social stratification complemented this fairly well organized circle of news-supply, production and distribution. Its influence on the booktrade cannot be measured because it entered into a complex relationship with the printers' or booksellers' own biography, viewpoints, and eco-

---

121 Ibid.

122 SP 16/464.57. These books were forbidden by the King's proclamation at Whitehall 13 March 1640 for being 'seditious pamphlets sent from Scotland'. Powell's address is reconstructed from Taylor's *Cosmographie*.

123 SP 16/450.91. See also Tessa Watt, 'Piety in the pedlar's pack: continuity and change, 1578–1630', in *The world of rural dissenters, 1520-1725*, ed. Margaret Spufford (Cambridge, 1995), pp 235–72.

124 SP 16/467.9.

nomic interests. At the same time the population had its share in the formation and reproduction of opinions, dictating as 'consumers' – to a certain extent – the 'market value' of books and pamphlets on offer. In spite of the mass of pamphlets produced in London in the early 1640s, it was always an individual's decision to adopt one of the many opinions and viewpoints on offer as his or her own conviction.

Bookshops and printing houses were not only a very visible and audible physical presence in their neighbourhood with colourful broadsides and title pages hanging by the door and the latest book titles cried out, they were also a meeting place where opinions could be exchanged and books or pamphlets debated: here the written and spoken word clashed, interchanged, and reproduced itself. Strongly held religious and political convictions frequently engaged men and women of all social backgrounds in controversial discussions at work, in the streets, in lodgings, or at home. These often ended in denunciation and subsequent examination before the various justices of the peace or even the King's Bench, as will be shown later.

Religious radicalism, which had a strong hold on extra-mural London, most certainly had a strong influence on the interest men and women showed in news and opinions about political and religious issues. The suburbs and some of the liberties very quickly earned a reputation for Puritanism, and, after 1640, for radicalism. 'Puritanism was, perhaps, particularly strong because the magistrates of these areas were much less well organized than the city Aldermen and less likely to report seditious preaching to the Privy Council.'[125] At the same time, there were many complaints in the early 1640s about 'the "great concourse" of Roman Catholics in the liberties and suburbs'.[126] A broadside called *A letter directed to Mr Bridgman, 4th January 1641*, printed by Joseph Hunscott, emphasized the strength of royalists and Catholics in extra-mural London:

---

125 Pearl, *London*, p 40.
126 Ibid., p 39 and p 42.

> The mischievious Londoners, and Apprentices, may do us some hurt
> for present, but we need not much fear them, they do nothing or-
> derly but tumultuously: Therefore we doubt not but to have them
> under our command after some brunt, for our Party is strong in the
> City, especially Holborne, the new Buildings and Westminster.[127]

Religious tension was further heightened by radical lecturers who performed before large crowds often in the immediate vicinity of bookshops and printing houses. 'The total number of lectur-ers in London had risen from 75 in 1641 to 93 a year later, and the number of Puritan lecturers had risen to a new high of 72.'[128] Thus, there was much potential for a clash of opinions in every-day encounters in the immediate proximity of bookstalls and printing houses. For instance, south of West Smithfield, in the parish of St Sepulchre, which was 'infamous for filth, crime and plague', the publishers Thomas Bates and Francis Grove had their shops near St Sepulchre church, and nearby in the Old Bailey.[129] The parish had a long tradition of radical preachers who, at times, attracted up to a thousand people.[130] When flocking to the church in the 1640s to hear Thomas Gouge, son of one of the most prominent London Puritan clergymen, men and women were likely to notice the advertisments outside Bates' and Grove's shops, and perhaps even to enter their premises to take a closer look at what was on offer.[131] It was quite possible that on lecture days Bates displayed outside his door some of the woodcuts in defamation of the Anglican High Church, which he had among his stock in the Old Bailey: seven bishops sitting around a table

---

127 *A letter directed to Mr Bridgman, 4th January 1641* (1641), BL 669.f.4.39; Pearl, *London*, p 39.
128 Seaver, *Lectureship*, p 268.
129 Brett-James, *Stuart London*, p 215. Thomas Bates had a shop in Maidenhead on Snow Hill, Holborn Conduit, in 1645, and a shop in Bishop's Court in the Old Bailey. Plomer, *Dictionary*, p 16.
130 Seaver, *Lectureship*, p 113, p 144, p 175, pp 233–37, p 248f, p 364.
131 Thomas Gouge was admitted to the vicarage of St Sepulchre in 1638, a living he held until his ejection in 1662. Seaver, *Lectureship*, p 175 and p 364.

and singing a 'Protestation', while from the window above eight ducks, led by a decoy duck (John Williams, Archbishop of York), are flying towards the Tower (in the lower left-hand portion of the picture).[132] Another of Bates' woodcuts showed Matthew Wren, Bishop of Ely, seated at a table. From his mouth protrude two speech-tags, one inscribed with 'Only Canonical Prayers' addressed to four men in black who are described as 'Altar-cringing-Priests', and one inscribed with 'No afternoon sermons' addressed to two laymen who are described as 'Churchwardens for Articles'.[133] In 1641, a 'disputation' between 'Master Walker' [probably Henry Walker], and 'a Jesuite' actually took place in Bates' shop in Bishop's Court in the Old Bailey.[134] The same year he was examined before the House of Lords for selling 'a booke called *The Dreame or newes from Hell*', which he had from '[Giles] Calvert [bookseller in St Paul's Churchyard]'.[135] The book had been printed by [Thomas] Fawcett in Grub Street, who had the copy from 'one of the City but refused to tell his name'.[136] Bates' stock, however, was far from representing solely anti-Anglican opinions. He also dealt in many of John Taylor's pamphlets and offered a number of satires on religious sects, among them the Puritans.[137] There were also pamphlets for sale which

---

132   *The Decoy Duck: Together with the Discovery of the Knot in the Dragon's Tayle called etc.* (1641), BL E.132.135.

133   *Wrens Anatomy. Discovering his notorious Pranks and Shameful Wickedness with some of his most Llewd Facts and Infamous Deeds* (1641), BL E.166.7. Bates reused this woodcut with only slight alterations in the reprint of William Prynne's *Newes from Ipswich* (1641), BL E.177.12.

134   *A True Copie of a Disputation held betweene Master Walker and a Iesuite, in the house of one Thomas Bates in Bishops Court in the Old Baily* (1641), BL E.172.9.

135   H.L.M.P. 4 March 1641. This 'booke' could not be identified but its title almost certainly classified it as one of the many politico-religious satires of the time. There are several pamphlets in the *Thomason tracts* which carry the phrase 'News from Hell' in their title, but they are all different and make no reference to a 'dream'.

136   Ibid.

137   For instance, *Religions Enemies*; *The Dolefull Lamentation*; John Taylor, *The Devill Turn'd Round-Head: or Pluto became a Brownist* (1642), BL E.1366.29;

were clearly royalist in tone, such as *The Just Reward of Rebels, or the life and death of Iack Straw and Wat Tyler*.[138] Francis Grove dealt chiefly in 'ballads and the lighter literature of the period', such as Tarlton's *Newes out of Purgatory* or *The pleasant history of Cawood the Rook*.[139] Among his stock were also political ballads that were made in immediate reaction to important events of his time. In 1641, he printed 'scandalous ballads made of the Departure of the Queen Mother' for the use and by the direction of one John Brookes. Brookes had the ballads from John Loukes, a poet.[140] Thomas Bates was closely associated with a number of neighbouring booksellers and publishers, who dealt in plays, ballads, jests, lampoons, broadsides, newssheets, and political pamphlets. One of them was Francis Coles, publisher in the Old Bailey, who was probably the chief ballad publisher of his time.

Apart from religious and political radicalism, the demographic and economic composition of extra-mural London, and the various kinds of public pastimes influenced the atmosphere surrounding the producers and distributors of news and opinions. By the early seventeenth century the northern suburbs, where a number of printers and publishers had their shops, and the eastern suburbs were 'developing most rapidly with a growing sector based on artisan work and small industries'.[141] Lower rents than in the

---

A *Three-Fold Discourse Between Three Neighbours Aldgate, Bishopsgate, and John Heyden the Late Cobler of Houndsditch, a professed Brownist* (1642), BL E.145.3.

138　*The Just Reward of Rebels, or the life and death of Iack Straw and Wat Tyler* (1642), BL E.136.1

139　Plomer, *Dictionary*, p 87.

140　LJ IV.374 and 377.

141　Roger Finlay and Beatrice Shearer, 'Population growth and suburban expansion', in *Metropolis*, ed. Finlay and Beier, pp 37–60, p 53. The general profile of trades in inner- and extra-mural London presents the following picture: the dominant industry throughout the period from 1500-1700 was clothing, despite the depression from about 1620. Then followed victualling, merchants of various types, distributive and transport trades, building, leather and metal trades, miscellaneous producers (basketmakers, bowyers, boxmakers, fletchers, limners, and watchmakers), and miscellaneous services (apothecaries, midwives, scriveners, soldiers, waterbearers and woodmongers).

City, the availability of 'plant', and the wish to avoid official restraints and the regulatory powers over trading and manufacturing of the City's guilds, inspired many industrious but also many poor people to leave the City and to set up in the 'leafy suburbs'.[142] Despite this movement out of the City centre, the principal cause of suburban growth was migration.[143] The rural exodus between 1560 and 1650, particularly to London, surpassed the City's housing and labour capacities, and the 'eastern, northern, and southern suburbs were taking the rural surplus into unskilled trades, labouring, the transport of goods and shipping'.[144] In line with this trend, the majority of apprentices who had been bound to the Stationers' Company between 1641 and 1700 had migrated to London from all over the country.[145] The same must have been true for those young men and women who worked in printing houses without being formally bound, and who are difficult to trace since they do not appear in the stationers' registers.[146] Formal apprenticeship and guild membership were relatively weak in the expanding suburbs.[147]

A third factor which contributed to the development of suburban areas was migration from overseas. Foreigners who came 'predominantly in two periods in the latter third of both the 16th

---

142 Beier, 'Engine', pp 156–57.
143 Finlay and Shearer, 'Population growth', pp 50 and 52.
144 Ibid., pp 52–3.
145 McKenzie, 'Apprentices'.
146 Beier has warned that 'Guild labels are imprecise and unrepresentative. Membership of the trading guilds did not always signify the actual practice of their trade because, by the custom of London, their members could take on any trade'. Beier, 'Engine', p 143. If we further take into account the tendency that the proportion of London workers who entered the guilds and took up the freedom declined as the seventeenth century progressed, it can be safely assumed that apart from the registered stationers a large number of men and women were engaged in the booktrade, especially in the suburbs.
147 Beier, 'Engine', p 143. After the Star Chamber Decree in 1637 had reduced the number of master printers to twenty, moving to the suburbs was for many probably the only way for them to continue their trade and to employ servants who would fulfill the function of apprentices or journeymen.

and the 17th century', tended to settle in extra-mural London.[148] Roger Finlay and Beatrice Shearer have pointed to some general features in the composition of this migrant group, which 'varied at different times over the period'. Migrants were predominantly single with an increasing proportion of females. They included people from all social backgrounds, and from all areas of the country. A decreasing number were apprentices 'as the significance of this institution fell away'. And the majority of migrants who came from overseas were refugees who had suffered from religious persecution on the Continent.[149] Thus they were people who had endured hardship for their personal convictions and they were most likely to defend their opinions in the future.

Furthermore, the suburbs had long been notorious as a refuge for rogues and vagabonds, and the lawless and rough population added an element of social dislocation and unrest to these areas.[150] Alarmed by the increase in crime in the suburbs, the Middlesex justices obtained in 1610 a licence from James I to build a House of Correction. 'This was the famous Hick's Hall, which was completed in 1612 at the south end of St John's Street, to be both a prison and a meeting place for the justices formerly using the Castle Inn near Smithfield Bars. It was on a large garden plot near the east end of Clerkenwell, and was for the "punishment and employment of rogues and vagabonds of Middlesex"'.[151]

However, it is important to note that the northern and north eastern suburbs were not a closed society of vagabonds, the poor, adventurous entrepreneurs, and newcomers. Clerkenwell, for instance, 'was a place of residence for many distinguished people all through the seventeenth century, and especially for magnates'.[152] At the same time, 'the Red Bull, in St John's Street, Clerkenwell, was well known for its turbulent audiences and in

---

148 Finlay and Shearer, 'Population', p 51 and Brett-James, *Stuart London*, p 24.
149 Finlay and Shearer, 'Population', p. 50-1.
150 Pearl, *London*, p 38.
151 Brett-James, *Stuart London*, p 217.
152 Ibid., p 218.

1638 it got into trouble for putting on a play lampooning one of the notorious monopolists of the City, Alderman William Abell'.[153] Not far away were the Fortune and the Curtain near Moor Fields. These suburban public playhouses were rivalled by as many as half a dozen inns commonly used for playing.[154] Public playhouses continued to offer a pennyworth of playgoing (or bearbaiting) until 1642, and its visitors represented the diversity and heterogeneity of the London (suburban) populace.[155] Plays were a favourite pastime and a welcome genre for the widespread circulation of political opinions in the combination of literate and oral forms of expression they offered: writing-reading, speaking-hearing, acting-seeing. Valerie Pearl has observed that 'situated in the liberties and outparishes, the playhouses were close enough to the people who flocked to them to express their opposition to authority and good order'.[156] A complaint against interludes ran:

> We do understand that certaine players that use to recyte their plays at the Curtaine in Moorfields do represent upon the stage in their interludes the persons of some gentlemen of good desert and quality that are yet alive under obscure manner, yet in such sorte as all the heavens may take notice both of the matter and the person that are meant thereby.[157]

However, 'some of the opposition to theatres arose not so much from the contents of the plays or the moral character of the players as from the political danger in permitting large and excited assemblies to gather'.[158] One of the most celebrated London ri-

---

153 Pearl, *London*, p 41. The play in question was probably *The New Whore Vamped*. For the sentence against the actors and details on the offending passages see SP 16/429.51–2.
154 Andrew Gurr, *The Shakespearean Stage 1574–1642* (1970, rpt. and enlarged London, 1980), (1970), p 117.
155 Gurr, *Stage* (1970), p 7 and p 144–45.
156 Pearl, *London*, p 41.
157 Gurr, *Stage* (1980), p 18.
158 Pearl, *London*, p 41.

ots was the pursuit and murder of John Lambe who was 'jostled and reviled as the "duke's [Buckingham] devil" by a crowd of apprentices and boys in Moorfields ... as he made his way home from the Fortune playhouse'.[159] This event left a lasting impression 'and was ominously recalled in May 1640 in the lines "Charles and Marie do what they will, We will kill the Archbishop of Canterbury like Doctor Lambe"'.[160] Men and women flocking to the playhouses until 1642 passed by a number of bookshops which were located in this area and sold seditious politico-religious pamphlets, perhaps including the lines against Laud. Because of their proximity, as well as their stock and repertoire, suburban playhouses and bookshops seem to have attracted the same mixture of people. By the beginning of the seventeenth century, John Webster wrote about the audiences of the Globe in the southern London suburb of Southwark:

> I have noticed most of the people that come to that
> playhouse resemble those ignorant asses
> who, visiting stationers shops, their use is not
> to inquire for good books, but new books.[161]

What, then, were these 'new books' and pamphlets that so attracted the common people and at the same time so worried the holders of power? Central to our understanding of public opinion and the development of a popular political consciousness is the analysis of what they were offered to read and listen to in terms of political and religious opinions and news. In the following chapter I will look at the most popular news genres of the time, namely ballads, satires, and woodcuts, analysing their contents and their modes of presentation.

---

159 Lindley, 'Riot Prevention', p 114.
160 Ibid., p 115.
161 John Webster, *The White Devil*, (1624), ed. John A. Symonds (London, 1959),
     p 20.

4 · Religion, Politics and Popular Literary Genres

Pens and presses in the 1640s were busy satisfying people's hunger for news, and their written and printed products were eagerly passed on from hand to hand and mouth to mouth around London and across the country. The presentation of news and opinions ranged from learned politico-religious tracts, newsbooks, speeches, letters, and proceedings of Parliament to satires, elegies, poems, dialogues, prophecies, plays, woodcuts, and ballads. Although there were clear distinctions between these genres with regard to the intellectual demands they made on their audience, they were consumed by men and women across the social scale. Educated people read and commented on ballads and pictures just as people of little learning obtained and commented on letters which communicated rather dry and highly specific political events.

In the 1640s, people of all classes and both genders had access in one way or another to more or less all genres of news presentation. This phenomenon is easily explained by the dynamics of communication discussed in the concluding chapter, and the 'reading' habits or 'reading culture' of people living in a society that was still immersed in its oral culture in spite of the rapid growth of literacy.[1] 'Reading' in mid-seventeenth-century Eng-

---

1   From David Cressy's work we know that the social structure of illiteracy which
     he defines on the basis of people using marks (instead of signatures) in the

land was still a social and communal affair with one person reading out a written or printed paper or interpreting a picture while
others stood by listening. On their title pages authors invited
people to hear what was written rather than to read: 'Brethren
and Sisters all give eare to what I shall tell you.'[2] It was not unusual for illiterate people to ask for help when trying to understand a written or printed text.[3] Statutes against seditious pamphlets actually encouraged the 'ignorant multitude' to present
suspicious prints they came across to a (literate) official to have
them read and examined for legality.[4] George Barnard testified
that after he had heard that Bartholomew Astin, 'an olde blinde
man almost a hundred yeares of age', had received a letter from
London in which 'letter he heard there was some dangerous
words', he went to see the letter.[5] He met Astin's wife early the
same morning and 'desired to see it, and readinge the said letter
and conceiving the wordes to be dangerous did forthwith repair
(as my dutie hee thought hee was bound) to Thomas Babington
the next Justice of the peace and acquainted him thereof and

---

diocese of London and Middlesex between 1580 and 1700 was as follows: marks
were used by about 76 per cent of women, 79 per cent of husbandmen, 78 per
cent labourers, 31 per cent of servants, 30 per cent of yeomen, 28 per cent of
tradesmen and craftsmen, 18 per cent of the apprentices, 2 per cent of the
gentry, and 0 per cent of the clergy and the professions. David Cressy, *Literacy
and the Social Order. Reading and Writing in Tudor and Stuart England* (Cambridge, 1980), p 121. In rural England the figures for illiteracy were generally
higher, especially among women, showing great regional variations. However,
it has been convincingly argued that since reading was taught prior to writing
these figures are gross underestimates of reading ability. See Margaret Spufford,
'First steps in literacy: the reading and writing experiences of the humblest
seventeenth-century autobiographers', *Social History*, 4 (1979), pp 407–35,
and Keith Thomas, 'The meaning of literacy in early modern England', in Gerd
Baumann (ed.), *The written word. Literacy in transition*, Wolfson College Lectures 1985 (Oxford, 1986).

2   Samuel Sheppard, *The Committee-Man Curried* (1647), BL E.398.21; also *A
     Diurnall of Dangers* (1642), BL E.112.4.
3   SP 16/16/373.61 (1637); see also Thomas, 'Literacy'.
4   Arber, *Transcript*, i, 452, 453.
5   SP 16/357.180 (1637).

delivered the said letter unto him'. Eager to learn the most recent news, people of different social background and gender – often complete strangers – spontaneously mixed and gathered around someone reading out a newsletter 'sent from a friend' or communicating what he or she had heard or read. In the same way official announcements and proclamations were either read out from the pulpit or they were posted in public places. One can easily imagine a group of people gathering around a newssheet hung on a wall, and listening to someone who was able to read.

'Reading' was not confined to the verbal utterance and reproduction of texts. It also comprised the performance of texts through specific intonations, gestures, and mimicry, which emphasized the speaker's interpretation of the news and opinions communicated.[6] Jests or 'jesting passages', for instance, came alive in performance, highlighting what was funny and encouraging others to laugh, and the same was true for the numerous highly provocative politico-religious satires of the period. Often only the contents of literary products were passed on by word of mouth without the original source at hand, thus turning literature into a communal good. Ballads were sung in the streets and in alehouses rather than read quietly at home, and they, too, were reproduced without their written or printed base. The same was true for jokes and rhymes, and for dialogues, which often invited performance.

Pictures were a central feature of news presentation in the seventeenth century.[7] They were either used in their own right with only brief printed explanations, trusting the onlooker to grasp their meaning, or they served to catch people's eyes to direct them to the printed word. These woodcuts were full of sym-

---

6   Richard Bauman, *Story, performance, and event. Contextual studies of oral narrative* (Cambridge, 1986).
7   For a valuable introduction to the significance of pictures in the early modern period see *Historische Bildkunde. Probleme – Wege – Beispiele*, Zeitschrift für Historische Forschung. Beiheft 12 (1991), ed. Brigitte Tolkemitt and Rainer Wohlfeil.

bolism drawing on both biblical and secular imagery, and they
were deeply imbedded in the political culture and everyday life
of their time. Public figures were portrayed, 'types' such as the
naked 'Adamite' or the 'Roundhead' were created, London sites
appeared such as Charing Cross, or the 'Nag-Head Tavern', a
meeting-place of religious nonconformists, and certain new images such as birds standing for Bishop Wren and Sir John Finch,
lord keeper, appeared and reappeared in ever new contexts, giving these pictures their own dynamic and inner dialogue. Some
pictures showed a natural realism when representing, for instance,
the burning of popish books and pictures, the execution of well
known figures such as Laud and Strafford, or the Irish rebellion.

Finally, manuscripts played an important role in the circulation of news and the formation of opinions during this period.[8]
They could be produced and spread on a private basis without
the help of printing presses, publishers, and hawkers, which made
them less vulnerable to searches and censorship than the more
exposed production of printed papers. As a result manuscripts
touching on the politico-religious conflicts of the time were often more daring and saucy than printed items. Furthermore, some
people still believed that manuscripts were 'more authentic' than
prints since no one could meddle with their content during the
production phase.[9]

The most obvious genre of written news was private letters.[10]
Written in the first person singular, these letters acquired the

---

8   The continuing influence of manuscripts in spite of the advance of printing
     has been underestimated if not wholly negated for a long time. See Harold
     Love, 'Scribal Publication in Seventeenth-Century England', *Transactions of
     the Cambridge Bibliographical Society*, 9 (1987), pp 130–54; and Don F.
     McKenzie, 'Speech-Manuscript-Print', *The Library Chronicle*, 22 (1990), pp
     87–109.

9   For 'some of the psychological anxieties associated with print' see McKenzie,
     'Speech-Manuscript-Print', esp. pp 96–98.

10   By 'private letters', I do not mean the well-known newsletters or 'separates'
     regularly sent to and fro between people of higher social standing and mem-
     bers of Parliament. Rather, I refer to occasional correspondence between or-

authority or at least gave the impression of an eye-witness reportage: interior, private, immediate and authentic. Their documentary status and their 'ability to personalize history' tempted people to read or listen to them.[11] Apart from being shared with friends and acquaintances, even strangers, letters were often offered to the presses, and during the 1640s a large number of printed letters circulated parallel to their written originals. The popularity of the genre most likely encouraged authors to invent letters, too, whereas satirists played with the genre, devising letters written by fictional, often demonic, characters such as Pluto or Satan.[12]

Manuscripts communicating news and opinions were not restricted to this 'natural' genre. Especially ballads and poems were circulated in writing. Libels were penned and put up in public places.[13] During his visit to Ipswich in July 1640, Sir Lionel Tollemache heard of a 'scandalous paper found nailed, together with the new book of Canons, on or near the pillory in the market-place [in Ipswich]'.[14] The paper had been taken down by the local apothecary, who carried it to the bailiffs of the corporation. Tollemache took a copy and sent it to Archbishop Laud. In his diary Laud frequently referred to short libels against himself. One was found posted on the cross in Cheapside saying: 'The Arch-Wolf of Canterbury had his hand in persecuting the saints and shedding the blood of martyrs.' Another, discovered 'at the south

---

dinary people touching among other things on recent news. For the former see Cust, 'News'.

11   See Patterson, *Censorship*, p 203.

12   See, for instance, *A true Copy of the Devills Letter* (1640), anonymous manuscript, SP 16/466.60.

13   On libels in seventeenth-century England see recently Adam Fox, 'Ballads, Libels and Popular Ridicule in Jacobean England', *Past and Present*, 145 (1994), pp 47–83; Alastair Bellany, '"Rayling Rymes and Vaunting Verse": Libellous Politics in Early Stuart England, 1603–1628', in Holstun, *Pamphlet*, pp 285–310, 367–71; and Croft, 'The Reputation'.

14   SP 16/461.27 (1640).

gate' of St Paul's, ran: 'The devil had let that house to me.'[15] An undated, astonishingly bold and ironic libel of the early 1640s against the King reads as follows:

> Change places Charles, and pat on Pym's grave gowne
> Whilst in the upper house he weares the Crowne
> Let Pym be king a whyle and be thou Pym,
> Then weele adore thee as we now doe him,
> Hang up the Bishops that soe proudly strive
> To uphold their owne and thy Prerogative
> And be content seing most of them are Romaines
> To have some Traytors in the house of commons
> Let us alone awhile and then thou shalt see
> Weele all be Kings as well as Pym and hee.[16]

I suggested earlier that the variety of news presentation reached people across social and gender divisions. The ways in which individuals appropriated news, however, differed greatly from one person to the next, and pamphleteers had to take into account the range of cognitive abilities and foreknowledge among their readership. The politicized everyday talk of men and women during this period shows that especially people of lower social status tended to 'fictionalize' their news reports rather than passing on straight facts, something that will be commented on in more detail in the following chapters. The same tendency can be observed in the most popular literary genres of the time which authors used for the presentation of news and opinions: woodcuts, ballads, satires, and dialogues. They incorporated many features that were familiar from the rich oral culture and religious imagery of early modern England, and presented news in the guise of wonder stories, magic, tales of folk heroes, journeys into hell, prophecies, and the Apocalypse.[17] Most of them were printed

---

15 Laud, *Works*, iii, pp 228, 229. Also pp 232, 234, 235, 237.
16 Ashm Ms 36.73r
17 See Jerome Friedman, *Miracles and the Pulp Press during the English Revolution. The Battle of the Frogs and Fairford's Flies* (London, 1993); Smith, *Literature*. Dorothy George, *English Political Caricature to 1792. A Study of Opinion*

and sold in London's northern suburbs near Smithfield, an area which, as already shown, was difficult for censors to check. The following paragraphs provide a survey of some forms and styles in which news and opinions were expressed, taking woodcuts, ballads, and pamphlets as an example.[18]

'Base Pictures Putting Me in a Cage': Woodcuts as Opinion Leaders

During the 1640s, woodcuts and to a lesser extent engravings played a central role in the presentation of news, and texts were regularly supplied with pictures. Archbishop Laud complained not only of libels and ballads 'sung up and down the streets as full of falsehood as of gall', but also of 'base pictures putting me in a cage and fasting me to a post by a chaine at my shoulder. And divers of these libels made men sport in taverns and ale-houses, where too many were as drunck with malice as with the liquor they sucked in'.[19] Contemporaries were quite aware of the power of pictures and their initial perceptual advantage: pictures were almost always different from their surrounding verbal context, and hence they were quickly perceived and imprinted on the mind. George Wither, a mid-seventeenth-century poet and illustrator of emblems, observed: 'When levity or a childish delight in trifling objects hath allured them to look on the pictures, curiosity may urge them to peap further, that they may seek out their meanings.'[20]

---

and Propaganda (Oxford, 1959), is still valid as an introduction to politico-religious satires and woodcuts of the period.

18   This chapter does not attempt to survey all printed ephemera and manuscripts from the early 1640s. Discussion is limited to those which focus on contemporary religious and political issues, and especially those which explore the political effects of religious polarization.

19   Hugh Trevor-Roper, *Archbishop Laud 1573–1645* (London, 1940), p 412.

20   Cit. in Francis Quarles, *Emblems Divine and Moral. With a Sketch of the Life and Times of the Author*, ed. George P. Marshall (London, 1859), p xv.

Apart from catching people's attention, arousing their curiosity, and emphasizing certain arguments in the text, these woodcuts bridged the gap between the literate and the illiterate. With
direct, punchy illustrations often closely resembling features of
the common stage (eye-catching, entertaining prints with characters in dramatic postures and speech tags, set against bare back-
drops), pamphleteers strove to appeal to the widest possible popular audience.[21] Whereas some woodcuts were merely decorative
and bore no relation to the text (printers often recycled woodcuts for economic reasons), others carried a full message, being
accompanied only by short commentaries or speech tags. 'Such
publications were emotive and not intellectual; the image-mak-
ers personalised difficult issues and featured everyday, familiar
stereotypes; they drew on such easily accessible verbal and visual
sources as popular literature, proverbs and the Bible.'[22] The question of whether people of very little or no learning were able to
grasp the political or religious message of such woodcuts is still
open to debate. Scholars have frequently pointed to the complex
cognitive processes involved in 'reading pictures'.[23] Furthermore,
individual responses to pictures cannot be generalized, nor is there
any guarantee that pictures were understood in 'the right way'
regardless of the observer's educational background. Yet the impression pictures made on people's minds, their mnemonic function, and the power they could exert over individuals have been
recognized since ancient Greek and Latin theories about the art

21   Tamsyn Williams,'"Magnetic Figures": Polemical Prints of the English Revolution', in *Renaissance Bodies. The Human Figure in English Culture c.1540–
1660*, ed. Lucy Gent and Nigel Llewellyn (London, 1990), pp 86–110, p 88.
22   Williams, 'Magnetic Figures', p 88.
23   Rudolf Schenda, 'Bilder vom Lesen – Lesen von Bildern', in *Internationales
Archiv für Sozialgeschichte der deutschen Literatur*, 12, ed. Wolfgang Frühwald,
Georg Jäger, A. Martino (1987), pp 82–106; Robert W. Scribner,
'Reformatorische Bildpropaganda', in *Bildkunde*, ed. Tolkemitt and Wohlfeil,
pp 83–106; and id., 'The Printed Image as Historical Evidence', *German Life
and Letters*, 48 (July, 1995), pp 324–37.

of memory, rhetoric, and the 'sense of sight'.[24] Cicero was already well aware that

> The most complete pictures are formed in our minds of the things that have been conveyed to them by the senses, but that the keenest of all our senses is the sense of sight, and that consequently perceptions received by the ears or by reflexion can be most easily retained if they are also conveyed to our minds by the mediation of the eyes.[25]

Pictures were a central feature of medieval culture, as has been demonstrated most recently by Horst Wenzel's impressive study of culture and memory in the Middle Ages.[26] Frances Yates had already shown that the growing practice of preaching in the vernacular to a lay audience in the Middle Ages inspired the creation of many new images for oral delivery. In particular, the vice-virtue scheme was filled out to reinforce ideas of salvation and damnation. In the seventeenth century pictures gained a new didactic significance. The 'Renaissance association of thinking with seeing, and the constant recourse to visual and pictorial explanations' instigated a reform of pedagogic and linguistic theories.[27] English schoolmasters increasingly tried to 'make our words as legible to Children as Pictures are', arguing that 'if the eye hath not seen that we are speaking of, it can make no report of it to the minde'.[28] From their first attempts at learning to read people became used to relating pictures to words and vice versa. The

---

24 The literature on this subject is vast. See especially the seminal study by Frances Yates, *The Art of Memory* (London, 1966); David Freedberg, *The Power of Images. Studies in the History and Theory of Response* (Chicago and London, 1989).

25 Cicero, *De oratore II*, Lxxxvii, 357. Cit. in Yates, *Memory*, p 4.

26 Horst Wenzel, *Hören und Sehen. Schrift und Bild. Kultur und Gedächtnis im Mittelalter* (Munich, 1995).

27 Forrest G. Robinson, *The Shape of Things Known. Sidney's Apology in Its Philosophical Tradition* (Cambridge/Mass., 1972), p 6; and especially Murray Cohen, *Sensible Words. Linguistic Practice in England 1640–1785* (Baltimore and London, 1977).

28 H. Woodward, *Light to Grammar and all other Arts and Sciences. With a Gate to Sciences opened by a Natural Key*, (1641). Cit. in Cohen, *Sensible Words*, p 7.

key principle of language acquisition and reading was the visualization of letters and words.[29] Often words were keyed by numbers to pictures, or a complex illustration corresponded to the integrated discourse of an enumerating commentary. This very method of carefully relating pictures to commentaries was frequently used in politico-religious and satirical woodcuts of the 1640s. Quite often, the author himself established the link between the text and the woodcut or engraving in a brief note:

> The Picture that is Printed in the front
> Is like this Kingdome, if you look upon't:
> For if you well doe note as it is,
> It is a Transformed Metamorphosis ...
> And this is Englands case this very day,
> All things are turn'd the Cleane contrary way.[30]

Authors also directly commented on the function of a picture, describing it as 'the emblem of the time'.[31] Others carefully numbered each item on the picture in order to explain them one by one in the text below.[32] There were, furthermore, picture stories which explained political or religious events by way of a series of woodcuts. A broadside entitled *The Malignants trecherous and Bloody Plot against the Parliament and Citty of London* consists of twelve small engravings beginning with the conspirators as they sit around a table devising their plan, and ending with their execution.[33] Political (or historical) picture stories also featured in one of the most popular games of the time, namely playing cards. Given the variety of cards that were advertised, it seems to

---

29   Ibid., pp 8–13 and pp 18–25.
30   *A Discovery of the Jesuits Trumpery, Newly Packed out of England* (1641), BL 669 f.4.10.
31   *Mad Fashions, Od Fashions, All out of Fashions, or the Emblems of these Distracted Times* (1642), BL E.138.30, *A Rot amongst the Bishops* (1641), BL E.1102.4
32   See for instance *Heraclitus Dream* (1642), BL 669.f.6.29 and *Behold Romes Monster on his monstrous Beast* (1643), BL 669.f.8.29.
33   *The Malignants trecherous and Bloody Plot* (1643), BL 669.f.8.22.

have been fashionable to own a specific set, and people could choose from 'Love cards, Fortification Cards, Military Cards, Heraldry Cards, Poetical & Philosophical Cards, Chronicle Cards, Ladies Cards, Classical Cards, Historical Cards, Masquerade Cards, and Habit Cards'.[34] These cards consisted of a picture and a brief description of what was shown. Best known for the mid-seventeenth century is the 'Rump Parliament Series' of playing cards. The playing card featuring the 'King', for instance, has a picture of Oliver Cromwell with the text saying 'Oliver declares himself and the Rebells to be the Godly Party'.[35] Another shows Oliver Cromwell and his followers praying to God while Charles I is beheaded in the background. No series of playing cards for the early 1640s is known to have survived, but there are individual cards which probably date from this time. One shows a 'Citty Constable' and a watchman, and the text underneath runs: 'I am a Citty Cunstable, be you mean or Worshipfull: tis late doe you prate some Tavern hunter, goe watchman, carry him to the counter'.[36] More important, there is direct evidence which demonstrates how people who played cards in the early 1640s related the pictures shown on their cards to the political and religious disputes of their time.[37]

A common and quite powerful device for the presentation of a particular viewpoint in condemnation of another was the 'opposition of concepts' such as 'Heresy' against 'Faith or Truth', which was applied throughout the 'pictorial politics' of the time and was based on the conceptual contrast of virtues and vices.[38]

---

34   Douce Misc. Playing Cards. Bodleian Library, Oxford.
35   Johnson Collection. Indoor Games. Playing Cards. Rump Series, Bodleian Library, Oxford. Also, J. R. S. Whiting, *A Handful of History* (Gloucester, 1978)
36   Douce Collection. Playing Cards, Bodleian Library, Oxford.
37   SP 16/469.95 and SP 16/470.33 (1640).
38   See the woodcut in *Englands Petition to her gratious King* (1643), BL 669.f.4.14 and *Three Figures Ecclesiastical described as Sound-head, Rattle-head and Round-head* (1642), BL 669.f.6.94. In general, Ernst H. Gombrich, *Symbolic Images. Studies in the Art of the Renaissance* (London, 1972).

Apart from comments on the function and meaning of pictures
and various typographical and artistic devices to help decode their
message, the familiarity of the images used was central for their
understanding. The 'audience was to be contacted through images and symbols familiar to them, which were then transformed
on the propagandists' terms'.[39]

A survey of pictorial representations of religious and political
conflicts of the period shows a rich variety of traditional symbols and images, some of which can be traced back to the Middle
Ages, early Christianity, and Greek and Latin mythology. There
are woodcuts, for instance, which show the Pope being attacked
by a unicorn, a mythical animal taken to represent Christ and his
invincible strength, signified by the horn.[40] The whale was not
only a symbol of the Resurrection (John 1:17, 2:1 and 10) and
Salvation in early Christian belief and art, but was also used as a
likeness of the devil who draws unbelievers into hell.[41] The devil
was pictured as a dragon, a composite winged beast with lion's
claws, eagle's wings, a serpent's tail, and fiery breath. The ship
was often used as a symbol of both the church and the state,
which had its origin in the Old Testament story about Noah's
salvation in the ark. Other symbols included the hour-glass to
signify time, the skull as a reminder of death, or a pair of scales to
signify justice. Often the 'true' church was presented as a castle,
already a favourite allegorical figure in medieval English sermons
and homilies, standing for defence, security and protection.[42] And
finally, the Seven Virtues and the Seven Vices or Deadly Sins were

---

39   Scribner, *Simple Folk*, p 9. In general, still Jacques Ellul, *The Formation of Men's Attitudes*. Trans. K. Keller and J. Lerner (New York, 1965).

40   *The Pope's Benediction* (1641), BL E.158.15; *The Lineage of Locusts or the Popes Pedegre* (undated), BL 669.f.4.21. The following definitions of symbols are based on Gertrude G. Sill, *A Handbook of Symbolism in Christian Art* (London, 1975).

41   See, for instance, *A True and Wonderfull Relation of a Whale, pursued in the Sea* (1645), BL E.308.24.

42   Gerald R. Owst, *Literature and the Pulpit in Medieval England. A Neglected Chapter in the History of English Letters and of the English People* (Cambridge, 1933; rpt. 1961).

used in woodcuts and texts to label the conflicting political and religious parties. Although these symbols and images carried fixed and thus recognizable meanings throughout the centuries, the message put forth depended on the overall composition of the picture and the way its various figures were related to each other.

The dynamics created in pictures through the use of familiar images in new contexts, and the creation of new symbols, can be nicely demonstrated by a Puritan tract of the year 1641 entitled *A Rot amongst the Bishops*.[43] It not only presents the 'ship of state and church', which was familiar through biblical imagery and reused many times in political woodcuts of the period, it also turns the ship into a symbol of the 'devilish' interrelation of the state with a popish church, and a corrupt ecclesiastical jurisdiction in the early 1640s. The sequence of four 'emblems' as a picture-story was in the narrative tradition of popular news presentation of the period, and the pictures showed apocalyptic imagery which was widely used in the political and religious prints of the Puritans. The story ends with a prophecy concerning the fate of Laud, thus resorting to a popular genre of mid-seventeenth-century England. The first 'emblem' shows a ship which seems to have been taken over by some of the most hated politicians, lawyers, and clergy of the time, namely Archbishop Laud, Sir John Lambe, Bishop Wren and Sir Arthur Duck. They were easily identifiable through their portraits and their written names, and their images were generally familiar from numerous other woodcuts of the time. At the right end of the ship near Wren stands a female-shaped devil with dangling bosoms, clawes, and horns.[44] At the other end, next to Laud, hangs a flag tied to the

---

43   *A Rot amongst the Bishops* (1641), BL E.1102.4.
44   For one of the many political attacks on Wren, Bishop of Norwich, see *Wrens Anatomy. Discovering his Notorious Pranks and Shameful Wickednesse* (1641), BL E.166.7, and especially the woodcuts in *The Wrens Nest Defild or Bishop Wren Anatomized, His Life and Actions Dissected and laid open* (1641), BL E.165.14.

Pope's staff which serves as a pole. The association with Rome is strengthened by the flag's symbol: the crossed key and sword, and the tiara. Between Laud and Wren stands Lambe, exercising jurisdiction in the widely hated ecclesiastical court, the High Commission. A wimple behind him is inscribed 'Licence', and below on one of the ship's planks is written 'high comission'. Above him on the top mast stands Duck holding on to a pole with a flag inscribed 'processe'. And finally, there are the three flags of the 'three kingdomes' representing the Commonwealth and secular power. The ship is heavily armed. One canon has just been fired, and from another hangs a knotted rope resembling that of the hangman. Above is written 'the oath et:cet:'.

This is a newly created and powerful symbol of the 'Canons and Institutions Ecclesiastical' introduced by Laud in 1640, and especially the controversial canon VI, which imposed on all clergymen the notorious 'etcetera' oath. The oath bound them not to consent to the alteration of 'the government of this Church by archbishops, bishops, deans and archdeacons, etc.'.[45] The image of the church canon as a cannon ball draws on the early modern love for word play. Furthermore, it hints at the destructive force – further emphasized by the hangman's rope – of the canon that imposed the 'etcetera' oath. Whereas the cannon ball hints at the Bishops' War with Scotland, the rope evokes individual suffering under the impact of Laud's blind insistence on uniformity. In the lower left corner of the picture the jaws of hell open, symbolized by the open mouth of a sea-monster (resembling a whale) and the inscription 'hell'. The second emblem shows God's hand of justice reaching out of the clouds and a storm – the tempest – blowing from above which finally drowns the ship and with it its popish crew, thus ending its influence over the 'three kingdomes'. The final two emblems show the former ship's crew delivered to the tower, and Archbishop Laud looking down from the tower on to the gallows, foreshadowing

---

45   Kenyon, *Stuart*, p 151.

his execution (he was sentenced to death in 1645) if he did not
repent. A passage in the text encapsulates the overall message:

> O would your little Grace had bin more wise
> You lov'd few words, and therefore would not preach,
> But silenc'd such as dayly us'd to teach.
> Your ayme was to have alterations
> And by your Altars thought to alter Nations.
> But God Almighty crost your enterprise.[46]

The cannon ball as a symbol of the church canons can also be
found in other woodcuts. There is, for instance, a broadside by
Wenceslaus Hollar entitled *Archbishop Laud firing a Cannon*.[47]
Laud fires a cannon which is marked 'oath'. As it flies through
the smoke, the ball bursts, and its pieces appear to hit those standing near the Archbishop. The bursting cannon symbolizes the
House of Commons' decision in 1640 to declare the church canons illegal.

Pamphleteers and people producing woodcuts and engravings
in the 1640s were quite inventive in their creation of new and
powerful symbols which seem to have been readily accepted. The
presentation of Bishop Wren and Lord Finch as a wren and a
finch, for instance, was widely used, once introduced. The woodcut on the title page of a tract called *Old Newes Newly Revived*
shows Lord Finch and 'Wren Winde ore the Banke' with wings,
hinting at their escape to France.[48] A different woodcut in *The
Wrens Nest Defild* crudely shows Bishop Wren's misconduct,
drawing on his bird image and scatological elements.[49] The picture reveals a three-storey house with a wren standing on its chim-
ney. The bird lifts its tail, and a speech tag says 'a Wren muting'.
A man, standing on a ladder which leans against the house, holds

---

46   *A Rot*, p 9.
47   Parthey's Wen. Hollar (1640), No.482. See picture section.
48   *Old Newes Newly Revived: Or, the discovery of all occurrences happened since
      the beginning of the Parliament* (1641), BL E.160.22.
49   *The Wrens Nest Defild*.

a nest beneath the bird's tail, saying: 'Rome is beguiled, this Nest defild'. Bishop Wren watches the scene standing near by, and with raised hands exclaims: 'For which I weepe, no further peepe'. Below the picture is a brief explanatory verse:

> The Wren's Nest is defild, for which he weepes, whilst that a Jesuite rudely in it peepes, that ruined house doth Norwich signify. Whose Doctrine ruined was by fallacy, Hatcht by the Wren; that vile polluted Nest, Doth specify; the Bishops uncleane Breast.

Texts, too, took up the theme: in a fictitious dialogue between Secretary Windebank and Lord Finch after their flight to France, Windebank informs Finch that 'the newes goeth in these parts, that in England they picture your Honour with wings', that 'the Ducks wings will be pluckt, and Lambe begins to be one of season'.[50] They also refer to the 'church canons', which have now 'murthered the canonists themselves'. The double-meaning of canons becomes even clearer when Finch specifies: 'You meane the Booke of Canons that was lately made'.

A recurrent symbol of religious sects and nonconformist preaching habits was the 'tub' both in pictures and in words, decrying sectarians as 'tub-preachers'.[51] The most popular 'tub-preachers' of the period were as famous as leading politicians and clergy such as Laud, Strafford or Pym. Their names regularly appeared in pamphlets and woodcuts, among them Greene, the feltmaker, Spencer, the groom or horse-keeper, Samuel How, the

---

50 *Times Alterations or A Dialogue betweene my Lord Finch and Secretary Windebancke; at their meeting in France, the eight of January 1641.* BL 669.f.4.5. At the top of the broadside is a portrait of Lord Finch with wings.

51 John Taylor, *A Tale in a Tub; or, A Tub Lecture, as it was delivered by Me-heele Mendsoale, an inspired Brownist, in a meeting house near Bedlam* (1641), BL E.138.27; *A Full and Compleat Answer Against the Writer of A late Volume set forth, entitled A Tale in a Tub or A Tub Lecture* (1642), BL E.141.19; *A Swarme of Sectaries, and Schismatiques: Wherein is discovered the strange preaching (or prating) of such as are by their trades Coblers, Tinkers, Pedlers, Weavers, Sowgelders, and Chymney-Sweepers* (1641), BL E.158.1.; *The Sheperds Oracles* (1645), BL E.310.20, see picture section. For an example of royalists meeting in a tavern see *The Malignant's Conventicle* (1643), BL E.80.5.

cobbler, 'Praisegod' Barebone, the leatherseller, John Heyden, the cobbler, and the 'prophet' James Hunt. Often, sects were shown assembling in the Nag's-Head Tavern in Coleman Street, a well-known meeting place of nonconformists, and various authors reused a woodcut which showed the tavern, carefully changing the names of the preachers in question.[52] Furthermore, pictures of sectarian assemblies usually showed a mixed group of men and women, partially accounting for the strong presence of women among nonconformists, but mainly discrediting the sects for sexual looseness and disorder, emphasized by lines such as: 'When Women Preach and Coblers pray, the fiends in Hell make Holiday.'[53] Best known are the illustrations of the Adamites and of the Ranters, where men and women were usually depicted naked. The scenes alternate between various forms of sexual behaviour, reproof, and whipping.[54] Typical also were illustrations such as the woodcut in *The Brownists Conventicle* which shows four men seated around a table after a meal listening to 'simple Robin'. On the right stands a man who kisses a woman and says 'A little in zeale good sister Ruth'.[55]

For Puritans and sects the Christian symbol of the cross had lost its sacred meaning and had become, instead, a symbol of

---

52 See, for instance, *Lucifer's Lacky, or, the Devils New Creature* (1641), BL E.180.3; *New Preachers New.* (1641), BL 180.26; and *The Sermon and Prophecie of Mr James Hunt of Kent* (1641), BL E.172.26.

53 *Lucifers Lacky.* See also *A Discovery of Six Women preachers. With a relation of their names, manners, life and doctrine* (1641), BL E.166.1; *The seven Women Confessors* (1642), BL E.134.15. For women among religious nonconformist groups in seventeenth-century England see Crawford, *Women and Religion*.

54 See, for instance, the woodcuts in *A Nest of serpents Discovered, or, a Knot of old Heretiques revived, Called the Adamites* (1641), BL 168.12; *A Sermon Preached the last Fast day in Leaden-Hall Street* (1642), BL E.91.32; *The Routing of the Ranters* (1650), BL E.616.9; *The Ranters Ranting* (1650), BL E.618.8; *The Ranters Declaration with Their new Oath and Protestation* (1650), BL E.620.2.

55 *The Brownists Conventicle* (1641), BL E.164.13, see picture section. For a survey of pamphlets on illicit sexual behaviour of sects see Friedman, *Miracles*, pp 83–113.

popery. Pamphleteers often ridiculed the 'cross-phobia' of the sects, as in a pamphlet called *A Three-Fold Discourse*.[56] John Heyden was said to loathe the cross-shaped arrangement of streets between Aldgate and Bishopsgate in London because they resembled popish crosses. Just as hated were Catholic relics including the rosary, the staff, and holy pictures. Two symbols are often used to express Puritan hatred of popery and its evil influence over the English state and church. The figure of 'Time' identified by the hour glass on its head is presented in the image of a pedlar carrying on his back a 'Sack-full of Knavery, Popery, prelacy, Policy, Trechery, Malignant Trumpery, Conspiracies, and Cruelties, filled to the top by the Malignants'.[57] Another woodcut on a broadside shows a pedlar, again in the figure of 'Time Carrying the Pope from England to Rome'.[58] The verse underneath the woodcut explains:

> Then up I took upon my aged backe
> This load of vanitie, this Pedlers packe
> This trunke of trashe and Romish Trumperies.

The second symbol which was quite vivid in describing the 'sickening' influence of popery in England was the vomiting of popish items and 'superstitious church innovations'. Best known is the play *Canterburys Change of Diot*, but there are also other woodcuts which take up the theme. In *The Bishop's Potion, or, A Dialogue betweene the Bishop of Canterbury and his phisitian* Laud vomits with the assistance of his physician.[59] Out come all the innovations in the Anglican Church ascribed to him. In the end the doctor says: 'Nay, if the Miter be come, the Divell is not far

---

56   *A Three-Fold Discourse Betweene Three Neighbours* (1642), BL E.145.3.
57   *The Devills White Boyes Or, A mixture of malicious Malignants with their much evill and manifold practices against the Kingdome and Parliament* (1644), BL E.14.11.
58   BM Parthey's Wenceslaus Hollar, No. 483 (1641).
59   *The Bishop's Potion, or, A Dialogue betweene the Bishop of Canterbury and his phisitian* (1641), BL E.165.1.

off. Farewell good my Lord.' Another woodcut shows Laud standing in his robes and vomiting books.[60] His head is supported by the Puritan Henry Burton, who was convicted by the Star Chamber in 1637 with Prynne and Bastwick. On the floor lie several volumes inscribed 'tobacco', 'Canons and Constitutions', and 'An Order of Star Chamber'. With reference to the treatment they had received, Burton's left ear is torn and blood drips down on his ruff.

Time and again pamphlets commented on the influence of the Catholic Queen Henrietta Maria over Charles I. These issues also cropped up in people's discussions of politics and religion during this period. Interestingly, woodcuts took up the theme, too, and represented these views quite vividly. In *The Great Eclipse of the Sun* Charles I is pictured sitting at a table with his sword drawn, pointing at the sun eclipsed by the moon.[61] The moon is the Queen who has 'over-clouded' Charles and is held responsible for the darkness and bloodshed. On the left a church is burning, and in the centre appears the ghost of Strafford. Verses beneath say: 'The subjects blood! With Fire and Sword cries vengeance, Lord.' Another woodcut makes believe that the King has submitted 'the crown to the distaff' under the influence of the Queen.[62] The picture shows Charles, Henrietta Maria and a 'Bishop-king'. The bishop wears the King's robe and crown and holds the sceptre towards the Queen. A naked child is hiding under his robe. The text satirizes the relationship of the Queen to both her husband and the priest.

Apart from images that were created under the influence of day-to-day-politics, the most popular imagery in the politico-religious satires of the 1640s was that of the Apocalypse of the *Book of Revelation*. In contrast to the medieval interpretation of

---

60   Untitled broadside (1645), BL 669.f.10.18
61   *The great Eclipse of the Sun, or, Charles his Wane Over-clouded By the evil Influ-ences of the Moon* (1644), BL E.7.30. See picture section.
62   *The Sussex Picture, or, An Answer to the SEA-GULL* (1644), BL E.3.21. See picture section.

the Apocalypse, which usually condemned an individual (a specific Pope, who for particular reasons was Antichrist), the Protestant interpretation condemned an institution (the papacy),
which in its false doctrine taught Antichrist's deceit, and it aimed
its attack at all Roman Catholics – the members of the false
Church ('Heresy') – for they knowingly supported Antichrist
and his ministers. Typical of the Reformation exegesis of the
Apocalypse was the Geneva Bible gloss, identifying the seven-
headed beast of the *Book of Revelation* with pagan Rome and the
two-horned beast with Antichrist, whose two horns symbolized
the Pope's religious and temporal power. Both images are amongst
the most prominent ones in politico-religious woodcuts of the
seventeenth century, and they are used to symbolize the evil power
of the Pope and his followers on earth. In England, the commentaries on the *Book of Revelation* in the Geneva Bible version
were written by Heinrich Bullinger and John Bale, two of the
most able writers for the anti-papal campaign and influential theo-
logians in the formation of the English Protestant apocalyptic
tradition.[63] The Geneva Bible enjoyed great popularity in England over half a century to the early 1640s, and because of the
great weight scriptural authority possessed, 'the Geneva Bible
proved an excellent vehicle for the widespread dissemination of
the apocalyptic tradition in England'.[64]

Many of the woodcuts and politico-religious satires of mid-
seventeenth-century England reflected its tone and its interpretation of apocalyptic imagery. The evil spirits, for instance, resembling frogs that come forth from the mouth of the dragon,
the seven-headed beast, and false prophets (Apoc.16:13) were
time and again identified with papal supporters in pamphlets and
woodcuts. Other popular symbols included a hand reaching out
of the clouds throwing lightning to earth, a head with round

---

63   Paul Christianson, *Reformers and Babylon. English Apocalyptic Visions from
     the Reformation to the Eve of the Civil War* (Toronto, 1978), p 13ff.
64   Ibid., p 38.

cheeks and rays protruding from its mouth signifying the tempest, the Whore of Babylon, the devil and the mouth of hell, and death in the figure of a skeleton. The opened mouth of hell, often in the shape of a monster resembling the dragon, was used to emphasize the pact between the Pope, bishops, priests, and especially Archbishop Laud, and the devil. The woodcut of a pamphlet called *Hell's Hurlie-Burlie* shows a huge monster with sharp teeth.[65] In its wide-open mouth resides the devil, wearing a crown and surrounded by dancing horned creatures. He receives the Pope, who is accompanied by bishops and cavaliers and claims his superiority over the devil on the basis of his and his servants' evil achievements on earth, especially in England. There is a continuous flow of the Pope's crew into hell: Jesuits, courtiers, malignants, citizens, country-men, and soldiers who had fought against the Parliament during the English Civil War. One of the 'malignants' introduces his train to the devil and seeks his approval to be admitted to the company in hell:

> We are of the number of those that stood stiffly for our King, and were forward, with the hazard of our lives to maintain an unlawfull and unlimited Prerogative, to the danger of our Countries ruine: We were they that call'd honest men Round-heads, and threaten'd their destruction, because they were better then our selves: wee by advice of our gracelesse Lord Bishops ... cry'd up superstition and formalitie.

Pictures of hell as found in many woodcuts and texts in the seventeenth century go back to the medieval tradition of hell imagery which is nicely summed up by the following description:

> There, in hell-mouth is stynke, and ther is all derkenes ... There is horribull syght off develes, dragons, wormes and serpentys to turment them. There is syghynge and sorowynge, wepynge and welynge, hideous cryynge and murnynge, hunger, thyrste irremediable, wyth gnagyng off tethe wyth-owte ende.[66]

---

65 *Hell's Hurlie-Burlie, or A Fierce Contention Betwixt the Pope and the Devill* (1644), BL E.11.4.
66 Owst, *Literature*, p 523.

Very popular with pamphleteers was the seven-headed beast which was frequently used to stress the evil influence of the Roman Catholic church over England and its rulers, and to contrast it with Puritan beliefs.[67] A good example is provided by the broadside *Behold Romes Monster on his monstrous Beast*.[68] Drawing on images of the Apocalypse, it is a powerful visual and verbal demonstration of the final downfall of the Roman Catholic church through God's intervention on earth. In order to ensure that the onlooker understood the picture, the various images were marked by letters that were explained below. The Pope is represented as the 'Whore of Babylon' riding on the seven-headed beast, with each head representing one of the seven deadly sins. The beast walks on stilts 'to raise him up aloft, in supreame Seate, Like Saturnes Sonne, ruling all Princes great', as the text explains under letter 'E'. Behind the 'barrell-bellied' beast wait 'Babels Bishops, Jesuits, Friers bace' eager to fill their cups with 'Romish Fornication' squirting out from the monster's anus in the form of skulls and bones, described as 'Romes all rotten Reliques' (letters 'G' and 'H'). Whereas the Pope's followers gradually get drunk on these 'rotten reliques' and 'in Destruction sleeping, snorting, die' (letter 'L'), the beast advances only to meet 'Death' sent by God. Out of the clouds blows the tempest, and three skeletons (letter 'N') attack the monster with 'death-wounding Dart'. The monster is about to step into the flames of hell opening up in the ground before it, and 'thus is prowd Babel fallen, and in her fall, Fallen are her Vassals, Sathans Vessels all' to perish and suffer for ever in hell (letter 'Q').

All of these images and symbols appeared both in texts and illustrations, and they were skilfully used to emphasize specific

---

67 For woodcuts see, for instance, *The Bishops Last Good Night* (1641), BL 669.f.4.61; *Newes from Rome, Or, a relation of the pope and his patentees Pilgrim into Hell* (1641), BL E.158.18. A variation on the theme is *The Kingdomes Monster uncloaked from Heaven* (1643), BL 669.f.8.24, which shows a three-headed beast, namely of papists, malignants and Irish Catholics.

68 *Behold Romes Monster on his monstrous Beast* (1643), BL 669.f.8.29. See picture section.

ABOVE. **Political Symbolism:** opinion represented as a woman (1642)

TAYLORS

Phyficke has purged the DIVEL.

OR,

The Divell has got a fquirt, and the fim-
ple, feame-rent, thredbare *Taylor* tranflates
it into railing Poetry, and is now
foundly cudgelled for it.

By *Voluntas Ambulatoria.*

Such is the lan-
guage of a beaft-
ly railor,
The Divels privi-
houfe moft fit
for *Taylor*.

Printed in the yeere 1641½

LEFT: **Political Symbolism:** John Taylor's railing poetry is caused by the squirt of a she-devil (1641)

Iconography of censorship: Archbishop Laud dining on the ears of the Puritan William Prynne (1641)

Censorship: the burning of the Book of Sports (1643)

This Canons feal'd, well forg'd, not made of lead,
Give fire. O noe I will breake and strike vs dead.

That I.I.B. doe fweare that I doe approve the Doctrine and Difcipline or Government eftablifhed in the Church of *England*, as containing all things neceffary to Salvation; And that I will not endeavour by my felf or any other, directly or indirectly to bring in any Popifh Doctrine, contrary to that which is fo eftablifhed: Nor will I ever give my confent to alter the Government of this Church, by Archbifhops, Bifhops, Deanes, and Arch-Deacons, &c as it ftands now eftablifhed, and as by right it ought to ftand: Nor yet ever to fubject it to the ufurpations and fuperftitions of the Sea of Rome. And all thefe things I doe plainly and fincerely ac knowledge and fweare, according to the plain and common fence, and underftanding of the fame words, without any equivocation or mentall evafion, or fecret refervation whatfoever. And this I doe heartily, willingly and truly, upon the faith of a Chriftian: So help me God in Iefus Chrift.

Prime, lay the Trayne, thus you muft mount, and levell,
then fhall we gett the day. *but freind the Devill.*
Turne, wheele about, take tyme, and ftand your ground,
this Canon cannot faile, *but tis not found.*
Feare not, weel caft it, tis a defperate cafe,
weel fweare it, and enjoyne it, *but tis bafe,*
The Mettalls brittle, and tis ram'd fo hard,
with an *Oath* &c. that hath fowly marr'd
All our defignes, that now we have no hope,
but in the fervice of *our Lord the Pope,*
Diffolve the Rout, each man vnto his calling
which had we kept, we had not now beene falling

Startling images: the controversial church cannons symbolized by a canon ball (1640)

A Behold *Romes* Monster on his monstrous Beast!
To fulnesse of his foulenesse (now) encreast!
How He in Papall Pride doth ride along,
And how his sonnes and shavelings thrust and throng
To see his sacred hollow-Holinesse
His Babylonish Blasphemies expresse.
B His Barrell-Bellied Beast on stilts doth stalke,
C And with 7 hideous Heads doth proudly walke.
D The heads,7 Hell-spawn'd deadly sins doe show.
Wherein *Romes* Rabble rankly rise and grow.
E Foure faithlesse Feet, Deceit, Debate and Pride,
With ill-got-Gaine, his steps on stilts do guide;
To raise him up aloft, in supreame Seate,
Like *Saturnes* Sonne, ruling all Princes great.
His long-cloud-threatning fierce advanced Tayle
F The very starres (Gods Saints) doth sore assayle:
Whereby is showne, *Romes* bloody Inquisition,
Wasting Gods Saints,halting their owne perdition,
G Then *Babels* Bishops, Iesuits, Friers bace,
About the Beasts Posteriours flocke apace,
H And from his Barrell-Breech, the Dregs and Lees
Of *Romes* all-rotten Reliques, deere Decrees,
I They fill full-Cups of Romish Fornication;
K Which,by the Princes of *Romes* domination,

L So fill'd, are swill'd, and They made drunke thereby,
And in Destruction sleeping, snorting die.
As(thus)proud *Babels* Band doth proudly prance,
In Blood and Blasfemy Her-selfe t'advance
M Gainst God and his deere Saints,Heau'ns indignation
Poures-downe the Vials of dire Desolation
Vpon *Romes* Whore, and with his nostrils breath,
N Sends his obsequious Seruant, Sergeant Death,
O Her to arrest,with his death-wounding Dart;
Who shoots his shaft and reaues and cleaues his heart.
Whom (as She in her hight of Pride did sit)
He,with his Rope of wrath, puls to the Pit
P Of Desolation and Destruction dire,
To burne in Hels all-euer-burning fire.
Q Thus is proud *Babel* fallen,and in her fall,
Fallen are his Vassals, Sathans Vessels all:
Euen now,this worke begins,for, *Rome* looks sickly,
Euen so Lord Iesus come,oh Lord come quickly;
To right the wrongs of thy distressed Saints.
To send an end to all their woes and plaints.

Most humbly, heartily prayeth,
IOHN VICARS.

Imprinted at London, and are to be sold by *William Peake* at his shop neere Holborne Conduit, next the San Tauerne. 1643.

alyptic imagery: the Whore of Babylon and the downfall of popery (1643)

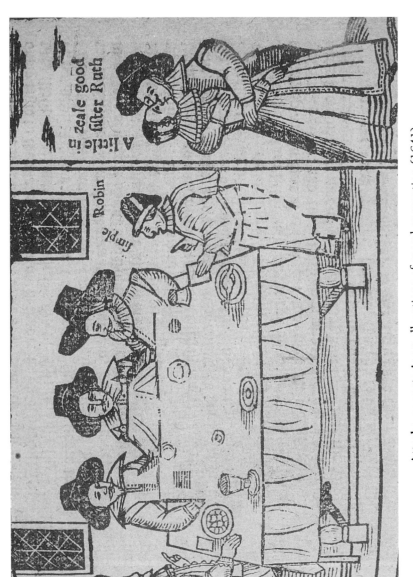

Attacks on sectarians: allegations of moral corruption (1641)

Clichés: Puritans represented as tub-preachers (1645)

ABOVE. **Popular allegations:** the King is ruled by his Catholic wife and her popish advisor (1644)

BELOW. **Guilt:** Charles I (the sun) threw his country into utter destruction overpowered by his Catholic wife (the moon) (1644)

Thy Subjects blood !
with fire and sword,
Cries *Vengeance Lord.*

views. Given the ease with which images and themes 'travelled' through the genres of news presentation they were central in shaping the public discourse on politics and religion. Pamphlets and illustrations in mid-seventeenth-century England engaged in a dialogue amongst themselves and with their audience. They not only evoked a specific meaning, but at the same time they referred back to other illustrations and pamphlets which all sprang from a shared cultural tradition. As popular as woodcuts and as easily accessible for the unlearned were ballads which had a central place both in popular recreations and moral teaching. Thus it is not surprising that authors readily used this genre for the dissemination of news and for confronting people with their own interpretations of the time.

'To Be Sung to the Tune of...':
Ballads as Popular Political Commentators

Ballads were among the cheapest and most accessible forms of print.[69] A pamphlet dating from 1641 advertised the works of one of the leading ballad writers of the period by claiming that 'For a peny you may have all the Newes in England, of Murders, Flouds, Witches, Fires, Tempests, and what not, in one of Martin Parkers Ballads'.[70] In her study of cheap print and piety, Tessa Watt traced the various uses of ballads and the 'myriad ways in which they may have been dramatized, localized and personalized by the singers'. 'The printed broadside ballad was only the visible tip of an iceberg. Ballads could be chanted out by petty chapmen, performed by travelling players, danced to at bride-

---

69 Watt, *Cheap print*, p 11, and Spufford, *Small Books*.
70 Henry Peacham, *The worth of a penny* (1641). Cit. in Watt, *Cheap print*, p 11. Martin Parker was one of the most prolific ballad writers of the 1640s. For details on his life and work, see Edward H. Rollins, 'Martin Parker, balladmonger', *Modern Philology*, 16 (January, 1919), pp 449–74.

ales, harmonized, or shouted as insults.'[71] Furthermore, ballads
infiltrated the contemporary musical culture, decorated the walls
in alehouses and private homes, were desirable objects of collection among the educated and were often copied into people's
commonplace books. Finally, broadside ballads left traces in domestic wall painting and painted cloth and vice versa. Contemporary references point to the ubiquity of ballads both geographi-
cally and socially.

Given the wide distribution and great popularity of ballads it
is not surprising that pamphleteers used the genre as a welcome
and effective medium for spreading news and opinions at the
outbreak of the Civil War. Men of letters such as John Cleve-
land, John Taylor, Alexander Brome, Sir John Berkenhead, and
Sir John Mennes discovered ballads, too, as 'an effective weapon
to use against Parliament and for the King'.[72] In 1640 about one
hundred ballads were entered in the stationers' register, mostly
in support of the King and his war against Scotland. In the following years the number of registered ballads decreased rapidly,
and in 1642 not a single ballad was entered. Yet their publication
continued, touching on more and more controversial issues,
openly siding with one or other of the conflicting parties or la-
menting the general distempers of the time. Clearly, printers and
publishers thought it wiser to produce ballads surreptitiously.
The new censoring authorities had expressed their strong dislike
of ballads and similar 'lascivious books' or 'vaine pamphlets', thus
discouraging any goodwill among publishers about registering
ballads at all, regardless of their content.

Ballads of the Civil War period are scattered through the
Thomason tracts in the British Library, the Wood and Rawlinson
collections at the Bodleian library, and the much neglected bal-

---

71   Watt, *Cheap print*, p 37.
72   Edward H. Rollins, *Cavalier and Puritan Ballads and Broadsides illustrating the
     period of the Great Rebellion, 1640–1660* (New York, 1923), p 14. For the fol-
     lowing observations see also pp 9 and 12.

lad collection at the Manchester Free Reference Library. Furthermore, there are three well-known editions of political ballads of this period published in the nineteenth century by Thomas Wright, William Walker Wilkins, and Charles Mackay, and finally, Hyder Rollins' edition of broadside ballads of the Civil War period.[73] A number of ballads, as yet little-known and under-explored, seem to have survived in manuscript and it will be an important task to try and locate them in full. Those I have used here are either scattered through the state papers, or in the Ashmolean collection at the Bodleian library in Oxford. Whereas some manuscript ballads were clearly copied from printed broadsides (or vice versa), such as *The New Medley*, others are only known in a hand written version, and it is difficult to judge whether or not they were also circulated in print.[74] Their subject matter ranged from immediate responses to specific political events to general comments on political and religious issues.

Whereas some ballads, in print or manuscript, gave straightforward news accounts, others abounded in witticisms, familiar stereotypes, sexual allusions, and biting comments. The latter presented their political and religious messages within the context of popular recreation scenes such as drinking and gambling or clad them in dreams or prognostications. Generally speaking, the topics of these ballads covered the whole range of opinions

---

73 Rollins, *Cavalier*; C. H. Firth, 'Ballads on the Bishops' Wars, 1638–1640', *The Scottish Historical Review*, 3 (1906), pp 257–73; Thomas Wright, *Political Ballads published in England during the Commonwealth* (London, 1841); William Walker Wilkins, *Political Ballads of the Seventeenth and Eighteenth Centuries*, 2 vols. (London, 1860); and Charles Mackay, *The Cavalier Songs and Ballads from 1642–1684* (London, 1863). For further bibliographical details, especially on edited ballads, see the introduction in Rollins. Also Natascha Würzbach, *Die englische Straßenballade 1550–1650: Schaustellerische Literatur, Frühform eines journalistischen Mediums, populäre Erbauung, Belehrung und Unterhaltung* (Munich, 1981); and Paul Denzer, *Ideologie und literarische Strategie. Die politische Flugblattlyrik der englischen Bürgerkriegszeit 1639–1661* (Tübingen, 1991).

74 Ashm Ms 36.157r–158r; Wood 401.154

and disputes of the period. There were ballads in support of the King and the Scottish war, and others that were critical, if not abusive of, Charles' politics. Whereas some ballads showed great sympathy for the Parliament, others opposed it and were full of contempt for Puritans and religious sects in general. There were also ballads about the general distempers of the time, and others that expressed concern at the (bad) opinions foreigners might have about 'Britannia'.

Due to censorship, the scarcity of ballads surviving from this period, and the fact that they circulated in manuscript and by word of mouth, any attempt to impose a chronology on the development of these themes must be misleading. Thus the following sequence of topics represents only what we can know on the basis of available sources. Generally speaking, the topics discussed in any news genre of the period mirrored the tide of political and religious anxieties in reaction to the execution of power as it was felt by the various groups involved. Most of the surviving ballads touching on the two Scottish wars supported the politics of the King, which is not surprising in view of the vigorous attempts to suppress anything in favour of the Scots during this period. Up to the end of 1641 there were ballads that still created a picture of harmony and possible understanding between the King and the Parliament and placed great hopes on the summoning of the Parliament. And even up to the outbreak of war ballad writers hoped for a settlement and expressed *A Good Wish For England* or warned of the horrors of the impending war.[75] At the same time, there were attacks on the evil councillors of the King in general, and in particular, on Laud, Strafford, Windebank and Finch. Likewise, the political involvement of bishops in general and the evil politics of individual bishops in particular came under attack. Since the beginning of 1642, the disillusionment of a number of people with the Parliament and its inability to solve long-standing grievances began to be mirrored in ballads. Now

---

75   *A Good Wish for England*, BL 669.f.4.40. Denzer, *Ideologie*, p 48.

'King Pym' , too, became a common target of criticism and was accused of misusing his power.[76]

In total, the ballad production of this period was characterized by conflicting arguments and a clash of opinions throughout rather than the dominance of one particular view at a time. A number of both printed and manuscript ballads have been chosen for discussion here in order to illustrate the range of opinions and the ways in which they were presented.

On 9 April 1640, a few days before the Short Parliament opened, one of the most prolific ballad writers of the period, Martin Parker, entered a ballad with a full description 'of the manner how his Maiestie and his Nobles went to the Parliament, on Munday, the thirteenth day of Aprill, 1640, to the comfortable expectation of all Loyall Subiects'.[77] Obviously basing his description and the accompanying woodcut on earlier accounts of similar processions, Parker claimed 'To publish what my selfe did see,/ That absent (Loyall) hearts may be Participants as well as wee'. The main function of his song, however, was 'to say and sing/ The praises of our royall King,/ Who now this present hopefull spring, Hath call'd a Parliament'. Throughout his fifteen verses Parker echoed the great expectations placed on the Parliament by the majority of people at this time. The weight of these expectations was typographically emphasized by printing the references to the Parliament (the refrain) in white letters to contrast with the black letters of the main text. The King and Parliament were seen as fruitful complements to each other, which probably made people identify with both. With the premature composition and publication of his ballad, Parker was sure to be the first to enter the market with an 'eye-witness account' of this great event. Most likely he did not put this ballad on the market before the 13th or 14th of April.

76   See also Denzer, *Ideologie*, pp 18–88.
77   Wood 401.140 and Rollins, *Cavalier*, pp 77–82.

In contrast to Parker's glorification of Charles I and his wise decision to summon a Parliament, the anonymous author of another ballad shifts perspectives and concentrates solely on the Parliament, which he calls 'the great Counsell of the King'.[78] While this 'great council' is presented as the long-awaited saviour from all hardships and injustices, Charles I is referred to only indirectly by listing the many grievances he was held responsible for. After cheering up his audience with an invitation to drink to the advent of better times, the author seeks to arouse people's sympathies for the Parliament. Throughout his verses he juxtaposes an impersonal 'they', representing those formerly in power with the people, including himself, who suffered long-standing grievances under their rule. Speaking in the first person plural he takes the oppressed as his mouthpiece and conjures up a like-mindedness which did not necessarily exist. Furthermore, when people sang this ballad they appeared to be identifying with its contents since they were singing about 'themselves':

> Like silly Sheepe they did us daily sheare,
> Like Asses strong our backes were made to beare,
> Intollerable burdens, yeare by yeare,
> No hope, no helpe, no comfort did appeare,
>   But from the great Counsell of the King,
>   And the Kings great Counsell.[79]

> Who did regard our povertie, our teares,
> Our wants, our miseries, our many feares,
> Whipt, stript, and fairely banisht as appeares;
> You that are masters, now of your owne eares
>   Blesse the great Counsell of the King,
>   And the Kings great Counsell.[80]

Interspersed with this personalized perspective on history were allusions to other issues: the Scots were 'unkindly' used by 'them';

---

78   Like in Parker's ballad, the refrain is printed in white letters.
79   Verse 2.
80   Verse 5.

'now the nest of filthy Birds are flowne';[81] 'their' opposition to proclamations issued by the Parliament; 'their' false propaganda against the Parliament; the destructiveness of mechanic preaching; or the plots of papists and prelates. In case of open conflict, which was already reckoned with, an uncompromising stand on the side of the Parliament was advocated: 'For my part I resolve to fall or stand,/ With the great Counsell of the King,/ And the Kings great Counsell.'

An undated ballad in manuscript of about the same time was even more powerful in its support for the Parliament and open in its agitation against the King.[82] Addressing men and women alike, the author summoned all those to the Guildhall 'that would noe longer To monarchs be subiected'. Encouraging people to disregard the King's proclamations he pressed the men to deliver their gold, silver, jewels, and money to the Parliament, and the women to bring their spoons. If the Parliament succeeded in overcoming the King they would be paid back with great profit. Furthermore, ropes should be bought for all the King's friends. 'Religious Sempstresse' were asked to donate their 'silver Thimble', for 'Twill be a fine thinge in deposing a King to say she had a finger (in it)'. Similarly, a manuscript ballad entitled *The Triumph of the Roundheads* joyfully announces that 'good days are comeinge on'.[83] Listing the various tasks yet to be fulfilled, such as crushing the 'Antichristian Crew', destroying everything 'Popish hands have built', or teaching the 'Nobles howe to Crouch', the author concludes each verse with the cheering phrase 'Hay then up goe wee'.

While the King and Parliament were still haggling about the grant for subsidies necessary to continue the war against Scotland, Martin Parker, too, published a ballad exhorting 'all loyall

---

81   This phrase refers to the escape of Sir Francis Windebank and John Lord Finch to France and Holland which is frequently depicted in words and pictures as birds flying away.
82   *Your Brethren Strange and Lusty*, Ashm Ms 36.76r-77r.
83   *The Triumph of the Roundheads*, Ashm Ms 36.81v.

subiects' to 'freely disburse,/ both person, purse,/ and all you
may to avoyd the curse,/ of lasting warre which will be worse'.[84]
He accused the Scots of having started the conflict 'under the
colour of religion' whereas in reality they were striving to overthrow the King's government and then 'Iocky with his bonnet
blew, /both Crown and Scepter would subdue'.[85] After claiming
that the Scots clearly 'rebell ith' high'st degree', Parker takes the
opportunity to make a strong point on a widely debated issue
which had for many become a case of conscience: the question
of whether it was lawful to take up arms against the King in matters of religion.

> No true Religion wil giue warrant,
> That any subiect arm'd should be,
> against his Prince
> in any sence,
> what ere he hold for his pretence,
> Rebellion is a foule offence.

A ballad entitled *Jockies Lamentation, Whose seditious work was
the loss of his Country, and his Kirk* took a completely different
perspective.[86] Pretending to describe the various phases of the
Scottish war through the eyes of a Scottish soldier, the author
misses no opportunity to ridicule and discredit the Scots by their
'own' testimony. Certain of victory, they fell to plundering, drinking, eating and whoring, only to be surprised and beaten by the
'Red-Coats'.[87] In one of the ten verses the author looked back to
the origins of the Scottish war:

84   *A True Subject's Wish*, (April 1640) Wood 401.142 and Rollins, *Cavalier*,
     pp 83–88. For other ballads in support of the King's army against the Scots see
     News from Newcastle (August 1640); *Good News from the North* (September
     1640, Wood 401.134); and *Britaines Honour* (Wood 401.132) all repr. in Rollins,
     Cavalier, pp 89–106. See also Firth, *Ballads*.
85   In many pamphlets and ballads the Scots were personified by a dumb fellow
     called Jocky. The Scottish soldiers were called the blew-caps while the King's
     army was referred to as the black-caps.
86   (S.S.) Wood 401.152
87   English soldiers, probably referring to the clothes worn by cavaliers.

The godly Presbyterian
That holy man a war began,
    in Scotland there,
Then Jocky gay, both Laird and Lad
Like people mad, were very glad
    in armes to appear;
They made a new covenant for to pull down
The crosses that stood in every Town
And the Rochet that the Bishop did bear
And the white smock his Chaplin did wear,
But now the good Covenant's gone to rack,
And quite out of date like an old Almanack,
And all the crosses are our own losse
For Jocky's gone home by weeping-cross.

According to the author, in the course of the war the Scots
lost both their freedom and their wealth to the English, and rue-
fully realized at the end that 'what covetousnesse doth bring/
Wee have lost our Kirk, and every thing'.

With the growing conflict between the King and the Parliament in the early 1640s ballad writers increasingly turned to the
immediate political issues of the day. An anonymous ballad of
1640 entitled *The Lofty Bishop, The Lazy Brownist, And The Loyall
Author* laments the troubles brought about in state and church
by religious sects, namely the Brownists, and the episcopal hierarchy with its Roman sympathies.[88] The opinions generally held
by each religious group and their arguments against each other
are personified in 'the Bishop' and 'the Brownist' respectively,
whereas 'the Author' claims to take the only sensible position
between these conflicting parties. In three separate songs typographically arranged in three columns the protagonists voice their
opinions and mutual accusations. Although each song is a kind
of soliloquy, the three characters nevertheless seem to communicate by addressing their opponent directly and commenting
on his or her opinions.

---

88   *The Lofty Bishop* (1640), BL 669.f.8.32.

The Bishop sings in verse one:

> What would yee lazie Brownists have,
> you rage and runne away;
> And cry us downe, our Church, and eke,
> the forme therein we pray.[89]

The Brownist replies in verse two:

> Sure yee be monsters, for such members
> of Christ his Church as yee,
> I have not read of in Gods word
> allowed by him to be.[90]

In his concluding verses the author assumes the role of a commentator on the preceding performances and demands the suppression of the two 'Monsters' to allow church and state to consolidate.

The Author laments

> The Brownists noses, want a Ring
> (to draw them with a Rope;)
> The Prelates wings doe cutting neede,
> (least they fly to the Pope).[91]

For 'the Author' the only answer to the religious conflicts was the Parliament which 'no doubt these Monsters will destroy'.

Occasioned by the passing of the Bishop's Exclusion Bill in January 1642, the well-known ballad *The Bishops Last Good Night* was published. Referring to the bishops' protestation that no laws, resolutions or orders which the Parliament passed during their absence were valid, the author demands the downfall of all prelates for this treacherous act. Each verse is devoted to one bishop who is referred to by his see (Canterbury, York, Durham etc.) and concludes with the imperative 'Come down'. Throughout,

---

89 Verse 1 out of 8 verses sung by 'the Bishop'.
90 Verse 2 out of 8 verses sung by 'the Brownist' who sings after 'the Bishop' has finished.
91 Verse 7 out of 8 verses sung by 'the Author'.

the ballad expresses a strong feeling of superiority and triumph over episcopacy, challenging bishops with rhetorical questions and threats such as 'how dare you ?' from the secure position of victory. The broadside is headed by two woodcuts facing each other. The picture on the left shows Archbishop Laud sitting at a table with his arms wide apart listening to the conflicting parties. Two speech tags protrude from his mouth, one saying 'Only Canonicall prayers' which is answered by a group of bishops standing below: 'So we desire it', the other saying 'No afternoon sermons' to which two citizens reply: 'Then no Bishops'. Below the woodcut is written: 'If they had ruld still, where had we been?' The woodcut on the right shows the Pope with his triple crown and staff, riding on the seven-headed beast and addressing three men, a 'Jesuit', a 'Fryer', and a 'Papist': 'Estote proditores Betraye your Country.' Above the woodcut a legend explains the picture: 'There Treason will by degrees come in.' And below is written: 'God keepe us from Prelates, Popish Prelates.' Similarly, a ballad of the same year called *The Organs Echo* heavily attacks the bishops, foremost among them Archbishop Laud.[92] A woodcut surmounting the broadside shows the archbishop tied to a post, with a pair of open wings on his shoulders, signifying his desire to escape.[93] Shortly after Strafford was beheaded on 12 May 1641, a ballad came out which ridiculed those followers of the King who had fled the country to avoid a similar fate, namely Secretary Windebank and Lord Keeper Finch.[94] Written as a drinking song with a jolly refrain, the ballad was less serious than the above although it touched on grave matters. After referring to one of the evil deeds performed by those now escaped to France

---

92   Repr. in Wilkins, *Political Ballads*, pp 3–6.
93   Ibid.
94   *Keep thy head on thy shoulders*, repr. in Rollins, *Cavalier*, pp 127–31. On the death of Strafford see also *The true manner of the Life and Death of Sir Thomas Wentworth*, Rollins, *Cavalier*, pp 120–24. This ballad especially addressed 'Country men' inviting them to listen so they 'shall heare and see … the obiect of mishap,/Caught fast in his own trap'.

or Holland, the author concludes each verse with the detached
and indifferent phrase 'For what is all this to thee or to mee?',
followed by the refrain:

> Then merrily and cherrily
> Lets drink off our Beere,
> Let who as will run for it
> Wee will stay here.

This technique of mixing serious political issues with the invitation to drinking allows the author to create a setting in which his
ballad could be performed naturally: in an alehouse or a tavern.
In 1644, probably shortly after the sentence imposed on Laud
had become public, a ballad was published which claimed to be *A
Prognostication Upon W. Laud* written originally in 1641.[95] In a
gloating tone the author addresses the archbishop as 'My little
Lord', expressing his 'bewilderment' that he 'should suffer such
a change, in such a little space' after he had ruled over the King
and state. In eighteen verses he refers to the various political and
religious events Laud was held responsible for, which he inter-
sperses with moral observations on the downfall of haughty
minds. A large woodcut shows a scaffold near the Tower, surrounded with crowds of people. Laud's dead body lies at the feet
of the hangman, who presents his head dripping with blood to
the people. From the hangman's mouth protrudes a speech tag:
'Behould a traytors head.'

The sympathies of ballad writers in favour of the King or the
Parliament were often quite pronounced. A ballad in manuscript
setting out to 'explain' the Commons' protestation, which was
issued on 3 May 1641, in defence of the true reformed Protestant religion against popery, criticizes the role of the Parliament,
and especially of John Pym:[96]

---

95   *A Prognostication Upon W. Laud* (1641), BL 669.f.10 and Wilkins, *Ballads*, pp
     13–18.
96   *An explanacon of the Protestacon*, Ashm Ms 36.92v.

Ile drinke a health to the King,
I meane the King in the North
But as for Pymm I esteeme of him
As a man of noe great worth
I know noe King but Charles
Protector of this Nation
And him Ile defend unto my lives end
By vertue of the Protestacon.

In premonition of rebellion, the author professes that 'noe Charmes shall make me take armes' against the King 'by vertue of the Protestacon'. If the King and the Parliament should fall out 'Tis easy to tell/I may not rebell/By vertue of the Protestacon'. He gives an assurance of his readiness to honour the Parliament and obey its laws as long as they are in keeping with the King. Valuing the 'liberty of my person as a subiect', he does not, however, 'for high to spire/As to make my Prince my Slave'. Although displaying a general tolerance towards the Parliament as an institution, the author does not share any of its political or religious positions. Throughout his seven verses he emphasizes his conformity to the existing order in state and church. Another ballad even speaks of *Pym's Anarchy*.[97] The supporters of Parliament spiced their political arguments with references to existing social injustices, encouraging the people to fight for better times. The achievements of the Long Parliament were celebrated by a ballad entitled *Thanks to the Parliament*.[98] In 1645 a ballad appeared which unmasked the machinations of both James I and Charles I over the past forty years.[99] The most serious allegation against Charles I, which expressed the feelings of many people, was voiced in the last but one verse:

Let no man believe him what euer he sweares;
Hee's so many Iesuits hangs at his Eares,

97   *Pym's Anarchy*, Repr. in Bishop Percy's Folio Manuscripts, ed. J. W. Hale and
       Frederick J. Furnivall (London, 1867), vii, p 37.
98   *Thanks to the Parliament*, Repr. in Rollins, *Cavalier*, pp 139–43.
99   *A Satire On James I And Charles I*, repr. in Rollins, *Cavalier*, pp 151–53.

> Besids an Indulgence procured from Rome
> To pardon his Sinnes both past and to come;
> Which is more then the whore
> Ere would haue granted
> But to see Poperie
> Here againe Planted.

In contrast, a jolly drinking song called *The Courtiers Health; Or The merry Boyes of the Times* expessed the singers' loyalty to the King.[100]

> We Boyes are truly Loyal,
> for Charles we'l venture all,
> We know his blood is Royal,
> his name shall never fall.
> But those that seek his ruine
> may chance to dye before him.
> While we that sack are woeing,
> for ever will adore him.

The refrain ran:

> Fill the Pottles and Gallons
> and bring the Hogshead in,
> We'l begin with a Tallen
> a brimmer to the King.

Since the author describes these loyal subjects as drunkards rather than as brave men defending the King, he might have intended to discredit the royalists in general rather than to portray them as a shining example. This would be an external perspective taken by someone who declined to join in with the singers. On the other hand, sung in a cheerful and relaxed company over a few jars of beer this song could just as well achieve its end of drumming up support for the King. In this case the drinking scene only fulfilled the social function of fixing a specific context for the performance of the ballad which would guarantee success. This view finds support in the succeeding verses which take up

---

100 *The Courtiers Health*, Firth b.19 (4), undated, probably about the mid-1640s.

the various well-known royalist positions: the dislike of 'those strange dissenters' and 'Phanatticks', a relaxed attitude towards alleged popish plots, or the enjoyment of the good life.

Typical of many popular news genres was a 'typology' of the conflicting parties which were often described with the help of pictures.[101] Using this technique a manuscript ballad from about 1641 creates 'types' for the main opponents of the period: the cavaliers and the Puritans.[102] With his details on appearance, apparel, and behaviour, the author virtually 'engraves' these people into the minds of his audience. Like a riddle each verse is introduced with a question asking who would match the subsequent description. People could just sing the riddle and wait for the audience to find the answer:

What Monsters here that thinks is good
To quench his heate with Country' s blood
That now in Armes appeare;
That lead the King about to be
A cloake to their faine knavery
Thats a damned Cavalier.

What Creatures that with his short hayres
his little Band and huge long Eares
That this new Faith hath founded,
The Puritans were never such
The saints themselves not halfe soe much
O such a mans a Roundhead.

Just as popular was the use of games as an allegory for conflicting parties. The most famous one was Thomas Middleton's scandalous play *A Game at Chess* (1624).[103] In 1642 the image was taken up again, when a pamphlet appeared under the same ti-

---

101 See, for instance, *Three Figures Ecclesiastical, Heads of all Fashions. Being a Plaine Desection or Definition of diverse, and sundry sorts of heads, Busting, Jetting, or pointing out vulgar opinion*, with a woodcut (1642), BL E.145.17.

102 Ashm Ms. 36.77r (about 1641).

103 Margot Heinemann, *Puritanism and Theatre: Thomas Middleton and Opposition Drama under the Early Stuarts* (Cambridge, 1980), pp 151–71.

tle.[104] A ballad entitled *A New Game at Cards* used the idea and presented the protagonists of the mounting internal and external crisis in the early 1640s as 'three Nimble Shuffling Cheaters': an Irishman, a Scot, and an 'English-man' who 'would play for an English Crown'.[105] The author directly addresses all people fond of playing cards, promising to teach them a new game they have not seen: 'Play with all the Knaves without King or Queen.' The 'secret in the thing' was 'That the Knave of Clubs should beat the King'. When this was finally achieved 'They all rejoyc'd now at this thing,/And glad they were they had left out the King'.

Once the war had broken out between the King and the Parliament, songs encouraging the soldiers were composed and circulated on both sides. The most famous song in support of the Royalists was Martin Parker's ballad *When The King Enjoys His Own Again* which appeared in 1643.[106] Conjuring up the picture of the good old times when the King and his train still resided in London and all were in their proper place, the author promises that 'All things will be well, When the King enjoys his own again'. In fact, no matter what happens the 'times will not mend' or the war cease unless the King is restored to his former place, power and fame. In the same year, *A Spirituall Song of Comfort* was published for the encouragement of the soldiers fighting on the side of the Parliament.[107] Abounding in biblical imagery the song describes the war as a crusade against the Antichrist on earth. In spite of possible defeats they will win a victory over their enemies because 'the battell onely is the Lords':

> Though here the beasts and the false Prophet,
> a little while doe seeme to thrive,
> Yet shortly shall they both be taken,
> and into the lake be cast alive.

---

104 *A Game at Chess* (1643), BL E.88.2.
105 *A New Game at Cards*, Wood 401.148. See also the politico-religious satire *Newes from Hell, Rome, and the Inns of Court* (1642), BL E.133.13, which also uses playing cards as an allegory for opinions and news.
106 Repr. in Wilkins, *Ballads*, pp 10–13.
107 *A Spiritual Song of Comfort* (1643), BL 669.f.8.44.

Apart from specially composed war songs which must have made a strong impact on soldiers gathering courage for the next fight, there were also ballads which ridiculed the war, or at least took the position of an uninvolved observer. A ballad in manuscript of the year 1642 sings of the 'strange Adventure and the sad fate/ which did befall a Colonell of late'.[108] The colonel, a man of impressive appearance, strong, 'portly' and of a 'warlike hardy weight', suffers an embarassing misfortune in the presence of 'the worthies and the rest beside' when mounting his 'courser': he 'beshitt his hose in every seame'. The smell is unbearable and people are warned to 'stand further of,/if it offend your nose'. When he returns in triumph from Finsbury to his home in Leadenhall, he desires to see 'his Helena'. She right away 'smelt out his knavery' and all worry that in 'the hott skirmish of the day/ his Paris might miscarry or in other way/ Meete with some wound', his 'sultanesse' called for a doctor. When the 'skilfull Sambrooke' started to examine his patient, he soon has 'the business on his fingers ends' and sends for the 'kitchen Queane/ with cloth in hand to make his worship cleane'. Worried about his payment the doctor exclaims:

> The divill a wound I see, is this the prime
> Of the six Cittie Colonells? In good tyme
> They say that shitten lucke is good and I
> will put it to the vote of chivildry
> Whether all be not likely well to Jumpe
> In the new Militia when a Curd is drump.

To sum up, politico-religious satires, broadsides, and short pamphlets (comprising up to eight pages) were a central genre for communicating news and opinions. Whereas ballads were still closely linked to performance and oral delivery, pamphlets relied more on being read. An exception were verse satires and dialogues which retained oral features of communication in the form of mnemonic devices such as (memory) rhymes, or the imita-

---

108 *Upon the valiant Colonel Alder[...]* (1642), Ms, SP 16/490.51.

tion of face-to-face communication in dialogues, which recalled
both ordinary talk among people and the tradition and popularity of the stage. Thus they also attempted to combine traditional
verbal elements of communication with professional news presentation.

'Religion's Made a Tennis Ball':
Satirical and Other Observations of the Time

Pamphlets of the early 1640s seem to have functioned almost
like a seismograph, carefully registering every political sensation
and reissuing it with biting satirical comments. There were hardly
any events or issues that did not feature in pamphlets of the period. The subjects discussed included a variety of aspects of public life, such as church canons, acts of Parliament (the exclusion
of the bishops from Parliament, the abolition of the Star Chamber and High Commission Court) the King's prerogative, Archbishop Laud's sympathies for the Catholic church and the ambi-
tions of the Catholic Queen Henrietta Maria, the imprisonment
of leading clergy and politicans (Laud, Strafford and others), the
conduct of individual bishops, the political atmosphere among
the governing bodies (the relationship between the Parliament
and the King, the Queen and Archbishop Laud, the King's evil
councillors, 'King' Pym), riots in London, rumours, general anxieties (fear of popery, fear of sects, disorder), the hopes placed on
Parliament and the final disillusionment, economic grievances
(land enclosure, the grant of patents, monopolies), the conduct
of the law courts (bribery), and the question of alliances in the
Civil War. Employed both by Puritans and cavaliers, satires and
short pamphlets made up the bulk of popular news presentation
of the period. In part their popularity was due to their wit and
irreverence, which enabled people to voice their opinions against
social superiors through laughter and jesting. In fact, satires shared
with libels and defamation (a central feature of social conflict) a
deeply irreverent tone which showed no respect for the existing

social hierarchy. The form of the satire, which was from its very beginning a kind of protest, a sublimation and refinement of anger and indignation and a guardian over morals and values, added a stir of dissent and revolt to the news presentation of mid-seventeenth-century England. This impression of political defamation in satires gains strength from the fact that pamphleteers often attacked individuals. At the same time, however, the satirical nature in which irreverence was expressed also served as a safety net. Pamphleteers could always claim they were only joking.

The issues picked upon in these pamphlets lay at the heart of the politico-religious conflicts of the early 1640s. Thus, with all their prejudices they played a central part in the formation of public political opinion. In the following survey I shall summarize the arguments of the main conflicting parties, starting with attacks on the state and church and concluding with satires on the Puritans and the various religious sects.

Pamphlets against episcopacy generally attacked bishops for their close allegiance with Rome and the Pope. In the eyes of many pamphleteers, bishops were the very embodiment of all evil that came from Rome. They were accused of idolatry and superstition, and described as fat and lazy hypocrites who led a luxurious and immoral life.[109] More specifically, bishops were induced by the Pope and his superior, the devil, to sow discord in the Parliament, to drive the church into heresy in order to weaken the kingdom, and finally, to subject England to Rome.[110] Bishops, so the argument continued, cared little or nothing about their spiritual duties and only strove for higher positions in church and state. Their 'sudden downfall' (for instance the exclusion of the bishops from the House of Lords; the imprisonment of Archbishop Laud) was heralded as the achievement of the 'wise' Parliament – and the judgement of God.

---

109 *Hell's Hurlie-Burlie, Or A Fierce Contention Betwixt the Pope and the Devill* (1644), BL E.11/4.
110 *Seven Arguments Plainly Proving That Papists Are Trayterous Subjects* (1641), BL E.156/1; *The Black Box of Rome opened* (1641), BL E.206.1

Although all pamphlets were based on these arguments, there was a variety of opinions concerning the reform or total abolition of episcopacy, and the identity of those in England and abroad who supported the bishops. In general, however, authors voiced their deep mistrust of any form of church hierarchy. The majority of pamphlets called for episcopacy to be abandoned in accordance with the *Root and Branch Petition* of 1640.[111] Some authors described the collaboration between the Queen and the bishops in state and church affairs.[112] The majority of pamphlets between 1640 and 1642 presented Charles I as the victim of his council and urged him to dismiss his evil councillors. 'For that the Cavaliers kill and fight and by their evill Counsell have made the King like an insenced Lion against his people and Parliament.'[113] Another author asked:

> Why then should we (who lay claim to the true Protestant Religion) long to be at peace with such as these; and summit to that discipline they will give us; who minde Whoring, Swearing, Idolatry, Drunkenesse, blasphemie, and all manner of vice, and prefer it before any thing that is truly good.[114]

As members of the King's council, bishops were accused of striving for authority superior to that of the King, and of acting against the King's prerogative, as became apparent in their canons, constitution etc.[115] They were frequently seen to be involved in bribery and the unjust proceedings of ecclesiastical and secular courts, and Parliament was praised for having put an end to all of them.[116] Together with lawyers, royalists and Jesuits they were the serv-

---

111 *A Decade of Grievances Presented and Approved to the Right Honourable and High Court of Parliament* (1641), BL E.172/5

112 *The Sussex Picture, The Great Eclipse.* See picture section.

113 *The Devills White Boyes.*

114 *The Cavaliers Bible, A Squadron of xxxvi Severall Religions by them held and maintained* (1644), BL E 4/24.

115 *A Copy of the Bill against the XIII Bishops, presented to the Lords by the Commons* (1641), BL E 173/21.

116 *News From Hell.*

ants of Rome who had been ordered by the Pope and the devil to
sow discord in England. In the same vein, authors argued that
the King's court, the clergy, foreign powers, the Pope and the
devil in a joint effort were aiming to destroy the kingdom. Others alleged that the collaboration between the devil, malignants,
cavaliers, papists, Irish rebels, bishops, the Star Chamber, and
the Queen was solely responsible for all evil.[117]

Politico-religious satires also commented on specific events
such as the exclusion of the bishops from the House of Lords.
Their most prominent target amongst individual clergy and politicians was Archbishop Laud. Throughout, Laud was associated
with popery and Arminianism. He was portrayed as someone
who ruthlessly struggled to subject the Anglican church to Rome,
who introduced and enforced 'superstitious innovations', who
supported the corrupt Court, and who prosecuted religious
nonconformists without pardon in the Star Chamber. Apart from
these general arguments, the most hated innovation attributed
to the archbishop was the placement of the communion table
altarwise in the east of the Church, and the 'etcetera' oath.[118] He
was held responsible for the introduction of the *Common Prayer
Book*, and for reissuing the *Book of Sports*, which legalized certain popular forms of recreation on Sundays and holidays, to the
fury of Puritans. He had had a hand in licencing Pocklington's
book *Sunday no Sabbath*, which was later burned – like the *Book
of Sports* – by order of the Parliament.[119] These measures were
taken as proof of the archbishop's influence over Charles I in
religious matters.[120] The fates of ministers who had suffered under Laud were repeatedly reiterated, the most spectacular cases

---

117 *The Kingdomes Monster* and *The Devills White Boyes*.
118 *Archbishop Laud firing a Canon*, see picture section and *Mercuries Message
     Defended* (1641), BL E.160.13.
119 LJ IV.160–1 and LJ IV.180 (1641); *The Bishops Potion* (1641), BL E.165.1. *The
     Book of Sports*. See picture section.
120 *Mercuries Message Defended*; *The Bishops Potion*.

being the trials of Prynne, Bastwick, and Burton.[121] The war with
Scotland was widely attributed to Laud's influence over the King,
and some pamphlets even accused the archbishop of seducing
the King to popery.[122] The rivalry between Laud and Williams
was ridiculed, presenting Laud as a loser, or at least as equally
unsuccessful.[123] Other topics included Laud's relationship with
the King and Queen, his influence at Court, his treatment of
disobedient bishops, his arguments against preaching, or even
his influence on the tobacco patent. Many pamphlets anticipated
Laud's death, and only a few showed pity when he eventually
died on the scaffold in 1645.[124] The woodcut on the title page of
A Prognostication Upon W: Laud foreshadows Laud's death sentence.[125] The author of a pamphlet entitled *A Charme For
Canterburian Spirits* claims after Laud's death: 'Laud play'd the
Devil on earth so well, That he since in-stalled Vice-roy of Hell.'[126]
The delivery of his last sermon from Tower Hill was taken by
pamphleteers as a case in point to prove that he had never been a
true Christian. In the pamphlet *The Full View of Canterburies
fall, from Pope deliver us all* he is accused of having read his sermon rather than of speaking freely, inspired by the word of God,
and of having shown no true signs of repentance.[127] A woodcut
shows Laud's severed head with blood dripping down from his
neck and an axe underneath symbolizing the hangman. The inscription above Laud's head reads:

---

121 *A New Play*, and *Canterburies Pilgrimage* (1641), BL E.172.28.
122 *A Discovery of the Notorious Proceedings of William Laud* (1641), BL E.172.37;
      The Last Advice of William Laud, late Archbishop, to his Episcopall Brethren
      (1645), BL E.269.10.
123 *The Organs Eccho* (1641), BL 669.f.4.32; *A New Disputation Betweene the two
      Lordly Bishops, Yorke and Canterbury* (1642), BL E.1113.2.
124 *An Answer To the most Envious, Scandalous and libellous Pamphlet, Entitled
      Mercuries Message* (1641), BL E.157.7 (the author condemned those who con-
      tinued to attack Laud even after he was imprisoned).
125 *A Prognostication Upon W: Laud.* See also *A Prophecie Of the Life, Reigne and
      Death of William Laud, Archbishop of Canterbury* (1644), BL E.18.8.
126 *A Charme of Canterburian Spirits* (1645), BL E.269.18.
127 *The Full View of Canterburies fall* (1645), BL E.26.1.

My head that wrought all misery
is smitten off, as you may see.
You Prelates be warned by me
the reward of evil just you see

To which the hangman replied:

Laud sought applaud
but justice turned the wheele
Hadst thou been good
Thou hadst been graced still.

In the centre of the woodcut was a final moral judgment over
Laud:

O Canterbury had you had grace For to beware
This preaching place
Then had you better provd to be
And praises gaind eternally.

In the tradition of the anti-Catholic drama, the author of *Canterbury's Will* devises a mock repentance of the archbishop.[128] In
a dialogue between Laud and his scrivener, the hated church innovations and the persecution of nonconformists are reiterated
in order to contrast this 'evil' policy with what Laud should have
done. He thus appears even more vicious. Laud asks his scrivener
what people thought of him and the reply is: 'Each schoolboys
mouth is filled with a "give little Laud to the Devill"'. Deeply
concerned, Laud condemns popery and vows to give away his
wealth to all those he had prosecuted. The dialogue finishes with
the scrivener exclaiming:

O my Lord, had your Grace been in this minde you now are in six
yeares since, you never had exchanged Lambeth Palace for a Tower
Lodging.

---

128 *Canterburys Will With a serious Conference betweene His Scrivener and Him*
(1641), BL E.156.5. See also *The Last Advice*. Rainer Pineas, *Anti-Catholic
Drama*, Bibliotheca Humanistica and Reformatorica (New York, 1972).

Pamphlets against Puritans and sects which mushroomed in the early 1640s equalled those against episcopacy in numbers. They were written by royalists and supporters of the bishops' church. There were also some pamphlets written by 'Protestants' against the evil influences of the sects. Puritans were attacked as a separate group, but more often they were subsumed under the attacks on religious sects and their 'ridiculous' practices.[129] Whereas bishops had been a clear cut political and religious target, the growing number of sects was treated in the early 1640s mainly as a curious phenomenon. After 1645, the picture changed dramatically. Attacks against the bishops and episcopacy were then replaced by attacks against the Assembly of Divines and the Presbyterian church government. At the same time, criticism of the sects became more urgent and powerful. For many people they had replaced the papists as the greatest enemy to state and church, and they were held responsible for the topsy-turviness of the world. Although biased in his report, Thomas Edwards expresses the feelings of many when he writes in 1645:

> You have, most noble Senatours, done worthily
> against Papists, Prelates and scandalous Ministers
> in casting down Images, Altars, Crucifixes,
> throwing out Ceremonies, etc. but what have you
> done against other kinds of growing evils, Heresie, Schisme,
> Disorder, against Seekers, Anabaptists, Antimonians (sic),
> Brownists, Libertines, and other sects? Should I speak
> against the pope and the papists and spare them, who are
> worse enemies, and doe overthrow the truth more?[130]

In the early 1640s, however, the problem of the sects in London appeared in a slightly different light. There were three ways in which woodcuts and pamphlets dealt with this phenomenon. Firstly, individual sects were analysed and described in a diction-

---

129 See, for instance, *English Puritanism* (1641), BL E.208.4, *A Discovery of 29 Sects here in London* (1641), BL E.168.7.

130 Thomas Edwards, *Gangraena* (London, 1645/46), p 5, p 211.

ary-like way. The historical and biblical background of their origin and their development was provided in a scholarly way, and ancient writers who had worked on the same issues were consulted:

> These Authors (Augustine, Damascus) are cited to shew that it is no feigned what is written of them (Adamites); now those that have taken up the same names here rather added to these fearfull points then any waies lessen them.[131]

Another pamphlet defines a number of sects in a rather dry and learned fashion 'each in their colours without any dissimulation in the world'.[132] The author encourages true-hearted Protestants that 'they may establish such things, and only such as may be pleasing to Almighty God'. The accompanying woodcut shows a man walking in the street among sectarians and a friar. The scene is explained in a short verse: 'The Protestant walkes up and downe the streete (with greefe) And in his sad distractions to God praies for releefe.'

Secondly, the various sects, their manners and beliefs, were rendered completely ridiculous. Satires dwelled especially on their stupidity and ignorance which resulted from their objection to learning as well as from their immoral behaviour and ideas. Amongst the most amusing pamphlets of this type is *A Threefold Discourse betweene three Neighbours*.[133] In the course of the dialogue, the cobbler John Hunt, a well known preacher in London, turns out to be embarrassingly stupid. His arguments and beliefs are unconvincing and he willingly accepts advice. At the same time some of the beliefs of Puritans are ridiculed:

---

131 *A Nest of Serpents Discovered Or, A Knot of old Heretiques revived Called the Adamites* (1641), BL E. 168.12.
132 *The Divisions of the church of England crept in At XV Several Doores* (1642), BL E.180.10.
133 *A three-fold Discourse.*

Cobbler: Talk no more. More-fields is a most profane place, they never meane to come thither againe

Aldgate: Why Moorfield so odious to you?

Cobbler: For the great offence they give to us the godly and sober-minded; first they are receptables of uncleane beasts.

Aldgate: Yes, they have horses there.

Cobbler: The walks are laid and made in the form of a cross. That is intolerable

Aldgate: Why John, are not your selfe made in the form of a crosse? Spred but your armes abroad and see.

The cobbler wearily admits:
But I shall like my selfe the worse for it as long as I live.

The dialogue continues in this way, and in the end the cobbler confesses 'I would have given all the shoes in my shop I had known so much before'. Even more irreverent was a description of the Adamites in 1641:

> Many of these were so conceited and so void of reason that they climbed naked to the tops of trees, and there would sit naked expecting Bread from heaven, until they fell downe halfe dead with hunger: a just punishment for such presumptions.[134]

Another way of ridiculing the sects were puns on the term 'roundhead', a derogatory word for Puritans. Authors came up with all kinds of interpretations of the meaning of roundhead and invented 'new heads': *Heads of all fashions, Being, A Plaine Desection or Definition of diverse and sundry sorts of heads, Burting, Jetting, or pointing at vulgar opinion*.[135] These 'heads' provided a typology of Londoners, such as Puritans, Bishops, Lawyers, Drunkards, or Pimps, thus disgracing the protagonists of both conflicting parties. The rejection of learning in favour of 'pure,

---

134   *A Nest of Serpents.*
135   *Heads of all fashions.*

God-inspired' preaching, the habit of sectarians of meeting in private houses, barns and fields, and the opportunities they gave to women preachers provided much material for criticism. Allegations of sexual misconduct have already been mentioned. Another way of discrediting the sects was to summarize sectarian sermons in print to demonstrate their stupidity and to warn people to beware of these religious groups.[136] One sermon extract nicely shows how sectarians used apocalyptic imagery to drive home their point:

> The Bishops function, deare brethren, is an Anti-Christian calling; the Deanes and Probends are the frogs mentioned in the Revelation: There is none of these Bishops but hath a pope in their bellies: I will tell you, deare brethren, they be papists in grain.[137]

Another pamphlet aptly captures the rhetorical force and atmosphere these sectarian preachers could create:

> The sayd Bareboone preached very nigh fire house; crying diverse times, as was audible heard, Hell and Damnation, telling them they were all damned, he did speake likewise much against the Booke of Common Prayer, against the Bishops, and many others.[138]

The spread of mechanic preaching was taken as a sign of the madness of the world. Sectarians were accused of sacrilege: 'But the substance which is Gods Ordinance hath bin sacrilegiously (sic) intruded and usurped upon by an impudent rabble of ignorant Mechanicks, who have dared to presume to preach.'[139] Similarly they were presented as *Religions Enemies*:

---

136 *Three Speeches, Being such Speeches as the like were never spoken in the City* (1642), BL E.240.31.
137 *The Brownists Conventicle.*
138 *The Discovery of a Swarme of Separatists, Or A Leatherseller Sermon Being a most true and exact Relation of the tumultous combustion in Fleet-street last Sabbath day being the 29 Dec* (1641), BL E.180/25. *The Brothers on the Separation; or, a relation of a company of Brownists* (1641), BL E.172.11
139 *A Cluster of Coxcombes* (1642), BL E.154.49

Religion's made a Tennis-Ball
For every foole to play withall
both which we have so many
That we disputed have so long
Bout which is right and which is wrong
till we have hardly any.[140]

Thirdly, sectarians eventually came to be seen as presenting a threat to the state and church. Whereas some pamphleteers believed episcopacy was indispensable for the kingdom and the church and that the sects were the only cause of friction, others were convinced that the bishops and the sects were equally bad. The threat posed by religious sects in the early 1640s was expressed in the same overall tone: the vast number of sects and the anarchy, instability and disorder they caused.

This sort of people were not once a handfull, and then crept in corners, but now they are like the Aegyptian Locust covering the whole Land and they will rule Religion, not Religion them, or else they will goe against Religion.[141]

Another author commented:

Now from these premises of discord and faction where truth is made the object of every contentious fancy and so become opinion, needes must there proceed much tumult, much division, and much distraction to the great disgrace and scandall of the true Protestant Religion.[142]

Sectarians were accused of mistreating the traditional values and manners of conduct and of striving to turn everything upside down.

Indeed they doe pretend faire colours for their soule intentions, strong proofes for their weake Assertions and scandalous Aspertions, their talke being reformation, rectifying, mundifying, clarifying of the

---

140 *Religions Enemies.*
141 *Lucifer's Lacky.*
142 *The dolefull Lamentation.* See also *A Discovery of 29 Sects.*

Church, and nothing is in their mouthes or pens but rayling against
our Church of England, the Booke of Common Prayer, preaching,
Sacraments, Ceremonies, Rites, Orders, Government and Governors.[143]

The prevailing notion that the growing number of sects caused
disturbance and anarchy was further strengthened by descrip-
tions of their gatherings and the crowds they attracted with their
preaching. Such gatherings usually ended in tumult when watch-
men arrived or when intruders interrupted the sermons.[144] Furthermore, sects were believed to object to any kind of order and
hierarchy. Authors made believe that they overthrew commonly-
held views of the social order and gender relations. Anyone could
be a preacher:

> Every Cobler and Button-maker will get into a Tub, and talk to the
> people of Divine matters, while Scholars walk up and downe in si-
> lence, or else are faine to cry small coale.[145]

Among these polemical pamphlets there were some thought-pro-
voking analyses of the time which related the rise of mechanic
preaching and Puritan attacks on anything that looked remotely
popish to their economic hardships. Consequently, the danger
of unrest in London lay in its economic impact: stagnation in
trade and production due to the feeling of insecurity about the
future.[146] A common denominator of all pamphlets regardless of
the author's political or religious background was an element of
fear and anxiety. It is, however, most interesting to see that fears
triggered off by the sects were mainly related to social order,
deference, and the church hierarchy, whereas those expressed by
Puritans and sects were related to religious issues and questions
of salvation. Thus, it seems that the pamphlet literature of the
early 1640s disseminated two incompatible perceptions of the

---

143 *Religions Enemies.*
144 *The Discovery of a swarme of Separatists.*
145 *Newes, True Newes* (1641), BL E.144.3.
146 *The dolefull Lamentation.*

nature of the conflict. Whereas it was for some a religious conflict which weighed on people's consciences and was experienced
through an apocalyptic world view, it was for others predominantly a conflict of political power and influence, and of social
order, deference and obedience. Both perceptions, however, created fears of an insecure future, which affected people in their
everyday life, either because of the impending loss of salvation
in an anti-Christian world, or because of the increasing disorder
which gave power to the unlearned and to women, thus shaking
the foundations of society. It was a curious mixture of personal
religious convictions which came under threat from uniformist
politics on the one hand, and complete 'religious freedom' on
the other. The experience of the dislocation of former securities
such as the King, the church, and the social hierarchy constituted the political discourse in most pamphlets and satires. The
impact of these experiences on ordinary people is hard to imagine today. However, the way in which people discussed the politics of their time – even under the threat of punishment – shows
how strongly ordinary men and women felt about these issues,
how informed they were about what was at stake, and how willingly they defended their own convictions.

5 · Talking Politics:
Opinions, Rumour and Gossip

To ask 'what's the news?' in early modern England was more than a customary greeting. Especially at times of crisis, people's hunger for news increased and politics spilled over into everyday life.[1] During the early phase of the English Reformation there was a noted increase in seditious speeches and the spread of rumours, which in turn led to the creation of an early form of policing system.[2] The Thirty-Years War accelerated the growth of the still young medium of the newspaper not only in the countries directly involved but also in England.[3] Here the interest in news at a time of crisis was paralleled by the development of a professional communication system which laid the foundations

---

1 For an exploration of the increase in mass-communication in times of major upheavals and crisis see J. Wilke, 'Geschichte als Kommunikationsereignis. Der Beitrag der Massenkommunikation beim Zustandekommen historischer Ereignisse', in *Massenkommunikation. Theorien, Methoden, Befunde*, Kölner Zeitschrift für Soziologie und Sozialpsychologie, ed. M. Kaase and W. Schulz (Opladen, 1989), pp 57–71.
2 Geoffrey R. Elton, *Policy and Police: The Enforcement of the Reformation in the Age of Thomas Cromwell* (Cambridge, 1972). For the German Reformation see Scribner, 'Oral Culture'. For the impact of the French Revolution see Lynn Hunt, *Politics, Culture, and Class in the French Revolution* (Berkeley and Los Angeles, 1984), and Arlette Farge, *Subversive Words. Public Opinion in Eighteenth-Century France* (Cambridge, 1994).
3 Frank, *The Beginning*.

for a continuing general public interest in politics.[4] On the eve
of the English Civil War newsbooks, pamphlets, broadsides,
woodcuts, and letters were disseminated throughout the City
and the country in order to inform people about the impending
crisis. Complaints about the boldness and frequency with which
ordinary people expressed their opinions in writing and speech –
'now all Humors utter what they please' – increased at the same
time, thus throwing light on the receivers' and also (re)producers'
end of news and opinions.[5]

Under the impact of the politico-religious conflicts of the
1640s there was a gradual politicization of everyday talk. People
across social and gender divisions time and again turned from
some 'general discourses' (a contemporary expression for everyday talk) to discussing the political and religious issues of their
time.[6] The topics of 'general discourses' were wide: neighbours
met for chit-chat, and masters and servants discussed their work.
There was talk about household affairs, the weather and the crops,
prices, illnesses, herbal remedies and the like. There was the exchange of news about local events and politics, and there was a
lot of gossiping. There were also neighbourly disputes, defama-
tions and libelling amongst all social groups as most recently
demonstrated by the works of Laura Gowing and Adam Fox.[7]

In contrast, the discussion of so-called high politics went beyond the immediate context of everyday life and the community, and it generally relied on the availability of information.
Men and women of this period displayed an active interest in

---

4   See Sharp, 'Popular Political Opinion' and Harris, *London Crowds*. At present
    there are no studies of seditious words for the interregnum period.
5   Peacham, *The World*.
6   Everyday life is constituted of those given facts, modes of perception, experi-
    ence, and behaviour, which are repeated every day, becoming a routine which
    is self-evident or even mechanical. It is defined as the totality of people's im-
    mediate reality, perception, and behaviour in contrast to a reflected, learned or
    scientific engagement with reality.
7   Laura Gowing, *Domestic Dangers. Women, Words, and Sex in Early Modern
    London* (Oxford, 1996) and Fox, 'Ballads'.

matters that were outside their immediate local context, and they had some basic 'knowledge' of national politics. In fact, during the crisis-ridden 1640s, national politics and religion became a matter of personal concern and – for many – of spiritual well-being. The politico-religious conflicts of the time were on everyone's mind.[8] At work, in alehouses, and at home men and women discussed the whole range of contemporary issues: the Scottish war, Charles I's religious policy, the political influence of his Catholic wife Henrietta Maria, the designs of the King's 'evil councillors', the alleged Catholic affiliation of Archbishop Laud, plots and riots in London, or the question of whether 'religion can be a lawfull cause for subjects to take Armes against their Prince'.[9]

At the same time, men and women seemed more willing to report 'seditious' words, often out of fear of punishment if they concealed what they had heard.[10] Greatly disturbed by 'Captain Napier's' remarks on politics and religion 'at the lodging of Mrs Cromewell, near Sherelane, in St Clement's parish', the physician Dr May said after Napier's departure: 'Many a man hath been laid upon a hurdle for less matters than this, and for concealment.'[11] And Mr Swadlin, vicar of Aldgate, who had overheard the whole conversation from a small 'closet' in the same room, 'came forth' and added: 'Yea, that he hath, this man speaketh treason confidently.' Having thus conceived the danger of the situation all the men and women present during the incident sat down together and reconstructed the whole dialogue

---

8   Court records present a cross-section of all social groups involved in political and religious disputes of their time which does not mean, however, that all actually participated. Yet it does mean that potentially, any person regardless of social status or gender could be informed and could voice opinions.

9   SP 16/457.129–130 (June 1640).

10 For a study of the general increase in litigation during this period see C. W. Brooks, *Pettyfoggers and Vipers of the Commonwealth: The 'Lower Branch' of the Legal Profession in Early Modern England* (Cambridge, 1986), esp. chs. 4 and 5.

11 SP 16/397.26–28 (August 1638).

step by step in writing, carefully noting who had said what.[12] Even such intimate affairs as dinner parties in a private home with invited guests could gain political significance if one of the company interpreted parts of the communication as seditious. In May 1640, James Smith, 'a man of good account and apothecary to Dr Longhan' had dinner at the house of Mr Clay at the lower end of Lombard Street.[13] There he met a merchant, a kinsman of Mr Clay, who reported 'that he had lately received certaine news out of Ireland'. His report included references to the 'Lord Lieutenant of Ireland' (Strafford) whose house 'was utterly raked and pulled down'. According to Smith's testimony, the merchant further claimed to have heard that if the 'Lord Lieutenant shall returne into Ireland his Lordship shall be in danger to be pulled in pieces, or to have his throat cut'. There was also talk of an 'Irish rebellion' similar to the 'Scottish rebellion'.

People across the social scale were well aware of the impending danger of legal prosecution if they uttered – or heard – something seditious.[14] At the same time men and women tried to find some privacy in which to speak their minds. In September 1641, Peter Wilkinson 'and his mistress' sent a letter from Essex to Mrs Elizabeth Beare in Fetter Lane, London, next to the Golden Lion tavern, expressing their relief at finally having found a 'good house' in 'dainty air', where they could 'laugh and talk nonsense' with familiar friends 'without fear or danger of censure'.[15]

The diversity and extent to which political and religious issues occupied the minds of the common people in their everyday encounters and communication cannot be assessed in the

---

12   This report has survived. For this unusually detailed account of several men and women immediately recording every step of the 'seditious speeches' they had heard, carefully checking whether or not they had remembered them correctly, see SP 16/397.27 (August 1638). Each recorded statement gives the name of the speaker and whether or not the others agreed.

13   SP 16/452.122 (May 1640).

14   SP 16/392.61 and SP 16/393.24i (June 1638).

15   SP 16/484.32 (September 1641).

way the inflationary pamphlet production of the early 1640s can be measured.[16] It is impossible to provide any statistics on the number of people engaging in political and religious discourses, the representation of social groups, or men to women ratios. The surviving evidence of 'actions on the case for words', on which the following two chapters are based, is incomplete, and its recordings are chance products rather than systematic collections.[17] Politico-religious discourses were indicted if they contained elements of defamation or seditious words.[18] In the period under discussion, cases of defamation were increasingly brought before common law courts and treated as a civil wrong causing damage to the person defamed, although ecclesiastical courts continued to exercise a concurrent jurisdiction if the imputed scandal fell solely into their realm. Seditious words and some cases of defamation were indicted as a crime in courts with a criminal jurisdiction on the grounds that they endangered the security of the state, tended to break the peace, or tended to provoke others to break it.[19] The evidence consists of informants' reports on

---

16   For some figures see the Preface to the *Catalogue of the Pamphlets, Books, Newspapers, and Manuscripts relating to the Civil War, the Commonwealth, and Restoration, Collected by George Thomason, 1640–1661, I, Catalogue of the Collection, 1640–1652* (Nendeln, 1969; repr.) p xxi.

17   For a brief analysis of seditious words for a later period (1660–1685) see Sharp, 'Popular Political Opinion'.

18   Compare Hamburger, 'The Development'; Roger B. Manning, 'The Origin of the Doctrine of Sedition', *Albion*, 12 (1980), pp 99–121; William S. Holdsworth, 'Defamation in the Sixteenth and Seventeenth Centuries', *Law Quarterly Review*, 40 (1924), pp 302–15; id., *A History of the English Law*, 17 vols. (London, 1903–72); Richard H. Helmholz, 'Canonical Defamation in Medieval England', *The American Journal of Legal History*, 15 (1971), pp 255–68; id., 'Selected Cases on Defamation to 1600', *Selden Society*, 101 (1985). In general, James F. Stephen, *A History of the Criminal Law of England*, 3 vols. (London, 1883).

19   The present study is based on records from King's Bench, Middlesex and Westminster Sessions of the Peace and Gaol Delivery, Surrey Assizes, Privy Council and state papers. Some cases tried in the Star Chamber survived for this period among the state papers. For the earlier period the records of the Star Chamber provide a rich source for the study of sedition and libel.

people's discourses, correspondence between secretaries of state, justices of the peace and local officials, examinations of suspects and depositions of witnesses, petitions and recognizances. One may object that these legal records were biased towards what was considered seditious and dangerous by the authorities and that, being court testimony, their accounts of people's opinions cannot be taken at face value. Defendants, plaintiffs and witnesses developed narrative strategies to make their case as strong as possible.[20] In the context of the law, allegations had to be plausible, convincing and chargeable, and the key adjectives used to describe the nature of spoken words – seditious, treasonable, heinous, or dangerous – recurred in nearly all cases. Sometimes the lines between neighbourly conflicts, personal animosities and revenge, which motivated an accusation, and the true intention, meaning and political weight of the alleged utterances were blurred. However, accounts of what people allegedly said reveal what the informants and witnesses considered dangerous among the many opinions on offer and worthy of legal prosecution. Furthermore, the diversity of the source material and the singularity of each surviving case with its clash of opinions among ordinary men and women suggest great approximity between recorded opinions and communicative processes including the interaction of people.

The court cases analysed here show a cross-section of all social groups for both genders, ranging from day labourers to lawyers, from maids to gentlewomen, ladies, and wives of labourers or justices. They certainly do not form a homogeneous picture of seditious utterances. Instead, they mirror the competing religious and political viewpoints and factions that surrounded the

---

20   Recently the impact which narrative strategies and the situation of the 'court room' had on the quality of testimonies has received much scholarly attention. See Natalie Z. Davis, *Fiction in the Archives. Pardon Tales and their Tellers in Sixteenth-Century France* (Stanford, 1987) and especially Gowing, *Domestic Dangers*.

power struggle in state and church, which can also be found in pamphlets, woodcuts and broadsides. These records provide evidence of the plurality of opinions held by ordinary men and women, the scope of possible interpretations of what was said and heard, and individual definitions of sedition. Given the chance nature of such talks being recorded, and the way the surviving material represents all social groups and both genders, these documents can safely be interpreted as the tip of an iceberg with many similar incidents unknown. In the context of the English Civil War the records about people's discourse are unique, for they provide an insight into how the conflicts at stake were perceived, seen, and presented from 'below' the arena of high politics and its formal political and religious discourses.

The following sections will pursue these various aspects, starting with an analysis of largely anonymous comments about the King, the Parliament, and the episcopacy. I will then look at genres of talk and people's interpretations of specific contemporary events.

Verbal Graffiti:
Discontent with High Politics in Statements from Below

Verbal utterances that were cited in court records without any information about the speaker, like graffiti, are products of the untraceable, spontaneous, and angry voice of the people. The records analysed here are mainly taken from King's Bench, Privy Council, Journal of the House of Commons, Middlesex and Westminster sessions of the peace, and Surrey assize records. The legal documents range from indictments and recognizances to 'billa vera', and the emphasis at present lies exclusively on the recorded speeches, not their legal implications. Some of the entries say nothing more than 'verbis scandalosis contra Regem', 'for cursing of the King's Majesty', 'for speaking violent treason against the King', 'for speaking scandalous words against the King, Queen and Prince', 'pro verbis scandalosis versus Parliament', 'for giving some base and scandalous speeches against the House of Commons now assembled in Parliament', 'for a song against the Parliament', 'for speaking divers contemptible words against the Bible and the Religion established and against the honourable House of Commons', 'charged with uttering of the most scandalous and reproachful speeches against the Professors of the true Religion established in this kingdom', or simply 'for words by him spoken, which wee conceave to be noe lesse than treason', or 'concerning speeches of a very high and dangerous nature charged to have been spoken by one Margaret Grigg'.

However, many entries are more precise, giving the full words that were allegedly spoken. Some statements share the contemporary language of insult, such as rogue or whore, and often verbal utterances and physical violence are not far apart. Like the political and religious satires of the 1640s, which were largely written in rhymes, imaginative narratives and fictitious dialogues, and employed a range of rhetorical persuasive techniques and sexual imagery, oral comments on political and religious events of the time were characterized by a highly figurative language which abounded in social types, personifications, symbols and sexual insults. People resorted to familiar stories and images which corresponded to the mental world of the illiterate or semi-literate to the extent that realities outside their immediate personal experience could be related to. At the same time both literate and illiterate people shared in part the same language when they drew, for instance, on folk heroes to emphasize their political likes and dislikes. Furthermore, some recorded speeches reveal images and figures which spring from everyday life, fiction, or the language of contemporary pamphlets. The majority of recorded utterances focus on the King, the Parliament, and the church, and therefore the following paragraphs will be confined to these.

The King's Crowne is the Whore of Babylon

The first Statute of Westminster of 1275 had already declared that

> from henceforth none be so hardy to tell or publish any false News
> or Tales, whereby discord or occasion of discord or slander may grow
> between the King and his People, or the Great Men of the Realm.[21]

Subsequent statutes and legal treatises reinforced and further elaborated possible offences in speaking about the King and Queen, the King's household, the nobility, and the various central office holders in state and church.[22] In his *Cases of Treason* Francis Bacon argued that 'where a man doth compasse or imagine the death of the King, the Kings Wife, the eldest Sonne, and Heire apparent, if it appeare by any overt act, it is Treason'. Likewise, 'where a man doth perswade or withdraw any of the Kings Subjects from his obedience, or from the religion by his Majestie established, with intent to withdraw any from the Kings obedience, it is Treason'.[23]

Cases on seditious words in the late 1630s and early 1640s did not explicitly refer to any statutes or laws but the respective judges were frequently admonished that the convict 'may receive condigne Punishment as his offence shall require that so others may bee deterred from doing the like libertie'.[24] On the back of one of the Middlesex gaol delivery books of 1640 was scribbled the following order issued under Queen Elizabeth. It probably served as a reminder:

---

21 3 Edw I, Stat. Westm. prim. c. 34, XXXIV. *Of Slanderous Reports.*

22 For the legal history of defamation and seditious words see Holdsworth, *A History*; id., 'Defamation'; and Helmholz, 'Canonical Defamation'.

23 Francis Bacon, *Cases of Treason* (1641), BL E.160.1.

24 SP 16/466.101 (September 1640). Often the assize judges or justices of the peace sent the information against the defendant, his or her examination, and the depositions of the plaintiffs and witnesses to the secretaries of state or the Privy Council, informing them of the steps taken so far and asking for further advice. See for instance SP 16/423.116, 1639; SP 16/417.97 (April 1639), and especially the correspondence in PC.2.48 to PC.2.53. It is not clear what procedure was followed after the outbreak of the Civil War.

> If any be convicted or attayned for speaking maliciously of his own
> imagination any false seditious and slanderous words sayeth or talketh
> of the King or Queen be sett on the pillory in some market place
> neere where the words were spoken, and have both his ears cutt off
> and also three months of imprisonment. This statute confirmed in
> the first year of Elizabeth.[25]

Clearly, irreverent words about the King and his family were forbidden and entailed legal prosecution and punishment. The forms
of punishment varied greatly, ranging from imprisonment, fines
and loss of all goods to public punishment and repentance. In
July 1640, one Puckeridge who had spoken 'scandalous words
against his Majesty' was fined '2,000l and condemned to stand in
the pillory in every market town throughout that county [Es-
sex]'.[26] While the official language of the period and most of the
polemical pamphlet literature of the early 1640s differentiated
between the King's person, his office, and his evil councillors,
thus drawing on the 'two body' theory, ordinary men and women
directly named the King as the source of all evil. In contrast to
statements against the Parliament or the church, nearly all recorded statements either announced a wish to kill the King, or
expressed disobedience to authority. In accusations against both
men and women the alleged words were often introduced with
phrases such as 'conspiring and designing to compass the said
King's death spoke these scandalous words', or 'intending to
overturn and disturb the government of the kingdom of England, and to bring the said King into hatred and contempt spoke
publicly these words against the King'.[27]

Joan Sherrard, spinster, of the parish of St Dunstan in the West,
allegedly uttered 'these words against the King to wit vizt His
Majesty is a stuttering foole. Is there never a Felon yett living? If
I were a man, as I am a woman, I would help to pull him to

---

25   MJ/GDB/8.32 (1640).
26   SP 16/461.32 (1640).
27   MJ/GDR (4 April 1645), Jeaffreson III, p 94; MJ/GDB/29.11, No. 5, (1644)
      repr. in Jeaffreson III, p 120.

pieces'.[28] Judith Castle, the wife of Percivere Castle, was charged
with having bidden her husband to go and kill the King. In her
examination at Hicks Hall she confessed, however, 'that she, out
of her distemper spoke such words because she wished the death
of her husband and she is very sorry that she spoke such words'.[29]
Mary Giles, wife of Edward Giles, lawyer, dwelling in the parish
of St Andrewes, Holborne, was charged with 'these scandalous
words vizt I will kill the King of England'.[30] And Anne Dixon,
daughter of John Dixon, Ipswich, was falsely accused of saying
'let the King be hanged if he will'.[31] Henry Sutton allegedly said
'he would kill the King',[32] Robertus Boys, gentleman, St Martin-
in-the-Field, finally was freed of the charge of having said 'hee
would be avenged of the King or his blood',[33] and Richard
Eigmion was committed to Newgate for 'speaking violent treason against the King'.[34]

Both men and women quite often employed violent images in
order to express criticism, and some evidence reveals how people perceived of the political contexts of their time. When Alice
Jackson 'sawe to sheeps head in a poll' she exclaimed that 'Shee
wished the Kinge and Prince Ruperts heads were there instead of
them, and then the Kingdome would be settled, and the Queene
had not a foote of land in England and the King was an evill and
an unlawfull King, and better to be without a Kinge than to have
him Kinge'.[35] Alice Jackson clearly blamed Charles I and Prince

---

28 MJ/GDB/29.11, No. 5 (27 May 1644).
29 MJ/SPB/15.34 (14 January 1640–41). The location of her dwelling in London
    (Middlesex) is not named.
30 MJ/GDR (4 April 1645) Jeaffreson iii, p 94.
31 SP 16/367.73 (September 1637). For the rest of the case see SP 16/367.73i-ii
    (September 1637); SP 16/378.30 (January 1638); and PC.2.48.499 (January
    1638).
32 MJ/GDB/15.7 (December 1642).
33 MJ/GDR (29 November 1642), Jeaffreson iii, p 84, and MJ/GDB/14.17, 15.7,
    15.15, 15.18 (December 1642).
34 MJ/SPB.51.9 (30 September 1644).
35 MJ/GDR (26 March 1643).

Rupert for the outbreak and conduct of war, and believed that only with both men safely 'locked away' would the kingdom be settled. The image resembles a scene of public punishment where offenders were sentenced to stand on the pillory, exposing them to the gaze and assaults of passers-by in order to make them repent of their sins and to deter others. In stressing that the Queen had not a foot of land in England, Jackson alluded to her French origin, and in doing so to her Catholicism.

A general unwillingness to accept the King's authority also found verbal expression and was severely prosecuted. Allan Morris, dwelling in St John's Street, yeoman, was charged before the King's Bench for saying 'That my master, Amarego Calvetto, are not the Kings subjects nor my master and we nor the Parliament'.[36] George Walker was 'charged to have uttered and delivered in a sermon by him preached the 4th of October last divers things tending to publique faction and disobedience to Authority'.[37] Thomas Aldberry, dwelling in East Smithfield, gunsmith, allegedly said 'there is noe King and that hee would acknowledge noe King'.[38] John Bassett of Stepney was examined 'for saying on Easter day last that hee did not care for the kinge, and that hee was as good a man as the kinge'.[39] Thomas Creede, dwelling in St Olave, Southwark, feltmaker, was imprisoned for saying, 'vizt. That the Kynge was fled. Whereas scandal and discord among the King and his people have arisen in very great infamy and depravement of the King'.[40] Similarly, Ansell Powlten was examined

> for saying that the Kinge was runne away from his parliament, and that hee was noe kinge, neither had hee a foote of land but what hee must winne by the sword, and being asked of one why the State did

36   KB.9.824, pt. 4 (1642).
37   P.C.2.49.540, 11 (November 1638).
38   MJ/GDR (1 July 1643), Jeaffreson iii, p 89.
39   MJ/SPR (4 October 1642), Jeaffreson iii, p 174.
40   Surrey Assi/35 84.45–46 (10 January 1641–1642).

impresse in the Kinge and Parliament name, for answearinge that they did that to cousen the subject.[41]

The question of obedience and loyalty to the King was a much debated issue during this period, and the surviving verbal graffiti signified more than rash unmeditated utterances. Manuscripts, printed works, and people in everyday encounters discussed the problem of which was to be followed, one's 'private conscience' or 'public dutie' in case of conflict. The central strand of Puritan thinking, 'the impulse to liberty of conscience, the individual's right to interpret God's word without priestly intervention' (or, as it were, the intervention of the crown) thus gained political momentum.[42]

After a long cross-examination in 1640 touching among other things upon his former schoolmaster and the authorship of a book in manuscript, the merchant Barny Reymes of Gracious Streete, London, was confronted with certain passages from the 'written book' in question. 'Being demanded his opinion of the first Question in the booke he sayth he holds that no pretext of religion can be a lawfull cause for subjects to take Armes against their Prince.'[43] By 1638 this question was a matter of everyday talk. On the occasion of a funeral feast in the house of 'one Mr William Baly of Mydleton in Westmoreland', Roger Moore, gentleman, was questioned by several men then present about the news his cousin had brought from the Low Countries. He answered that there was no news but that all things prospered well. 'And upon further dyscourse Moore sayd that they did well and

---

41 MJ/SPR (4 August 1646), Jeaffreson iii, p 97. To 'cousen' should read 'to cozen', meaning 'to cheat, to defraud'. *The Concise Oxford Dictionary of English Etymology*, ed. T. F. Hoad (Oxford, 1991), p 102.

42 Underdown, *Revel, Riot and Rebellion*, p 239. Cf. Thomas, 'Cases of Conscience', and the Introduction above. For a brief note on Calvinist 'resistance theory' see Glenn Burgess, 'The Impact on Political Thought: Rhetorics for Troubled Times', in *The Impact of the English Civil War*, ed. John Morrill (London, 1991), pp 67–83, p 69.

43 SP 16/457.129–130 (June 1640).

that they might lawfully take Armes against ther Prince in matters of conscience or Religion.' Being asked by John Bayliffe
'whether we, yf the King should come to alter Religion (which
God forbid) might Revolt from our Prince and take Armes against
him', Moore remained silent. According to another witness,
William Baly demanded of Moore: 'How can any king be pros-
perous with them that have rebelled against ther king. I would
know of you what you would do if our king should command
his subjects to change Religion.'[44] Another asked Moore 'what
he would doe if the King should command him to turne Papist
or doe a thing contrary to his conscience'. Moore allegedly replied that 'he would rise up against him and kill him'.[45] The ex-
amining justices of the peace were especially interested in Moore's
answer. They questioned all witnesses 'whether Moore say anything either in generall, that any subject might in such a case,
either take Armes or kill ther prince or in pertyculer that we
might in the like case kill our king.'[46] Whereas some witnesses
claimed Roger Moore remained silent, others disagreed about
the causes Moore had seen as justifying the taking up of armes
against the King. However, at the end of the examination all witnesses testified the following accusation: 'His opinion was that
in cause of Religion, subjects though private men, might with
good conscience take arms against their kinge and kill him.'

Finally, some of the verbal graffiti was insulting. An accusation against John Buckwell ran: 'In an humour of distraction
which he maketh showe of', he 'hath misdemeaned himselfe in
the house of the Queene her Majesties Mother at Cheswicke,
both in uttering of divers distracted and offensive speeches, and
in assaulting some of her Majesties servants, and in committing
of other outrages in the houses of some of the adjoyning neigh-

---

44 SP 16/409.102–102ii (1638). The 'low countrymen's' rebellion 'against ther
    king' mentioned by Baly, referred to the Netherlands' fight for independence
    from Spain. See also SP 16/410.6.
45 SP 16/404.64.
46 SP 16/409.102–102ii.

bours'.[47] The only instance of language of insult being used against the King discovered so far is that of the 'pretended scandalous words' of Robert Hand of Whitecross Streete, London, 'bodyes-maker' (sic). Using words that referred to a person's honour mixed with apocalyptic imagery familiar from contemporary Puritan pamphlets and woodcuts, Hand allegedly said 'That the King was a traitor and his Crowne was the Whore of Babylon'.[48] The image clearly shows the alliance between the state and church, emphasizing the King's dependency on the latter. The central symbol of power, the crown, was in the hands of the church, signified in the 'Whore of Babylon', which was a popular image employed by nonconformists against the Anglican High Church. Since the King allowed himself to be controlled by representatives of a religion that was hostile to many subjects, threatened the freedom of religion, and was suspected of popery (another implicit meaning of the Whore of Babylon image) he was betraying his people.

All our Bishops and Parsons are Rogues.

Verbal graffiti against the church and religious views touched upon all shades of religious opinion and sects, depending on the speaker's personal belief. It was marked by threats of divine punishment against followers of the 'wrong' religion, contempt of the religious enemy, and verbal assaults which sometimes resulted in physical violence.

John Blake of the parish of St Martin-in-the-Fields was examined before the King's Bench for the following conviction and 'prophecy':

> Then are you all damned, all your bishops and parsons are rogues and rascalls and you have no bishops and over a while there shall be no bishops in England and if you be not Romane Catholickes within

---

47   MJ/SPR (1 October 1640), Jeaffreson iii, p 170–71.
48   MJ/GDR (11 March 1643), Jeaffreson iii, p 87.

a week, nay within two days or by Thursday next you shall all dye, and that within a week there should be a great alteracon and that all should be of his religion.[49]

James Wayle and Robert Hammond, two shoemakers dwelling in the parish of St Martin-in-the-Fields, London, were charged 'for not going to church during the two years last past, and for saying that the Church is noe true Church'.[50] In the early 1640s, numerous charges appear to have been brought against men and women from all over London for not going to church, meeting instead in 'unlawfull assemblies' in 'contempt of the religion established in this realm'.[51] The stationer Walter Wasse of Little Britain in St Botolph, Aldersgate, for instance, was summoned before the Middlesex sessions of the peace because he preferred to 'heere a sermon under a tree then out of a pulpitt'.[52] Susan Platt and her husband, John Platt, yeoman, dwelling in St Giles Cripplegate, allegedly adhered to views of the Anabaptists. They were both accused of having said: 'That to baptize an infant was to no more effect than to baptize a catt or a dogge.'[53]

Religious practices were not only ridiculed in words. One incident narrated in Thomas Edwards' *Gangraena* 'involved a blasphemous parody of the sacrament of baptism, in which soldiers took a hare into a parish church, filled the baptismal font with urine, and then poured it over the helpless animal while reciting from the book of common prayer'.[54] Although Edwards' account needs to be treated with caution, as it was probably written mainly to shock his contemporaries, it nevertheless mirrored other stories of his time. A similar episode is known from a small village in Huntingdonshire. In June 1644, the troopers of Captain Ri-

---

49   KB 9.817 pt. I (1641–42).
50   SP West.R., 20 (October 1645), Jeaffreson iii, p 181.
51   See, for instance, KB 9.823.113 pt. 2.
52   MJ/SPR (20 July 1641), Jeaffreson iii, p 173.
53   MJ/GDR (January 1645), Jeaffreson iii, pp 92–3 and pp 110–21.
54   Ian Gentles, *The New Model Army* (Oxford, 1991), p 89, quoting Thomas Edwards' *Gangraena*, 3 vols. (London, 1646) iii, p 18 ff.

chard Beaumont led a horse into the parish church and, after pissing in the font, they baptized the horse in a coarse parody of the Anglican service with a corporal acting as priest and a soldier playing the god-mother.[55] Such attacks on Anglican baptism rites, Anglican liturgy, and the representatives of episcopacy were not an exception. In one of several letters which Nehemiah Wharton sent to his master, George Willingham, merchant at the Golden Anchor in St Swithin's Lane, London, Wharton described the following incident: 'This morning our soldiers sallied out about the country and returned in state, clothed in surplice, hood and cap, representing the Bishop of Canterbury.'[56] Like the parody of baptism, hardly any verbal utterance could have been more powerful in demonstrating the soldiers' contempt of the Anglican High Church than this non-verbal dramatization of disrespect and ridicule. David Underdown has shown that 'people on both sides in the civil war often engaged in symbolic behaviour, used recognizable cultural codes to assert their identities, to provoke or ridicule their enemies'. Whereas for royalists the obvious target were 'roundheads', often symbolized by a picture of a 'man in a tub', the symbolic targets for the other side were 'usually vestiges of Laudian rituals'.

Much verbal (and printed) discontent with the Anglican High Church and Laud's religious innovations was focused on the *Book of Common Prayer*, and the King finally issued a proclamation in December 1641 'commanding the severe execution of the laws against the contemners of the common prayer book'.[57] However, it was of little effect. When John Waterton, dwelling in Shadwell in the parish of Stepney, heard the *Book of Common Prayer* read, he said: 'There were more soules damned then died of the plague and that he would mayneteyne the same.'[58] William

---

55   Capp, 'Popular Culture', p 35.
56   SP 16/492.2 (3 September 1642), Northampton. See also Underdown, *Revel, Riot, and Rebellion*, p 177.
57   SP 16/486.63 (16 December 1641).
58   KB 9.823.123 pt. 2 (14 September 1642).

Turner of the parish of St Clement Danes 'spoke publicly these words to the depravation and contempt of the Book of Common Prayer, to Wit: That the Book of Common Prayer is all lyes and that they were fools and knaves that will maynteine it'.[59] The charge against Thomas Creede for commenting on the King's escape from London also included his 'contempt of the common prayer book in saying ... vizt. that the book of common prayer was popish and that the Lords prayer contained in the same book was also popish'.[60] Likewise, John Bassett, who was charged with uttering words against the King, had to answer for 'many other wild speeches both against Mr Stampe viccar and Mr Edgworth curate of Stepney and agaynst the book of Common Prayer and sayinge that all that heard and read it were damned'.[61]

It was not unusual, in a local parish context, for discontent with religious practices to turn into insults against individual office-holders. Rachel Weaburne of Lymehouse, Middlesex, spinster, had to answer a charge 'for sayeinge that Mr Edgworth curate of Stepney parish was a damned dogg and that she would rather goe to hear a cart wheele creake and a dogge barke then to hear him preach'.[62] Verbal assaults against individual representatives of the hated religion could easily turn into physical violence. During the baptizing of a child 'at the Fount' in the parish of Halsted, Essex, Robert Howard struck the *Book of Common Prayer* out of the curate's hand saying it was a popish book, and kicked it up and down the church.[63] At the same time, Jonathan Poole, an 'Excommunicated Person', took the clerk by the throat, forcing him to 'deliver unto them the Hood and Surplice, which they immediately rent and tore in pieces'. When those involved

59   MJ/SPR (20 April 1642), Jeaffreson iii, 80.
60   Surrey Assi/35 84.45–46 (10 January 1641–42).
61   MJ/SPR (4 October 1642) Jeaffreson iii, p 174.
62   MJ/SPR (19 July 1642) Jeaffreson iii, p 174.
63   LJ IV.100–101 (30 November 1640); LJ IV.107 (10 December 1640); LJ IV.109 (14 December 1640); LJ IV.113 (18 December 1640).

in the riot were ordered to be attached by virtue of a warrant, they 'were immediately rescued by a Multitude of People'.

After the Puritans had gained the upper hand in Parliament and revised some of Laud's church innovations, assaults on Puritan religious politics now caught people's attention and started to busy the courts. In December 1642, the parishioners of 'St Dionis Back-Church, London', sent a petition to the House of Commons complaining about alterations to the interior of their church made by 'Dr John Warner, now Bishop of Rochester, rector of the said church'.[64] Furthermore, they accused him of having used 'unseemely speeches – as Puritanical knave; and in his pulpit has compared lecturers to ballad singers and hobby-horse sellers, for that they in the fair or market have the most crowd, while mercers and goldsmiths who sell rich commodities have nothing to do'.[65] In contemporary pamphlets on poets, authors, and printers, ballads were described as one of the meanest literary products 'formed in every part of the City, and then chanted from Market to Market, to a vile tune, and a worse throat'.[66] Hobby-horses were toys consisting of a stick with a horse's head, and playing with them was a favourite pastime in seventeenth-century England.[67] In comparing lecturers with ballad singers and hobby-horse sellers, Warner denied that they had any profound Christian message, describing their lectures instead as 'items of mass-amusement' more apt for fairs or markets than churches. According to Warner religion had degenerated to the level of a commodity which sells best if it is cheap and popular rather than valuable and demanding like the 'rich commodities' of mercers and goldsmiths who stood for the representatives of the Anglican High Church. In creating this analogy between religious messages and economic goods, Warner evoked and exploited both

---

64 SP 16/493.28, 28 December 1642.
65 Ibid.
66 *A true Description.*
67 In the fourteenth and fifteenth centuries a hobby-horse was either a small horse in the morris dance or a figure of a horse manipulated by a performer.

the economic and cultural meaning of 'cheap' as inexpensive and vulgar, and of 'rich' as well supplied with wealth and of great worth. The mass of people was allegedly unable to differentiate between the value of '*cheap* commodities' and '*rich* commodities', or, in Warner's analogy, the false and true word of God.

When some people took down a cross at St Clement Danes in May 1643, Roland Kelinge exclaimed 'Round it, Round it, make it all Round'. Bystanders claimed that these words were spoken 'in a disdainful manner', probably interpreting them as an assault against Puritan politics. Since this period was extremely versatile in word-plays, and people were familiar with this art through proverbs, jokes, plays and satires, the utterance 'to make it round' might have been read as 'making it according to the wishes of round-heads'. As already demonstrated, there were many satires which ridiculed the roundheads' obsession with popish items, above all the crucifix.[68] However, the judges at Hick's Hall ruled that Kelinge's utterance harboured no dangerous meaning since he had taken the oath of allegiance.[69] Robert Lockyer was called before the Westminster sessions of the peace in 1644 'for saying and justifying it in open court that the ministers of the church of England were anti-Christian ministers, and that Mr Marshall and Mr Hill taught anti-Christian doctrine or the doctrine of divells, or some such words.'[70] The reference to Stephen Marshall and Roger Hill, two 'of the most distinguished Puritans of the time', discloses Lockyer's anti-Puritan sentiments and his disapproval of the church government established under the Parliament.[71] In September 1645, Mr Darley informed the House of Commons of 'some seditious passages delivered in a sermon by one Mr Volchier yesterday at Lincoln's Inn, derogatory and scandalous to the Honour and Proceedings of Parlia-

---

68   See, for instance, *The Dolefull Lamentations.*
69   MJ/SPB.33.33 (17 May 1643).
70   MJ/SPB.51.12 (30 September 1644).
71   Seaver, *Lectureship*, p 269.

ment'.[72] Volchier was sent for as delinquent, and those who had heard the sermon were requested to meet,

> and upon Conference amongst themselves, set down in writing, as near as they can, what the words were which Mr Volchier delivered in his Sermon, any way scandalous to the Parliament, and which they can testify.[73]

The Pox confound the Parliament.

Verbal graffiti against the Parliament employed either sexual slander, or some implicit political meaning revealing the speaker's perception of the role of Parliament. In contrast to verbal graffiti against the King and the church, verbal assaults on the Parliament appear to have been much more part of everyday language as it was used in conflicts among men and women. Its central ingredient was that of 'defamation of character' which incidentally made up the bulk of slander suits in the first half of the seventeenth century, touching upon a person's credit, honour, and sexual reputation. In the seventeenth century there was a noted increase in the number of defamation cases in all courts as a result of an excessive concern with honour and reputation.[74] The various social consequences for victims of slander always boiled down to humiliation and loss of face. The verbal strategy against the Parliament which was treated as one body seems clear: the emphasis on immorality, which every man and every woman could relate to and understand in its devastating consequences. It was aimed at undermining the Parliament's integrity, trustworthiness, and authority by undermining the honour of its

---

72   CJ IV.293 (29 September 1645).
73   Ibid.
74   Martin Ingram, *Church Courts, Sex and Marriage in England, 1570 – 1640* (Cambridge, 1987), pp 292, 304; James A. Sharpe, 'Defamation and Sexual Slander in Early Modern England: The Church Courts at York', *Borthwick Papers*, 58 (York, 1980). See also the introduction in Helmholz, 'Select Cases'.

members through scandalous sexual allegations. Thus, verbal criticism of political opponents by ordinary men and women operated within the same paradigm of a political language that linked moral corruption with political threats, a paradigm also at work in popular pamphlets, ballads, and verse libels of the period. At the same time, allegations of moral corruption which were expressed through sexual slander such as 'whore', 'whoremaster', or sexual diseases such as the pox were a forceful tool in neighbourly conflicts and were employed to dishonour foes. The choice of slanderous language against the Parliament in support of political arguments reveals what was probably closest to people's experience of expressing spontaneous discontent and anger. An attack on people's honour was most effective when it homed in on their sexual behaviour. Laura Gowing has demonstrated that the image of loose women and prostitutes served as a means of insulting both men and women in neighbourly disputes and of discrediting people's reputations and trustworthiness.[75] In his study on eighteenth-century France, Martin Dinges has shown that the insult of prostitution was for both men and women a universal symbol for harming the social order.[76] Reformation studies have already pointed to the continuous confrontation of the religious sphere with the profane, namely the sexual and scatological sphere.[77]

For the political context of the 1640s, the assault on authority through the common language of sexual insult suggests, furthermore, a loss of deference towards authority and a strengthening of individual viewpoints and self-confidence. This view is supported by the fact that communication and the formation of

---

75   Gowing, 'Gender' and idem, *Domestic Dangers*.
76   Martin Dinges, '"Weiblichkeit" in "Männlichkeitsritualen"? Zu weiblichen Taktiken im Ehrenhandel in Paris im 18. Jahrhundert', *Francia* 18 (1991) pp 71–98, p 89.
77   Pia Holenstein and Norbert Schindler, 'Geschwätzgeschichte(n). Ein kulturhistorisches Plädoyer für die Rehabilitierung der unkontrollierten Rede', in *Dynamik der Tradition*, ed. van Dülmen, pp 41–108, p 65.

opinions in mid-seventeenth-century England were characterized by the subjective interpretation of reality on the basis of
religious convictions and personal judgement rather than official policy – in spite of a basic knowledge of the law. Whereas the
Catholic Elizabeth Thorowgood, for instance, thought that the
King was sympathetic to the Catholics because of his Catholic
wife, Mary Cole, also a Catholic, was convinced of the opposite,
wondering how the Queen could endure his attitude.[78] Furthermore, the use of slander in political disputes reveals a consistent
pattern of the 'language of conflict' in seventeenth-century England which was entrenched in concepts of honour, morality, and
sexual reputation. Recently, scholars including Richard Cust,
Alastair Bellany, Ann Hughes, Susan Wiseman and others have
started to emphasize the politico-religious nature of assaults
which appear at first to be merely scandalous allegations. Alastair
Bellany has pointed to the 'sexual and scandalous sides of Stuart
politics' in verse libels, arguing that they nevertheless disseminated political attitudes. He showed that 'at a time when religious standards of morality were tightening, libels reflected and
transmitted representations of the court and its courtiers as sexu-
ally, politically and religiously corrupt'.[79] Similarly, Susan Wiseman
has shown that sexual satire was applied to political objectives
throughout the Civil War, and demonstrates how it interacted
with political theory.[80] At the same time these verbal assaults seem
to suggest that people failed to defer to parliament men, treating
them as equals.

---

78   SP 16/457.3–4 and SP 16/392.61, SP 16/393.24i.
79   Bellany, 'Raylinge Rymes', p 295; Richard Cust, 'Honour and Politics in early
     Stuart England: the case of Beaumont v. Hastings', *Past and Present*, 149 (1995),
     pp 57–94; id., 'Honour, rhetoric and political culture: the Earl of Huntingdon
     and his enemies', in *Political Culture and Cultural Politics in Early Modern
     Europe*, ed. Susan D. Amussen and Mark A. Kishlansky (Manchester, 1995),
     pp 84–111; Ann Hughes, 'Gender and politics in Leveller literature', in *Politi-
     cal Culture*, ed. Amussen and Kishlansky, pp 162–88; Croft, 'Reputation'.
80   Susan Wiseman, '"Adam, the Father of all Flesh": Political Rhetoric and Politi-
     cal Theory in and after the English Civil War', in *Pamphlet Wars*, ed. Holstun,
     pp 134–57.

That defamation and slander of the Parliament was quite popular is also apparent in the performance of ballads. Dorothy Crowch had 'to answeare the complaint of Dr Symon Digby, for scandalizeinge him and keepinge a disorderly taverne and sufferinge her sonne and others to singe reproachfull songs in her house against the parliament'.[81] Some fiddlers, who sang 'a scurrilous song against the Parliament' in Gratious Street, London, were caused to be apprehended 'by some well-disposed Men' and sent to the House of Correction.[82]

The surviving evidence of verbal assaults provides rare insights into political comments and the language people used to express their opinions. John Scullard of the parish of St Mary's in Islington, labourer, 'spoke publicly these wicked and devilish words, to wit, the "Pox confound the Parliament"'.[83] John Parker of Whitecross-street, brickmaker, had to answer the complaint of Robert Hand 'for the pretended scandalous words against the Parliament, vizt That the Parliament were all rogues and rascalls'.[84] 'Intending to bring the Parliament into hatred and contempt', Mark Istleberry dwelling at South Mimms, Middlesex, 'uttered these scandalous words, That the Parliament doe maintaine none but a company of rogues'.[85] John Voysey, merchant of Dartmouth, Devon, had to answer before the Middlesex sessions of the peace 'for speaking certeine scandallous and disgracefull wordes against this present Parliament in his drink, vizt That some of the Parliament men had the pox and were whore-masters, and some of them were rogues and rebells'.[86] William Harmon of St Leonard's Shoreditch, gardener, allegedly said 'the Parliament were all rogues and thieves and they would be the confusion of the Kingdome'.[87]

---

81   MJ/SPR (3 September 1644), Jeaffreson iii, p 178.
82   CJ II.604 (3 June 1642).
83   MJ/GDR (5 October 1642), Jeaffreson iii, p 82.
84   MJ/GDR (19 March 1643), Jeaffreson iii, p 87–8.
85   MJ/GDR (30 March 1645), Jeaffreson iii, p 94.
86   MJ/SPR (1 March 1646), Jeaffreson iii, p 98.
87   MJ/SPR (3 September 1644), Jeaffreson iii, p 178.

Judith Pheasant, wife of Azarias Pheasant, tailor, of the parish of St Clement Danes, was charged 'to have bidd a pox of God take the Parliament and all those that belong to them, and to have sworne severall oathes also shee would invent a new curse for them, being drunke, and other offences'.[88] According to information presented to the House of Commons, Edward Jeffery of Southminster, clerk, had said 'A Pox upon the Parliament; That by God, he would first cut the Parliament's Throats, before they should take a Course with such Priests as himself'.[89]

The following words spoken by Nicholas Browne, vintner, show how people used traditional figures to defame the Parliament. These figures were known from history, popular literature, ballads, plays, and pamphlets as symbols of popular protest and revolt – in this case since the fourteenth century: 'The Parliament was nothing but a Company of Robin Hoods and Little Jacks'.[90] The identity of Robin Hood as the famous English folk hero and 'Little Jack', alias 'Little John', as his ally is apparent. Similarly, in 1640 the candidate for Parliament in Somerset was known as 'Robin Hood' and his chief supporters as 'Little Robins'.[91] Robin Hood was a familiar sight because he was commonly represented on domestic wall hangings in the seventeenth century.[92] Furthermore, Robin Hood and 'Little John' were popular figures in the mid-seventeenth-century pamphlets and ballads. Interestingly enough these pamphlets were printed and published by stationers who had their shops in the suburbs and dealt chiefly in the lighter literature of the period, including ballads.[93] In 1632, Martin Parker published for 'gentlemen and yeomen bold' the *True Tale of Robin Hood* as a small merry book, and a cycle of twelve Robin Hood stories in a quarto double-book selling at

---

88   SP.West.R. (14 January 1646), Jeaffreson iii, pp 183–84.
89   CJ II.728 (1642).
90   CJ III.17 (1643).
91   Capp, 'Popular Culture', p 34.
92   Fox, *Aspects*, p 18.
93   Francis Coules, John Wright, Thomas Banks, and Thomas Bates.

3d.[94] Margaret Spufford has pointed to the ambivalence of the Robin Hood figure throughout history, including his representation in seventeenth-century chapbooks: 'He gives nothing to the Beggar but the offer of a fight, and when he finds himself losing, he draws his sword on his poor opponent, who is armed only with a quarter staff.'[95]

In the light of these contemporary representations of Robin Hood and Little John, Nicholas Browne seems to have associated the Parliament with rebels and outlaws who – in this negative interpretation – threaten to upset the existing order to promote their own unlawful interests while claiming to act on behalf of the people. The negative view of folk heroes and the allusion to them as a rhetorical device was also shared by people of very different social standing and education. In a warning against the promotors of equality and social justice, Joseph Hall, Bishop of Norwich, warned the House of Lords in November 1641:

> My lords, if these men (sectaries and mechanical preachers) may, with impunity and freedom, thus bear down ecclesiastical authority, it is to be feared they will not rest there, but will be ready to affront civil power too. Your lordships know, that the Jack Straws, and Cades and Wat Tylers of former times, did not more cry down learning than nobility.[96]

People in mid-seventeenth-century England must have easily recognized Jack Straw and Wat Tyler as the leaders of the great revolt in 1381 in reaction to the heavy taxation levied upon the poor under Richard II.[97] In 1642, a pamphlet entitled *The Rebellious Life and Death of Wat Tyler and Jack Straw*, was published

---

94 Spufford, *Small Books*, p 231. See also P. R. Coss, 'Aspects of Cultural Diffusion in Medieval England: The Early Romances, Local Society and Robin Hood', *Past and Present*, 108 (1985), pp 35–79.

95 Spufford, *Small Books*, p 232.

96 *The Parliamentary or Constitutional History of England* (London, 1762), x, pp 132–3. Cit. in Brian Manning, *The English People and the English Revolution* (Harmondsworth, 1976), p 56.

97 Owst, *Literature*, p 291.

and sold in the northern suburbs of London. It can be traced back to a 'lively play' on the theme of Jack Straw of the year 1593: *The Life and Death of Jacke Straw, A notable Rebell in England: who was kild in Smithfield by the Lord Maior of London.*[98] The recollection of folk heroes or rebels – depending on the viewer's perspective – and the reference to the earlier play was emphasized by a woodcut which showed four ghosts standing on a stage. They were wrapped in winding sheets and carried torches. A skeleton stood near a man in the costume of the sixteenth century, who was terrified by the ghosts and skeleton. Written under the impact of the conflict-ridden 1640s, the pamphlet version cut out all sympathy with the requests of the rebels including the heroic and well known 'watchword of revolt' – 'when Adam delved and Eve span Who was then a gentleman?'[99] Instead, the anonymous author gave a very detailed historical account of the 1381 revolt with the penitent ghost of Jack Straw appearing at the end as a bad example to any potential rebel. Throughout the narration moral points were made about the horrors of any rebellion, the unlawfulness of the rebels' requests, and the necessity to obey the King. Here the question of 'private conscience' and 'public duty' is raised again and answered in favour of unconditional obedience to the King. Already at the outset of the tract it was stressed that 'The Prince is supreame head of all Authority, and the subject is injoyn'd to obey God, the lawes, and his Prince; for Treason can have no place where Obedience claimeth principality'. The author of *The Resolution of the Women of London to the Parliament* took a different stand while also evoking the images of Jack Straw and Wat Tyler.[100] The great-

---

98   *The Rebellious Life and Death of Wat Tyler and Jack Straw* (1642), BL E.136.1 (1642). The play *The Life and Death of Jacke Straw, A notable Rebell in England: who was kild in Smithfield by the Lord Maior of London* is repr. in *The Tudor Facsimile Texts* under the supervision and editorship of J. S. Farmer (New York).

99   Owst, *Literature*, p 291.

100 *The Resolution of the Women of London to the Parliament* (1642), BL E.114.14.

est concern that was expressed on behalf of 'the women of London' was that 'It is most true, that the King hath raised an Army to destroy us all'. The pamphlet continues: 'Now I pray you consider who it is that raiseth these forces, it is not Wat Tiler or Jack Straw, or any such rebellious company that in former times did rise against the King, but the King doth intend to make warre against himselfe, or on those that love him as wel as himselfe, that is his loving subjects and Parliament.'

The appeal to Jack Straw and Wat Tyler in the seventeenth century demonstrates once again that the meaning of familiar images, symbols and tales depended essentially on the way they were contextualized. Although these two figures – like Robin Hood – were part of England's tradition and collective memory, and were easily recognizable in a specific historical and communicative context, this did not imply that they carried a fixed meaning. Instead, the message they carried depended on both the author's and the viewer's perspective. Furthermore, these two references to Straw and Tyler show how easily political symbolism could distort political realities.

People also evoked local heroes in order to express their political opinions. In the early phase of the Civil War, the inhabitants of a small village in Worcestershire remembered the baronial revolt against Henry III, which had been led by Simon de Montfort, Earl of Leicester. While hardly hiding their criticism of the present monarchy, their story related how his dead body had been found there and how he was revered as a martyr for his fight for the commonwealth, but not for the King.[101] In general, social types enjoyed great popularity in seventeenth-century England, and they played a central role in everyday communication.[102] As already shown, 'social types' such as gossips, rogues,

---

101 Cit. in Fox, *Aspects*, p 33–4.

102 For the history of 'social types' or 'characters' and their significance in oral cultures and homiletic preaching see Owst, *Literature*, and Yates, *The Art*. For an actualisation of old familiar social types in seventeenth-century England see Joseph Hall, *Character of Virtues and Vices* (1608); Sir Thomas Overbury,

knaves or whores or well known historical figures helped to evaluate behaviour and reputation; they provided a 'label for a style of behavior, a kind of person, and the associated evaluation of the moral worth of that behavior'.[103]

Quite a few men and women based their views on the political role of the Parliament on specific interpretations of the time. In May 1641, one Thomas Wickes informed the House of Commons of 'very dangerous words spoken by Doctor Howell'. When they met in Grays Inn on the 3 May 1641, 'He told me that Things were ripe and grown to a Head; we should know within Three or Four Days, whether the king should be King or no King; and that he was sure I would stand right; and that the Kingdom would not be governed by a Company of giddy-headed People'.[104] William Spencer, alias William Pigge, of St James Clerkenwell 'spoke publicly these scandalous words to the defamation of Henry Earl of Holland, Knight of the Garter and one of the Privy Council, to wit, That the Earl of Holland was raysed from a beggar by the Kinge and that now he did what he could to cutt the King's throat'.[105] When the lord mayor, Richard Gurney, was impeached by the two Houses of Parliament in July 1642 for his active support of the King, William Pigge disapprovingly commented 'that the Parliament had imprisoned the Lord Maior for nothing else but because he was an honest man and did the King's service'.[106] Joseph Brandon, dwelling in St Giles-in-the-Field,

---

Character (1614), and the character-building in Ben Jonson's works, and John Dekker, Seaven Deadly Sinnes of London (1606), reprinted in A.B. Grosart (ed.), The Non-dramatic Works of Thomas Dekker, 5 vols. (New York, 1963), ii, pp 1–86.

103 Sally E. Merry, 'Rethinking Gossip and Scandal', in Toward a General Theory of Social Control, 2 vols. (Cambridge, Mass., 1984), ed. Donald Black, i, pp 271–302, p 178.

104 CJ II.478 (May 1641).

105 MJ/GDR (5 October 1642), Jeaffreson iii, p 82.

106 Ibid. In July 1642, 'the Commons sent up a request to the Lords to join with them in an impeachment of the Lord Mayor'. At the opening of his trial on 22 July 1642, Gurney was described as 'one of the greatest offenders of his pre-

gentleman, expressed a similar opinion about the trial against Gurney and the election of the new lord mayor, Sir Isaac Pennington. Obviously quite angry, he said 'That he wished the Parliament Howse to fall on the Right Honourable the Lord Saye, Mr Pymme and all other traytors to theire Kinge as they were, and wishing the nowe Lord Mayor of London, callinge him *the supposed Mr Mayor* hanged, and hoped to see him drawne in peeces.'[107] In calling Gurney's successor 'the supposed Mr Mayor', Joseph Brandon used a phrase which had been coined by the crown and the royalist party who refused to accept the election, referring hereafter to Pennington as 'the pretended Lord Mayor'.[108]

Another political event caught the imagination of the public. By special order of Parliament the King's letters, which had been taken at Naseby Field by Thomas Fairfax, were published in 1645. This aroused much public interest and a number of pamphlets commented on the content and authenticity of the letters.[109] The Parliament claimed that the King's letters laid open 'many Mysteries of State' which justified their war against him – a claim which was for some people only a propaganda device.[110] Thomas Sampson of Spittlefield, turner, argued 'that the letters that were

---

decessors' and as 'a great burthen and nuisance to the City and Commonwealth'. The charges against him included his support for the Commission of Array and his open sympathy for the King against the Parliament. Valerie Pearl, *London and the Outbreak of the Puritan Revolution. City Government and National Politics, 1625–43* (Oxford, 1961), p 156. In August 1642, he was succeeded by Alderman Isaac Pennington.

107 MJ/GDR (1642/1643), Jeaffreson III, p 87. The date given by Jeaffreson for the recognizance, 18 March 1642, is wrong. Brandon could not have commented on the Lord Mayor's election before this event actually took place.

108 Pearl, *London*, p 157.

109 For references see footnote 1 in *The King's Cabinet opened: Or certain Pacquets of secret Letters and papers. Written with the King's own Hand, and taken in his Cabinet at Naseby Field, June 14, 1645, by victorious Sir Thomas Fairfax*, repr. in *Harleian Miscellany*, ed. T. Parker, 12 vols. (London, 1808–1811), vii, pp 544–77. See also Patterson, *Censorship*, p 209–10.

110 *The King's Cabinet opened. Harleian Miscellany*, vii, p 544.

taken in the King's cabinet were not of the Kinges owne hand-writinge, but that the State did counterfeit his hand', thus imply-ing a political plot on the parliament's side.[111]

The question of allegiance and Civil War directly affected the people, and it is not surprising that it weighed on their minds. William Kendall of St-Martin-le-Grand, button-maker, said 'that all the souldiers who went on the parliament's side were traytors'.[112] According to the information sent by a Suffolk man, Mr Throne, to the House of Commons, Mr Leech, minister, asked him whether his brother 'had associated'. When Throne affirmed, Leech asked: 'Does he find Arms?' Throne answered: 'Yes', and Leech replied: 'He wondered at That they were Traitors by the King's Proclamation.'[113] Some people outrightly refused to ac-cept the Parliament's authority, or boldly expressed their con-tempt for its members. In May 1641, Grace Weaver, mistress of the Spread Eagle in Gracechurch-Street, told Thomas Shawbery, a university student, that 'she hoped to see him upon his Knees, for some Words spoke by him against Mr Pym, a Member of this House'.[114] Shawbery replied 'that he would cut his Throat, and his Sinews in pieces before he would down on his Knees in that sort'. According to witnesses he further called Pym 'King Pym, and Rascal' and said that 'he could find in His Heart to cut King Pym in pieces'. In his choice of language, referring to John Pym as 'King Pym', Shawbery joined the ranks of conservative ob-servers such as Sir Peter Wroth who deeply disapproved of the Puritan influence in Parliament and used the same 'title' in his correspondence.[115] Ballads, too, talked of 'King Pym'.

---

111 MJ/SPR (24 March 1646), Jeaffreson iii, p 99.
112 MJ/SPR (11 October 1642), Jeaffreson iii, p 175.
113 CJ III.27 (3 April 1643).
114 CJ II.478 (15 May 1641).
115 Fletcher, *The Outbreak*, p 129. The term 'King' was attached to Pym as chair of the committee given executive power while the King was in Scotland and the Parliament in recess (September to October 1641). It was used contemp-tuously by critics about his heavy-handed behaviour in that committee.

During 'some Discourse concerning the Parliament' between Nicholas Tabor and John Lindsey, Tabor allegedly said 'That the said Mr John Lowry was an Ass and a Fool'. When Lindsey 'desired him to forbear, telling him he was a Parliamentman', Tabor replied that 'he cared not if Mr Lowry and he both were hanged'. Lindsey 'told him he might be brought upon his Knees for these Words' but Tabor answered that 'the Parliament should not bring him upon his knees'.[116] At a get-together in the Balcony Tavern in Covent Garden on a Saturday night in March 1642, Colonel Francis Edmund made the following statement in the presence of Colonel Gobreth, Serjeant Major Hamilton, Sir Piers Crosby, Mr Bayly, a minister and his father, 'and all Scotts': 'That he was glad his Majesty gave no other Answer to the Militia; and that he did hope his Majesty would display his Banner: And, if Strode, Pym, and Hampden, were in a convenient Place, they should not trouble his Majesty any longer; He would dispatch them.'[117] In an inn at Bromesgrove, in Worcestershire, Robert Smyth declared 'But now that his Majesty had proclaimed that no Ordinance of Parliament did bind without his Majesty's assent unto it; he cared not a Fart for the Parliament Orders: And that a Company of Asses had sat above a twelve month together for nothing but to set Division between his Majesty and his People'.[118] When the collectors William Hawkins and Giles Coxe demanded the weekly assessment of Joseph Griffith, dwelling in Wapping, he answered 'That he cared not, if those Parliamentmen were hanged whose Hands were on the Warrant'.[119] Towards the end of the first phase of the Civil War, Thomas Fellow, dwelling in Monken Hadley in Middlesex, yeoman, was ordered to appear at the next sessions of the peace to be held at Hick's Hall 'to answer for causing his sonne John Fellow to beate Henry Hoare, and for calling the said Henry Hoare roundheaded rogue, and at the same time for

---

116 CJ II.252 (11 August 1641).
117 CJ II.471 (1642).
118 CJ II.530 (April 1642).
119 CJ III. 27 (3 April 1643).

sayinge to bystanders I would the roundheads would rise, we should find as many partakers as they shall; I will spend the dearest blood I have against the Roundheads'.[120] John Draycott of St James Clarkenwell, yeoman, allegedly 'spoke these opprobious and scandalous words 'vizt This Parliament heere is only a parliament of roagues, for they have plundered all honest men, and have not left above three or four honest men in the Cittye of London, but what they have plundered and imprisonment'.[121]

Vox Populi:
Genres of Talk and Common Interpretations
of Politics and Religion 1637 to 1645

People not only commented on the various political and religious phenomena of their time, simply 'calling them names' and placing them on their individual scale of judgement between good and bad, but they also interpreted and analysed contemporary events or passed value judgements on public figures. The interpretation and representation of events or persons which transgressed the immediate everyday life horizon entailed a complex cognitive and communicative process which engaged speaker and hearer alike. The speaker had to relate his or her 'memorized information' of the different components of the 'event' to the actual happening. For instance, memorized information of the conflicts between England and Scotland had to be activated to grasp the outbreak of the Scottish war. In a second more complex cognitive step the event had to be judged with the help of the individual's value and belief system. In turn, the hearer had to deconstruct what was said about the 'event' into its possible interpretations to decide what underlying viewpoint could provoke the offered representation of action or person. In order to

---

120   MJ/SPR (3 September 1644), Jeaffreson iii, p 178.
121   MJ/GDR (4 December 1644), Jeaffreson iii, p 90.

communicate in a meaningful way, both speaker and hearer thus had to share a certain foreknowledge of the issue talked about, a readiness to appropriate new information and a knowledge of the possible ways of interpreting the related incident according to personal background and experience. Sperber and Wilson have convincingly argued that the 'empirically inadequate notion of "mutual knowledge" and the conceptually vague notion of "shared information"' needs to be complemented with an analysis of the individual ways in which humans share information.[122] A person's 'total cognitive environment' (facts that are perceptible or inferable) consists of the fact he/she is aware of *and* capable of becoming aware of. Memorized information thus is a component of cognitive abilities. Consequently, even identical so-called shared information will produce different cognitive results in different individuals. This has already been demonstrated by the various political meanings that were associated with folk heroes in the seventeenth century. The same is true of the various meanings that traditional symbols such as the cross acquired in specific contexts. The interpretation, appropriation, and representation of social and political reality challenged people who engaged in political discourses to transfer experience and knowledge, to contest viewpoints, and to establish personal opinions as a guideline to one's own comprehension and ordering of reality.

Genres of Talk

As national conflicts grew, personal viewpoints gained an additional meaning which went beyond their mere communicative function, signifying further the speaker's or hearer's ('forbidden') political and religious allegiance. At this time of uncertainties and competing belief systems at all levels of society, includ-

---

122 D. Sperber and D. Wilson, *Relevance. Communication and Cognition* (Oxford, 1986), p 39.

ing those in power, individual interpretations of high politics were immediately subject to control. In other words, they were censored. Communication research has shown that under conditions of high excitement and anxiety 'there is usually a relaxation of conventional norms governing communicative behaviour' and rumours spread across subgroups and class boundaries.[123]

It is not surprising that rumours and gossip thrived in the tense atmosphere of the 1640s, and the genres found most frequently in everyday talk were gossip, rumour, (religious) dispute, and news report.[124] In the actual communicative processes of the time, these genres were not always clearly separated. Gossip could often bear elements of story-telling and reports could easily turn into gossip or rumour. However, important characteristics and social functions distinguish these genres from each other. Whereas the meaning of dispute and report is quite straightforward, denoting either the contest of people's viewpoints in direct encounter or the exchange of information, the characteristics of gossip and rumour are more complex. In her essay 'Rethinking Gossip and Scandal', Sally Engle Merry has defined gossip as 'informal, private communication between an individual and a small, selected audience concerning the conduct of absent persons or events'.[125] For gossip to occur, the people involved have to be familiar with the person or event talked about, which requires a certain degree of intimacy, confidence, loyalty, and

---

123 Ralph L. Rosnow and Gary A. Fine, *Rumor and Gossip. The Social Psychology of Hearsay* (New York, Oxford, and Amsterdam, 1976), p 35.

124 Until recently the analysis of genres and styles was the sole domain of literary critics and it was confined to written literary products only. However, in the late 1970s – after some pioneering work by anthropologists on the social functions of gossip (Max Gluckman) – the use of certain genres of talk in everyday spoken language was discovered by neighbouring disciplines. A number of interesting case studies based on field work have been conducted since, and various theories of genres of talk have been developed by linguists, anthropologists, ethnographists, ethnomethodologists, etc.

125 Sally Engle Merry, 'Rethinking Gossip', pp 271–302. The following observations on gossip are based on this article unless otherwise indicated.

exclusiveness on the part of the audience. Gossip can either contain value-free information about a third known party, or it may contain information couched in moral terms with reference to how people should act.

In the context of the 1640s, gossip became politicized and served a double function: it could manifest the speaker's conformity to state and church while passing value judgements on the nonconformist behaviour and opinions of an absent third party, and it could unmask nonconformists among the audience in the communicative process of finding a consensus for the ascribed moral, political, or religious standing. Whereas gossip typically deals with the personal affairs of individuals and their moral or (sometimes far-reaching) political implications, rumours can also deal with events and issues of great importance or magnitude.[126] Furthermore, rumour is a communication constructed around unauthenticated information. Consequently, someone who repeats a rumour is transmitting suspect evidence. The early modern term 'noise' or 'flying speech' for rumour catches this idea of quickly spreading communication whose author and truth value remains in the dark. In contrast, gossip is small talk with or without a known base in fact.

Both gossip and rumour circulate around ambigious situations where the application of conventional cultural meanings (moral/religious/folk belief etc.) is uncertain and people strive to generate shared interpretations of the new meaning of events or behaviour. They thus create cognitive patterns of norms, reputations, and social identities, often resorting to social types as part of a group's shared culture, which denote the moral worth or unworthiness of a specific behaviour or person. In the 1640s these included 'whore' or 'whoremaster', 'rascall', 'knave', 'papist' or 'roundhead'. This aspect of rumour-mongering and gossiping has been described as 'a problem solving transaction in which a form of collective critical ability is operating. It is a means of adapting

---

126   Rosnow and Fine, *Rumor and Gossip*, p 11.

to change, and it facilitates social control when the existing order is believed to be in jeopardy'.[127] This is certainly true for the
communicative behaviour of people in the late 1630s and early
1640s, when everyday talk was increasingly censored. However,
especially at times of social upheaval and war, gossip and rumour
also tend to have disruptive, oppressive, divisive, and destructive
implications.[128] Inauthentic information can intensify people's
general uneasiness while unsustained fears turn into 'facts' and
spread like a contagion from person to person until a whole population has become contaminated.[129] In her study *Rumors, Race,
and Riots*, Terry Ann Knopf has developed a process model of
rumour, which emphasizes the functional basis within certain
contextual features. Using 'racial rumours' as an example she
shows that 'these rumors serve multiple functions: they confirm
hostility as "fact"; and they intensify the underlying emotions.
The social structure, the political climate, and opportunities available for the emergence of a certain rumor – all are contextual
features which assist in determining rumor themes'.[130]

---

127 Ibid., p 55. In his article 'Gossip and Scandal', *Current Anthropology*, 4 (1968),
     pp 307–15, Max Gluckman was the first to stress the harmonious social func-
     tion of gossip. For subsequent studies see the references in Sally Engle Mer-
     ry's article and Don Handelman, 'Gossip in Encounters: The Transmission of
     Information in a Bounded Social Setting', *Man*, 8 (June 1973), pp 210–27, and
     E. B. Almirol, 'Chasing the Elusive Butterfly: Gossip and the Pursuit of Repu-
     tation', *Ethnicity*, 8 (1981), pp 293–304.

128 Engle Merry was one of the first who criticized the assumption that social
     conflict creates social cohesion and order by showing that it 'exaggerates the
     harmonious consequences of gossip while ignoring its disruptive, oppressive,
     divisive, and destructive implications', Engle Merry, 'Rethinking Gossip'. As
     early as the 1930s, studies of war-time rumours pointed to the destructive
     impact of rumour in a society forced to close ranks and to create and segregate
     scapegoats in confronting a common danger. See esp. G. W. Allport and L.
     Postman, *The Psychology of Rumor*, (New York, 1948) and Rosnow and Fine,
     Rumor and Gossip, pp 23–25.

129 Rosnow and Fine, *Rumor and Gossip*, p 34.

130 Terry A. Knopf, *Rumors, Race, and Riots* (New Brunswick and New Jersey,
     1975), quoted in Rosnow and Fine, *Rumor and Gossip*, p 58.

In the early 1640s the politico-religious conflicts and the growing anxiety about national politics let to the rise of 'religious
rumours'. Especially fear of popery and popish plot rumours
flared up between 1640 and 1642 and coincided with the ebb and
flow of political crisis. Catholicism was 'a lurking peril in an un-
prepared country' until war broke out in 1642, the lines between
friend and enemy were clarified, and Catholics became an identifiable group within the opposing army.[131] These 'popish plot rumours' were no isolated phenomenon but belong to a long tradition of Protestant distrust and fear of Catholics in early modern
England. 'Common to all these alarms over Catholics was some
form of crisis or political disaster, sometimes present but often
predicted for the future, and involving anything from foreign
affairs to relations between King and Parliament.'[132] The disruptive impact of these kinds of 'bogey' and 'wedge-driving' rumours
on society is generally attributed to their intensification of la-
tent anxieties and the creation of images of an enemy which di-
vide groups and give rise to aggression and physical violence.[133]

The following case dating from 1640 demonstrates how la-
tent anxieties about Catholics could produce quite vivid rumours
in small-town communities when ambiguous official sympathies
for Catholicism coincided with local novelties in Catholic behaviour. At times of tension no Catholic behaviour was above
suspicion and people carefully observed the houses of Catholics.

---

131 Robert Clifton, 'Popular Fear of Catholics During the English Revolution',
     Past and Present, 52 (1971), pp 23–55, p 33.
132 Clifton, 'Popular Fear', p 43. The background, nature, and disruptive impact
     of anti-popery rumours is well documented in the works of Clifton; Carol Z.
     Wiener, 'The Beleaguered Isle. A study of Eizabethan and early Jacobean Anti-
     Catholicism', Past and Present, 51 (1971), pp 26–62; Caroline Hibbard, Charles
     I and the Popish Plot (Chapel Hill, 1983); Anthony J. Fletcher, A County
     Community in Peace and War: Sussex, 1600–1660 (London, 1980); and John
     Miller, Popery and Politics in England, 1660–1688 (Cambridge, 1973).
133 Rosnow and Fine, Rumor and Gossip, pp 23–25. A well-known typology of
     rumours differentiates between pipe dream or wish rumours which express a
     person's hopes, bogey rumours which mirror fears and anxieties, and wedge-
     driving or aggression rumours which divide groups.

The evolving 'anti-popery' rumours easily created social tension, divided neighbours, and threatened to result in violence. In June 1640 a rumour spread in the neighbouring villages of Woolwich and Plumstad that the high constable 'of the hundred' had searched 'Burridge House meaning Mrs Ratcliff's house' and found ten beds still warm but nobody in them.[134]

Sodowick Pool, dwelling in Woolwich, passed this rumour on to the blacksmith Timothy Scudder in his shop in Plumstead. He further related that he had heard 'that there were fourty to fifty men lately landed on the backside of Mr Voltes warfe [=wharf] at Woolwhich and they went towards Mrs Ratcliffes house called Burridge house'.[135] The rumour about men secretly landing at Woolwich was repeated by several other people with slight variations: Susan Curris, also from Woolwich, claimed to have seen men land at the end of Mr Voltes' wharf on Sunday a fortnight ago between ten and eleven o' clock at night. Some of them carried swords but she did not know whether or not they went towards Burridge House.[136] While loading his cart with bricks Allen Churchmen watched twenty men at least make their way into Mrs Ratcliff's orchard at Plumstead 'but whether they had anie weapons or no he knoweth not'.

When Zacheris (sic) Musgrave, gentleman, and one Brickstock who was in his company, entered George Taylor's victualling house in Woolwich, Taylor's wife Sarah told them about the warm empty beds found in Burridge House. She further said that she 'much wondered what should become of them (who had been in the beds) unless they were in the vault'. For she had heard from

---

134 In the surviving documents Burridge House is never explicitly called a Catholic household. However, hints at 'the papists' at Burridge House and the whole unfolding of the rumour strongly suggest that it was a Catholic household, most likely run by local Catholic gentry. Robert Clifton has shown that 'fears centred repeatedly upon one particular Catholic house or individual Catholic', in 'Popular Fear', p 48.

135 SP 16/456.14 (2 June 1640). Under examination Poole denied 'that he named fortie or fiftie men, but confesseth thirtie men and no more'.

136 SP 16/456.14 (2 June 1640).

Avis, now the maid of Thomas Bartram from Woolwich, that a 'vault was beginning to be made' while Avis was still living at Burridge House.[137] According to Sarah Taylor, the said Mr Musgrave had told her 'in a jesting manner' (obviously appealing to her anti-Catholic sentiments) that the gentleman 'in the grey stokens' was a priest 'if we have anie'. Zacheris Musgrave was the master of one Ralph Henshaw, and both seem to have had ties with Burridge House. Furthermore, there was apparently some tension between the staff of Burridge House and the master workmen, among them one Thomas Bartram, at the King's ropery in Woolwich. When Bartram and Henshaw met one evening in Woolwich and went to the local tavern, Bartram questioned the latter about the most recent news at Burridge House. Henshaw answered that 'there is small news there, you heare all the vaults are founde, and therefore I hope you will nowe be quiet'. According to Bartram, Henshaw had asked him whether or not he was one of the master workmen in the 'king's rope yard', and when Bartram affirmed, Henshaw replied: 'There will shortly be a hott day in the rope yard, and the men there shall rue for it by reason of the Papists at Burridge house.' Henshaw's testimony declares that 'Bartram said unto one Artyn Buck, go with this fellow (Henshaw) home to his Masters house, for feare that he and the rest that belonge to Burridge house should sett the kings rope yard on fire to revenge them selves for the report that have bine raised against them'.[138]

The rumours that were spread about Burridge House took a final turn when Richard Symes, dwelling in Woolwich, told Zacheris Musgrave that 'he heard it was reported' that Archbishop Laud had recently visited Burridge House.[139] Laud's alleged visit most likely supported the rumours about mysterious activities in Burridge House. In popular hearsay he 'was turned papist'

---

137 SP 16/456.13 (2 June 1640).
138 SP 16/456.14 (2 June 1640).
139 SP 16/456.15 (2 June 1640).

himself, and his contact with the inhabitants of Burridge House must have intensified the widespread rumour that in Burridge House men in arms, 'papists', were hiding ready to overturn the state and church.

Rumours in the 1640s, however, did not spring from traditional animosities and stereotypes alone; the political issues of the day caught the public imagination just as well. Events which occupied pamphleteers, dominated political debate, and were a recurrent theme in correspondence and newsletters also spilled over into everyday life talks: the Scottish war, the dissolution of the Parliament and riots in London, the Irish rebellion, and the political role of Archbishop Laud. In a particular study of discourses about the Scottish war and riots in London the following sections will look at the various ways and genres in which these events were interpreted and represented by ordinary men and women in the pursuit of their everyday tasks.

Common Interpretations of Politics and Religion

The government's nervousness about the political deadlock between England and Scotland, the 'rebellious' behaviour of many women and 'the rude sort of people in Edinburgh [who] made a tumultous outcry that they would have no bishops',[140] and the outbreak of war found expression not only in more severe censorship of pamphlets and manuscripts touching on the 'Scottish affair' but also in a heightened sensitivity to discourses about these issues. In 1639 a hectic inquiry was launched by the Privy Council concerning the whereabouts of Scots in London and 'disorderly gatherings' which were liable to breed seditious talks. The justices of the peace duly returned notes listing the various

---

140 SP 16/425.22, 1639. In her letter to Secretary Windebank, Mary Countess of Westmoreland referred to the hearsay about women's participation in the Scottish war: 'They say the women of Scotland are chief stirrers of this war.' SP 16/420.70 (May 1639).

dwellings of Scots, among other places at Blackfriars, Lombard
Street, Rood Lane, and Mill Dock.[141] Furthermore, the lord mayor
of London and the justices of the peace for Middlesex were ordered to suppress certain victualling houses after the councillors
provided them with information about 'many disorderly gatherings at the house of John Carr, in St Mary-at-Hill, at the sign of
the Ball; at Mrs Ramseys near the same place, adjoining to the
Pied Dog; at James Nemock's at Young's Quay; and at Andrew
Adamsons at the Scottish Arms by the Millbank, at the further
end of St Katherine's, in which houses are kept ordinaries for all
sorts of people.'[142] Nemock must have been denounced to the
Privy Council as a harbourer of the King's Scottish enemies, in-
dicating anti-Scottish feelings. That this was not one of the routine actions against unlicensed victualling houses is conveyed by
the reiterated question about seditious discourses or speeches
during the examinations of the householders.[143] John Carr replied that 'he never heard any seditious discourse used in his
house, which he conceives is not a proper place for it'.[144] Nevertheless, his house was searched and a 'great trade with all Scottish ships' was discovered.[145] Furthermore, Carr was 'in great
suspicion to have received and scattered some of the Covenanters seditious pamphlets'.

James Nemock, tailor, kept a house in the parish of St Dunstan
in the West 'to lodge such guests as come thither, and so has

---

141 SP 16/418.85, 1639. For 'the return of the Justices of the Peace of the countie
     of Middlesex' of Irish residents living in the suburbs and Middlesex see H.L.M.P.
     13 November 1641; For the 'return of the Justices of the Peace for the Citty
     and liberty of Westminster' of Irish residents living in the city see H.L.M.P. 13
     November 1641.

142 SP 16/420.154–54i (1639); SP 16/421.26 (1639).

143 See, for instance, the report of the justices of the peace for Middlesex about
     unlicensed alehouses within Covent Garden. SP 16/421.26 (1639). For the
     regulation and licensing of alehouses in general see Peter Clark, *The English
     Alehouse* (London/New York, 1983), pp 166–94.

144 SP 16/418.37 (1639).

145 SP 16/418.99 (1639).

done for 30 years past'.[146] He explained that his guests sometimes ate at his house, 'they being for the most part Scottish
skippers and seamen'. Since the 'beginning of the troubles in Scotland', he had no constant lodgers in his house, 'but sometimes
some would desire to lodge there, whom he always entertained'.
Nemock assured the examiners that 'he never had any munition
laid in his house to be shipped, or any packs of buff or other
leather, nor never knew any such things shipped by his own countrymen'. He never heard any seditious discourse used in his house.
Andrew Adamson admitted that his victualling house was sometimes frequented by Scots who also took lodging there. Yet he
also claimed never to have heard 'any seditious discourse used in
his house'.[147] He further said that 'Scottishmen' mainly lodged
with one Taylor 'at the sign of the Flushing in Wapping or St.
Katherine's', and in the house of 'the keeper of the Star Tavern
there'.

Although these examinations might not have proved very successful from the point of view of the examiners, the authorities
certainly were on the right track. During his visit to London in
May 1639, two months after the King and his army had moved
North towards the Scottish border, Edward Thursby of Gatewick,
Essex, heard 'some newes concerning the Scottish business',
which he told the 'chief women' of his parish who were visiting
his wife 'that lyes in': 'That divers of our men were gone into the
north to provide for defence against the Scotts, and that some
verses were made which came to my Lord of Hollanders [sic]
hand, seven libells as he heard wherein the Scots desired some of
the Bishops and that thereupon the King sent for the Archbishop
of Canterbury.'[148] Being pressed with further questions about the
meaning of his words, Thursby 'denyeth that he ever said my
Lord Grace of Canterbury was gone out of the way onely he said

---

146 SP 16/418.42 (1639).
147 SP 16/418.55 (1639).
148 SP 16/423.132 (29 May 1639).

he heard that His Grace was to goe to the King about the 14th of May'. He further claimed that 'he rememberes not from whom he heard this newes *but that it was spoken about the Towne*'. However, in the course of the examination 'he called to mind that one Rowland Keely, taylor, dwelling in Sheere lane told it him'. In an attempt to ease his case Edward Thursby emphasized that Keely 'reported it to him for truth, which made this examinant tell it with the more confidence'.

From its very beginning the conflict between England and Scotland was accompanied by a wave of propaganda pamphlets struggling to win English sympathies for the Covenanters' cause.[149] These pamphlets were tailored to fit a popular English audience, emphasizing their mutual interest in fighting popery while launching a fierce attack on episcopacy in both countries. Especially English bishops were presented as capable of incensing the King so much that he would go to war. In spite of rigorous attempts to intercept pamphlets and letters at the Scottish border they reached England, often via the Low Countries, in large numbers.[150] The libels 'wherein the Scots desired some of the Bishops' obviously reached a large popular audience, 'being spoken about the town' and passed on to men and women outside the City by word of mouth and in private letters. The wife of Mr Dove and Mrs Hiegate, 'who is now at London', had been among the women visiting Mrs Thursby when her husband returned from London with his news. Mrs Dove passed on Thursby's news to her husband who informed an acquaintance of his, Dr Robert Aylett, about it in a letter.[151] The content of these libels seems to have stirred people's imaginations when they

---

149 See P. Donald, *An Uncounselled King. Charles I and the Scottish troubles, 1637–1641*, Cambridge Studies in Early Modern British History (Cambridge, 1990), especially chps. 4 and 5.

150 For the printing of Scottish pamphlets under cover in the Low Countries see P. Donald, *An Uncounselled King*, p 188.

151 SP 16/421.21 (1639).

drew their own connections between Laud's departure to York and the Scots' demand for English bishops.

In April 1639, William Goward of Lambeth, waterman, testified under examination that he went into the house of Robert Harrison of Lambeth to drink a cup of beer. While he was sitting there a stranger came in about eight or nine o' clock at night, called for a mug of beer and said 'there was a Scotch two pence for you'. After the stranger had taken a seat he suddenly said 'I must or will have this Bishops head'. When William Goward inquired which bishop he meant 'whether it were any of the Bishops of Scotland because he heard one was coming up' the former replied 'noe not he but the little Bishop of Lambeth or Canterbury which of them this Informant knoweth not but he was sure one was spoken'. The stranger further informed that Marquis Douglas was come up to the King with a submission 'as he conceiveth And the kinge was graciously pleased, if they did all submit by the 10th of May they should have a pardon'.[152] Apart from Goward there were two women present in the room, Jane Grubie, servant to Robert Harrison, 'sitting at her work when the stranger came in', and Joane Liggs, a lodger.[153] Both affirmed that the guest asked for the bishop's head calling him 'the little man of Lambeth', a popular reference to Archbishop Laud who was known to be very short. The stranger turned out to be one Anthonie Botheway of the parish of St Sepulchre near Smithfield, who was a clothworker by trade 'but followeth day labour and hath lived this three yeares in Cow lane and hath beaten Tobacco with John Smart of the libertie of the Tower this half yeare and with Mr Pease of St Lawrence lane six yeares before'. During his examination Botheway vehemently denied having spoken of the bishop at all, emphasizing that he truly 'detests and abhors' the words alleged against him. The only reason why he came to Lambeth was to demand 10 shillings which were owed to him by one

---

152 SP 16/417.97i (14 April 1639).
153 SP 16/417.97ii (14 April 1639).

William Glen, Mr Freeman's man. However, as for the other statements he had made, Botheway disclosed how he had obtained the
relevant information:

> He saith that there was a gentleman one Mr Fardell who lives in
> glasiers house at long lane and next to the sign of the beare who read
> a letter sent from Yorke unto him some times this last weeke import-
> ing that the castle of Edingburgh was taken and that Marquis Doug-
> las was come up to his Majesty at York and submitted himselfe And
> that the king was gratiously pleased that if all the rest of the Scotts
> would submitt he would grant them pardon and their lands again.[154]

With slight distortions this letter probably referred to a proclamation written by Sir John Hay, 'one of the many now in exile
from Scotland', after the King had reached York.[155] It 'offered
pardon to all those in Scotland who would submit on certain
terms'.[156]

Disagreement arose in everyday life talks about the true causes
of the Scottish war and the Scots' intentions, and rumours spread
across the whole country. In July 1640, when walking from King-
ston to Wanting, Thomas Webb of the county of Wiltshire, clothier, was overtaken by the husbandman William Horne of South
Fowl, Berkshire. He asked Horne whether there were any soldiers coming that way, which Horne denied, adding that some
soldiers had passed by Hungerford the week before. After some
talk about wool prices in their respective home counties, they
exchanged the most recent news. Whereas Webb denied knowing any, Horne said 'that he had heard that the apprentices did
rise in London and would destroy the Bishop'.[157] When Webb
inquired after the reason for this rising, Horne answered 'that

---

154 For references to the Marquis of Douglas see P. Donald, *An Uncounselled*
     King, p 71, p 129, p 227.
155 Ibid., p 139.
156 Ibid., p 138.
157 SP 16/461.46ii (26 July 1640). This statement refers to the Lambeth riots after
     the dissolution of the Short Parliament in May 1640.

there was a *noise* in the country that it was thought it was because my Lord Canterbury was turned papist'. According to
Webb's testimony, Horne had further said 'that he thought we
should have a pitiful time'.[158] And when Webb asked 'why', he
replied 'that it was Bishop Laud who was the cause of the rising
of all this army and that the king was ruled by him'. For further
clarification Webb wanted to know which of the bishops the said
Bishop Laud was and Horne explained 'that Bishop Laud was
Bishop of Canterbury, and that he was turned papist and that it
was well known'. Obviously disagreeing and aware of the potential danger inherent in such seditious words, Webb inquired after
Horne's name and address and reported the whole case to Secretary Windebank.

The rumour that Laud 'was turned papist' spread across the
country during the Scottish war and took different forms including fictitious elements.[159] The following case demonstrates
the way in which a craftsman reproduced this 'noise' in translating 'facts' into little 'images and stories' which seem to have been
closer to his mental world and his way of appropriating the world
around him. At the same time he used symbols signifying popery (the cross and the crucifix), which were well known during
this period through woodcuts and pamphlets. In this particular
case popular ideas about monster births which were interpreted
as signs of divine displeasure might also have influenced the rumour.[160] While in Maiden Bradley on 6 June 1640, the clothier

---

158 SP 16/461.46i (25 July 1640).
159 In this context 'fictitious' elements in everyday talk does not mean lies, which
     they are usually classified as in communication research. See, for instance, W.-
     D. Stempel, 'Fiktion in Konversationellen Erzählungen', in *Funktionen des
     Fiktiven*, Poetik und Hermeneutik, 10, ed. D. Henrich and Wolfgang Iser
     (Munich, 1983), pp 331–56. Instead they are cultural expressions which con-
     vey the cognitive ability of people who need to translate 'facts' into codes
     (little stories or images) which correspond to their own mental world.
160 Although the explanations of monster births as final causes (divine will) started
     to give way to proximate ones (physical explanations and the natural order) in
     the seventeenth century, broadsides, ballads, religious literature and sermons

Thomas Webb met William Collyer, a starchmaker from Bristol. They traded a horse, and during the habitual exchange of news Collyer related that there was news in Bristol that Archbishop Laud 'was turned Papist, and that the King and his jester had found the cross and the crucifix in his breast'.[161] At a meeting of ministers in Kettering at the sign of the Swan in August 1640, Mr [James ?] Cranford, parson of Brocball [sic], passed on the following rumour about the Scots 'in the hearing of Samuel Lynell, host of the Red Lyon, and John Baxter, host of the Swan'.[162] He reported that the Scots had invaded England as far as a 'certain days journey' with an army and 10,000 beasts and 40,000 sheep. Referring to the Scottish army as the source of information, Cranford further explained that 'the intent of the Scots' coming was only to have two men ready vizt. the Archbishop and the Lord Lieutenant of Ireland'.[163] Before crossing the Tweed in August 1640, the Scots had prepared their invasion by issuing pamphlets which emphasized the mutual aims of England and Scotland in their struggle against popery, and called for the English authors of the troubles (Laud and Strafford) to be tried and punished in an English Parliament.[164]

---

continued to emphasize the spiritual and apocalyptic implications of prodigies. Katherine Park and Lorraine J. Daston, 'Unnatural Conceptions: The Study of Monsters in Sixteenth- and Seventeenth-Century France and England', *Past and Present*, 92 (1981), pp 20–54.

161 SP 16/456.36 (6 June 1640). Thomas Webb is the same as the above-mentioned Thomas Webb who discussed the cause of the Scottish war with one William Horne. Both cases ended with Webb informing about someone who accused Laud of having turned papist. He possibly was an official informant.

162 SP 16/465.65 (28 August 1640). See also the pamphlet *The Liar*, which reports of the birth of a child with a mark on its breast like a crucifix.

163 'The Scots invaded England, routed the English at Newburn and on 29 August took Newcastle.' J. P. Kenyon, *Stuart England*. The Pelican History of England (London, 1978; 2nd edn, 1985), p 130. Mr Cranford is almost certainly James Cranford, one of the Scottish ministers who attended the peace negotiation in London and the author of *The Scots Intentions*.

164 Donald, *An Uncounselled King*, pp 245–48.

One of the most widely spread pamphlets was *The Intentions of the Army of Scotland* on which Cranford's information was probably based. His rumour about the Scots' intentions provides further evidence that 'sympathies ran between the nations' with regard to the 'popish plot theme' which 'easily linked upset of religion with upset of state'.[165] For a long time Laud had been accused of popery, and Strafford lost all public sympathy when it became known that he was negotiating with Catholic Spain for military assistance against Scotland and intended to bring over the Irish army into England. One of the ways in which the notorious *Intentions of the Army of Scotland* were passed on in print or writing is shown in the following case. Likewise in August, John Fryer, carpenter, who was billeted in the White Hart Inn in Bocking, a village in Essex, was asked by one Edward Cole of Barfolk, Suffolk, whether he was a soldier. Fryer affirmed, and Cole asked him to walk down the street with him. When they entered Braintree churchyard, Cole told Fryer 'that there were books come from the Scots, signifying what they intended to do in England, and asked him what he would say if he should show him one of them, adding that he would warrant that if he and the rest of the soldiers had such a book amongst them they would make fine sport with it'.[166] Fryer answered 'that he would go a mile to see such a book', whereupon Cole bade him to wait and disappeared behind the church 'to see if he could find one'. Returning shortly afterwards he told Fryer 'that there lay a paper which he believed was such a book' and handed him 'a groat [four pence] and bade him good night'. Before departing he warned the soldier not to tell anyone from where he had the book nor to disclose his name 'for it were known that [if] a rich man had such a book it were as much as his living were worth, but that the soldiers might use it'. Fryer went to the appointed place and 'found the book rolled up and lying in one of the arches of the church'.

---

165 Ibid., p 132.
166 SP 16/465.43 (29 August 1640).

Doubts about the justification of the war against the Scots were freely expressed. On 20 August 1640, Samuel Cole and John Crosse, both clothiers of Dedham in Essex, ate their supper in the common dining room of the Green Dragon in Bishopsgate Street in London, where a footpost arrived every Wednesday carrying letters between London and Bury St Edmunds, Suffolk.[167] Cole and Crosse were frequent guests here, and the mistress of the house, Anne Anderson, and a 'stranger' sat with them at the same table. Edward Rand of Lougham, Essex, also a clothier and well acquainted with Cole and Crosse, had already finished his supper and was leaning against the board. Statements about other people present varied, but seemed to agree that there were, besides the tapster and the servant, Ingleby Proctor who came later, one or two ministers, one of them called Mr Cooper, one person all in black, one Nicolas whose surname was not known, and 'many other people' at a long table in the room 'among whom at the upper end sat a minister'.[168] 'About supper time', captain John Watt being 'very merry and pleasant' entered the 'ordinary room' of the Green Dragon, and joined Cole and Crosse at their table.[169] They asked him whether the King had gone north. And when Watt 'told them, yes', the two clothiers replied that they would not believe it, and inquired laughingly 'what should he do there?'[170] According to Watt's testimony the following dialogue developed:

Watt:
I told them I met his Majesty upon the road near and the report was that the Scottish Army was marching in England; and I believed his Majesty's care was for theirs and all his other English subjects' safety.

Cole and Crosse 'pished and gearingly said' among 'many more disloyal and disaffecting words of his Majesty':

---

167 Taylor, *Cosmographie*.
168 SP 16/466.114 (9 September 1640).
169 SP 16/464.57 (20 August 1640); SP 16/466.114 (9 September 1640).
170 SP 16/464.57 (20 August 1640).

What need the King trouble himself so much, the Scots are honest people and will do us no harm but rather good.

Watt answered:
I told them they were base fellows to speak so much against their own souveraign, and applaud the Scots which had been so disobedient against their native King; and said I believed they were of that Puritan faction which would rather side with the Scots than with their own King, if they were near them.

Cole and Crosse responded:
Sirrah, it is no matter if you were hanged. The other called me rascall, continuing their censorious and abusive speeches of the King's acts in his proceedings against the Scots. And said they were honest men as any that spake against them.

Biased in his report, Watt missed out on a few details to which all the other people examined had testified. He allegedly spoke 'of certain Puritans here about London and elsewhere that would furnish the King with no money, nor lend any thing'. Furthermore, when he accused Cole and Crosse of being of the Puritan faction, they asked him 'what a Puritan was', whereupon he lost his temper, threw a trencher and a beaker at them and struck Cole with his sword. The evidence suggests that Watt had walked into one of the many London alehouses or taverns which were frequented mainly by Puritans and 'appear to have been centres of political agitation at this time'.[171] All the surviving depositions support Cole's and Crosse's account, which was unusual for a mixed tavern company, especially in the case of such allegations.[172] There was, furthermore, the professed 'well acquaintance' among most of the people, the presence of at least one minister, and the seating arrangement at a long table with the minister at one end. The assurance of like-minded friends prob-

171 Pearl, *London*, p 233.
172 Furthermore, their petitions to Secretary Windebank were supported by a letter written by their neighbour in Dedham, who testified to Cole's and Crosse's good fame, SP 16/466.93 (8 September 1640).

ably encouraged Cole and Crosse to be so frank in uttering their opinions.[173] Nevertheless, on 11 September 1640 the Privy Council ordered that Cole and Crosse 'who were formerly committed to the Gatehouse upon the complaint of Captain Watt shall not be released until they under their hands have acknowledged their offence'.[174]

On Tuesday, 18 September 1640, at about three o'clock, several people had already assembled in Robert Stone's warehouse in Bartholomew Lane, when he entered his shop, coming from an upper floor of his house. Richard Bateman, son of Robert Bateman, city chamberlain and treasurer of the East India Company, and Robert Bowles, beadle of Breadstreet ward, had come to look at Stone's armour. Anthony Dyett, a gentleman, had entered the shop eager to pass on the most recent news about the Scottish war. Stone later testified that 'at my saluting Mr Dyett he took out a letter or the copy of a letter which he told me was written from his father Sir Robert Dyott'.[175] Dyett invited Bateman to listen, too, since he was a man 'that looked with an honest face and one that seemed to wish well to his Majesty's design'.[176] Bowles claimed that he arrived at the shop when Dyott was already reading the letter to Stone while Bateman was standing by listening. Although he did not pay much attention to what was being said 'coming in there about other business and having his mind also full of grief for the loss of his eldest son in the war',[177] Bowles gave the following account:

---

173 It seems less likely that Cole and Crosse had simply taken the opportunity to get first-hand information from an army officer, only uttering slight doubts which provoked Watt to defame them as Puritans (the logical 'opposite' to himself as a loyal subject to the King) and finally to physical violence.

174 PC.2.52.725 (11 September 1640).

175 SP 16/466.248 (September 1640). Within the documents the spelling of this name alternates between 'Dyett' and 'Dyott'.

176 SP 16/466.285 (September 1640).

177 Bowles' son 'served as a horseman under the Lord Conway, and was slain in the face in counter with the rebels' SP 16/466.286 (September 1640).

When he (Mr Dyett) came to that passage of the letter which mentioned a petition that had been delivered to his Majesty by some
lords to his best remembrance the said gentleman said that such as
did advice the King to pacify with the Scots did dishonour the King;
or to that effect. Whereunto Mr Bateman (as this examinant
remembereth) answeared that they that were the first cause of this
dissention betwixt the two kingdomes did more dishonour the
King.[178]

Other witnesses disagreed with Bowles' testimony, accusing
Bateman of having said 'that the King was gone upon a dishon-
ourable action against the Scots' and that 'he could wish those
were hanged that were the plotters to set the kingdomes of England and Scotland together by the ears'.[179] Again pleading inno-
cence because of his grief, Bowles admitted that in answer to
some comments about Puritans uttered by Dyett he said that for
his part he thought them honest men. According to Robert Stone
and Anthony Dyett, both Bateman and Bowles had said that the
letter was written by some Jesuit or papist which probably provoked the talk about Puritans.[180]

For some people the absence of the King from London created the impression of a power vacuum. On 16 May 1639, Mr
Arnold and Mr Stephens met at the house of Christopher
Bawcock, victualler, in Thames Street, London, to sign an agreement.[181] There they overheard the following discourse about meat
between the victualler, one Robert Griffin, glover, of St Giles
Cripplegate, Peter Johnson, mariner, of East Smithfield, and John
Hame likewise of East Smithfield. When Griffin stated that there
was a law forbidding any sale of meat on Fridays and Sundays,

---

178 Ibid. On 28 August 1640 a petition had been sent to Charles I by twelve Eng-
     lish peers asking the King 'for redress of particular grievances and especially
     for an end to the war'. Donald, *An Uncounselled King*, p 248.
179 Francis Beller, Stone's servant; Benjamin Stone, Stone's son, SP 16/466.286
     (September 1640); Anthony Dyett, SP 16/466.250 (September 1640).
180 SP 16/466.250 (September 1640) and SP 16/466.248 (September 1640).
181 SP 16/422.69 (16 May 1639).

Bawcock 'earnestly' asked who made those laws?[182] Griffin replyed 'the king and the Counsell', whereupon Bawcock said 'that those lawes were made but by ill conditioned men'. Griffin's warning 'to take head what he said' only provoked the victualler to bolder language. And when Griffin tried to caution him a second time, saying 'he would not say so much for all the wealth that ever he saw', Bawcock answered 'that one may say any thing for the king was now at York'. Whereas Bawcock felt a new freedom of speech, other people went further and saw a chance for action during the King's preoccupation with the Scots. In August 1640, while the King summoned a Great Council of the peerage to York to discuss the political situation, Mrs Anne Hussey, exhausted from sleepless nights, was desperate 'to impart some secret business concerning the state of this kingdom to her husband now at Southhampton'.[183] Unable to reach him, and probably encouraged by Mrs Streeter, the mistress of her present lodging in Drury Lane, she decided to inform one Philip Bainbridge of Shire Lane about the 'business'. Bainbridge had already been given the gist of the news by Mrs Streeter: Mrs Hussey was an Irish woman from the family of Lord Hussey, and had received some news from a Mr Conyard (= William O' Connor), an Irish priest and confessor to the Queen.[184] Bainbridge was reluctant to listen to Anne Hussey's account but finally gave in to Mrs Streeter's request, and they retired to an upper room of the house 'where Mrs Hussey spoke these words privately to me, and asked my advice therein vizt':

> That Mr Conyard told her the Catholics were glad the King went speedily into Scotland, for ere he returned there would be a great change, and he was assured the Catholics in England would flourish more in England than they had these many years, for some good reasons that he would show. To which Mrs Hussey replied, as she told me, and demanded how that could be, he answered his Queen

---

182 SP 16/422.70 (16 May 1639).
183 SP 16/464.31 (18 August 1640).
184 William O' Connor was a servant to the Queen Mother.

was no fool, for there were 7,000 men and more in readiness to perform her designs (help the Catholics), and the end of last month he brought another man with him, and said he was one of the officers of war, and thereupon he drew out a pipe and began to sound, and said within 20 days she would see more. Mrs Hussey further saith that last month he came to her and told her he was going to the Spanish, Venetian, and French ambassadors, to send messages to the Pope, and he then said he had three letters about him directed to the Pope. She saith that at that time she said to him that it was impossible to overcome the King by the sword, to which she answered if it could not be done otherwise his hand should do it. All this was said in Irish.

The case soon reached the ears of the Privy Council, and Anne Hussey and William O'Connor, who was already committed to the Gatehouse, were referred to the justices of the peace for Middlesex for examination.[185] Furthermore, special order was given 'to the sheriffs of London to receave into their charge the person of the said Mrs Hussey and to dispose of her in some such safe place as she may be free from any violence or danger'. The background of these unusual security measures was 'credible' information that Anne Hussey had been threatened by 'certaine Irish people to bee mischieved, and that there have been some Irish to inquire after her as it is strongly suspected to offer some violence' because she had given testimony 'of certaine lewd and traiterous speeches uttered by one William O' Conner an Irish Priest'.[186]

On the occasion of Strafford's impeachment on 11 November 1640, Pym 'began to educate his colleagues in the full horror of the papist design'.[187] In this context he referred to William O'Connor's relation about the impending Catholic upheaval against the English Protestants. In the summer of 1641, several

---

185 PC 2.52.725, 11 September 1640. For an earlier examination of William O'Connor see SP 16/420.50 (May 1639).
186 Ibid. The order to protect Anne Hussey was renewed on 4 October 1640. PC 2.53.15.
187 Fletcher, *The Outbreak*, p 4.

pamphlets appeared with a full account of the discourse between Anne Hussey and the Irish priest, thus lending further support to the flourishing popish plot theories spread by Pym's circle.[188] The increasing anxiety on the outbreak of war not only prepared the ground for rumours and provoked heated discussions, but also triggered off unrest and riots, especially in London.

Riots in London

Disorder and riots were a familiar scene in seventeenth-century London and were part of the everyday experience of traditional holidays and festivals.[189] The authorities anticipated trouble and took precautionary measures so that the 'insolencies *usually* committed in London on May Day [could] be suppressed'.[190] However, disorder in the early 1640s entered a new dimension for various reasons which have been well summarized by Keith Lindley.

> The period from the dissolution of the Short Parliament to Charles's final departure from London witnessed disorder on an unprecedented scale as an explosive combination of political crisis, trade depression and plague, and a resurfaced and newly confident religious radicalism was ignited by rumour and panic fears, and the population of the cities of London and Westminster, the suburbs and the south bank of the Thames took to the streets in their thousands to demonstrate or take direct action.[191]

---

188 *A Discovery To the prayse of God, and joy of all true hearted Protestants, of a late intended plot by the Papists to subdue the Protestants. Being a true Copie of a Discourse between William O' Conner a Priest, and Anne Hussey an Irish Gentlewoman.* Printed Anno, 1641. William Clark Collection BB.I.14 (28); a different edition with a woodcut: William Clark Collection BB.W.4.(28); BM E.158.4.

189 For a general survey of traditional acts of 'ritualized' violence in Stuart London see Peter Burke, 'Popular culture in seventeenth-century London', *The London Journal*, 3 (1977), pp 144–6.

190 PC.2.52.450 (1640) For precautions against disorders on Shrove Tuesday see PC.2.51.300. On riot prevention in general during this period see the superb article by Lindley, 'Riot Prevention', pp 109–26.

191 Ibid., pp 115–16.

These riots are well documented and details need not be reiterated here.[192] Panic fears, however, were not only expressed in demonstrations and endless rumours about plots, but became a daily physical reality which changed people's everyday life routines and the familiar scenes around them, causing a constant sense of emergency with psychological consequences that we can only speculate about. One of the most visible reminders of danger was the fortification of London in 1642 and 1643. The Venetian Ambassador reported home:

> There is no street, however little frequented, that is not barricaded with heavy chains, and every post is guarded by numerous squadrons. At the approaches to London they are putting up trenches and small forts of earthworks at which a great number of people are at work, including the women and little children.[193]

Furthermore, orders were issued to set up double watches who became a visible presence about London 'which fills every one with fear and apprehension of greater evils';[194] vagrants and 'idle' persons were more severely prosecuted, in each case creating a great stir when they were apprehended with many people watching;[195] companies were ordered to provide the City with an additional 200 barrels of gun powder;[196] householders were held responsible for the quiet behaviour of their apprentices and servants;[197] the names of the participants in 'rebellious assemblies' were published in proclamations and posted up in markets, the chief streets of London, and the suburbs;[198] and finally, in De-

---

192 Lindley, 'Riot Prevention'; Pearl, *London*; and Manning, *The English People*.
193 Brett-James, *Stuart London*, p 270.
194 SP 16/486.90 (December 1641). For orders of double watches see, for instance, Rep. of the Court of Aldermen, May 1640, p 192, and August 1640, p 272; PC.2.52.482–484, May 1640; and especially Lindley, 'Riot Prevention'. For an example of riot prevention in an individual ward in London, see *Precepts from the Lord Mayor to the Aldermen of Aldersgate ward*, Guildhall MS.1509.
195 For instance PC.2.52.483 (May 1640).
196 Rep. of the Aldermen (May 1640), p 192.
197 SP 16/480.16 (May 1640).
198 PC.2.52.493 (15 May 1640).

cember 1641, the King ordered the lord mayor to raise trained bands in case people refused to retire home peaceably, explicitly approving the use of brutal force if necessary: 'You command the captains and officers of the bands by shooting with bullets or otherwise to slay and kill such of them as shall persist in their tumultuary and seditious ways and disorders.'[199]

The participation of many people, men and women, in such 'rebellious assemblies' is an established fact.[200] However, hardly anything is known about individual participants, their motives for participation, and their individual perceptions of these tumults.The following case studies of the tumults of May 1640 may perhaps stimulate the debate about whether the demonstrators were an apolitical rabble or thinking individuals.

On 6 May 1640, one day after the Parliament had been dissolved, papers appeared throughout the City urging the apprentices to join in a hunt for 'William the Fox' – Archbishop Laud – who was held responsible for the dissolution of Parliament.[201] Three days later a libel appeared exhorting all apprentices to sack the archbishop's house at Lambeth on the following Monday: 'Come now and help us that we may destroy this subtle fox and hunt this ravening wolf out of his den which daily plotteth mischief and seeks to bring this whole land to destruction by his popish intentions, Canterbury we mean.'[202] At the opening of Parliament in April 1640 rumours had already been circulating about possible acts of revenge in case the Parliament should be dissolved. Samuel Plumley, servant of James Bowyer, 'one of the clerks in the office of the six clerks in Chancery lane', was accused on 7 April 1640 of having spread the following rumour:

---

199 SP 16/486.99 (28 December 1641). For similar orders to raise trained bands see PC.2.52.490–494
200 For the participation of women see Higgins, 'The Reactions of Women', in *Politics, Religion*, ed. Manning, pp 179–222.
201 Pearl, *London*, pp 107–108.
202 Lambeth Laud Misc 943, 717, cit. in *Stuart Royal Proclamations*, II, ed. J. F. Larkin (Oxford, 1983), p 711.

'That if the parliament should be dissolved, he heard that his Graces house of Canterbury at Lambeth should be fixed, and that they would keep his Lordship in until he should be burnt, and that thousands would say as much as he sayd who spoke these words.'[203] Refusing at first 'to discover of whom these words were spoken or in whose company besides himself',[204] Plumley finally made a full confession.[205] About six or seven days before the dissolution of the Parliament he sat down to dinner in the cellar of 'Symons Inns' with 'some gentlemen' and Samuel Day of Dowgate, skinner, Edward Symons, tailor in Lombard Street, and William Hicks, clerk under Mr May's clerks of the warrants in the court of Common Pleas in Middle Temple Lane. One of the gentlemen, William Knight, clerk under Mr Farmor in the Supreme office, said 'that if the Parliament were dissolved it was reported that Blackhall would be fired and by this Black Hall he *conceaves* is meant my Lord Archbishop of Canterbury his house. And that they would keep his Grace in it till he were burnt'.[206] Under examination Knight acknowledged part of the charge without remembering any talk about the burning of Laud 'nor any discourse upon the name of Blackhall'.[207] He himself had heard it reported as a 'flying speech' and could not remember who had told it to him.

During the tumultuous weeks of May 1640, Richard Beaumont, servant and apprentice of James James, a London apothecary, heard 'the report of the tumult in Southwark on Thursday night from three or four in Southwark who were called up to support them' when he was carrying some 'physick' to one of his

---

203 SP 16/458.182 (7 April 1640).
204 Ibid., (1 May 1640).
205 SP 16/451.81ii, (5 June 1640).
206 Ibid. Blackhall was a joke on 'Whitechapel', the royal palace. Black was the symbol of evil, and hall formed a minimal pair with hell: Blackhall thus signified the 'mouth of hell' which was frequently pictured in woodcuts in association with the papists including Archbishop Laud.
207 SP 16/451.183 (5 June 1640).

master's patients there on Friday morning.[208] Back in the City he heard more news in the house of Elizabeth Williamson, a perfumer dwelling behind the Old Exchange. Her servant, John Flagmore, and two other men were discussing 'the tumult at Lambeth on Monday afternoon', stating that the apprentices did not pull down the bishop's house on the holiday last but would do so during the Whitsun holiday.[209] Mrs Williamson and Beaumont's sixteen-year-old fellow-servant, Edmund Wilson, who had heard the following rumour in a grocer's shop near their master's house, informed them that the apprentices planned to pull down the Queen Mother's house and Somerset House Chapel because they were houses of popery. They further related that the apprentices had sent word to the Lord Arundel who dwelt in the Strand that they heard he had mounted ordinance against them in George Field, and therefore 'if he did shoot they would pull down his house and not leave one stone upon another'.[210] Beaumont passed these rumours straight on to Richard Spratt, a waterman. He further testified that he heard from one Gerrard Oglethorpe, an attorney's clerk dwelling in Lawrence Lane, that Archbishop Laud had a crucifix on the communion table in his chapel, and that he bowed toward the altar, and that Oglethorpe claimed to have actually seen 'that crucifix and pictures there'.[211] Under examination Oglethorpe denied the alleged words but confessed that he did say to Richard Beaumont 'that he had seen some pictures at the chapel which were the pictures of Christ and of the 12 disciples going to Emanes'.[212]

On 15 May 1640, the King published a proclamation for the repression and punishment 'of the late rebellious and traiterous assemblies in Lambeth, Southwark, and other places adjoyning',

---

208 SP 16/454.96 (16 July 1640).
209 SP 16/453.112 (17 May 1640).
210 SP 16/453.97 (16 May 1640) and SP 16/454.96 (16 May 1640).
211 SP 16/454.96 (16 May 1640).
212 SP 16/454.96, (17 May 1640). The road to Emmaus is where Jesus met the disciples after the Resurrection (Luke 24).

and particularly for the apprehension of John Archer, George Seares, William Seltrum, and 'divers other Rebellious persons'.[213] People in London showed different reactions to this proclamation and they did take notice. When Robert Maynard was examined about his relationship with John Archer, a glover in Southwark, he denied having had any contact with him since he last saw Archer two weeks ago. Their only contact was through Archer's deceased uncle who appointed Maynard as the executor of his will and left a legacy of fifty pounds for his nephew. Maynard claimed that he 'never heard of his the said Archer's imprisonment nor of any matter that he was questioned for until he saw his Majesty's proclamation set up at the court gate at Whitehall on the last Monday in which proclamation the said Archer was named and was to be apprehended as a traitor'.[214] The stationer Thomas Homer of Seacoal Lane in London was imprisoned because he professed ignorance of the proclamation against tumultuous people, showing great sympathy with their aims and refusing to assist one of the provost marshalls at Court in his attempt to apprehend a 'lewd women'.[215] On 26 May 1640, the same provost marshall, Thomas Smith, heard in the King's Head tavern some 'discourse in a room adjacent concerning the Rebels'. When he stood near by listening he was invited to join the party although he did not know them. They 'pursued their discourse' saying that Seltrum, the shoemaker mentioned in the proclamation, together with some glovers and others, 'did live about Pickhatch, Golden lane and Oldstreet'. These men had apparently tried to pull down a bawdy house in that neighbourhood, destroying some windows and taking away a few goods. They now planned a second attack on Thursday after the plays in the Red Bull and the Fortune had finished and they could hope for support from people walking home from the theatre.

---

213 Larkin, *Proclamations*, p 710.
214 SP 16/454.81 (21 May 1640).
215 SP 16/455.7–8 (1640).

If we bear in mind the politicization of everyday talk, the riots in London in the early 1640s reveal a gradual shift away from spontaneous, event-oriented, and frequently ritualized modes of protest such as feasts and holidays or hunger riots, which were highly dependent on performance, towards more rational forms of protest.[216] Riots were premeditated, and the reasons for particular tumults were expressed in the slogans of the participants. People did not act in mere panic, but the felt and seen omnipresence of danger which threatened to change their lives, depending on their individual standpoints, made men and women think and talk about the causes of crisis, and finally induced them to act.

The formation of opinions which could lead to various forms of action – the presentation of petitions, demonstrations or political unrest – was the result of a complex process of communication, involving various media. It created its own political culture through the coinage of a new political symbolism and language, and it depended on the interaction of various genres of communication and of the people involved. The dynamics of communication inherent in these interactions will be the topic of the concluding chapter.

---

216 On hunger riots and their legitimization see John Walter, 'Grain riots and popular attitudes to the law: Maldon and the crisis of 1629', in *An ungovernable People. The English and their law in 17th c. and 18th c.*, ed. John Brewer and J. Styles (London, 1980), pp 47–84.

6 · The Dynamics of Communication

The dynamics of communication in mid-seventeenth-century England sprang from the interplay of textual, oral, and performative aspects of communication. There was also a historic dimension. As evident from the preceding chapters, communication was deeply influenced by the survival and recognition of traditional knowledge and images from past centuries. Furthermore, both in print and in speech the political language of the period was influenced by common speech packed with proverbs and colloquial sayings, and the use of concrete and sometimes coarse images from everyday life.

On the purely textual level, orality and literacy were interwoven. Oral residues in print, such as oral speech patterns, the images and tales of collective memory, and the imitations of dialogues, were quite frequent in popular news genres. If we look at the various media involved, the flow of ideas among different news genres, and the interaction of oral and print culture, pictures and performances were equally important. On the performative level, the dynamics of communication were influenced by the ways in which people interacted and related to each other on the grounds of what was being said and discussed. The court cases on sedition on which part of this chapter is based are a rich source for questions which go beyond the immediate factual relevance of communication for the socio-political history of the period. The singularity of many cases allows an inquiry into the process of communication which does not stop at the mere exchange of news but addresses questions of the dynamics of talk, the underlying motives, intentions and attitudes in communicative processes, the interchange of various media such as commenting on a ballad or discussing parts of Scripture as possible explanations for actual events, the various genres of talk, non-verbal communication, and social interaction. Furthermore, when we look at the social interaction of people in communication, the active and well-informed role of women in political and religious discourses raises a number of questions about gender roles, and the discrepancies between contemporary literature on women's speech and their role in everyday verbal encounters.

In the following paragraphs the dynamics of communication will be analysed by looking in turn at oral residues in print, the interplay of various media, the interaction of men and women, and the impact of gender on communication.

Interfaces of Orality and Literacy

In spite of the influence of the printing press and growing literacy rates, seventeenth-century society retained many of its traditional aids to memory. These included landscape memory verses which helped people to find their way around without maps, proverbs, songs, and visual representations, including the popular religious wall hangings found in most – even poorer – households and alehouses that Tessa Watt has brought to light in her book on cheap print and piety.[1] Furthermore, the stories about past heroes, magic figures, fairy tales and nursery rhymes which were passed on from generation to generation, custom and ritual, were central to the collective memory and communal wisdom of early modern English society. As already shown, the pamphlets and pictures of the 1640s were full of such communal wisdom which

---

1   Watt, *Cheap print*. For a discussion of memory aids in seventeenth-century
     England see Fox, *Aspects*, p 12f.

helped people to relate political issues to their mental framework, and which, furthermore, served as mnemonic devices when the contents of pamphlets were passed on by word of mouth.

The use of traditional knowledge and everyday life scenes to express political or religious opinions for both the literate and the illiterate can be traced back to pulpit oratory and homilies of fourteenth- and fifteenth-century England. English homilies of this period all 'set out to give the common people that simple instruction in points of ritual and religious duties that the church deemed needful for the ordinary man and woman to know'.[2] According to Gerald Owst, the homilist was, in fact, the first to take up everyday life scenes and grievances and to clothe them for the first time with a deep spiritual and social significance for ordinary people. He 'linked them with great religious themes and moral principles'.[3] From early times the whole sermon was metrical throughout, and it abounded in fantastic verbal imagery which, in its vivacity and directness, must have had a considerable impact on its medieval audience. Furthermore, a crucial feature of medieval pulpit oratory and homilies was the combination of satire and complaint, a device which later became prominent in the pamphlet literature of the 1640s.

Among the pictorial topics of pulpit orators were the figures of Faith, Wisdom, Truth, the four Virtues of Prudence, Justice, Temperance and Fortitude, the picture of Lust (Venus, Drunkenness), Death, the tragedy of Fortune's wheel and of Devildom. Furthermore, there were the images of the Ship, the Castle, the Sinner as a Horseman, the Whore of Babylon who gave birth to the Seven Deadly Sins, the Devil and the Mouth of Hell, the

---

2   Owst, *Preaching in Medieval England. An Introduction to Sermon Manuscripts of the Period c. 1350–1450*, (Cambridge, 1926), p 243. There were different types of sermons including 'sermones ad status' (visitation sermons), sermons on Our Lady, sermons at funerals, sermons in verse etc. One of the most outstanding examples was the *Festivall* by John Myrc, a popular festival sermon book of the 14th century, with anecdotes about sacred people, who are fascinated by the lurid and painful.

3   Owst, *Literature*, p 46.

humble Pilgrimer with his Burden on his back, the moralization and allegorical use of the Game of Chess, Corruption, Gluttony, the Chameleon, the Sick Stomach, the Sun-Eclipsed, the Anti-Pope, Avarice and Pride.

In medieval preaching there was a strong tendency to identify a specific topic with an illustration. Images were inherited from classical rhetoric and were gradually popularized. Abstract figures such as Lust (Venus) or Pride were personified. 'The Vices themselves now strutted upon the scene as well-known types and characters of the tavern or market place.'[4] Under the impact of the moralizing and pedagogical aims of English preachers and homilists, man was classified into specific characters which became quite influential in popular culture. They were gradually standardized in order to 'stick in the memory' as a good or bad example, and they proceeded through the centuries with little modification. These characters featured in medieval morality plays, in Elizabethan drama and pamphleteering, and they were used in the politico-religious satires of the 1640s.[5]

In addition to orally preserved traditional knowledge and imagery in pamphlets, 'metrical' and 'formulaic' memory aids familiar from oral societies also found their way into the print culture of the seventeenth century. As early modern England was as yet only a partially literate society, communication was still dominated by oral habits of thought and expression, including the extensive use of formulaic elements, clear diction, short sentences, rhyme schemes, and metre. These oral habits gradually found their way into written language which started with the practice of writing down what had been originally composed and delivered orally. This was increasingly the case with sermons in medi-

---

4   Ibid., p 87.
5   Sandra Clark, *The Elizabethan Pamphleteers. Popular Moralistic Pamphlets 1580–1640* (London, 1983), p 145 ff. Also Eric Sirluck, 'Shakespeare and Jonson among the pamphleteers of the Civil War', *Modern Philology*, 53 (1955–56), pp 38–99.

eval England, and the process climaxed with the advent of printing and the gradual transition of society from orality to literacy.
Throughout the seventeenth century this process was still
underway.

These written testimonies of oral habits of thought and expression in combination with evidence from still existing oral
societies have allowed modern researchers to reconstruct the basic characteristics of a culture such as early modern England which
still had a massive oral residue. The most decisive feature was to
'think memorable thoughts', that is, 'to do your thinking in mnemonic patterns, shaped for ready oral occurrence' in order to
solve effectively the problem of retaining and retrieving something without immediate resort to chirographically or typographically fixed and thus 'readable thoughts'.[6] Memory relied on specific formulaic stylings which Walter Ong subsumes under the
heading of the 'psychodynamics of orality':

> Your thought must come into being in heavily rhythmic, balanced
> patterns, in repetitions or antithesis, in alliterations and assonances,
> in epithetic and other formulary expressions, in standard thematic
> settings (the assembly, the meal, the duel, the hero's helper and so
> on), in proverbs which are constantly heard by everyone so that they
> come to mind readily and which themselves are patterned for reten-
> tion and ready recall, or in other mnemonic form.[7]

If we compare Ong's inventory of the characteristics of orally
based thought and expression with oral residues found in the
pamphlet literature of the 1640s, we can add the following features: an additive pragmatic style rather than a subordinative analytic style; an aggregative style, that is, clusters of integers such
as parallel terms or phrases, clauses or epithets; redundancy, that
is, the repetition of what has just been said, keeping both the
hearer and the speaker on the track; certain conservative or tra-

---

6   Walter J. Ong, *Orality and Literacy. The Technologizing of the Word* (London
     and New York, 1982), p 34.
7   Ibid.

ditionalistic elements, 'since in a primary oral culture conceptualized knowledge that is not repeated aloud soon vanishes, and societies must invest great energy in saying over and over again what has been learned arduously over the ages;'[8] a closeness to the human world 'assimilating the alien objective world to the more immediate familiar interaction of human beings' since in the absence of writing there were no analytic categories to structure knowledge at a distance from lived experience;[9] and finally, for the same reason, orally based thought and expression as it found its way into printing and writing was agonistically toned, empathetic and participatory, homeostatic (words acquire their meanings only from their always insistent actual habitat), and situational.

Almost all popular politico-religious pamphlets and ballads of the 1640s were metrical throughout, and, significantly, a large number were written in the same metrical pattern of the heroic couplet, usually employing the simple rhyme scheme (AA BB CC). This was the most favoured form of the verse satirist from about the middle of the seventeenth century, and had been extensively and successfully used by popular poets since the fifteenth century, above all by Geoffrey Chaucer. It had also been common in homiletic preaching. Milman Parry was the first to coin and explore the concept of the metrical formula as a characteristic of oral societies in his study of Greek hexameter verse.[10] His definition of the formula as 'a group of words which is regularly employed under the same conditions to express a given essential idea' is also illustrated by some of the pamphlet literature of the 1640s. The following excerpts taken from two different pamphlets provide an example.

---

8   Ong, *Orality*, p 41.
9   Ong, *Orality*, p 42. See also Jack Goody, *The Domestication of the Savage Mind* (Cambridge, 1977), p 11ff.
10   Milman Parry, *The Making of Homeric verse*, ed. Adam Parry (Oxford, 1971), p 272.

Behold Romes Monster on his monstrous Beast!
To fulnesse of his foulenesse (now) encreast!
How He in Papall Pride doth ride along,
And how his sonnes and shavelings thrust and throng
To see his sacred hollow Holinesse
His Babylonish Blasphemies expresse.[11]

A warning to all that are Nursers of pride,
For Justice is knowne to be Eagle-ey'd;
Those that will climb must look to have a fall,
For Fortune will pat down her Tennis-ball.
Let no man frown, for ile have all know it,
This wicked age must have a biting Poet.[12]

The steady recurrence of the same rhythm in connection with specific messages certainly helped to reinforce certain ideas, and to make them orally transmittable once separated from their written source. We find the repetition of the simple rhyme pattern AA BB CC in both examples. Furthermore, the author of the first stanza operates with rhetorical figures such as alliterations (*How He*; *Papal Pride*; *hollow Holiness*; *Babylonish Blasphemies*) and with sound patterns which often form minimal pairs (fulnesse and foulnesse; pride doth ride; Monster on his monstrous Beast; thrust and throng; hollow Holinesse). The second stanza demonstrates the incorporation of proverbs, which was very common: 'Those that will climb must look to have a fall.' It also uses the popular image of Fortuna (fortune) and the idea of a tennis-ball bouncing up high to be patted down again. Throughout the examples cited above, 'characters', for instance the personification of Pride and Justice, occur and there is a good deal of biblical imagery especially from the Apocalypse.

Finally, there were also verses which, both in their rhythms and in the images they used, recalled traditional sayings, or, as in the case below, popular 'watchwords of revolt' coined in previ-

---

11   *Behold Romes Monster.*
12   *Fortunes Tennis-Ball* (1641), BL E.160.5.

izd by Opinion

ous centuries. The following example, taken from a pamphlet of
the year 1641, is a case in point:

> When Women Preach and Cobblers Pray
> The Fiends in Hell make Holiday.[13]

These lines were written in the simple metre of the heroic couplet. More interesting, however, is their striking resemblance in
metre, rhyme, overall composition, and theme (the overturn of
traditional social degrees) with the popular and old familiar
'watchword of revolt' of the fourteenth century:

> When Adam delved and Eve span
> Who was then a Gentleman.[14]

This case provides a good example of how one theme travelled
through the centuries reappearing in various genres and slightly
adapting new meanings while, however, preserving its key message of social injustice and revolt. The most influential account
of the great revolt in 1381 to which these lines refer, and which
had started in the counties of Kent, Essex, and Suffolk in response to heavy taxation levied on the poor by Richard II, was
that by St Albanes. Originally, according to Owst, the 'watchword of revolt' was 'in the first instance nothing more or less
than a popular rhyming couplet based directly on a favourite
homiletic argument, in this case one which English preachers of
the fourteenth century were wont to use in support of their in-
nocent diatribes upon the Pride and Life and emptiness of human boasting'.[15] There were typical pulpit references to this very
rhyme in Bromyard, and in a sermon by Bishop Brenton of
Rochester. At the same time the theme was taken up for the first
time in a vernacular poem by Richard Rolle until it was habitu-
ally associated with revolt and the struggle for social justice:

---

13 *Lucifers Lacky.*
14 White, *Social Criticism*, pp 119–20.
15 Owst, *Literature*, p 291.

When Adam delf and Eve span
Spir, if thou ill spede,
Ware was than the pride of man
That now merres his mede?
Of erth and slame, als was Adam,
Maked to noyes and nede,
A we, als he, maked to be
Whil we this lyf sal lede.[16]

The fact that this 'apparently innocuous pulpit theme' became, in Owst's wording, the 'popular watchword of revolution' strongly supports the argument that medieval preaching had a strong impact on the populace which in turn influenced the gradual popularization – and politicization – of religious and classical images and themes. In the 1593 stage version of the 'great revolt', the theme of popular revolt expressed through the above two-line stanza reappears in a condensed form in a speech by Parson Ball:

England is growne to such a passe of late,
That rich men triumph to see the porre beg at their gate.
But I am able by good scripture before you to prove,
That God doth not thi dealing allow nor love,
But when Adam delved and Eve span
Who was then a Gentleman,
Brethren, brethren, it were better to have this Communitie
Then to have this difference in degrees.[17]

An abbreviated version of the theme also featured again in Shakespeare's *Hamlet*.[18] And finally, the theme is taken up once more under the impact of the Irish rebellion. Here it was used, however, in an attempt to conjure up the horrors of rebellion rather than its moral goals.[19] In general, the metrical presentation of

---

16   Cit. in Owst, *Literature*, p 291.
17   *The Life and Death of Jacke Straw.*
18   William Shakespeare, *Hamlet*, The Arden Edition of the Works of William Shakespeare, ed. Harold Jenkins (2nd ed. 1984; rpt. London, 1985), Act V, Scene I.
19   *The Rebellious Life and Death of Wat Tyler.*

highly figurative texts in the popular pamphlet literature of the 1640s adopted the oral habit of rhythmic presentation for the sake of memory, and it was thus easily picked up by those who were listening.

Another characteristic feature of mid-seventeenth-century print culture was the presentation of news and opinions in the form of dialogues. It has already been stressed that one of the central features of ballads was their performance, which linked them to popular recreation and customs. In a similar vein, printed dialogues were the very image of face-to-face communication mirroring the way people talked about political and religious issues of their time. As a genre, dialogues represented most impressively the interfaces of orality and literacy in their apparent paradox of being a printed oral exchange of ideas. This impression is further emphasized by the fact that some dialogues had really taken place and were turned into print subsequently.[20] Just as in 'real life', the actors of printed dialogues often belonged to different social classes, genders, religious convictions, and professions. There were dialogues 'betwixt a Protestant and a Papist', a 'Citizen and a Country Gentleman', a 'Pedlar and a Romish Priest', or a 'Gentlewoman and a Priest'. Furthermore, those engaged in talking commented on the ways in which news was circulated in mid-seventeenth-century England, and they freely discussed pamphlets and illustrations of the period.

At their meeting in France, two famous refugees, Lord Finch and Secretary Windebank, referred to opinion leaders – 'the poets in England' – and to various sources from which they were

---

20 For instance, *A Discovery of the praise of God, and joy of all true hearted Protestants, of a late intended plot by the Papists to subdue the Protestants. Being a true Copie of a Discourse between William O' Connor a Priest, and Anne Hussey an Irish Gentlewoman*. Printed Anno, 1641. William Clark Collection BB.I.14 (28) and BB.W.(28) (a different edition with a woodcut). BL E.158.4. For references to the actual dialogue as it took place in London see SP 16/464.31 (1640). *A True Copie of a Disputation held betweene Master Walker and a Jesuite, in the house of Thomas Bates in Bishops Court in the Old Baily* (1641), BL E.172.9.

receiving the most recent news. Asked by Windebank what people in England were thinking 'about me', Finch answers: 'Newes
more than I can relate, thinke you and I have bin the best ben-
efactors to the ragged Regiment of Poets, that ever came since
Noah's flood.'[21] And when asked 'why', Finch continues: 'Why
I beleeve there hath bin more Impressions of severall kinds of
lamentable Ballads and Pamphlets (made upon us two) then ever
was of (the Puritan treaties) *The Practice of Piety* or *Crums of
Comfort*.' Finch finally puts an end to their conversation, explaining that he can stay no longer as he has to go to the post to
receive letters from England. In parting he assures Windebank
that 'at our next meeting I will informe you all other newes my
letters affords'. In a different dialogue, one of the speakers refers
to a ballad when he suggests that the 'chiefe commissioner' must
visit 'Tyburne, choose them whether, as the ballad saies, they have
a very bad time of it now I can assure you'.[22] He furthermore
passes on hearsay when introducing one piece of information by
saying 'I heard say'.

In a 'discourse' on the 'civill Wars of England and Ireland' in
which the role of the Parliament was heavily criticized, one of
the speakers used a proverb (which was typographically emphasized by being printed in italics) to mark his point. He said: 'There
is an old Proverb, From a blacke German, a white Italian, a red
Frenchman, I may adde one member more, and, from a Roundheaded Englishman, The Lord deliver us.'[23] In an attempt to explain why the King had left London, the second speaker in this
dialogue tells a fable 'for the further illustration of it'. In reply,
the first remarks that 'there is nothing that illustrates things better, or fasteneth them more firmly in the mind and makes the
memory of them more pleasing to the fancie, then Apologues,
Emblemes, Allegories and Parables'. He continues: 'And now that

---

21   *Times Alteration.*
22   *Old News Newly Revived.*
23   *A Discourse, or Parly, continued betwixt Partricius and Peregrine* (1643), BL
     E.60.14.

you compare a Monarch to the Sunne, I remember to have read'
of a similar comparison before.

Typical of nearly all printed dialogues was the almost ritual
inquiry after news. A traveller who meets a scholar near
Moorfields in London invites him to follow him into the fields
for 'I am a traveller, and can tell you strange news and much
knowledge'.[24] Whereupon the scholar replies: 'We scholars love
to hear news, and to learn knowledge.' He then inquires 'what
good news do you hear of the parliament?'

The predominance of printed dialogues among the most popular news genres of the 1640s not only reflected 'real discourses'
of the period. They often resembled plays with different characters such as 'a Citizen' and 'a Gentleman' and at times there were
even stage directions such as 'enter'.[25] In his book *Theatre and
Crisis* Martin Butler has already pointed to the continuity of 'opposition drama' in the politico-religious pamphlet literature of
the 1640s. He argues that 'with the collapse of the censorship in
1641, the satirical devices and political concerns of the popular
stages were assimilated into the work of purely political pamphlets'.[26] Although this argument is too sweeping to be sustained
because it simplifies the complexity of communication and the
interplay of various themes and genres, there are nevertheless
examples in support of it. Indeed, a number of pamphlets and
tracts were written in the form of plays and drew upon topics
and characters of popular plays of the late sixteenth and seventeenth centuries. A tract issued in 1642, for instance, bore the
title of Middleton's scandalous play *A Game at Chess*, which enjoyed great popularity and caused much distress until it was forbidden after its ninth night on stage.[27] The pamphlet was a 'meta-

---

24   Gabriel Plattes, *A Description of the famous Kingdom of Marcaria* (London,
     1641).
25   *The Downfall of Temporizing Poets.*
26   Martin Butler, *Theatre and Crisis 1632–1642* (Cambridge, 1984), p 231.
27   Heinemann, *Puritanism.*

phorical discourse shewing the present estate of this Kingdome',
that is, two combatants in battle: the black army of the King,
which was marked with blood and cruelty, an army of malignants
with a King who blindly followed the advice of the 'Queen, of
knights, prawns, and rocks'; and the white army of the Parliament which fought for the security and well-being of the Commonwealth.[28] Another pamphlet, *The Copie of a Letter sent from
the Roaring Boyes in Elizium*, made a direct reference to Ben
Jonson and Sejanus, the latter being the main character of his
play *Sejanus*.[29] There appears to have been some correspondence
between a pamphlet entitled *A True and Wonderful Relation of a
Whale, pursued in the Sea* which was said to have carried papists
in its belly, and some allusions in Ben Jonson's comedy *Volpone*
to a whale which was discovered in the Thames and 'twas either
sent from (Catholic) Spain, or the archdukes'.[30]

In contrast to private, indoor theatres of the period, which
saw the performance of the majority of new plays, for instance
by Francis Beaumont or John Fletcher, public playhouses, most
of them in the suburbs, relied mainly on the established repertoire of Elizabethan and Jacobean plays until the closure of the
theatres in 1642.[31] The majority of the London working population could afford regular visits to a playhouse and to other popular recreations such as bear-baiting or a prize-fight. Playhouses
attracted a total of up to 25,000 visitors weekly, which accounted
for quite a mixed crowd. A contemporary observer wrote:

> I doubt but you have heard of our famous play of Gongomar, which
> hath been followed with extraordinary concourse, and frequented
> by all sorts of people old and younge, rich and poore, masters and
> servants, papists and puritans, wise men etc., churchmen and states-

---

28   *A Game at Chess. A metaphorical discourse shweing the present estate of this
     Kingdome* (1643), BL E.88.2.
29   *The Copie of a Letter sent from the Roamy Boyes in Elizium* (1641), BL E.156.8.
30   *A True and Wonderful Relation of a Whale, pursued in the Sea* (1645), BL
     E.308.24; Ben Jonson, *Volpone* (1605).
31   Compare Gurr, *Shakespearean Stage*.

men, as Sir Henry Wotton, Sir Albert Morton, Sir Benjamin
Ruddier, Sir Tomas Lake, and a world besides; the Lady Smith wold
have gon yf she could have persuaded me to go with her. I am not so
soure nor svere but I could not sit so long, for we must have been
there before one a clocke at farthest to finde any roome.[32]

Until the 1640s – and for a large section of London society – the
public stage thus kept alive the implicit acceptance of social mo-
bility in these plays, the wide-ranging heroics of adventure stories, 'good and bad' characters, topoi of social topsy-turviness
such as Thomas Heywood's *Four Prentices of London*, which de-
picts four nobles all disguised as apprentices, satirical attacks on
social upstarts or on much hated professions standardized in social types such as 'the lawyer', 'the quack, or 'the merchant', or
the personifications of such malefactors as Pride, Lust, Drunkenness, Gluttony etc. Whereas the continuity of themes and characters familiar from plays in the pamphlet literature of the 1640s
testifies to the interplay of various genres and the role of traditional images in communication, the style of dialogues modelled
on plays seems to invite performance even after the closure of
theatres. Thus the vividness of printed dialogues in their imita-
tion of everyday talk had a further performative dimension: the
enactment of verbal exchanges.

There is evidence to suggest that in spite of the ban on theatres in August 1642, plays were still performed in back streets or
in the back rooms of alehouses and taverns.[33] Five years after the
closure of the London theatres a second ordinance for the suppression of all stage plays and interludes had to be issued. It
explicitly stated that in spite of earlier prohibitions, stage-
playing 'is presumed to be practiced by divers in contempt

---

32   Cit. in Gurr, *Shakespearean Stage*, p 144–45.
33   The best known dialogue/play was *A New Play called Canterburie his Change
     of Diet*. Also *The Downfall of Temporizing Poets*. For examples of the numer-
     ous close associations between plays and pamphlets during this period see
     Butler, *Theatre* and E. Sirluck, 'Shakespeare and Jonson'.

thereof'.[34] On 22 October 1647, the Parliament required the appointed authorities 'to enter into all houses, and other places within the City of London, and liberties thereof, and other places within their respective jurisdiction, where stage plays, interludes, or other common plays are or shall be acted'.[35] Furthermore, the tradition of drolls enjoyed renewed popularity in the 1640s since puppets were easy to handle, highly effective in their dramatization of texts, and they were exempt from the ban on theatres. Puppet-plays continued to be staged at Holborn Bridge.[36] In their remonstrance London actors complained about the closure of theatres whereas 'the motions of Puppets being still in force and vigour'.[37] We still know very little about these puppet-plays or drolls. In 1650, Francis Kirkman began to collect small farces 'usually known as drolls' and plays which were written and performed by actors after the closure of the theatres. In 1672, he published his collection in *Wits or Sport upon Sport* which throws some light on this kind of acting in the 1640s. In his description of the comedian Robert Cox, who was active in the 1640s, Kirkman gives a vivid account of the ways in which the ban on the stage was successfully undermined: 'An Excellent Comedian that liv'd in the Reign of Charles First, One, who when the Ringleaders of the Rebellion, and Reformers of the Nation supprest the stage, betook himself to making Drolls or Farces ... which under the Colour of Rope-dancing, were alow'd to be acted at the red Bull Play-house by stealth, and the connivance of those straight lac'd Governors'.[38] Thus means existed to perform small plays which were first published in the guise of printed dialogues,

34   *The English Drama and Stage under the Tudor and Stuart Princes 1543–1664. Illustrated by a Series of Documents, Treatises and Poems*, ed. William C. Hazlitt (London, 1869), p 67.
35   Ibid. p 64.
36   *The Actors Remonstrance.*
37   Ibid.
38   Francis Kirkman, *Wits or Sport upon Sport* (1672), ed. J. J. Elson (New York, 1932), p 12.

and to vent political and religious criticism in the traditional and popular forum of the 'stage'.

The distribution of news, the interplay of various news genres, the impact of pictures and the vividness of traditional symbols, tales and images can be reconstructed without too much difficulty for seventeenth-century England. The same is true for interfaces of orality and literacy. The ways, however, in which identifiable individuals used news genres, what they made of the information they received, and how they reacted to pictures can only occasionally be reconstructed from surviving documents. The preceding chapter has shown that ordinary men and women voiced their opinions as a result of the politicization of everyday talk and the availability of news. The following examples of 'people in communication' provide a rare insight into people's individual appropriation of news and their interaction with others in political discussions. They allow glimpses into the way political ballads could spark off laughter and subsequently political discussions, the associations pictures could evoke, the impact of hearsay on news circulation, the resort to defamation when criticizing political opponents, and the ways in which people consulted the Scripture in order to understand the politics of the day. Furthermore, they tell about neighbourly disputes, gossip and defamation, and the strategies employed to resolve conflicts or to save one's reputation. Finally, they tell the story of a man and a woman who re-enact in their small private world the religious conflicts of the period, one being a convinced Catholic, and the other a fierce Anabaptist.

While paying less attention to the content of opinions expressed, this section will look more closely at the cognitive and interactive aspects of communication. Emphasis will be put on the instigation and conduct of talk, verbal and non-verbal communication, attitudes of speakers and hearers, the interplay of visual, oral and printed or written elements in communication, and the interaction of people with special emphasis on gender relations and social status.

People in Communication

On the afternoon of Thursday, 13 October 1640 – at a time when
Charles I was struggling to make up for the defeat of his
unmotivated and badly equipped army by the Scots – Dr Seaton
and Mr Leviston met in the house of the widow Barbara Black in
St Martin's Lane, London, for a game of cards with Mrs Black.[39]
Their play was interrupted by the arrival of two women, Lady
Willoughby, the daughter of the Bishop of Worcester, and one
Mrs Melvin.[40] Their visit encouraged Dr Seaton to read out a ballad 'lately printed' about two Welshmen, which provoked laughter and joking remarks. Seaton declared he had sent this ballad to
Scotland, 'where it would make very good sport', and 'in a grin-
ning manner' he added that 'he wished he had but the Nouts[41]
head to send away with it for that would make sport indeed'.

    When Mrs Black inquired which 'Nouts head' he meant, Seaton
replied 'the Archbishop of Canterbury'. 'That indeed is as fatt as
your owne', was the widow's comment. Now Dr Seaton turned
to Leviston and urged him 'to speak something against his Grace',
and telling him 'that he durst (dared) not'. Unable to withstand
the provocation, a seemingly exasperated Leviston said: 'The
Divell take him, what would you have me say?' At this stage the
widow Black took over the initiative and told some news about
the Court, which she had probably received through old contacts – most likely with the King's shoemaker – dating from the
time when her late husband had been the King's tailor:[42] 'My
Lord Dorset the day before had said in open Councell, it were a

---

39   SP 16/469.95 (1640).
40   SP 16/470.33 (1640). At that time the Bishop of Worcester was John
     Thornborough, a pre-Laudian and probably anti-Laudian bishop. See Ann
     Hughes, 'Thomas Dugard and his circle: a puritan-parliamentarian circle',
     Historical Journal, 20 (1986), pp 771–94.
41   Nought: nothing OE; bad, good for nothing. *The Concise Oxford Dictionary
     of English Etymology* (1991), p 315.
42   During her examination Mrs Black clarified that 'she heard that when the kings
     shoemaker was before the Councell Board that the Earl of Dorset should say

good deed to have some of the Noses slitt viz. of the Scotts'. But she personally hoped that his nose would be slit first, adding 'if it had not bene for the Scotts, he had not bene where he is'.[43] A deliberately deformed face in early modern Europe signified the loss of one's honour, a 'loss of face'. Usually, only a whore was threatened by the wife of her lover: 'I will slitt your nose and mark you for a whore'.[44] The threat to slit men's noses seems to have accompanied accusations of homosexuality.[45] Turning her talk to the Scottish army, Mrs Black wondered 'that the English should presume to stand against so great an Army'. Whereupon Seaton remarked: 'Let them alone the Parliament wille coole their courages shortly'. After this interlude they returned to their game of cards. However, when two 'knaves' were put on the table, Seaton commented 'there wanted but the third vizt the Arch-bishop of Canterbury'. Addressing Mrs Black he continued and said: 'I have a little business with the Archbishop and must wayte on him ere it be long, I would thou wert but by, to see what cringes I shall make him.'[46]

Not much is known about Mrs Barbara Black apart from the details mentioned above and her examination before the Star Chamber Court.[47] She had probably enjoyed a basic education since she signed her written examination with her full name, in contrast to many other men and women examined for seditious words who signed with their mark only. It is most likely that her house in St Martin's Lane, London, was an alehouse or a tavern. As a widow she had to earn her own living, and running an ale-

---

that the shoemaker deserved to have his nose slitt and this Examinant denyeth that she ever said she hoped his Lordships nose should be first slitt or any thing to that purpose', SP 16/470.33 (1640).

43 Lord Dorset was Chamberlain to Queen Henrietta Maria.

44 Gowing, 'Gender', p 10.

45 Valentin Groebner, 'Losing Face: Noses and Honour in the late Medieval Town', *History Workshop Journal*, 40 (Autumn 1995), pp 1–15.

46 Fall in battle, creep along, weaken. *The Concise Oxford Dictionary of English Etymology* (1991), p 105.

47 SP 16/470.33 (1640).

house was typical for women of her status.⁴⁸ This assumption is
further supported by the card game, which was one of the most
popular recreations in alehouses, and the unceremonial entrance
of the two other women. Dr Seaton's harsh remarks against Archbishop Laud and his title identify him as a Puritan divine or as an
anti-Laudian lawyer. Both Seaton and Leviston might have been
Scots since their names point to Scottish origin. Too little is
known about Leviston to allow any assumptions about his background.

During the 1640s, ballad writers took up contemporary politics again after a phase of predominantly apolitical ballads. Among
the ballads touching on the Bishops' War was one which celebrated the valour of the Welsh soldiers, who were said to be
'extremely zealous for the King'.⁴⁹ The Welsh army was recruited
under the Earl of Bridgewater to support England against the
Scots. However, a saying made its rounds that it consisted of ten
horsemen only, five of whom were local drunkards.⁵⁰ The ballad
on the two Welshmen, which Dr Seaton read out to his small
audience, might have been similar to the following:

> There is a kind of beagles runs up and down the town
> yelping out your destruction crying:
> "O the valour of the Welshmen!
> Who are gone to kill the Scots."
> But give the Welshmen leeks and good words,

---

48 In her case study on the economic situation of women in Oxford from 1500
to 1800, Mary Prior shows that running an alehouse or tavern was the most
widespread work among widows unless they took over their husband's shop.
Since similar studies are as yet lacking for London, the same occupational
structure may be assumed for London for the time being. Mary Prior, 'Women
and the urban economy: Oxford 1500–1800', in *Women in English Society*, ed.
ead. (London, 1985), pp 93–118.

49 Firth, 'Ballads', p 262. For an example see M[artin] P[arker], *Brittaines Honour. In the two valiant Welchmen, who fought against fifteene thousand Scots*,
Wood 401.132 (1639–40).

50 Mockery of Welsh people, especially of their 'intelligence' and dialect, was
very popular in early modern England and a frequent topic of ballads and broadsides.

and call them "bold Britons",
and then you may do with them what you will.[51]

Barbara Black later admitted 'that there was some jesting att that tyme upon reading of the ballad' which was most likely provoked both by its content and by the listeners imagining what the Scots would make of it. The fact that the audience reacted with jesting remarks rather than with reproval suggests that there was some consensus about the opinions expressed in the ballad. The sympathetic reaction of his audience spurred on Dr Seaton to make more witty comments. In anticipation of more agreement and laughter he transgressed the immediate content of the ballad, alluding in 'a grinning manner' to contemporary politics and his own interpretation of events. His conviction that Laud's head would amuse the Scots – and the idea of sending it to the Scots would amuse his audience – implied that Seaton presupposed a commonly accepted perception of Laud as the (justified) arch-enemy of the Scots and the cause of the war. Seaton certainly gave away his own opinion about the archbishop and his political fate (death) by characterizing him as a 'Nout' before even naming him and wishing his head to be sent to Scotland rather than Laud in person. However, the 'telling-name' he had chosen for Laud was not immediately identified by all those present, which becomes evident in Barbara Black's inquiry which 'Nout's' head he meant. Furthermore, not all seemed to agree with Seaton's view of the archbishop, or at least, they did not want to risk any trouble and preferred to remain silent. Yet Seaton's daring speeches encouraged – or provoked – sympathizers to give vent to their political views.

Probably trying to impress her audience with her knowledge and connections to the King's circle, Barbara Black gossiped about events at Court which she then gave her own personal comments on. Finding an attentive listener at least in Dr Seaton, Mrs Black

---

51   Firth, 'Ballads', p 262.

turned to more general questions such as the chances of the English army against the Scots, demonstrating her knowledge about the weakness of the former and expressing her disapproval of the whole affair. Appearing as a well-informed political analyst, Seaton almost 'heroically' destroyed Barbara Black's worries about a positive outcome of Laud's designs by telling her to trust in the strength of the Parliament.

When they returned to their game of cards their talk was incited anew by the picture on one of the playing cards, the jack. Playing with the double meaning of 'knave' – a dishonest fellow or rogue, and another word for jack (a playing card) – Seaton used the occasion to express once more his utter dislike of Archbishop Laud. Now it was his turn to impress his listeners when he informed Mrs Black about the 'little business' he had to do with the archbishop and wishing her to be present to witness his power over Laud. The instigation of talk through a picture, the exploitation of its double meaning by translating the picture into a word – knave – and its subsequent association with a known contemporary person is a unique example of the way pictures were integrated into the communicative processes of the period under discussion. This case is especially revealing since the picture in question was 'unintentional', that is, it carried no specific (political) message, unlike the complete picture stories about political events which were frequently found on the backs of playing cards during this period. Their impact on the players has always been difficult to judge and was often doubted altogether. However, the present case demonstrates that people were obviously prepared to interrupt their game if a picture caught their attention and evoked certain associations which they wanted to communicate.

The communicative process that followed the reading of the ballad in Barbara Black's house fell into different phases. These phases were characterized by changes in the role of the speaker (Dr Seaton, Mrs Black), by changes in the topic talked about (the Welsh role in the Scottish war, Archbishop Laud, opinions at Court, and the strength of the English army), by various forms and genres of communication (reading aloud, jesting, provocation, defamation, question and answer, gossip), and by various media influencing the flow of communication (a ballad, a picture on a playing card). The dynamics that could develop from the recital or singing of a provocative and funny ballad and the interchange of various media can only be guessed at for many similar situations in London and across the country.

In the second example the question of 'private conscience and public duty' and disputes about the causes of the Scottish war and the meaning of certain passages in the Bible made up the core of the argument which developed in a small village.

'About lent last past', in 1640, John Oneby from Leicester went to Isabell and Bartolomew Byarn's (gentleman) house in Ashby Magna (Leicester) 'wherein he hath an interest in parte and purpose to speake with some clyents there present'.[52] Having 'dispatched his clients' Oneby came into the hall where he met his sister Rose Cooper, wife of a dyer, Isabell Byarn, Byarn's brother Humphrey, gentleman, Mary Brooksby and William Musson, yeoman, all from Ashby Magna. 'After some other discourse' Mary Brooksby, who was originally from Stepney, London, but had been living in Ashby Magna for twenty-two years, asked John Oneby if he had any news about the Scottish war and 'what he heard was the cause that moved the Scottishmen to make warre agaynst us'.[53] As far as she could remember Oneby answered

> That the Church of Scotland would not have any bishops that they would not receive the booke of common prayer and that they (?) upon Religion and oposed the Bishops there and their Rule over them, not only in matters ecclesiastical but so what the Bishops intended in matters of the state there. And the said Mr Oneby then and there

---

52   SP 16/430.10 (1639). This document comprises testimonies by several people. Unfortunately the original is not carefully numbered. Therefore each reference will also provide the examinant's name to make identification of the quoted passage easier.

53   SP 16/430.10 (1639) and SP 16/423.44iii (1639).

said that those were the causes of the Scottish warr which as he had
read would break out into open Rebellion.[54]

Isabell Byarn and William Musson further testified that Oneby
said that 'if thes were the causes of the Scottish mens warrs, then
theire warrs were there priests warrs'.[55] Musson added that he
heard Oneby say 'These priestly warrs but now the king (meaning therby our Gracious Sovereign king Charles) pleased to make
them his warrs'.[56]

Having explained the causes of the Scottish war, John Oneby
recited the prophet Jeremiah 5.31 which 'as hee said contained
such warrs: "Wonderful and horrible things is done in the land.
The prophets prophesy falsely and the priests beare rule by their
meanes, and what will they doe in the end thereof".[57] When he
'then and there discourse and comment upon the said words'
Mary Brooksby started arguing with Oneby and said 'I would
wish that Mr Mason (meaninge Mr Thomas Mason the vicar and
curate of Ashby Magna) was here to answere you about this
text'.[58] While they were discussing the prophet's words William
Musson left and went straight home to look up the said passage
in his Bible. He was awaited there by Richard Bent, gentleman,
of the parish of Crosby, Leicester, whom he had met on his way
to the examination, John Moore, and the local vicar Thomas
Mason.[59] Unable to find the quoted text, Musson was assisted

---

54   SP 16/423.44iii (1639).
55   SP 16/430.10 (1639) and SP 16/423.44ii (1639).
56   SP 16/423.44ii (1639).
57   Ibid. The full text quoted from the so-called King James' Bible is as follows:
      'The prophets prophecy falsely and the priests bear rule by their meanes; and
      my people love to have it so; and what will ye do in the end thereof?' Jeremiah
      directed these verses against the profit-oriented, organized 'professional proph-
      ets' and the priests of his time. They had formed a pact which required the
      prophets to prophesy according to the priests' wishes for which they received
      good payment in return. The Holy Bible, conteyning the Old Testament and
      the New: Newly Translated out of the Original Tongues. Appointed to be
      read in Churches, R. Barker (1613).
58   SP 16/423.44ii (1639).
59   SP 16/423.44ii (1639); SP 16/430.10 (1639).

by Moore and Mason. He then 'did declare and make knowen to them the wordes of the said Mr Oneby and the whole narration and all passages of the said matter in discourse which was then fresh in this examinants remembrance'.[60] In their later testimony both William Musson and Thomas Mason stressed that Oneby had talked about the Scottish war *although* Mason had recently read ('as he was enioyned') the King's proclamation 'against the sedition through some in Scotland' in the parish church of Ashby Magna and also the 'Homilies sett out by publick order to be read – viz: against disobedience and wilfull Rebellion'.[61] Musson claimed that it was this proclamation and the homily which had caused him 'to take more speciall notice of the said wordes spoken by Mr Oneby'.[62]

Not all witnesses supported the allegations against John Oneby. Isabell Byarn affirmed that Oneby 'said that he never heard or read that all such like warrs as were begun under pretence of religion ended either in Rebellion or such like ill'.[63] Likewise, Oneby's sister Rose Cooper told the jury that Oneby had said

> that he had read manie histories, but he never heard of anie where the beginning of differences betwixt the kyng and his subjects were grounded upon Religion but then ended in open Rebellion but for the present occasion he hoped the ministers would labor to make peace because they are preachers of the gospel of peace.[64]

According to Isabell Byarn, Oneby spoke solely of the war of Scottish priests and bishops without any reference to England. She recalled that Oneby quoted the prophet Jeremiah only after explaining 'that the Scotts and those of their faction did use to alledge two places of scripture which she now remembereth not'.

---

60 S 16/234.44ii (1639).
61 SP 16/423.44ii, iv (1639).
62 SP 16//423.44ii (1639).
63 SP 16/430.10 (1639) (Isabell Byarn).
64 SP 16/430.10 (1639) (Rose Cooper).

Rose Cooper was more precise in her testimony, providing the examiners with exact references to those passages Oneby had quoted in order to show what the Scottish faction based their arguments on: 'the 5 of Jer and the last verse and the 5th chapter of the first epistle of St Peter and the 2 & 3 verses.'[65] Both women agreed that he 'did not make any exposicon, application or coment at all upon the same'. Finally, Isabell Byarn declared that 'she hath often heretofore heard the said Mr Oneby argue against Puritans and their tenenth and against such as have endewured to sett upp a presbiterall government and hath ever expressed his dislike against them'. Her view was shared by Richard Bent who wondered 'that the said Mr Oneby should speake any such wordes in defence of Puritans for he this examinant has knowne him at the least twentie yeares during all which tyme he hath ever byn opposite to the Puritans and those of that faction'.[66]

Oneby's case quickly made its rounds in the neighbouring villages of Crosby and Willoughby Waterless and the rumour spread that John Moore had informed against John Oneby 'because he the said Mr Oneby had given testimonie against him the said Mr Moore concerninge his parsonage and had byn an Enemie of his'.[67]

It is significant that those people who probably had long-standing reservations about John Oneby presented him in their testimonies as a disloyal subject who disapproved of the King's politics and sympathized with the Scots' cause. They argued along the politico-religious divisions of their time, associating Oneby with Puritanism, which in their eyes equalled treason against the established church and state. This point was further stressed by

---

65 Jeremiah 5.31 (see above) and Peter 1.5 v. 2–3: (2) 'Tend the flock of God which is among you, taking the ... thereof, not by constraint, but willingly; not filthy lucre, but of a ready mind. (3) Neither as being lords over God's heritage, but being examples to the flock.' *King James' Bible*.
66 SP 16/430.100 (1639) (Richard Bent).
67 SP 16/430.10 (1639) (John Kynde of Willoughby Waterless in the county of Leicester, husbandman; Richard Bent).

the emphasis put on the King's proclamation and the 'prescribed' homilies against 'wilfull rebellion' which allegedly had no effect on Oneby. Although both texts had recently been read in public John Oneby disobediently spread seditious words about the Scottish war. In the light of these accusations and the seemingly biased interpretation of his statements about the Scottish war it was central for Oneby's reputation to dissociate himself from Puritanism. This was the prerequisite for making a more favourable interpretation of his statements possible which would take his words for a mere report of the Scots' opinions rather than for a plea in favour of the Scots' cause.

Throughout the whole communicative process in the Byarn's house, Oneby appeared as a learned man who responded to a very precise inquiry. Rather than confining her question to general news about the Scottish war, Mary Brooksby wished to know what Oneby had heard about the causes of this war. She thus not only instigated a political discussion among a group of men and women but determined its content: the causes of the Scottish war. After summarizing the main arguments of the Scots, Oneby drew his own conclusions about the meaning and impact of this war. Whereas some bystanders claimed that he personally called it a 'priestly war' which had been taken over by the King and would break out into open rebellion, others stressed that Oneby had only repeated what he had read without ever talking about any rebellion. Of special interest is Rose Cooper's statement about the many *histories* Oneby had read and his conclusion from history that religious conflicts could not break out into open rebellion. Her testimony reveals a central but hardly ever 'visible' aspect of communication: the application of personal knowledge gained from reading (and experience) to a specific political context.

In a way Oneby was practising the vital interchange of various media in the formation of opinions and in communicative processes when he quoted those texts from Holy Scripture on which the Scots based their arguments. That the appropriation of written texts allowed much variation according to individual and contextual factors became evident in Mary Brooksby's objection to Oneby's interpretation. Trying to give her arguments more weight she appealed to some higher authority on questions of religion and exegesis, the local vicar, who alone, she claimed, could come up with the right meaning. Others were obviously incited by Oneby's illustrations to look up the respective passages themselves and check on Oneby's report about the relevance of these texts for the Scots' behaviour – in other words, they wanted to form their own opinions.

The next case demonstrates how the dynamics of communication were influenced by temper, and how disputes degenerated into defamation or violence. Furthermore, this surviving dispute gives rare insights into the role of symbolic gestures as part of commmunication. And finally, the concept of male honour and revenge can be observed in practice and, in this case, it can be seen how it was gradually undermined by a woman's verbal appeasement strategies.

When Edmund Woodward, gentleman, and Stephen Edgby, constable from Bewdly (Worcs), entered the house of the former in Camburne (Worcs) on Thursday afternoon, 2 January 1639, Woodward's eldest daughter came running into the room and 'cried to her Mother that there were gents with theire swords drawn calling for her father'.[68] A moment later Woodward could see a gentleman 'in a scarlett Coate' unknown to him 'with his hatt under his Arme and his sworde drawne in his hand' repeating several times 'Com out thow Rogue Bastard and cowardly Rogue'. While his wife quickly locked the door, Woodward prepared to go out and defend himself and his family 'but was forcibly prevented by the said Constable and children crying about him hanging'. So Mrs Anne Woodward told them 'I will goe and answer them' and left the house to bolt the outer gate.[69] There a fair-haired gentleman sitting on his horse with his sword drawn

---

68   SP 16/441.36ii (1639).
69   SP 16/441.36i (1639).

demanded that her husband come out to fight with him 'if he durst'. When she replied that he was away in Bewdley the gentleman 'swore Wounds and Blood that my husband was in the house and he was a coward and durst not come forth and he would kill me and said thow art a whore and thy husband a coward'.

After this outburst he wanted to know the name of Mrs Woodward's husband, whereupon she 'desired him to tell me his name and I would tell him my husbands name'. It turned out that the gentleman and his companion were the two sons, John and William, of one Mr Blunt from Billington, whom she and her husband both honoured as she assured John Blunt. Gradually it became clear that one of Woodward's employees, a miller named William Sewne, had insulted John Blunt, and Blunt was asking for revenge. Desiring 'him to be pacient' Anne Woodward promised him full satisfaction and said 'whatsoever the Miller had wronged him my Husband should set him right and if he please to come when my husband was att home'. Blunt asked her to hold out her hand to him over the pale, and Anne Woodward 'gave him her hand that the Miller Should be putt out of his House'. Blunt seemed satisfied, and Mrs Woodward returned towards the house when she was suddenly called back by the gentleman who now demanded in renewed rage her husband's 'hart [heart] blood'. She asked John Blunt 'what good his hart blood doe you shall he spend his hart blood for a Miller?' Her pleading for patience went unheard and Blunt insisted on his revenge.

In the meantime Edmund Woodward and Stephen Edgby 'fynding her stay very long' went into the garden to call her inside the house.[70] From the lower end of the garden they saw one of the brothers throw stones at the mill windows and 'put their swordes in at the window and called the Miller Cowardly slave and cokold slave'.[71] Obviously undeterred by their status, the

---

70   SP 16/441.36ii (1639).
71   SP 16/441.36i (1639).

miller shouted 'that if they would kill a man when they were drunke they must hang when they are sober be their lords or knights or whatsoever they were'.[72] Equipped with a sword and a 'poleaxe' Woodward and Edgby went down immediately to speak with them.[73] However, in spite of Woodward's friendly greeting, his 'faire language entreating him to be pacified', and his promise that he 'should have anie satisfaction which was fitting for a gent', Blunt 'grew more outragious and said he could have no satisfaction but on him'.[74] Asked for his reasons Blunt replied that the miller had wronged him 'and you must and shall make me satisfaction for I will not meddle with base Rogues and fellowes and began to grow againe into a passion'. Woodward's suggestion that Blunt's man could beat the miller instead was rejected, too, on grounds that only Woodward himself could offer him satisfaction.[75]

In another attempt to pacify Blunt Anne Woodward 'had beare brought from the house', and desired the men to be quiet and drink.[76] She drank to John Blunt whereupon he drank to her husband 'upon condicion that he should owe him satisfaction'. But Edmund Woodward objected 'that it was an ill time and place among women and children but desired him to be content until his returne back' next Saturday. Blunt was not convinced and replied that he would call Woodward a coward if he did not keep his word. Even Woodward's confession that his friendship with Blunt's father made him hesitate to fight John Blunt had no effect on him. Likewise, Woodward's affirmation that 'what she said he would performe', referring to his wife's promise to turn

---

72 SP 16/441.36iii (1639). There were different opinions on whether or not John Blunt was drunk. Whereas some people were not quite sure, others claimed that they saw him mount and dismount his horse without any signs of drunkenness. John Blunt himself denied having drunk anything.

73 SP 16/441.36ii and SP 16/441.36vii (1639).

74 SP 16/441.36ii (1639).

75 SP 16/441.36i (1639).

76 SP 16/441.36ii (1639).

out the miller, enraged John Blunt only further. He replied that 'he would fight and swore he would kill us all, and he would put fire on the Mill and on the towne and if he could the whole kingdome and swore by godds precious wounds if the king were there and he had a knife in his hand he would kill or stabb him'.[77] Ready to 'go out of the gate unto him' had not his wife and children and the constable stopped him, Woodward answered: 'Take heade what you say'.[78] Blunt's only reply was 'I have spoken treason but I care not'. Anne Woodward's renewed pleadings 'to pray to god for patience I know no cause for you to be in this manner' only received angry words from the parting John Blunt.[79] His brother, however, was seemingly ashamed by the whole affair and addressing Anne Woodward he said 'that he was sorry that he had offended her in words and desired to salute her and so he did'.

Although Blunt had admitted instantly that his words were treasonable, the inquiring jury favoured a different reading, obviously siding with the accused gentleman. In their eyes the question at stake was not so much the words uttered *per se* but their true meaning in their specific context. Consequently, the justices tried to shift the blame to the audience, accusing them of having 'mistaken', that is, misunderstood, Blunt's utterance and of having construed a false meaning. A memorandum gave the following summary and interpretation of the whole case:

> Concerning Mr John Blunt whereupon hee is accused ther on two principal points. The one that hee should say if the king were ther hee would kill him.
>
> The other that hee should say hee had spoken Treason but hee cared not.
>
> For the first it was *rather mistaken then spoken* for hee vowed to kill a miller who it seemes had angered him (…) but hee would kill him,

---

77   SP 16/441.36i (1639).
78   SP 16/441.36ii (1639).
79   SP 16/441.36i (1639).

and if the king were ther he would kill him meaning the miller, though the king were present.

Blunt's own confession that he had spoken treason was interpreted by the justices as a sign of distress: 'It seems the poor gentleman tooke himself hardy and sayd I have spoken treason … fearing it seemes it had been Treason'. Thus, the misunderstanding was on John Blunt's side, too, who believed that his opponents had taken his words for treason. Only those witnesses who had not been directly involved in the verbal exchanges between Blunt and the Woodwards but watched the whole encounter from a distance tended to support the jury's view by admitting that 'whom he meant to stabb either the king or the Miller' they knew not.[80]

The underlying force of the whole communicative process between Mr and Mrs Woodward and John Blunt was the attempt by the former to pacify Blunt and the blind wish of the latter for revenge as it was appropriate among gentlemen. Whereas the language of John Blunt was characterized by defamation and sexual slander of both his male and female counterparts, by swearing, provocations and the threat of physical violence, Edmund and Anne Woodward's language was characterized by friendly greetings, pleadings, promises, patience, assurances of friendship, and a willingness to satisfy. The attitude of both parties was underlined by various forms of non-verbal communication. John Blunt arrived on horseback with his sword already drawn, a menacing gesture which was rightly interpreted by Woodward's children who rushed inside to warn their parents about the impending danger. In contrast Anne Woodward sealed her promise to dismiss the miller by holding out her hand to John Blunt in a very old form of verifying a verbal agreement.[81] Furthermore, when

---

80 SP 16/441.36iv-vi (1639).
81 Herman Roodenburg, 'The "hand of friendship": shaking hands and other gestures in the Dutch Republic' in *A Cultural History of Gesture*, ed. Jan Bremmer and Herman Roodenburg (Cambridge, 1991; pbk 1993), pp 152–189.

the discussion threatened to become violent she encouraged the men to have some beer and drink to each other, obviously hoping for the appeasing effect of communal drinking which was commonly a sign of friendship and togetherness.[82] Finally, Blunt's brother William desired to express his shame about the whole affair and especially the sexual slander against Anne Woodward by 'saluting' her. The phrase 'and so he did', getting back on his horse afterwards, clearly refers to a specific gesture performed by William Blunt which was the essential part of his salutation. In this context Blunt's ceremonial salutation was meant as an apology for his brother's bad behaviour.

Apart from these open gestures there were more subtle moves designed to pacify the raging gentleman. It was certainly a tactical consideration on Anne Woodward's part to go out and meet the stranger rather than to let her husband confront him in arms. Her appearance was bound to force Blunt to refrain from fighting and talk instead, since he could not inflict any physical violence on an unprotected woman. Although he uttered verbal threats against her and attacked her honour through sexual slander, he did not do her any physical harm. This gave Anne Woodward the chance to distract and mollify the gentleman. Incapable of using force, she had to fall back entirely on her wits and come up with various schemes. Her first strategy was to make Blunt believe that her husband was not at home, thus encouraging Blunt to give up his plans for revenge. She then flattered the young gentleman by telling him how much she and her husband honoured his father. Without arguing about the justification of Blunt's anger against the miller, she readily promised Blunt to turn the miller out of his house, sealing her promise with a handshake. Anne Woodward seemed to have achieved her aim when Blunt suddenly grew violent again, and all she could do then was plead with him to be patient. Later she even desired him to pray for

---

82   For the meaning of communal drinking see Clark, *Alehouse*, pp 1–20.

patience, obviously realizing that he lacked this virtue. Asked at one stage of the dialogue whether he was drunk, Blunt admitted that he was driven by 'passion rather than drink'. His whole behaviour and senseless rage create the impression of a man of a choleric disposition.

Throughout her encounter with John Blunt, Anne Woodward appeared as a firm, determined, courageous, and independent woman. She had suggested meeting Blunt alone, obviously knowing that her sex would stop him from violence. This argument was brought into play again by her husband, who tried to stop Blunt from fighting by claiming that he could not fight him while a woman and children were present. During her argument with John Blunt, Anne Woodward remained unimpressed by his verbal abuse and threats, sticking to her aim of solving the whole conflict in a peaceful way. She influenced the direction of talk just as much as Blunt did. When Blunt, for instance, desired to know her husband's name, she insisted on learning his name first. Furthermore, she confronted Blunt's conception of revenge with her own idea of a peaceful way of satisfying him by dismissing the miller – a proposal her husband later fully supported, arguing that he would do what she had promised. Even when her husband and Edgby had joined them she did not disappear into the house but still took the iniative in certain phases of the communicative process. She invited all men to drink to each other, and when Blunt dishonoured the King, she prevented her husband from attacking the gentleman.

When Edmund Woodward and Stephen Edgby appeared on the scene they both carried weapons. Their ability to use physical force against Blunt if words of pacification failed was the central difference between them and Anne Woodward. Consequently the option to turn from talking to fighting loomed over the subsequent communicative process although Woodward continued his wife's verbal appeasement strategy. With Woodward actually present Blunt could renew his demand for revenge among equals, dismissing any proposals of satisfaction as 'unfitting' for a gentleman. His consciousness of status became most evident when he refused to beat up the miller himself, arguing that he would not meddle with people of a different social standing. For Blunt the whole affair had boiled down to a question of honour, and he seemed to insist on social codes that had largely died out among the gentry – the duel. Although a duel was never mentioned, Blunt's whole behaviour and his insistence on Edmund Woodward's 'heart blood' strongly points to this upper-class male ritual of re-establishing honour.[83] Apart from the invaluable references to non-verbal forms of communication which hardly ever survive, the most striking feature of this case is the impact of gender differences on the pacification strategies of the Woodwards.

The final case of 'people in communication' provides an idea of chance encounters between men and women in London and the nature of religious disputes that could develop between initial strangers. It furthermore shows how people were aware of events around themselves, and how they incorporated news and opinions into their arguments.

Thomas Parkman and his wife regularly had lodgers in their house in the parish of St James, Clerkenwell. Among them were Elizabeth Thorowgood, a Roman Catholic, whose husband served in the King's army under John Digby, and Alexander West, an Anabaptist. During their stay Mrs Thorowgood and West met frequently in the house and had several arguments about the 'popish and protestant Religion'.[84] On Tuesday, 2 June 1640, Alexan-

---

83   For general treatment of the code of honour, see Lawrence Stone, *The Crisis of the Aristocracy* (Oxford, 1965), pp 242–50; Anthony J. Fletcher, 'Honour, Reputation and Local Officeholding in Elizabethan and Stuart England', in *Order and Disorder in Early Modern England*, ed. Fletcher and John Stevenson (Cambridge, 1985), pp 92–115; Melvyn James, *English Politics and the Concept of Honour, 1485–1642*, Past and Present Supplement, 3 (Oxford, 1978). Most recently Cust, 'Honour' and similarly, id., 'Honour, rhetoric and political culture: the Earl of Huntingdon and his enemies', in *Political Culture and Cultural Politics in Early Modern Europe*, ed. Susan D. Amussen and Mark A. Kishlansky (Manchester, 1995), pp 84–111.

84   SP 16/457.3i–4i (1640).

der West argued 'in a mild and Calme way' with Elizabeth Thorowgood about 'certeine Popish Tenenth' and referred to the 'Papists many treacheryes against this Nacon', especially 'that divillish conspiracy of the Gunpowder Plott'. 'By way of ostentacon' Mrs Thorowgood replied: 'But now the kinge loveth the Papists better then Puritans and hee would sooner trust them (meaninge the papists) then hee would the Puritans.' When West reproved her for these words 'bidding her have a care what shee says', Elizabeth Thorowgood told him that she would 'answere the words before the kinge, and the Councell'. Telling her 'it were a good deed', West expressed his readiness, which 'hee could finde in his heart', to inform the King about her speeches. But all Mrs Thorowgood answered was: 'Die alas! poore silly fellowe will the kinge say My wife is a Papist shall I not love them?' Now West spoke of the 'Multitude of Papists that were in this kingdome, and of their Arrogancy and Bouldness'. Whereupon she replied: 'Yee shall see within this little while there will bee more Papists then now there are.' According to West he had heard Elizabeth Thorowgood report on many earlier occasions in Parkman's house 'that shee hath heard diverse of his own Sort, meaninge the Protestants say that now the kinge comonly went to Masse, and was turned to bee a Papist'. West answered her 'that hee thought shee rather spoke it by way of Scandall to the Protestants thus to Traduce and scandal their kinge then for any reall matter of Truth that shee att any time heard such worde'.

One of Alexander West's frequent visits to Elizabeth Thorowgood's chamber took place during the 'comotion at Lambeth and Southwarke'. Under the impact of this event the following dialogue developed between them. Elizabeth Thorowgood said: 'I wished some order might be taken with those tumultous fellowes before they had done any harm.' Whereas Alexander West replied: 'I wish that he whoe was the cause of it were hanged.' When Mrs Thorowgood demanded 'whoe he was', West answered in a slanderous way: 'My Lord Canterbury a pox on hym for he was the cause of the dissolution of the parlament, but they will have him erre they leave.'[85] Trying to give his argument greater authority, West gossiped about occurrences in the King's chamber that supported his view of Archbishop Laud: 'My Lord Chamberline and my Lord Canterbury being together in the kings chamber, my Lord chamberline threw a booke at my Lord of Canterburys heade in the presence of his majesty and sayd god damne me, goe, for thou art a traytor.' Elizabeth Thorowgood later remembered that West's 'ordinary discourses with me before I forbid my lodging' were either verbal assaults against Catholics or arguments in favour of Anabaptism. Apparently, he had tried to convert her to Anabaptism on several occasions 'telling me that baptisme was not necessary to salvation, for sayd he, was not Enocke and Elias saved, and yett were they ever baptized'.[86] West, on the other hand, accused Mrs Thorowgood of persuading two women 'to forsake religion', which, however, proved to be false.

Although Alexander West and Elizabeth Thorowgood met quite frequently to discuss religious topics and day-to-day politics, their encounters were characterized by tension and animosity. Their tone was often arrogant, sharp, complacent, ironic and despising. When West said 'that were a good deed' in answer to Mrs Thorowgood's announcement that she would defend her words before the Privy Council, one can almost hear him laugh arrogantly. In turn Elizabeth Thorowgood signalled her scant regard for West by addressing him in a tone of compassionate

---

85 These verbal exchanges have been recorded in direct speech in Elizabeth Thorowgood's testimony. The only change from the original document is their typographical arrangement as a dialogue.

86 Enoch was the eldest son of Cain after whom the first city was named. He was the representative of wisdom in the rich apocalyptic literature of the period 150 B.C. until the year of Christ's birth. The apocalyptic literature of the Old Testament was very popular among sectarians and Enoch was thus a familiar figure. This probably accounts for the fact that he is chosen among the many other possible Old Testament figures who had not been baptized but were saved.

irony as a 'poore silly fellowe' who was unable to draw the correct conclusions from the existing politico-religious constella-
tions at Court. Although under examination West prided himself with his 'mild and calm' way of talking, his tone must have
struck Elizabeth Thorowgood as extremely biting. After all, he
was telling her 'mild and calmly' something which was outra-
geous in her eyes, namely, that the adherents of her religion were
traitors. West's generalizations about Catholics (*their* arrogance
and boldness) and his unqualified exaggerations (*multitudes* of
papists) certainly aroused Mrs Thorowgood's anger, provoking
her to defend her co-religionists against defamation. The most
effective way was to present Catholics as the King's favourites.
In a way the personal differences between West and Mrs Thorowgood marked the two extremes of the religious spectrum in the
1640s – Catholics and sectarians – and they obviously shared the
incompatibility and hostility of their beliefs.

Whereas West claimed to have talked in a 'mild and calm way',
he accused Elizabeth Thorowgood of provocative language.
Throughout his testimony against Mrs Thorowgood, West created the picture of a perfect 'gossip' who spoke 'by way of ostentation' and 'by way of scandal' full of malice without 'any real
matter of truth'. The term 'ostentation' implied 'vulgar display'
or 'false appearance' and West probably intended to describe
Elizabeth Thorowgood as a loose woman. This was a strong argument against women in the moral and legal climate of seventeenth-century England, and would have supported his accusation of her lack of credibility. However, West's disbelief in the
truth value of her claim that Protestants were spreading news
about Charles I going to mass was unfounded. A month earlier,
in May 1640, Mrs Chickleworth had gossiped about this very
incident in the neighbourhood of their lodging.[87] Elizabeth
Thorowgood, who had been committed to 'the new prison in

---

87   SP 16/454.42 (1640).

Clarkenwell, and her goods seized', presented herself in her petition as a model of chastity, loyalty and integrity. Describing West as a person 'which hath been branded for divers misdemenours, and of a scandalous disposition' her plea further read:

> Shee humbly prayeth your Lordshipp shee beinge very poore, gettinge her livinge by spinninge and in the nature of a widdowe, her husband beinge in the service of his Majestie in the troope of John Digby, you will bee pleased to give order that shee may bee enlarged.[88]

The fact that her husband was serving in the King's army demonstrated her loyalty to the state. After her imprisonment Elizabeth Thorowgood was re-examined by the justices of the peace for Middlesex and before the King's Bench, where she defended her own position with great self-confidence. Confessing that she had had several 'speeches' with Alexander West about Puritans and Catholics, she further admitted that 'shee used theis wordes': 'That the kinges Majestie might as well trust the Papists as the puritanes they were as good subiectes as the puritanes, And that shee said shee might speake theis words before any bodie.'[89]

The determination with which Elizabeth Thorowgood justified her opinions and religious beliefs was not unusual for Catholic women in early modern England.[90] In her essay 'Recusant Women 1560–1640', Mary Rowlands has shown that women – spinsters, wives, and widows – figured prominently among Catholics who refused to attend church or take the oath of allegiance in spite of severe penalties.[91] Under examination they were well able to speak for themselves and justify their reasons with religious arguments. According to Rowlands, 'the ability to learn, expound and teach religious knowledge was encouraged' among

---

88   SP 16/457.3 (1640).
89   SP 16/457.4ii (1640).
90   For another well documented case see SP 16/392.61; SP 16/393.2, 24–24i (Mary Cole).
91   Mary B. Rowlands, 'Recusant women 1560–1640', in *Women*, ed. Prior, pp 149–81.

Catholic women and 'episodes in which women successfully debated with "heretics" were recounted with approbation'.[92] The
King's Bench jury came to the conclusion that Elizabeth Thorowgood 'is a poore painfull woman, and laboreth for her living, and
hath never no cause of suspicon, that she is dangerous'.[93]

The above stories about men's and women's political and religious disputes in the early 1640s are unique examples of how
communication worked in everyday life. In view of the preceding chapters these stories demonstrate how the various aspects
of communication – censorship, the dissemination of news, the
impact of different news genres and pictures, the role of tales
and images of the past, interfaces of oral and print culture, and
the colloquial and slanderous nature of the political language of
the period – all played their part in every one of these communicative encounters. They thus bring together the various segments
of communication that have been discussed in turn throughout
the book, demonstrating the complex nature of the emerging
public sphere and its own seventeenth-century dynamics and
structures. Apart from fascinating detail about the interfaces of
print and oral news in these stories, perhaps most striking is the
evidence of floating borders between the private and the public
sphere and the ways in which 'some general discourse' turned
into a political and religious discussion.

Throughout there are numerous examples of women taking
part in communication. Furthermore, there has been evidence of
the gendered nature of political symbolism and 'political slander'. In this final section some of the material already discussed
will be looked at again in order to press the question of gender
and communication.

---

92 Ibid., p 175. Furthermore, women were 'prominent in the felonious activity'
    of harbouring priests, exploiting 'their supposed frailty and innocence', and
    pleading bodily infirmity when pursuivants arrived. Ibid., p 157.
93 SP 16/457.4, June 1640. 'Painful' is now obsolete and meant 'laborious'.

Gender and Communication

A striking feature of most everyday discussions about politics and religion in this period which have come down to us through numerous court records is the fact that women of all social classes, and regardless of their marital status, actively participated and that they were well informed.[94] In fact, it was quite often women who put forward important news and who instigated a discussion. John Oneby and Mary Brooksby talked about all kinds of 'general' things, when she confronted Oneby with a very precise question about the cause of the Scottish war, thus changing the topic of their 'general discourse' to politics, and she readily disputed his interpretation of the Bible.[95] Anne Hussey, an Irish woman, informed Philip Bainbridge about plots the Catholics were planning in England. She had received this news from 'Mr Conyard [O' Connor], an Irish priest and confessor to the Queen'. The case soon reached the ears of the Privy Council and Hussey and O' Connor were examined by the justices of the peace for Middlesex.[96] When Anne Hussey was threatened by 'certaine Irish people to bee mischieved', special order was given to the sheriffs of London 'to receave into their charge the person of the said Mrs Hussey and to dispose of her in some such safe place as she may be free from any violence or danger'.[97] A few months later the whole dialogue between William O' Connor and Anne Hussey appeared in print.[98]

---

94   Part of this section has previously appeared in a different form: 'The King's Crown is the Whore of Babylon: Politics, Gender and Communication in Mid-Seventeenth-Century England', in 'Presentations of the Self in Early Modern England', *Gender and History*, Special Issue, 7/3, ed. Amy L. Erickson and Ross Balzaretti (November, 1995), pp 457–81.

95   SP 16/430.10 (1639) and SP 16/423.44ii-iii (1639).

96   PC 2.52.725. For an earlier examination of William O' Connor see SP 16/420.50.

97   PC 2.52.725. The order was renewed a month later. PC 2.53.15.

98   *A Discovery of the prayse of God, and joy of all true hearted Protestants, of a late intended plot by the Papists to subdue the Protestants. Being a true Copie of a*

Men readily passed on news which they had received from women, and, in turn, they informed women about politics. On his return from a trip to London in May 1639, Edward Thursby of Gatewick, Essex, informed 'the chief women' of his parish who were visiting his wife 'that lyes in' about 'some newes concerning the Scottish business' that 'was spoken about the towne'.[99] One of the women passed the news straight on to her husband, who sent a letter to a friend telling him about his wife's relation.

In a society with norms that placed the greatest weight on men's words and deeds and condemned women to be quiet, associating honesty with chastity, obedience, and silence, women's public voicing of their opinions raises a number of questions about what we think of as women's 'traditional role' in history. The central role women played in everyday discussions of politics and religion on the eve of the English Civil War stands in sharp contrast to early modern conduct books which advised women not to engage in politics, but to confine their activities to the household. Similarly, women who transgressed the proper rules of conduct and talked about issues they were not entitled to pronounce upon were represented as lewd women, gossips, and scolds. These negative female stereotypes enjoyed great popularity in the sixteenth and seventeenth centuries, and they reappeared as symbols of disorder and unreliability in both learned and popular texts as well as in neighbourly disputes, signifying the defamation of private or public opponents. Furthermore, politics was traditionally seen as a male domain, and the few female rulers were considered an exception to the rule. Consequently, the question of women and politics in early modern Europe has been neglected, which is partially due to a rather narrow definition of the political as the politics of official institutions which excluded women.

Discourse between William O' Connor a Priest, and Anne Hussey an Irish Gentlewoman. Printed Anno, 1641. William Clark Collection BB.I.14 (28) and BB.W.(28) (a different edition with a woodcut). BL E.158.4.

99   SP 16/423.132.

More recent research has broadened the perspective by pointing to various informal ways through which women could shape
politics.[100] Noble women, for instance, could influence politics
through personal networking.[101] Women of varying social status
expressed their concerns in petitions to the state or organized
riots and demonstrations.[102] Studies on women and politics
during the English Civil War have tended to look at women's
special role within society at war.[103] Only recently, Ann Hughes
has convincingly demonstrated the necessity to take a broader
perspective and to undertake a cultural analysis of radical politics including gender rather than singling out specific episodes
in women's activism. Taking the Levellers as a case in point, she
can show that Leveller women and Leveller presentations of gender were part of the Leveller movement itself.[104] In England,
publications by women, mainly on religious issues, increased
considerably after the early 1640s, and women's opinions became known to a larger public.[105] Recently, historians have started

100 In general Natalie Z. Davis, 'Women in Politics', in *A History of Women*, iii,
     Renaissance and Enlightment Paradoxes, ed. George Duby, Michelle Perrot et
     al. (Cambridge/Mass. and London, 1993), pp 167–83.
101 Susanna Burghartz, 'Frauen-Politik-Weiberregiment. Schlagworte zur Bewäl-
     tigung der politischen Krise von 1691 in Basel', in *Frauen in der Stadt. Les
     femmes dans la ville*, ed. A.-L. Head-König und A. Tanner (Zürich, 1993), pp
     113–34.
102 Rudolf M. Dekker, 'Women in revolt. Popular protest and its social basis in
     Holland in the seventeenth and eighteenth centuries', *Theory and Society* 16
     (1987), pp 337–62; Walter, 'Grain riots'.
103 Paula Higgins, 'The Reactions of Women, with Special Reference to Women
     Petitioners', in *Politics, Religion and the English Civil War*, ed. Brian Manning
     (London, 1973), pp 179–222; Ann Marie McEntee, '"The [Un]civill-sisterhod
     of Oranges and Lemons": female petitioners and demonstrators, 1642–53',
     Prose Studies, 14 (1991), also published as a separate volume: *Pamphlet*, ed.
     Holstun.
104 Hughes, 'Gender and Politics'.
105 *Women and the Literature of the Seventeenth Century*, An Annotated Bibliogra-
     phy based on Wing's Short-title Catalogue, Compiled by Hilda L. Smith and
     Susan Cardinale (New York and London, 1990); *A Bibliographical Dictionary*,

to analyse women's religious radicalism and its impact on politics.[106]

In the past, historians have sometimes confused women's role
in history with the symbolic system describing politics. Joan Scott
has urged scholars to 'look for the ways in which concepts of
gender legitimize and construct social relationships'.[107] Thus, in
the light of women's engagement with politics in the conflict-
ridden 1640s, historians ought to pose the question of women's
participation in politics differently. First, we need to reconsider
our concept of the political. Politics in the early modern period,
I want to argue, is centrally connected to communication, information and rumour.[108] And second, we need to bring the literature on women's conduct and gossip into consideration of the
political in order to 'develop insights into the reciprocal nature
of gender and society and into the particular and specific ways in
which politics constructs gender and gender constructs politics'.[109]
Since negative representations of women and their speech play
such a prominent role and are used in order to discredit political

---

ed. Bell, Parfitt and Sheperd; Crawford, 'Women's published writings'; Graham
et al. (eds.), *Her own Life*.

106 At the University of Kassel, Germany, Heide Wunder, Helga Zöttlein, and
Barbara Hoffmann have started a joint project on various aspects of women's
religiosity and politics in late 16th to 18th century Germany: *Konfession,
Religiosität und politisches Handeln von Frauen vom ausgehenden 16. bis zum
Beginn des 18. Jahrhunderts*.

107 Joan W. Scott, 'Gender: A Useful Category of Historical Analysis', *AHR*, 91
(1986), pp 1053–75, p 1070.

108 In his essay 'The shaming of Margaret Knowsley: gossip, gender and experience of authority in early modern England', *Continuity and Change*, (1994),
pp 391–419, Steve Hindle has stressed both the political and social-historical
significance of gossip. An interesting survey of the uses and meanings of gossip and its social function has been published by Pia Holenstein and Norbert
Schindler: 'Geschwätzgeschichte(n). Ein kulturhistorisches Plädoyer für die
Rehabilitierung der unkontrollierten Rede', in *Dynamik der Tradition. Studien
zur historischen Kulturforschung*, ed. Richard van Dülmen (Frankfurt, 1992),
pp 41–108.

109 Scott, 'Gender', p 1070.

developments and opponents in the seventeenth century, the question of gender needs to be pressed further.

In order to tackle the interdependence of politics, gender, and communication in early modern England, the complex process of communication at the peak of political crisis in mid-seventeenth-century England is a good sample case to analyse, first, for the density of the surviving records on (seditious) speech of ordinary men and women, and second, for the acute concern with 'public opinion' and 'correct' opinions on the part both of the authorities and the people. The singularity and complexity of each case provides an insight into how men and women interacted when exchanging and defending their views. Various aspects of politics, gender, and communication and their interaction will be analysed by looking in turn at the representations of women and speech, the discourse on 'public opinion', communication and women's engagement with politics, and, finally, the self-perception of women who engaged in the exchange of opinions in the early 1640s.

Early modern representations of women are now quite familiar through numerous studies and anthologies, and I shall recapitulate only some of their main characteristics in order to show how they interacted with discourses on communication and 'public opinion', and how they influenced women's self-perception.[110] Conduct books, marriage manuals, and proverbs time and again emphasized 'silence' as the 'best ornament of women'.[111] 'For there is nothing that doth so commend, avaunce, set forthe, adourne, dercke, trim and garnish a maid, as silence.'[112] The 'space'

---

110 For the best known attack on women see Thomas Tel-troth alias J. Swetnam, *Arraignment of Lewd, idle, forward and unconstant women* (London, 1615). Ian Maclean, *The Renaissance Notion of Women* (Cambridge, 1980); and Katherine Usher Henderson and Barbara F. McManus, *Half Humankind. Contexts and Texts of the Controversy about Women in England 1540–1640* (Urbana and Chicago, 1985).

111 *A Collection of English Proverbs* (Cambridge, 1670), p 24.

112 Kelso, *Doctrine*, p 50.

for women's speech was confined to the domestic sphere; likewise, the topics on which women were allowed to speak were connected with the household. In his instructions to gentlewomen, Richard Braithwaite wrote about speech:

> Touching the subject of your discourse when opportunity shal exact it of you, and without touch of immodesty expect it from you; make choyce of such arguments as may best improve your knowledge in household affaires, and other private employments.[113]

This view of women's role in society is echoed in the reaction of the Parliament to Leveller women petitioners in 1649. They were 'desired to go home, and look after your owne businesse and meddle with your housewifery'.[114] Even the tone of women's speech and their gestures were prescribed by male guidelines: 'not to be cutted, sharpe, sullen, passionate, teechie; but meeke, quiet, submissive.'[115] Furthermore, women were to refrain from any 'discourse of state matters' or 'high points of divinity' since not understanding them 'they would labour to intangle others of equall understanding to themselves'.[116]

Obviously, conduct books and marriage manuals reached mainly educated women, yet ballads and proverbs also picked up the issue, and male rules for female talk showed a large variation on the same theme addressing all social groups.[117] There were

---

113 Braithwaite, *The English Gentlewoman*.
114 Hughes, 'Gender and Politics', p 163.
115 W. Whately, A *Bride-Bush, or Wedding Sermon: compendiously describing the duties of married persons*, (London, 1624).
116 Braithwaite, *The English Gentlewoman*.
117 Throughout the early modern period, marriage ballads frequently presented women as verbally or physically aggressive and uncontrollable, thus posing a threat to the existing social order and value system of society as well as to the honour and social position of their husbands. For the 'Ladie at Court' there were different rules guiding their talk and conversation as well as gestures and the topics of their speech etc. See A. R. Jones, 'Nets and bridles: early modern conduct books and sixteenth-century women's lyrics', in *The ideology of conduct. Essays on Literature and the History of Sexuality*, ed. N. Armstrong and L. Tennenhouse (New York, 1987), 39–72.

also numerous tracts in early modern England which defended women's independent utterance of opinions, though within limits.[118] Religion, traditionally a space which allowed women some 'room of their own', increasingly became a sphere where women's opinions were tolerated if not welcomed by men. Nevertheless, it would be misleading to conclude that *at the level of representation* women were granted more freedom of speech because of the emphasis on lay piety. In fact, the shift from the domestic space to that of religious activity meant merely a change of rules, demanding submission to a new set of values created by men, and partly reproduced by women. Although women could and did read and interpret the Bible from their own point of view, and although they were prepared to defend their religious convictions, as a number of important studies on women and religion have shown, the 'official interpretation' of God's word was, and still is, primarily masculine.[119] It was mainly in nonconformist religious groups that women could exercise their religious beliefs freely, but for the toleration of these religious sects they depended on the male governing bodies in state and church. However, research in progress on women's religious radicalism and their political influence promises to throw new light on the impact that women's religious views might have had on politics and state. To what extent various forms of folk religion and magic were influenced by female religiosity is as yet another open question. The main point for the present argument is that at all levels

118 For an example see S. Geree, *The Ornament of Women* (London, 1639) as well as the increasing number of female authors who defended women's writing and publishing in the seventeenth century. See for instance Angeline Goreau, *The Whole Duty of a Woman. Female Writers in Seventeenth-Century England*, 2 vols. (Washington, 1984) and Simon Shepherd (ed.), *The Women's Sharp Revenge. Five Women's Pamphlets from the Renaissance* (London, 1985).

119 Bonnelyn Young Kunze, *Margaret Fell and the Rise of Quakerism* (London, 1994); Crawford, *Women and Religion*; Phyllis Mack, *Visionary Women. Ecstatic Prophecy in 17th c. England* (Berkeley, 1992). See also the issue on 'Religion' in *L'Homme*, 1 (1990).

of religious practice, women's religious views could be rejected on the grounds that they were against 'God's word', which was defined by men.[120]

At the normative level of women's speech there was only one area where women's voices were granted some kind of authenticity of their own, and that was prophecy. Apart from biblical arguments in favour of female prophets it was thought that 'women were suited to be prophets because of their nature, being irrational, emotional, and unusually receptive to outside influences'.[121] The editor of the works of Antonia Bourignon wrote: 'In her conversations with God she used neither ideas nor meditations, but was in an admirable vacuity of all her desire of knowing either this or that; having no will of her own.'[122] In their role as prophetesses, women may have found an infinite space for their speech, yet they were deprived of their own voice. They were reduced to 'empty vessels' resonating with the words of God in the eyes of their male contemporaries. And it was men who sentenced prophetesses to imprisonment if their visions did not meet the political ends or threatened the power of men.

Regardless of the freedom of speech women were granted under certain conditions in early modern England, any deviation from the rules governing their talk turned the image of the chaste, obedient and graceful woman into the image of 'women on top': discordant, disruptive, unruly. Female speech was intrinsically suspect, and women who left the domestic or religious space threatened to overthrow the social order which depended on their general submissiveness. Norbert Schindler and Pia Holenstein have argued that the growing concern with women's uncontrolled

---

120 In her study on women and religion, Patricia Crawford has shown that the relative religious freedom women enjoyed during the turmoil of the mid-seventeenth century experienced a backlash during the Restoration when religious nonconformity came under criticism.

121 Phyllis Mack, 'Women as Prophets during the English Civil War', *Feminist Studies*, 8 (1982), pp 19–45, p 23.

122 Cit. in Mack, 'Prophets', p 23.

speech and sexuality in the sixteenth century went hand-in-hand with the introduction of marriage as the only acceptable status for women and attempts to combat prostitution and celibacy. Women were confined to the house, and public places were associated with a lack of chastity.[123] The continuing obsession with women's conduct, speech, and gossip in the early seventeenth century has been attributed by scholars to growing female assertiveness due to socio-economic changes which strained gender relations.[124] The majority of men in the seventeenth century, for instance, considered female disorder as one of the worst effects of the English revolution.[125]

The free utterance of opinions by women was equated with sexual looseness and disorder. 'Speech in public, especially with strangers, is not suitable to women, whose voice is no less to be dreaded than their nakedness, since habits and emotions are easily betrayed in speech.'[126] The image of the seductress evoked here introduces the irrational, incomprehensible, and uncontrollable in women as it was seen by many male contemporaries. The power of women's free speech is intertwined with their 'overpowering' sexual lust and desire, which men often felt to be threatening. This perception of women's unguarded speech is reinforced by the focus on the female tongue as a woman's main strength.[127] The tongue was depicted as her only weapon against men, and a number of tracts evoke the parallel between the female tongue and the male penis referring to 'original sin'. Lisa Jardine has

---

123 Holenstein and Schindler, 'Geschwätzgeschichte(n)', p 60.

124 David E. Underdown, 'The Taming of the Scold: the Enforcement of Patriarchal Authority in Early Modern England', in *Order and Disorder*, ed. Fletcher and Stevenson, pp 116–36.

125 Patricia Crawford, 'The Challenges to Patriarchalism: How did the Revolution affect Women?', in *Revolution and Restoration. England in the 1650s*, ed. John Morrill (London, 1992), pp 112–28, p 126.

126 Kelso, *Doctrine*, p 101.

127 See, for instance, a ballad printed in 1638: *The Anatomy of a woman's Tongue, divided in five parts: A Medicine, a Poison, a Serpent, Fire, and Thunder*. Harleian Misc., ed. T. Parker, 12 vols. (London, 1808–1811).

shown how the two metonymic uses of 'tongue' in the 'Taming of the Shrew' get 'drawn together in its bawdy use as the specifically female sexual instrument, the female counterpart of the penis'. She argues that 'throughout the literature of the period we find a willingness to slide provocatively from one sense to another: scolding=active use of the female tongue=female sexuality=female penis'.[128]

Inseparably connected with these images were those of the scold, shrew, or gossip. The popular early modern comic genre of the 'gossips' meeting', for instance, is full of stories such as the following: a company of women meets in a tavern, drinks and freely discusses their husbands' (sexual) behaviour, thus undermining men's authority and personal integrity.

> Three Gossips in a Tavern, chatting over a pint of Sherry, said one of them: I muse whereabouts a cuckolds hornes growes; quoth the second: I thinke they doe growe in the pole oor nape of the necke; verily, quoth the third, I doe thinke it bee true, for my husbands bands are always worne out behind.[129]

The gist of these and many similar stories was men's fear that their privacy might be hurt by women who spread information about their person that was not meant for a larger audience and might tarnish their public image. Here, too, women's speech which transgressed male rules and left the 'private sphere' threatened to upset the existing order. I have argued earlier that these negative and limited representations of women's speech with their subtexts of social disorder acquire new meaning in the mid-seventeenth century, when the rise of popular opinion and the public voice is heavily criticized in the wake of the gradual professionalization of the newstrade and the sudden growth in the

---

128 Lisa Jardine, *Still Harping on Shakespeare's Daughters. Women and Drama in the Age of Shakespeare* (Brighton, 1983), p 121.
129 John Taylor, 'A Ribble-Rabble of Gossips. Wit and Mirth. Chargeably Collected out of Taverns, Ordinaries, Innes, Bowling-Greenes and Allyes, in *Shakespeare Jest-Books*, ed. William C. Hazlitt, 3 vols. (London, 1864), iii, p 75.

number of pamphlets at the beginning of the English Civil War. The negative female identity of 'opinion' in the 1640s was influenced by the familiar image of women as 'scolds', 'shrews' and 'gossips', who violated the social order with their loathing, lust, and lies. 'Public opinion' thus threatened to transform society into a world turned upside down, bare of its traditional hierarchies, rules and morals.

In the preceding chapters it has been shown that politics repeatedly drew upon negative images of women, constituting a political symbolism which equated opponents with women's vices and sexuality. As we have seen, these negative images were paralleled by conduct books and marriage manuals which listed silence, obedience, and chastity among the top female virtues. Representing the model of female conduct, these virtues were always implicit in their inversion: the negative representations of women's behaviour. Vice versa, negative female images were an inversion of honest subjects and an ordered society. The concept of subversive female sexuality as a symbolic system signifying the insurgency of opponents, whether public figures or private persons, male or female alike, seems to have permeated all layers of society and discourse, both popular and learned.

The same applies to a genderized perception of gossip as malicious or trivial female talk which is condemned on moral grounds and plays down its social function. Men across the centuries and cultures have attributed the disruptive impact of gossip in their own times to exclusively female speech incapable of any positive outcome. Early modern England makes no exception. Originally a positive term deriving from the Old English 'godsibb' (godparent), which came to be applied to familiar friends, especially a woman's female friends gathering and tittle-tattling around her bed at a birth, the term 'gossip' acquired negative connotations once applied to exclusively female company outside the family.[130] Rooted in the image of tittle-tattling women

---

130 Old English Dictionary, i (1988), 873, and A. Rysman, 'How the "Gossip" became a woman', *Journal of Communication*, 27 (1977), pp 176–80.

at birth where men's presence was not permitted, in seventeenth-century England exclusively female company – 'gossips' – was associated with light talk that threatened to undermine men's honour – if not authority – since it was outside their control.[131] When gossip is acknowledged as a part of public opinion, it becomes part of the political and offers a way of seeing women as intricately involved in politics. In the guise of a seemingly trivial story, political gossip about the King and his family could signal personal and collective disapproval of his religious sympathies. In May 1640, Mrs Chickleworth told the following story to Mr Leonard and William Mayle, when she met them in the house of Mr Cledell in London:

> As she has heard 'the Queens Grace went unto the communion table with the King'. And the Queen had asked 'your grace whether that she might not be of that religion the King was – yes or no'? Whereupon his Grace answered her Majesty 'you are very well as you are, and I would wish to keep you there. And now the King goes to Mass with the Queen'.[132]

This little story encapsulates the fears of many people, namely, that Charles I might turn Catholic under the influence of his Catholic wife and Archbishop Laud (his 'Grace'), who was believed to be plotting the re-Catholicization of England.[133] The story reappears in the same year in Mrs Chickleworth's neighbourhood when the Anabaptist Alexander West accused the Catholic Elizabeth Thorowgood that he had heard her report on many occasions that 'shee hath heard diverse of his own Sort, meaninge the Protestants say that now the kinge comonly went to Masse, and was turned to bee a Papist'.[134] On 17 June 1640,

---

131 See, for instance, S. Rowland, *A Crew of Gossips* (1613); Taylor, *A Ribble-rabble of Gossips*, iii, 83–6; and esp. Philogenes Panedonius [R. Brathwaite], *Ar't asleep Husband? A Boulster Lecture; Stored with all variety of witty jeasts, merry Tales, and other pleasant passages* (1640).

132 SP 16/454.42.

133 Hibbard, *Charles I*.

134 SP 16/457.3i-4i.

William Mayle, a clothier from Wiltshire, overheard the following political gossip told by Mrs Wood in the presence of Mr Lowther and 'two other persons' in her own house, the Three Cranes in Thames Street, London. Mayle remembered that

> The said Mrs Wood reported that our Gratious prince hath byn these five days weeping bitterly and with dreams in the night. And that the King's Majesty came unto him at the last and asked him what was the matter. And the Prince did reply, your Majesty should have asked that sooner, then his Majesty requested the Prince tell him, the Prince answeared and said My Grandfather left you four kingdomes, and I am afraid your Majesty will leave me never a one. Whereupon the king should ask the prince who have been your relator in this?[135]

The political background to this story was Charles I's attempt to make up for his previous defeat in the Scottish war with an unmotivated and poorly equipped army in the autumn of 1640. Mrs Wood was obviously informed about the military strength of the two armies and voiced her scepticism of a royal victory by 'gossiping' about the King's family. The idea for her story probably came from a contemporary joke by one of the most popular and best known pamphleteers of the time, John Taylor:

> A Man beingly deeply in play at dice having lost much money, his sonne (a little lad) being by him, wept. Quoth the father: Boy, why dost thou weepe? The boy answered, that hee had read that his father (King Philipp) had conquered many Cities, Townes, and Territories, fearing that hee would leave him nothing to winne and I weepe the contrary way (quoth the boy) for feare that my father will leave me nothing to loose.[136]

Men, too, used pictorial language in order to explain their opinions. Yet they do not seem to have employed exemplary stories or personal details to the same extent as women. Furthermore, men's disputes, regardless of their social status, often ended up

---

135 SP 16/454.42
136 Taylor, 'Wit and Mirth', p 79.

in fighting, whereas women used violent images but were less inclined actually to fight.[137]

Although the source material recording political disputes is rather sketchy, it suggests that there was a tendency for women to voice their opinions about the political and religious conflicts of their time by telling stories which exemplified the issues in question, and to add spice to their arguments by drawing on personal details about the people involved. In other words, by interweaving narrative, gossip, and political facts they passed (moral) judgement.[138] Without dismissing the disruptive aspects of gossip and rumour in society, researchers working on women and gossip have only just started to take away the exclusively negative overtones of 'gossip' by pointing to the importance of female networking for the exchange of (personal) news, which could gain political momentum if it was 'publicized', thus blending the private and the public spheres.[139] In the case of the politico-religious opinions of the 1640s that were exchanged by word of mouth, gossip functioned as a genre that was familiar to women through their informal networks and talk. In order to exemplify their political views, women made up stories, often drawing on the large tradition of popular literature and imagery, which they then turned into 'political gossip' as an effective genre for passing judgement. This does not imply, however, that women did not use other ways of expressing their views, nor that men did not also gossip. Often women presented straightforward news

---

137 That women were less inclined to violence than men has been demonstrated by J. Bohlstedt, 'Gender, Household and Community Politics: Women in English riots 1790–1810', Past and Present, 120 (1988), pp 88–122.

138 On women's memory and narrative patterns see also some stimulating observations in James Fentress and Chris Wickham, Social Memory (Oxford, 1992), esp. pp 137–43.

139 Most recently Hindle, 'The shaming'; Carola Lipp, Schimpfende Weiber und patriotische Jungfrauen (Baden-Baden, 1986); and M. B. Norton, 'Gender and defamation in Seventeenth-Century Maryland', William and Mary Quarterly, 3rd series, 44 (January 1987), pp 3–39.

and facts and asked precise questions, as already demonstrated. Despite the normative impact of conduct books, social status and gender did not in practice restrict people from uttering their minds, an attitude which conflicted with the existing social hierarchy and gender roles. How, then, did women view their own participation in political and religious discussions? Did the role models of conduct books and the negative representations of women's speech have any impact on women's self-perception and agency? Did male contemporaries employ these images in discussions with women or in the court? And finally, did women feel that their sex imposed limits on the expression of their opinions? Did they, perhaps, profit from being women in verbal disputes?

In the politicized everyday talk of the 1640s, women did not feel inhibited from expressing their opinions by the rules set forth in conduct books. It could be shown that regardless of their social status women actively engaged in politico-religious discussions, and readily defended their opinions. Nevertheless, they and their male counterparts were conscious of these images, and time and again they cropped up in the course of their arguments.[140] Elaine Hobby has argued that women who published their works or sent petitions to the Parliament justified their conduct as a 'virtue of necessity', being aware that they were acting immodestly and transgressing prescribed rules of conduct.[141] The distinction between 'conventional phrases of modesty' is familiar from epistles in male publications, too, and women's justifications of their writing is not always clear.

Whereas there was pressure on women who published their works, this was less so for women who sent private letters. Nevertheless, depending on the topic they were addressing, there is

---

140 An important question that needs addressing through more research on different issues is whether women and men of a higher social status were more 'gender conscious' than those lower down the scale, and if so, how did it show?
141 Elaine Hobby, *Virtue of Necessity*. Similarly Goreau, 'Introduction', in *Duty*, i, p 1–20.

evidence that women knew they were acting contrary to the rules. On the outbreak of the Scottish war in 1639, Mary Countess of Westmorland sent the following letter to Secretary Windebank. Aware that she was transgressing gender boundaries, she justified her behaviour by reference to a woman's wish for peace:

> My noblest friend, into whose hands I dare put my life I know that to meddle in things above us is dangerous, but my interest and that of the children unborn enforces me to utter my mind (...). They say the women of Scotland are chief stirrers of this war. I think it not so shameful for women of England to wish well to the peace of these nations, whether it be by word or writing; yet I pray, when you have read this letter, to burn it, that it may not rise up in anybody's judgement but yours against me, to tax my zeal with ignorance or arrogance, who would willingly sacrifice my own life for the quenching of this fire.[142]

Women's speaking was a different story. In political and religious discussions of the period women's arguments were only occasionally rejected on the grounds of their sex, evoking the image of the unchaste gossip or unruly woman. The Anabaptist Alexander West defended himself in court by describing his way of discussing the 'popish and protestant Religion' with the Catholic Elizabeth Thorowgood as 'milde and calme' whereas she allegedly spoke in an 'ostentacious manner' and by 'way of Scandall to the Protestants thus to traduce and scandal their kinge then for any reall matter of Truth that shee att any time heard such worde'.[143] In the course of several discussions between West and Thorowgood while lodging at the house of Thomas Parkman in London, Elizabeth Thorowgood presented herself as a self-confident woman convinced of the justification of her opinions and her right to express them. When West threatened to report her to the King, she answered 'Die alas! poore silly fellowe will the kinge say My wife is a Papist shall I not love them'. And when

---

142 SP 16/420.5.
143 SP 16/457.3–4.

West complained about the 'Multitude of Papists that were in the kingdome, and of their Arrogancy and Bouldness', Thorowgood replied 'Yee shall see within this little while there will bee more Papists then now there are'. Eventually, Elizabeth Thorowgood forbade West her lodgings, and when she was tried before the King's Bench she admitted that 'shee used theis wordes': 'That the kinges Majestie might as well trust the Papists as the puritanes they were as good subjects as the puritanes, And that shee said shee might speake theis words before any bodie.'[144] In her plea to the King's Bench jury Elizabeth Thorowgood described West as a man 'which hath been branded for divers misdemenours, and of a scandalous disposition', whereas she was careful to present herself as a loyal subject whose husband was serving in the King's army whilst she earned her living by spinning. After several imprisonments and with all her goods seized, Elizabeth Thorowgood was finally released on the grounds that she 'is a poore painfull woman, and laboreth for her living, and hath never no cause of suspicion, that she is dangerous'.

At the symbolic level of representation, gender-specific images had been used: a male way of speaking was described as 'mild and calm', implying a rational and balanced argument, versus a female way of lying 'in an ostentacious manner' which evoked the negative image of the lusty and untrustworthy gossip, 'ostentacious' meaning 'vulgar display' or 'false appearance'. However, these gender constructions did not prevent the woman involved from expressing or defending her opinion. Likewise, West had continued his discussions with Thorowgood in spite of their opposing views, and the justices could be convinced that she was not 'dangerous'. The determination with which Elizabeth Thorowgood justified her opinions and stood up for her religious beliefs was not unusual for Catholic women in early modern England. During a discussion with her fellow servant Thomas Poulter about the Gunpowder Plot and the examina-

---

144 SP 16/457.4ii.

tion of Samuel Pickering before the Star Chamber, Mary Cole, a Catholic widow from Camden Hall in Essex, grew angry and exclaimed: 'If shee wear as the Queene shee would quickly make away with king Charles for dealing so hardly with that Religion.'[145]

In everyday life contexts men seem not only to have tolerated the participation of women in political and religious discussions, but they also respected their opinions and were keen to hear their views. When Barbara Black, one Seaton, and one Leviston discussed the Scottish war, the King's Council and his religious policy at great length in Black's house, the widow dominated their talk throughout. Furthermore, Seaton was trying to impress her with his courage and strength and said that he was going to make the Archbishop of Canterbury, William Laud, 'cringe' and hoped 'thou wert but by'.[146] A different image was evoked when Mrs Chickleworth defended the rumour and gossip she had spread about the King's Catholic sympathies by saying 'that she did not believe it but that these things came upon us for our sins'.[147] The belief that evil thoughts and deeds including suicide entered man's mind in a state of sin was very widespread in early modern England and was frequently used to explain unnatural things.[148] The woman's justification thus expressed a conviction of her own time, and as a woman in the traditional image of an 'empty vessel' she might have been considered especially suitable to receive and express such ideas. Furthermore, in her plea she presented herself as free of any guilt since it was not her own opinion that she had expressed. She claimed that she had merely reproduced the bad opinions that were flourishing as a result of collective sin.

---

145 SP 16/392.61 and SP 16/393.2, 24–24i.
146 SP 16/469.95, SP 16/470.33 (1640).
147 SP 16/454.42.
148 Seaver, *Wallington's World*; id., *Lectureship*; and esp. Michael MacDonald and Terence Murphy, *Sleepless Souls. Suicide in Early Modern England* (Oxford, 1990).

The following statements and cases suggest that women were aware of belonging to the 'weaker sex'. Whereas some women felt restricted in their actions because they were women, which involved both physical and political weakness and exclusion from such male activities as office-holding or, in one particular case, war, others did not experience the same lack of freedom. On the contrary, the image of the 'weaker vessel' could serve, for instance, as a means of imposing a specific female mode of communication which drew its own strength from the fact that it ruled out physical violence. At the height of the Civil War, Joan Sherrard, spinster, allegedly uttered 'these words against the King to wit vizt his Majesty is a stuttering foole. Is there never a Felon yett living? If I were a man, as I am a woman, I would help to pull him to pieces.'[149] Sherrard not only appears to have taken sides in the war as so many of her sex had done but also wished to join in the fighting. Being a woman this was impossible unless she dressed in men's clothes, thus changing her female identity to a male appearance. From her statement it is not quite clear whether she related the lack of agency she experienced to her prescribed social role as a woman, or to her lack of physical strength, or to both. In contrast, another woman, Mary Giles, wife of a lawyer, was accused of having said 'I will kill the King of England'.[150]

A well documented case of 1639 demonstrates that a woman was very powerful in imposing a mode of communication which kept a dispute that threatened to turn into physical violence within the realms of verbal warfare. The source of her power lay, in fact, in the image of women as the 'weaker vessel'. This case further shows that communication was not restricted to speaking, listening or reading, but that tone, gestures, posture, demeanour, and symbolic action were just as important. Throughout the argument with John Blunt, Anne Woodward remained unimpressed by his insults and threats. She was determined to solve the whole

---

149 MJ/GDB/29.11, No. 5 (1644).
150 MJ/GDR, (4 April 1645).

conflict in a peaceful way, exploiting her weakness into strength. Incapable of using any force and thus able to compel the two men involved in the dispute to talk rather than fight, she had to rely completely on her own wits, and she employed various strategies to appease the men involved. The behaviour of Anne Woodward shows that gender constructions which were negative *per se* did not necessarily restrict female agency. In this case, the image of the 'weaker sex', its corresponding gender roles and modes of conduct served as a means of de-escalating conflict by keeping the argument in the realms of verbal warfare rather than physical violence.[151] In a recent article Ulinka Rublack has discussed a similar instance in which pregnant women in early modern Germany were very powerful in fending off violence.[152]

All of the above cases suggest that it is important to analyse more carefully and on a larger scale, how representations of women and men interact with the self-presentation and self-perception of both sexes, and to look at male and female agency as it accords with or contrasts with gendered roles and social status. The negative images of women, namely that of the whore, gossip or scold, did not only legitimize the asymmetries of an early modern patriarchial society. These images served, furthermore, to discredit political opponents and private enemies. Arising from the subordinate position of women, these stereotypes were universally applied by both sexes to signify the breach of social taboos which threatened to overturn the existing social structure and value system. It has been shown that the images of women as gossips and scolds were instrumentalized for political ends, that is, they constructed politics. With the help of a political symbolism based on the female identity of 'opinion' with all its con-

---

151   In early modern Europe it was a widespread and popular theme that women, due to a lack of physical strength, could nevertheless outwit men. A famous case in point is Chaucer's *Wife of Bath*. Courtship ballads are full of women outwitting men when trying to protect their virginity.

152   Ulinka Rublack, 'Pregnancy, Childbirth and the Female Body in Early Modern Germany', *Past and Present*, 150 (1996), pp 84–110. Also M. Dinges, 'Weiblichkeit', esp. pp 94–96.

notations of unchastity and disorder, 'public opinion' was condemned for undermining the existing hierarchies and privileges. In other words: politics constructs gender.

In the context of communication in seventeenth-century England, it has become clear that gender constructions of women and speech had been largely internalized by men and by women. They influenced and recreated gender relations through the common interpretation of images and meaning, yet they did not determine and condition specific male or female behaviour to the extent of not allowing any 'alternative behaviour'. In the various instances of everyday life discussions of religion and politics, women, regardless of their social status and sex are found engaging in disputes with men. In court they had to justify the opinions they had voiced, not the fact that they had spoken 'as women'. The settings where these talks were conducted differed greatly, ranging from lodgings, alehouses, and workplaces to 'private' homes. Although there were signs that women were aware of certain gendered expectations of conduct, it did not seem to have prevented them from voicing their opinions both 'publicly' outside their home, and on issues upon which they were not entitled to pronounce. However, in the course of arguments and the conduct of talk, gender-specific images such as 'irrationality' and 'disorder' for women, or 'rationality' and 'violence' for men crept in and were readily used by both sexes. Yet the uses the various images of men and women were put to in a specific context differed with each instance. Since these images were functional rather than a mirror of reality, their employment was arbitrary and served private and political ends.

Women's central role in political everyday life discussions of the 1640s demonstrates that men and women acted within a gendered and classed society and political system both by adhering to and reproducing gendered and social roles of conduct, *and* by ignoring them. Gender constitutes itself as a process, and its various meanings and significations depend on specific historical contexts, everyday life situations, social status, and male and female agency.

7 · Conclusion

To the Reader
Distracted fame throughout the world so spreads
That monster-like, she now hath many heads
A man can goe to no place, but shall heare
Things that may make him hope, and make him feare.[1]

The rise of public opinion in seventeenth-century England troubled contemporaries and it was recognized as a new social force which had a strong impact on the political culture of the time. In fact, politics in the seventeenth century cannot be understood fully without recognizing that it is centrally connected to communication, information, rumour and gossip. Thus, women's conduct and gossip were brought into consideration of the political to 'develop insights into the reciprocal nature of gender and society and into specific ways in which politics constructs gender and gender constructs politics'.[2] The political symbolism of the period, representing public opinion as a woman, associating it with the negative qualities of gossip and 'fama', and the slanderous nature of 'the language of conflict' both in print and speech, has often led historians to confuse women's role in history with the symbolic system describing politics. In contrast, women actively engaged in political disputes; they were well informed and, although aware of gender stereotypes, they were not restrained by them. In fact, gender stereotypes such as the

---

1   *Heads of all Fashions.*
2   Scott, 'Gender', p 1070.

'weaker vessel' often served as a powerful means to negotiate the terms of conflict.[3]

To home in on people's honour and, in the case of politics, on the honour of those in power, by using slanderous imagery such as whoremaster, whore and rogue, signified contempt, criticism, and the loss of deference. It was often expressed in the harsh colloquialism of neighbourly conflicts, which penetrated politics in print and speech and were probably closest to people's experience of expressing discontent in an effective way. Furthermore, it was consistent with the overall pattern of the 'language of conflict' in the seventeenth century as found in verbal disputes, libels, pictures, pamphlets, political discourse, and the language of the courts. The 'language of conflict' appears to be modelled on gender conflicts expressed through moral corruption and the violation of the patriarchal hierarchy of the family. These violations were seen to equal upheaval in state and society, and they served as a powerful and widely understood political symbolism. Thus any attempt to define politics by confining it to institutions and an elite minority fails to understand the complexity of political processes and the interaction of conflicting social, cultural, and political norm systems and tradition. Furthermore, when we look at the central role of communication in politics in the early modern period it becomes clear that in practice there was no rigid division between the private and the political. Borders were fluid, and especially in view of the dynamics of communication various 'public' and 'private' spheres overlapped and interacted.[4]

---

3   See also Hughes, 'Gender and Politics'; Rublack, 'Pregnancy'; and Nicole Castan, 'La criminalité dans le ressort du Parlement de Toulouse, 1690–1730', *Crimes et criminalité en France sours l'Ancien Régime. 17./18. siècles. Cahiers des Annales*, 33 (Paris, 1971), pp 91–107.

4   Robert Scribner has developed a whole typology of places for sixteenth-century Germany where what he calls 'private public opinion' could occur. See Scribner, 'Kommunikation und Alltag'.

Central to the understanding of public opinion in the seventeenth century are the dynamics of communication which sprang from the professionalization of the news trade, the penetration of politics by print and oral cultures, censorship, and a readiness of the people to appropriate and pass on national news. In other words, a static perception of the public sphere, a narrow, legal definition of censorship rather than a conceptual reassessment of the meaning of censorship, and a Habermasian definition of public opinion as characterized by rational discourse alone, fall short of grasping the complexity of communication processes in a society with a massive oral residue. Censorship in the seventeenth century essentially meant interpretation and it was arbitrary by nature. Thus meanings were negotiable. This meant that the law could not simply be applied but that authors, readers, and state authorities alike were required to engage with the meaning of words and texts in order to censor. Public opinion 'happened' when ordinary discourses at home, at work, when trading or travelling, among lodgers, in alehouses, and in the streets turned to discussing the politics of the day. Neither the source of information – gossip or rumour, newsletters, ballads, print, manuscripts or pictures nor the place where a discourse 'became public' was closely defined. Similarly, the language used to express political or religious discontent cannot be judged on grounds of its *rationale* but must be understood in the context of a society that witnessed the penetration of politics by the traditions, images, and colloquialisms of orality.

Pamphleteers of mid-seventeenth-century England were part of the visual and oral culture of their time, and popular news genres such as satire formed a synthesis between a shared collective memory and day-to-day politics. In recent years, research on collective memory in past and present societies, especially in France and Germany, has emphasized the role of collective memory for the creation of meaning and culture within societies. A number of studies have shown how the collective memory of society evolves in a continuous dialogue between the past and the present, as becomes apparent in society's values, rituals, fes-

tivities, and historiography.[5] This dialogue is a central feature in
the presentation of news and opinions in seventeenth-century
England. It was quite common for authors to weave new messages into familiar and extremely popular slogans and images.
Similarly, familiar tunes were reused for different ballads. This
was usually pointed out in a note below the title, such as, 'to be
sung to the tune of *When the King enioys his own again*'.[6] Both in
print and in verbal exchanges, news and opinions were presented
in the guise of tales and wonder stories. Startling images of the
devil and hell, death, the monster of Rome, the Whore of Babylon,
monster births, or folk heroes such as Robin Hood and Jack Straw
were employed to express political and religious views. The same
was true for biblical images such as the ship, divine intervention
symbolized by the hand of justice and a face blowing a storm
from heaven, or even the cross, which acquired a new meaning
when serving particular political and religious ends, namely to
attack popery. The presentation of news abounded in references
to a rich variety of cultural expressions including the ritual and
routine of everyday life such as gender disputes, defamation,
drinking and gambling, cock fights or charivaris.

This complexity of communication and the synthesis of past
and present social and individual knowledge and values, coupled
with the image-filled language and its resort to a variety of cultural expressions, perhaps best exemplifies what Marshall Sahlins
argued years ago, namely that culture must be understood as a
process.[7] Central to this process and, in fact, central for any cul-

---

5   Pierre Nora (ed.), *Les Lieux de mémoire*, 7 vols. (Paris 1984/92); Aleida
     Assmann, *Arbeit am Nationalen Gedächtnis. Eine kurze Geschichte der deutschen
     Bildungsidee* (Frankfurt, 1993); Otto Gerhard Oexle (ed.), *Memoria als Kultur*
     (Göttingen, 1995); Etienne Francois, Hannes Siegrist and Jakob Vogel (eds.),
     Nation und Emotion. Deutschland und Frankreich im Vergleich (Göttingen,
     1995); Chris Wickham and James Fentress, *Social Memory* (Oxford, 1992);
     and Jay Winter, *Sites of Memory, Sites of Mourning: The Great War in European
     Cultural History* (Cambridge, 1995).
6   *The World Is Turned Upside Down* (London, 1646).
7   Marshall Sahlins, *Islands of History* (London, 1985).

ture to be meaningful is, as Aleida Assmann has argued, the function of collective memory as manifest in language, ritual, and symbolism, and the interaction of everyday culture with 'culture as a monument', that is, of what we remember, preserve, and reconstruct of the past in order to understand the present and conceptualize the future.[8]

In the political culture of the seventeenth century and the emergence of public opinion, elements of what has usually been described as 'popular culture' with all its tradition, communalism, and memory of the past merged with the discourse on national politics. With the emergence of public opinion, elements of popular culture present in these pamphlets and dialogues underwent an 'internal modernization' which implied a change of meaning and function. Rather than being traditional and communal, it gained new force in the expression of political discontent, social mobilization, and the development of an independent political awareness.[9] If we bear this in mind, the dynamics of communication in a society that, from a modern perspective, was on the verge of changing from orality to literacy no longer can be dismissed as unpolitical and as lacking any political *rationale*, an element of politics which, according to Habermas, was the prerequisite for the emergence of public opinion and the public sphere.[10]

One vital link in this picture is still missing, namely, the people and their role in the emergence of the public sphere. I have suggested that the power vaccum of the 1640s forced ordinary men and women to form their own opinions on politics and religion out of necessity. Significantly, this development was paral-

8 See, for instance, the introduction in *Kultur als Lebenswert und Monument,* ed. Aleida Assmann and Dietrich Harth (Frankfurt, 1991).
9 Compare Kaschuba, 'Ritual'.
10 For figures on rates of orality and literacy see Cressy, *Literacy.* Also J. Barry, 'Literacy and Literature in Popular Culture: Reading and Writing in Historical Perspective', in *Popular Culture in England, c. 1500–1850,* ed. Tim Harris (London, 1995), pp 69–94.

leled by the professionalization of the news trade, but at least as importantly, by numerous discussions in print and speech of the problem of 'public duty and private conscience'. Cases of conscience flared up throughout the public debate on politics and religion in the late 1630s and early 1640s. A paper of 1642, entitled *A Question answered, how Laws are to be understood, and Obedience yielded*, argued that human laws do not bind the conscience.[11] In a conflict among local office-holders about which proclamation should be published in their village, that of the King or that of the Parliament, one of the party argued: 'By God's word I am commanded to obey the King; I find no such Command for the Parliament.'[12] Ballads took up the theme, too. In *A True Subiects Wish* Martin Parker sang: 'No true Religion wil giue warrant, That any subiect arm'd should be, against his Prince in any sense, what ere he hold for his pretence, Rebellion is a foule offence.'[13] When questioned about the meaning of certain passages in a book, the London merchant Barny Reymes answered: 'he holds that no pretext of religion can be a lawful cause for subjects to take Armes against their Prince.'[14] A pamphlet dating from 1642 stressed that 'The King is supreame head of all Authority, and the subject is injoyn'd to obey God, the lawes and his Prince'.[15] The student Thomas Shawbery exclaimed that 'he could find in his heart to cut King Pym in pieces'.[16] Some people were convinced that the Scots were using religious grounds to justify their war against England.[17] When asked during a funeral feast 'whether we, yf the King should come to alter Religion (which God forbid) might Revolt from our Prince and take Armes against him', Roger More according to witnesses answered:

---

11   LJ V.14 (1642).
12   CJ II.622 (1642).
13   *A True Subiects Wish.*
14   SP 16/457.129–30 (1640).
15   *The Rebellious Life.*
16   CJ II.478 (1641).
17   The case of John Oneby above, SP 16/423.44 ff. (1639).

'His opinion was that in cause of Religion, subjects though private men, might with good conscience take arms against their kinge and kill him.'[18]

These references to cases of conscience demonstrate perhaps most forcefully that in the seventeenth century it was impossible to distinguish between private and public fully in politics, as it also became more difficult to accept the (increasingly apologetic) distinction between the King's private person and public body. Confronted with 'opinions in every house and street' and a King and Parliament utterly divided, ordinary men and women had to fall back on their 'private conscience' in order to discern their 'public duty'. In other words, people's personal and subjective opinions emerged into the public and became part of the political culture of the period. These cases further show the centrality of religion and especially the political effects of religious polarization during this period.

Public opinion is characterized by division, and it poses a potential challenge to authority, questioning its monopoly on the definition of meaning. Furthermore, it causes friction among those in power and those who are ruled. The growing distrust of the King's political designs, and the power struggle between Charles I and the Long Parliament had serious consequences for the attitude of the 'humble' towards state authority. Although criticism of the King and Queen had not been unheard of before, the increasingly incompatible positions – both political and religious – of King and Parliament undermined the very roots of authority. England's political culture was rapidly changing. Communication in seventeenth-century England helped demystify authority and laid the foundations for the emergence of a political awareness among the common people. The parameters of political debate had to be redefined. The legitimacy of the monarch no longer was based on divine authority but judged by his or her deeds and (religious) convictions. Throughout the rest of

---

18   SP 16/409.102–102ii (1638).

the century, politics, the church, and the monarchy remained issues of public debate. Those in power had to reckon with popular protest that was based on a critical assessment of political and
religious affairs. What we have been addressing here is not the
old question about the political emancipation of the people, but
rather the broader and more fruitful question of the changing
political culture of seventeenth-century England as part of early
modern state formation. In this sense the 1640s were revolutionary.

Bibliography

A Bibliographical Dictionary of English Women Writers 1580-1720, ed. Maureen Bell, George Parfitt, and Simon Sheperd, (New York, 1990)

A Breefe of M. Foxleys papers, for so much as is questioneable in the H. Commission SP 16/422.127

A Charme of Canterburian Spirits (1645), BL E.269.18

A Cluster of Coxcombes (1642), BL E.154.49

A Collection of English Proverbs (Cambridge, 1670)

A Collection of English Proverbs (Cambridge, 1670)

A Copy of the Bill against the XIII Bishops, presented to the Lords by the Commons (1641), BL E 173/21

A Decade of Grievances Presented and Approved to the Right Honourable and High Court of Parliament (1641), BL E.172/5

A Discovery of 29 Sects here in London (1641), BL E.168.7

A Discovery of 29 Sects here in London (1641), BL E.168.7

A Discovery of Six Women preachers. With a relation of their names, manners, life and doctrine (1641), BL E.166.1

A Discovery of the Jesuits Trumpery, Newly Packed out of England (1641), BL 669 f.4.10

A Discovery of the Notorious Proceedings of William Laud (1641), BL E.172.37

A Discovery of the prayse of God, and joy of all true hearted Protestants, of a late intended plot by the Papists to subdue the Protestants. Being a true Copie of a Discourse between William O' Connor a Priest, and Anne Hussey an Irish Gentlewoman. Printed Anno, 1641. William Clark Collection BB.I.14 (28) and BB.W.(28) (a different edition with a woodcut)

A Discovery of the prayse of God, and joy of all true hearted Protestants, of a late intended plot by the Papists to subdue the Protestants. Being a true Copie of a Discourse between William O' Connor a Priest, and Anne Hussey an Irish Gentlewoman. Printed Anno, 1641. William Clark Collection BB.I.14 (28) and BB.W.(28) (a different edition with a woodcut). BL E.158.4.

A Discovery To the prayse of God, and joy of all true hearted Protestants, of a late intended plot by the Papists to subdue the Protestants. Being a true Copie of a Discourse between William O' Conner a Priest, and Anne Hussey an Irish Gentle-

308 GOVERNED BY OPINION

woman. Printed Anno, 1641. William Clark Collection BB.I.14 (28); a different
edition with a woodcut: William Clark Collection BB.W.4.(28); BM E.158.4

A Diurnall of Dangers (1642), BL E.112.4

*A Full and Compleat Answer Against the Writer of A late Volume set forth, entitled A
Tale in a Tub or A Tub Lecture* (1642), BL E.141.19

A Game at Chess (1643), BL E.88.2

A Game at Chess. A metaphorical discourse shweing the present estate of this Kingdome
(1643), BL E.88.2

A Good Wish for England, BL 669.f.4.40, repr. in Rollins, *Cavalier*

A letter directed to Mr Bridgman, 4th January 1641 (1641), BL 669.f.4.39

A Nest of Serpents Discovered Or, A Knot of old Heretiques revived Called the Adamites
(1641), BL E. 168.12

A Nest of serpents Discovered, or, a Knot of old Heretiques revived, Called the Adamites
(1641), BL 168.12

A New Disputation Betweene the two Lordly Bishops, Yorke and Canterbury (1642),
BL E.1113.2

A New Game at Cards, Wood 401.148

*A new Play called Canterburie His Change of Diot. Which sheweth variety of wit and
mirth: privately acted neare the Palace-yard at Westminster* (1641), BL E.177.8

A New Play, and *Canterburies Pilgrimage* (1641), BL E.172.28

A New Sect of Religion Descryed, Called Adamites (1641)

A Parallel Between the Proceedings of this Present King and this Present Parliament
(1648)

A Presse Full Of Pamphlets (1642), BL E.142.9

A Prognostication Upon W. Laud (1641), BL 669.f.10

A Prognostication Upon W: Laud. See also *A Prophecie Of the Life, Reigne and Death
of William Laud, Archbishop of Canterbury* (1644), BL E.18.8

A Rot amongst the Bishops (1641), BL E.1102.4

A Rot amongst the Bishops (1641), BL E.1102.4

A Satire On James I And Charles I, repr. in Rollins, *Cavalier,* pp 151–53

A Sermon Preached (1643)

A Sermon Preached the last Fast day in Leaden-Hall Street (1642), BL E.91.32

A Spiritual Song of Comfort (1643), BL 669.f.8.44

A Swarme of Sectaries and Schismatiques (1641), BL E.158.1

*A Swarme of Sectaries, and Schismatiques: Wherein is discovered the strange preaching
(or prating) of such as are by their trades Coblers, Tinkers, Pedlers, Weavers,
Sowgelders, and Chymney-Sweepers* (1641), BL E.158.1

*A Three-Fold Discourse Between Three Neighbours Aldgate, Bishopsgate, and John
Heyden the Late Cobler of Houndsditch, a professed Brownist* (1642), BL E.145.3

A Three-Fold Discourse Betweene Three Neighbours (1642), BL E.145.3

A True and Wonderful Relation of a Whale, pursued in the Sea (1645), BL E.308.24

A True and Wonderfull Relation of a Whale, pursued in the Sea (1645), BL E.308.24

*A True Copie of a Disputation held betweene Master Walker and a Iesuite, in the house
of one Thomas Bates in Bishops Court in the Old Baily* (1641), BL E.172.9

A True Copie of a Disputation held betweene Master Walker and a Jesuite, in the house of Thomas Bates in Bishops Court in the Old Baily (1641), BL E.172.9

A true Copy of the Devills Letter (1640), anonymous manuscript, SP 16/466.60

A True Description Of The Pot-Companion Poet (1642), BL E.143.6

A True Subject's Wish, (April 1640), repr. in Rollins, *Cavalier*

Achinstein, Sharon, 'The Politics of Babel in the English Revolution', in *Pamphlet Wars. Prose in the English Revolution*, ed. James Holstun (London, 1992), pp 14–44

Achinstein, Sharon, *Milton and the Revolutionary Reader* (Princeton/New Jersey, 1994)

Act of Common Council, BL 669.f.7.49

Acts and Ordinances of the Interregnum 1642–1660, 3 vols. (London, 1911), ed. Charles H. Firth and R. S. Rait

Allport, G. W., and L. Postman, *The Psychology of Rumor*, (New York, 1948) and Rosnow and Fine, *Rumor and Gossip*, pp 23–25

Almirol, E. B., 'Chasing the Elusive Butterfly: Gossip and the Pursuit of Reputation', *Ethnicity*, 8 (1981), pp 293–304

An Answer To the most Envious, Scandalous and libellous Pamphlet, Entitled Mercuries Message (1641), BL E.157.7

An explanacon of the Protestacon, Ashm Ms 36.92v.

Anthony Dyett, SP 16/466.250 (September 1640)

Archbishop Laud firing a Canon, see picture section and *Mercuries Message Defended* (1641), BL E.160.13

Archy's Dream, Sometimes Jester to his Maiestie (1641), BL E.173.5.

Assmann, Aleida, *Arbeit am Nationalen Gedächtnis. Eine kurze Geschichte der deutschen Bildungsidee* (Frankfurt, 1993)

Bacon, Francis, *Cases of Treason* (1641), BL E.160.1

Barnes, Thomas G., 'Due Process and Slow Process in the late Tudor and early Stuart Star Chamber', *American Journal of Legal History*, 6 (1962)

Barry, J., 'Literacy and Literature in Popular Culture: Reading and Writing in Historical Perspective', in *Popular Culture in England, c. 1500–1850*, ed. Tim Harris (London, 1995), pp 69–94

Bauman, Richard, *Story, performance, and event. Contextual studies of oral narrative* (Cambridge, 1986)

Behold Romes Monster on his monstrous Beast (1643), BL 669.f.8.29

Behold Romes Monster on his monstrous Beast (1643), BL 669.f.8.29

Beier, A. L., 'Engine of manufacture: the trades of London', in *Metropolis*, ed. Beier and Finlay, pp 141–67

Bell, Maureen, 'A dictionary of women in the London book trade, 1540-1730' (unpublished Master's Dissertation, Loughborough University of Technology, 1983)

Bell, Maureen, 'Hannah Allen and the Development of a Puritan Publishing Business, 1646–51', *Publishing History*, 26 (1989), pp 5–66

Bellany, Alastair, '"Rayling Rymes and Vaunting Verse": Libellous Politics in Early Stuart England, 1603–1628', in Holstun, *Pamphlet*, pp 285–310, 367–71

Ben Jonson, *Volpone* (1605)

Berghaus, Günter, *Die Aufnahme der englischen Revolution in Deutschland 1640–1669*, vol. 1., Studien zur politischen Literatur und Publizistik im 17. Jahrhundert mit einer Bibliographie der Flugschriften (Wiesbaden, 1989)

Bill of Attainder of the Earl of Strafford, see *Sir John Evelyn his Report*, BL E.163.6 and CJ II.208, 209

Bill of Printing, CJ II.402

Bladgen, Cyprian, 'The Stationers' Company in the Civil War Period', *The Library*, 5th ser., XIII, 1 (1958), pp 2–17

Blanning, Timothy C. W., Review of "Andreas Gestrich, *Absolutismus und Öffentlichkeit. Politische Kommunikation in Deutschland zu Beginn des 18. Jahrhunderts*" in *Bulletin of the German Historical Institute London*, Vol. XVIII, No. 1 (February, 1996), pp 32–5

Bohlstedt, J., 'Gender, Household and Community Politics: Women in English riots 1790–1810', *Past and Present*, 120 (1988), pp 88–122

Bond, John, *The Poet's Recantation having suffered in the Pillorie* (London, 1642)

Book of Sports, BL 669.f.7.12

Braithwait, Richard, *The English Gentlewoman, Drawne out to the Full Body: Expressing what Habilliments do Best Attire her, What Ornaments Do best Adorn her, What Complements Do Best Accomplish her* (London, 1631)

Britaines Honour (Wood 401.132), repr. in Rollins, *Cavalier*

Brooks, C. W., *Pettyfoggers and Vipers of the Commonwealth: The 'Lower Branch' of the Legal Profession in Early Modern England* (Cambridge, 1986)

Burgess, Glenn, 'The Impact on Political Thought: Rhetorics for Troubled Times', in *The Impact of the English Civil War*, ed. John Morrill (London, 1991), pp 67–83

Burghartz, Susanna, 'Frauen-Politik-Weiberregiment. Schlagworte zur Bewältigung der politischen Krise von 1691 in Basel', in *Frauen in der Stadt. Les femmes dans la ville*, ed. A.-L. Head-König und A. Tanner (Zürich, 1993), pp 113–34

Burke, Peter, 'Popular culture in seventeenth-century London', *The London Journal*, 3 (1977), pp 144–6

Butler, Martin, *Theatre and Crisis 1632–1642* (Cambridge, 1984)

Calhourn, Craig, (ed.), *Habermas and the Public Sphere* (Boston, 1992).

Canterburys Will With a serious Conference betweene His Scrivener and Him (1641), BL E.156.5

Castan, Nicole, 'La criminalité dans le ressort du Parlement de Toulouse, 1690–1730', *Crimes et criminalité en France sours l'Ancien Régime. 17./18. siècles. Cahiers des Annales*, 33 (Paris, 1971), pp 91–107

Catalogue of Prints and Drawings in the British Museum, ed. F.G. Stephens, completed by Dorothy M. George, 7 vols. (London, 1870-1954)

Catalogue of the Pamphlets, Books, Newspapers, and Manuscripts relating to the Civil War, the Commonwealth, and Restoration, Collected by George Thomason, 1640–1661, I, Catalogue of the Collection, 1640–1652 (Nendeln, 1969; repr.)

Certain Grievances or Errors of the Service Book, LJ IV.478.

Chartier, Roger, *The Cultural Uses of Print in Early Modern France*, tr. Lydia G. Cochrane (Princeton, 1987)

Christ, Timothy, *Francis Smith and the Opposition Press in England, 1660-1688* (unpublished PhD dissertation, University of Cambridge, 1977)

Christianson, Paul, *Reformers and Babylon. English Apocalyptic Visions from the Reformation to the Eve of the Civil War* (Toronto, 1978)

Clarendon, Edward H., *History of the Rebellion and Civil Wars in England*, ed. William D. Macray, 6 vols. (Oxford, 1888)

Clark, Peter, *The English Alehouse* (London/New York, 1983)

Clark, Sandra, *The Elizabethan Pamphleteers. Popular Moralistic Pamphlets 1580–1640* (London, 1983)

Clifton, Robert, 'Popular Fear of Catholics During the English Revolution', *Past and Present*, 52 (1971), pp 23–55

Cobbett's Parliamentary History of England from the Norman Conquest in 1066 to the Year 1803, 2 vols. (London, 1807), ed. Richard Bagshaw

Cohen, Murray, *Sensible Words. Linguistic Practice in England 1640–1785* (Baltimore and London, 1977)

Collinson, Patrick, *De Republica Anglorum. Or, History with the Politics Put Back* (Inaugural Lecture, Cambridge, 1990)

Conceits, Clinches, Flashes and Whimzies; a jest-book of the 17th century, hitherto unknown to bibliographers, repr. from the unique copy of 1639, ed. James O. Halliwell (London, 1860)

Corns, Tom, and D. Loewenstein (eds.), 'The Emergence of Quaker writing' *Prose Studies*, 18 (1995)

Coss, P. R., 'Aspects of Cultural Diffusion in Medieval England: The Early Romances, Local Society and Robin Hood', *Past and Present*, 108 (1985), pp 35–79

Crawford, Patricia, 'Public Duty, Conscience, and Women in Early Modern England', in *Public Duty*, ed. John Morrill et al, pp 57–76

Crawford, Patricia, 'The Challenges to Patriarchalism: How did the Revolution affect Women?', in *Revolution and Restoration. England in the 1650s*, ed. John Morrill (London, 1992), pp 112–28

Crawford, Patricia, 'Women's published writings 1600-1700', in *Women in English Society 1500-1800*, ed. Mary Prior, (London/New York, 1985

Cressy, David, *Literacy and the Social Order. Reading and Writing in Tudor and Stuart England* (Cambridge, 1980)

Croft, Pauline, 'The Reputation of Robert Cecil: Libels, Political Opinions and Popular Awareness in the early Seventeenth Century', *TRHS*, 6th ser., 1 (1991), pp 43–69

Crofts, J., *Packhorse, Waggon and Post. Land Carriage and Communications under the Tudors and Stuarts* (London, 1967)

Cromartie, Alan D. T., 'The Printing of Parliamentary Speeches November 1640 – July 1642', *The Historical Journal*, 33 (1990), pp 23–44

Cust, Richard, 'Honour and Politics in early Stuart England: the case of Beaumont v. Hastings', *Past and Present*, 149 (1995), pp 57–94

Cust, Richard, 'Honour, rhetoric and political culture: the Earl of Huntingdon and his enemies', in *Political Culture and Cultural Politics in Early Modern Europe*, ed. Susan D. Amussen and Mark A. Kishlansky (Manchester, 1995), pp 84–111

Cust, Richard, 'News and Politics in Early Seventeenth Century England', *Past and Present*, 52 (1985), pp 60–90

Darnton, Robert, *Edition et sédition: L'univers de la littérature clandestine au xviii siècle* (Paris, 1991)

Darnton, Robert, *The literary underground of the Old Regime* (Cambridge/Mass., 1982)

Davis, Natalie Z., 'Women in Politics', in *A History of Women*, iii, *Renaissance and Enlightment Paradoxes*, ed. George Duby, Michelle Perrot et al. (Cambridge/Mass. and London, 1993), pp 167–83.

Davis, Natalie Z., *Fiction in the Archives. Pardon Tales and their Tellers in Sixteenth-Century France* (Stanford, 1987)

Dekker, John, *Seaven Deadly Sinnes of London* (1606), reprinted in A.B. Grosart (ed.), *The Non-dramatic Works of Thomas Dekker*, 5 vols. (New York, 1963), ii, pp 1–86

Dekker, Rudolf M., 'Women in Revolt. Popular Protest and Its Social Basis in Holland in the Seventeenth and Eighteenth Century', *Theory and Society*, 16 (1987), pp 337–62

Denzer, Paul, *Ideologie und literarische Strategie. Die politische Flugblattlyrik der englischen Bürgerkriegszeit 1639–1661* (Tübingen, 1991)

Dinges, Martin, '"Weiblichkeit" in "Männlichkeitsritualen"? Zu weiblichen Taktiken im Ehrenhandel in Paris im 18. Jahrhundert', *Francia* 18 (1991) pp 71–98

Donald, P., *An Uncounselled King. Charles I and the Scottish troubles, 1637–1641*, Cambridge Studies in Early Modern British History (Cambridge, 1990)

Dunn, Kevin, 'Milton among the monopolists: *Areopagitica*, intellectual property and the Hartlib circle', in *Samuel Hartlib and Universal Reformation, Studies in intellectual communication*, ed. Mark Greengrass, Michael Leslie and Timothy Raylor (Cambridge, 1995), pp 177–236

Edwards, Thomas, *Gangraena*, 3 vols. (London, 1645/46)

Eisenstein, Elisabeth L., *The printing press as an agent of change*, vol. 2 (Cambridge, 1979)

Eisenstein, Elisabeth, *Grub Street Abroad. Aspects of the French Cosmopolitan Press from the Age of Louis XIV to the French Revolution* (Oxford, 1992)

Ellul, Jacques, *The Formation of Men's Attitudes*. Trans. K. Keller and J. Lerner (New York, 1965)

Elton, Geoffrey R., *Policy and Police: The Enforcement of the Reformation in the Age of Thomas Cromwell* (Cambridge, 1972)

Englands Petition to her gratious King (1643), BL 669.f.4.14

English Puritanism (1641), BL E.208.4

Farge, Arlette, *Subversive Words. Public Opinion in Eighteenth-Century France* (Cambridge, 1994)

Finlay, Roger, and Beatrice Shearer, 'Population growth and suburban expansion', in *Metropolis*, ed. Finlay and Beier, pp 37–60

Firth, C. H., 'Ballads on the Bishops' Wars, 1638–1640', *The Scottish Historical Review*, 3 (1906), pp 257–73

Fletcher, Anthony J., 'Honour, Reputation and Local Officeholding in Elizabethan and Stuart England', in *Order and Disorder in Early Modern England*, ed. Fletcher and John Stevenson (Cambridge, 1985), pp 92–115

Fletcher, Anthony J., *A County Community in Peace and War: Sussex, 1600–1660* (London, 1980)

Fletcher, Anthony, *The Outbreak of the English Civil War* (London, 1981)

Fortunes Tennis-Ball (1641), BL E.160.5

Foster, Steven, *Notes from the Caroline Underground. Alexander Leighton, the Puritan Triumvirate, and the Laudian Reaction to Nonconformity* (London, 1978)

Fox, Adam P., *Aspects of Oral Culture and its Development in Early Modern England* (Cambridge University PhD, December 1992)

Fox, Adam, 'Ballads, Libels and Popular Ridicule in Jacobean England', *Past and Present*, 145 (1994), pp 47–83

Francois, Etienne, and Hannes Siegrist and Jakob Vogel (eds.), *Nation und Emotion. Deutschland und Frankreich im Vergleich* (Göttingen, 1995)

Frank, Joseph, *The Beginning of the English Newspaper* (Cambridge, Mass., 1961)

Frearson, Michael, *The English Corantos of the 1620s* (Cambridge University PhD, 1993)

Freedberg, David, *The Power of Images. Studies in the History and Theory of Response* (Chicago and London, 1989)

Freist, Dagmar, 'The King's Crown is the Whore of Babylon: Politics, Gender and Communication in Mid-Seventeenth-Century England', in 'Presentations of the Self in Early Modern England', *Gender and History*, Special Issue, 7/3, ed. Amy L. Erickson and Ross Balzaretti (November, 1995), pp 457–81

Friedman, Jerome, *Miracles and the Pulp Press during the English Revolution. The Battle of the Frogs and Fairford's Flies* (London, 1993)

Gentles, Ian, *The New Model Army* (Oxford, 1991)

George, Dorothy, *English Political Caricature to 1792. A Study of Opinion and Propaganda* (Oxford, 1959)

Geree, S., *The Ornament of Women* (London, 1639)

Gestrich, Andreas, *Absolutismus und Öffentlichkeit. Politische Kommunikation in Deutschland zu Beginn des 18. Jahrhunderts*, Kritische Studien zur Geschichtswissenschaft, 103 (Göttingen, 1994)

Gluckman, Max, 'Gossip and Scandal', *Current Anthropology*, 4 (1968), pp 307–15

Gombrich, Ernst H., *Symbolic Images. Studies in the Art of the Renaissance* (London, 1972)

Good News from the North (September 1640, Wood 401.134), repr. in Rollins, *Cavalier*

Goody, Jack, *The Domestication of the Savage Mind* (Cambridge, 1977)

Goreau, Angeline, *The Whole Duty of a Woman. Female Writers in Seventeenth-Century England*, 2 vols. (Washington, 1984)

Gowing, Laura, *Domestic Dangers. Women, Words, and Sex in Early Modern London* (Oxford, 1996)

Greg, William W., 'Licensers for the Press * to 1640', *The Bibliographical Society*, n.s., 41 (Oxford, 1962), p 105–6

Greyerz, Kaspar von, *Vorsehungsglaube und Kosmologie*, Publications of the German Historical Institute, 25 (Göttingen/Zurich, 1990)

Groebner, Valentin, 'Losing Face: Noses and Honour in the late Medieval Town', *History Workshop Journal*, 40 (Autumn 1995), pp 1–15

Habermas, Jürgen, *The Structural Transformation of the Public Sphere*, tr. Thomas Burger and Frederick Lawrence (Cambridge, Mass., 1989), first published in Germany as *Strukturwandel der Öffentlichkeit* (Darmstadt, 1962)

Hall, Joseph, *Character of Virtues and Vices* (1608)

Hamburger, Philip, 'The Development of the Law of Seditious Libel and the Control of the Press', *Stanford Law Review*, 37 (1984–1985), pp 661–765.

Handelman, Don, 'Gossip in Encounters: The Transmission of Information in a Bounded Social Setting', *Man*, 8 (June 1973), pp 210–27

Harris, Tim, *London Crowds in the Reign of Charles II*, Cambridge Studies in Early Modern British History (Cambridge, 1987)

Hartlib, Samuel, *A briefe discourse concerning the accomplishment of our reformation* (London, 1647)

Heinemann, Margot, *Puritanism and Theatre: Thomas Middleton and Opposition Drama under the Early Stuarts* (Cambridge, 1980

Hell's Hurlie-Burlie, Or A Fierce Contention Betwixt the Pope and the Devill (1644), BL E.11/4

Helmholz, Richard H., 'Canonical Defamation in Medieval England', *The American Journal of Legal History*, 15 (1971), pp 255–68

Helmholz, Richard H., 'Selected Cases on Defamation to 1600', *Selden Society*, 101 (1985)

Henderson, Katherine Usher, and Barbara F. McManus, *Half Humankind. Contexts and Texts of the Controversy about Women in England 1540–1640* (Urbana and Chicago, 1985)

Her Own Life. Autobiographical writings by seventeenth-century Englishwomen (London/New York, 1989), ed. Elspeth Graham, Hilary Hinds, Elain Hobby and Helen Wilcox

Heraclitus Dream (1642), BL 669.f.6.29

Hetet, John S. T., *A Literary Underground in Restoration England: Printers and Dissenters in the Context of Constraints 1660-1689* (unpublished PhD dissertation, University of Cambridge, 1987)

Hibbard, Caroline, *Charles I and the Popish Plot* (Chapel Hill, 1983)

Hic Mulier; or, The Man-Woman (1620), and *Haec Vir; or, The Womanish Man* (1620)

Higgins, Paula, 'The Reactions of Women, with Special Reference to Women Petitioners', in *Politics, Religion and the English Civil War*, ed. Brian Manning (London, 1973), pp 179–222

Hill, Christopher, 'Society and Literature in 17th century England', *Collected Es-*

says of Christopher Hill; I: Writing and Revolution (Brighton, 1985)

Hindle, Steve, 'The shaming of Margaret Knowsley: gossip, gender and experience of authority in early modern England', *Continuity and Change*, (1994), pp 391–419

Historische Bildkunde. Probleme – Wege – Beispiele, Zeitschrift für Historische Forschung. Beiheft 12 (1991), ed. Brigitte Tolkemitt and Rainer Wohlfeil

Hobbes, Thomas, *Leviathan* (London, 1651), ed. Crawford B. Macpherson (1951, repr. 1984)

Hobby, Elain, *Virtue of Necessity. English Women's Writing 1649–88* (London, 1988)

Holdsworth, William S., 'Defamation in the Sixteenth and Seventeenth Centuries', *Law Quarterly Review*, 40 (1924), pp 302–15

Holdsworth, William S., *A History of the English Law*, 17 vols. (London, 1903–72)

Holenstein, Pia, and Norbert Schindler: 'Geschwätzgeschichte(n). Ein kulturhistorisches Plädoyer für die Rehabilitierung der unkontrollierten Rede', in *Dynamik der Tradition. Studien zur historischen Kulturforschung*, ed. Richard van Dülmen (Frankfurt, 1992), pp 41–108

Holmes, Clive, 'Drainers and Fenmen: the Problem of Popular Political Consciousness in the Seventeenth Century', in *Order and Disorder in Early Modern England*, ed. Anthony Fletcher and John Stevenson (Cambridge, 1985), pp 166–95

Hughes, Ann, 'Gender and politics in Leveller literature', in *Political Culture*, ed. Amussen and Kishlansky, pp 162–88

Hughes, Ann, 'Thomas Dugard and his circle: a puritan-parliamentarian circle', *Historical Journal*, 20 (1986)

Hunt, Lynn, *Politics, Culture, and Class in the French Revolution* (Berkeley and Los Angeles, 1984)

Ingram, Martin, *Church Courts, Sex and Marriage in England, 1570 – 1640* (Cambridge, 1987)

James, Melvyn, *English Politics and the Concept of Honour, 1485–1642*, Past and Present Supplement, 3 (Oxford, 1978)

Jardine, Lisa, *Still Harping on Shakespeare's Daughters. Women and Drama in the Age of Shakespeare* (Brighton, 1983)

Jones, A. R., 'Nets and bridles: early modern conduct books and sixteenth-century women's lyrics', in *The ideology of conduct. Essays on Literature and the History of Sexuality*, ed. N. Armstrong and L. Tennenhouse (New York, 1987), pp 39–72

Jonson, Ben, *Newes from the New World* (1620), reprinted in *The Complete Masques*, ed. Stephen Orgel (New Haven and London, 1969), pp 292–305

Kaschuba, Wolfgang, 'Ritual und Fest. Das Volk auf der Straße. Figurationen und Funktionen populärer Öffentlichkeit zwischen Frühneuzeit und Moderne', in *Dynamik der Tradition. Studien zur historischen Kulturforschung*, ed. Richard van Dülmen (Frankfurt, 1992), pp 240–67

Kelso, Ruth, *Doctrine for the Lady of the Renaissance* (Urbana, 1956)

Kenyon, J. P., *Stuart England*. The Pelican History of England (London, 1978; 2nd edn, 1985)

Kenyon, John P., *The Stuart Constitution 1603–1688. Documents and Commentary* (Cambridge, 1966)

Kirkman, Francis, *Wits or Sport upon Sport* (1672), ed. J. J. Elson (New York, 1932)

Knights, Mark, *Politics and Opinion in Crisis 1678–1681* (Cambridge, 1994)

Knopf, Terry A., *Rumors, Race, and Riots* (New Brunswick and New Jersey, 1975)

Kultur als Lebenswert und Monument, ed. Aleida Assmann and Dietrich Harth (Frankfurt, 1991)

Lambert, Sheila, 'Printing for Parliament 1641–1700', *List and Index Society*, Special Series (1984)

Lambert, Sheila, 'Procedure in the House of Commons in the Early Stuart Period', *EHR*, 95 (1980), pp 753–81

Lambert, Sheila, 'Richard Montague, Arminianism and Censorship', *Past & Present*, 124 (1989), p 36–68

Lambert, Sheila, 'The Beginning of Printing for the House of Commons, 1640–1642', *The Library*, 6th ser., III, 1 (March, 1981), pp 43–61

Lambert, Sheila, 'The Printers and the Government, 1604–1637', in *Aspects of Printing from 1600*, ed. Michael Harris and Robin Myers (Oxford, 1987), pp 1–29

Lanthorne and Candle-Light (1609), reprinted in *The Non-Dramatic Works of Thomas Dekker*, 5 vols. (New York, 1963), ed. Alexander B. Grosart

Laslett, Peter (ed.), *Patriarcha and Other Political Works by Sir Robert Filmer* (Oxford, 1949)

Laud, William, *Constitutions and Canons Ecclesiastical, Treated upon by the Archbishop of Canterbury and York* (1640)

Laud, William, *Works*, ed. W. Scott and J. Bliss, 7 vols. (Oxford, 1847–60)

Levy, F. J., 'How Information Spread among the Gentry, 1550–1640', *Journal of British Studies*, xxi (1982), pp 20–24

Lilburne, John, *England's Birth-Right* (1645)

Lindley, Keith J., 'Riot Prevention and Control in Early Stuart London', *TRHS*, 5th ser., 33 (1983), pp 109–26

Lipp, Carola, *Schimpfende Weiber und patriotische Jungfrauen* (Baden-Baden, 1986)

Long, Helen A., *Appearance into Public Light: Aspects of the Control and Use of Print in London in the 1640s* (unpubl. D. Phil. dissertation, University of La Trobe, Melbourne, 1984)

Love, Harold, 'Scribal Publication in Seventeenth-Century England', *Transactions of the Cambridge Bibliographical Society*, 9 (1987), pp 130–54

Lucifer's Lucky Or, The Devil's new Creature (1641), BL E.180.3

MacDonald, Michael, and Terence R. Murphy, *Sleepless Souls. Suicide in Early Modern England* (Oxford, 1990)

Mack, Phyllis, 'Women as Prophets during the English Civil War', *Feminist Studies*, 8 (1982), pp 19–45

Mack, Phyllis, *Visionary Women. Ecstatic Prophecy in 17th c. England* (Berkeley, 1992)

Mackay, Charles, *The Cavalier Songs and Ballads from 1642–1684* (London, 1863)

Maclean, Ian, *The Renaissance Notion of Women* (Cambridge, 1980)

Mad Fashions, Od Fashions, All out of Fashions, or the Emblems of these Distracted Times (1642), BL E.138.30

Mahony, Michael, 'Presbyterianism in the City of London, 1645–1647', *Historical Journal*, 22 (1979), pp 93–114

Manning, Brian, *The English People and the English Revolution* (Harmondsworth, 1976)

Manning, Roger B., 'The Origin of the Doctrine of Sedition', *Albion*, 12 (1980), pp 99–121

'Mary Westwood, Quaker Publisher,' *Publishing History*, 23 (1988), pp 5–66

McEntee, Ann Marie, '"The [Un]civill-sisterhod of Oranges and Lemons": female petitioners and demonstrators, 1642–53', Prose Studies, 14 (1991)

McKenzie, Don F., '"The Staple of News" and the late Plays of Ben Jonson', in *A Celebration of Ben Jonson*, Papers presented at the University of Toronto in October 1972, ed. William Blissett, J. Patrick and Richard W. van Fossen (Toronto, 1973), pp 83–128

McKenzie, Don F., 'Speech-Manuscript-Print', *The Library Chronicle*, 22 (1990), pp 87–109

Mendle, Michael, 'De Facto Freedom, De Facto Authority: Press and Parliament, 1640–43', in *Historical Journal* 38 (1995), pp 307–32

Merry, Sally E., 'Rethinking Gossip and Scandal', in *Toward a General Theory of Social Control*, 2 vols. (Cambridge, Mass., 1984), ed. Donald Black, i, pp 271–302

Miller, E. H., *The Professional Writer in Elizabethan England* (Cambridge/Mass., 1959)

Miller, John, *Popery and Politics in England, 1660–1688* (Cambridge, 1973)

Miller, W. E., 'Printers and Stationers in the Parish of St. Giles Cripplegate 1561–1640', *Studies in Bibliography* (1966), p 15–38

Milton, Anthony, *Catholic and Reformed: Roman and Protestant Churches in English Protestant Thought, 1600–1640*, Cambridge Studies in Early Modern British History (Cambridge, 1996)

Milton, John, *Areopagitica* (London, 1644)

Morrill, John, and John D. Walter, 'Order and Disorder in the English Revolution', in *Order and Disorder in Early Modern England*, ed. Anthony Fletcher and John Stevenson (Cambridge, 1985), pp 137–65

Morrill, John, Paul Slack and Daniel Woolf (eds.), *Public Duty and Private Conscience in Seventeenth-Century England. Essays Presented to Gerald E. Aylmer* (Oxford, 1993)

Myers, Robin, *The Stationers Company Archive 1554–1984*, St Paul's Bibliography (London, 1990)

Nash, F., 'English Licenses to Print and Grants of Copyright in the 1640s', *The Library*, 6th ser., IV (1982), pp 174–84

New Preachers New. (1641), BL 180.26

Newes from Hell, Rome, and the Inns of Court (1642), BL E.133.13

Newes from Rome, Or, a relation of the pope and his patentees Pilgrim into Hell (1641), BL E.158.18

Newes, True Newes (1641), BL E.144.3

News from Newcastle (August 1640), repr. in Rollins, *Cavalier*

No Pamphlet But A Detestation Against all such Pamphlets As are Printed Concerning the Irish Rebellion (1642), BL E.134.3

Nora, Pierre (ed.), *Les Lieux de mémoire*, 7 vols. (Paris 1984/92)

Norton, M. B., 'Gender and defamation in Seventeenth-Century Maryland', *William and Mary Quarterly*, 3rd series, 44 (January 1987), pp 3–39

Oexle, Otto Gerhard (ed.), *Memoria als Kultur* (Göttingen, 1995)

Old Newes Newly Revived: Or, the discovery of all occurrences happened since the beginning of the Parliament (1641), BL E.160.22

Ong, Walter J., *Orality and Literacy. The Technologizing of the Word* (London and New York, 1982)

Overbury, Sir Thomas, *Character* (1614)

Owst, Gerald R., *Literature and the Pulpit in Medieval England. A Neglected Chapter in the History of English Letters and of the English People* (Cambridge, 1933; rpt. 1961)

Owst, Gerald R., *Preaching in Medieval England. An Introduction to Sermon Manuscripts of the Period c. 1350–1450*, (Cambridge, 1926)

Panedonius, Philogenes [R. Brathwaite], *Ar't asleep Husband? A Boulster Lecture; Stored with all variety of witty jeasts, merry Tales, and other pleasant passages* (1640)

Park, Katherine, and Lorraine J. Daston, 'Unnatural Conceptions: The Study of Monsters in Sixteenth- and Seventeenth-Century France and England', *Past and Present*, 92 (1981), pp 20–54

Parker, Henry, 'Observations', in *Revolutionary Prose of the English Civil War*, ed. Howard Erskine-Hill and Graham Storey (Cambridge, 1983), p 50

Parker, Martin, *Brittaines Honour. In the two valiant Welchmen, who fought against fifteene thousand Scots*, Wood 401.132 (1639–40)

Parker, Martin, *The Poet's Blind mans bough* (1641), BL E.172.6

Parry, Milman, *The Making of Homeric verse*, ed. Adam Parry (Oxford, 1971)

Patterson, Annabel, *Censorship and Interpretation. The Conditions of Writing and Reading in Early Modern England* (Madison, 1984)

Peacham, Henry, *The worth of a penny* (1641)

Peacham, Henry: with an engraving by Wenceslaus Hollar, *The World is Ruled and Governed by Opinion* (1641), British Museum, Department of Prints and Drawings BM 272

Pearl, Valerie, *London and the Outbreak of the Puritan Revolution. City Government and National Politics, 1625–43* (Oxford, 1961)

Pennington, Donald, and Keith Thomas (eds.), *Puritans and Revolutionaries. Essays in Seventeenth-Century History presented to Christopher Hill* (1978, repr. pb. 1989)

Phillips, Henry E. I., 'The Last Years of the Court of Star Chamber, 1630–1641', *TRHS*, 4th ser., xxi (1939), pp 103–31

Pierce Penniless (1592), reprinted in Thomas Nashe, *Works*, 5 vols. (London, 1904–10), ed. Ronald McKerrow

Plomer, Henry 'More Petitions To Archbishop Laud', in *The Library*, 3rd ser., X, 39 (July, 1919)

Plomer, Henry, 'Secret Printing During the Civil War', *The Library*, n.s., V (1966), pp 374–403

Plomer, Henry, 'Some Petitions for Appointment as Master Printers called forth by the Star Chamber Decree of 1637', *The Library*, 3rd ser., X , 39 (1919), p 101–16

Plomer, Henry, *A Dictionary of the Booksellers and Printers who were at work in England, Scotland, and Ireland from 1641 to 1667*, The Bibliographical Society (Oxford, 1968)

Power, M. J., 'The social topography of Restoration London', in *The Making of the Metropolis. London 1500-1700*, ed. A. L. Beier and Roger Finlay (London, 1986), pp 119–223

Precepts from the Lord Mayor to the Aldermen of Aldersgate ward, Guildhall MS.1509.

Prior, Mary, 'Women and the urban economy: Oxford 1500–1800', in *Women in English Society*, ed. ead. (London, 1985), pp 93–118

Prose Studies 18 No. 3. Special Issue: 'The Intersections of the Public and Private in early modern England', ed. Paula A. Backscheider and Timothy Dykstal (December, 1995).

Prynne, William, *Canterburies doome. or the first part of a compleat history of the commitment, charge, tryall, condemnation and execution of W. Laud late Archbishop of Canterbury* (London, 1646)

Prynne, William, *Newes from Ipswich* (1641), BL E.177.12.

Pym's Anarchy, Repr. in Bishop Percy's Folio Manuscripts, ed. J. W. Hale and Frederick J. Furnivall (London, 1867)

Quarles, Francis, *Emblems Divine and Moral. With a Sketch of the Life and Times of the Author*, ed. George P. Marshall (London, 1859)

Religions Enemies, The Devil Turn'd Round-Head: Or, Pluto became a Brownist (1642), BL E.136.29

Religions Enemies; The Dolefull Lamentation; John Taylor, *The Devill Turn'd Round-Head: or Pluto became a Brownist* (1642), BL E.1366.29

Robinson, Forrest G., *The Shape of Things Known. Sidney's Apology in Its Philosophical Tradition* (Cambridge/Mass., 1972)

Robinson, Howard, *The British Post Office. A History* (Princeton, 1948)

Rollins, Edward H., 'Martin Parker, balladmonger', *Modern Philology*, 16 (January, 1919), pp 449–74

Rollins, Edward H., *Cavalier and Puritan Ballads and Broadsides illustrating the period of the Great Rebellion, 1640–1660* (New York, 1923)

Roodenburg, Herman, 'The "hand of friendship": shaking hands and other gestures in the Dutch Republic' in *A Cultural History of Gesture*, ed. Jan Bremmer and Herman Roodenburg (Cambridge, 1991; pbk 1993), pp 152–189

Rosnow, Ralph L., and Gary A. Fine, *Rumor and Gossip. The Social Psychology of Hearsay* (New York, Oxford, and Amsterdam, 1976)

Rostenberg, Leona, *The Minority Press and the English Crown: A Study in Repres-*

sion, 1558–1625 (Nieukoop, 1971)

Rowlands, Mary B., 'Recusant women 1560–1640', in *Women*, ed. Prior, pp 149–81

Rublack, Ulinka, 'Pregnancy, Childbirth and the Female Body in Early Modern Germany', *Past and Present*, 150 (1996), pp 84–110

Rysman, A., 'How the "Gossip" became a woman', *Journal of Communication*, 27 (1977), pp 176–80

Sahlins, Marshall, *Islands of History* (London, 1985)

Schenda, Rudolf, 'Bilder vom Lesen – Lesen von Bildern', in *Internationales Archiv für Sozialgeschichte der deutschen Literatur*, 12, ed. Wolfgang Frühwald, Georg Jäger, A. Martino (1987), pp 82–106

Scott, Joan W., 'Gender: A Useful Category of Historical Analysis', *AHR*, 91 (1986), pp 1053–75

Scribner, Robert W., 'Flugblatt und Analphabetentum. Wie kam der gemeine Mann zu reformatorischen Ideen?', in *Flugschriften als Massenmedium der Reformationszeit*, ed. Joachim Köhler (Stuttgart, 1981), pp 65–76

Scribner, Robert W., 'Heterodoxy, Literacy and Print in the German Reformation', in *Literacy and Heresy 1000–1530*, ed. Peter Biller and Ann Hudson (Cambridge, 1994), pp 255–78

Scribner, Robert W., 'Mündliche Kommunikation und Strategien der Macht in Deutschland am Anfang des 16. Jahrhunderts', in *Kommunikation und Alltag im Spätmittelalter und in der frühen Neuzeit*, Österreichische Akademie der Wissenschaften, Phil.-hist. Klasse, Sitzungsberichte Bd. 596 (Vienna, 1992), pp 183–98

Scribner, Robert W., 'Oral Culture and the Diffusion of Reformation Ideas', in *Popular Culture and Popular Movements in Reformation Germany* (London, 1987), pp 49–69

Scribner, Robert W., 'Reformatorische Bildpropaganda', in *Bildkunde*, ed. Tolkemitt and Wohlfeil, pp 83–106

Scribner, Robert W., 'The Printed Image as Historical Evidence', *German Life and Letters*, 48 (July, 1995), pp 324–37

Scribner, Robert W., *For the Sake of Simple Folk – Popular Propaganda for the German Reformation* (London, 1994)

Seaver, Paul S., *The Puritan Lectureship. The Politics of Religious Dissent 1560–1662* (Stanford, 1970)

Seaver, Paul S., *Wallington's World: A Puritan Artisan in Seventeenth-Century London* (Stanford, 1985)

Seven Arguments Plainly Proving That Papists Are Trayterous Subjects (1641), BL E.156/1

Shakespeare, William, *Hamlet*, The Arden Edition of the Works of William Shakespeare, ed. Harold Jenkins (2nd ed. 1984; rpt. London, 1985)

Sharp, Buchanan, 'Popular Political Opinion in England 1660–1685', *History of European Ideas*, 10 (1989), pp 13–29

Sharp, Buchanan, 'Popular Protest in Seventeenth-Century England', in *Popular Culture in Seventeenth-Century England*, ed. Barry Reay (1985, repr.

London, 1988)

Sharpe, James A., 'Defamation and Sexual Slander in Early Modern England: The Church Courts at York', *Borthwick Papers*, 58 (York, 1980)

Shepherd, Simon (ed.), *The Women's Sharp Revenge. Five Women's Pamphlets from the Renaissance* (London, 1985)

Sheppard, Samuel, *The Committee-Man Curried* (1647), BL E.398.21

Siebert, Frank S., *Freedom of the Press in England, 1476–1776* (Urbana, 1952)

Sill, Gertrude G., *A Handbook of Symbolism in Christian Art* (London, 1975)

Sir James Cambels Clarks Disaster, By Making Books (1642), BL E.122.22

Sirluck, Eric, 'Shakespeare and Jonson among the pamphleteers of the Civil War', *Modern Philology*, 53 (1955–56), pp 38–99

Smith, Nigel, *Literature and Revolution in England, 1640–1660* (New Haven and London, 1994)

Sparkes, Michael, *Scintilla or a Light Broken Into Dark Warehouses* (1641)

Sperber, D., and D. Wilson, *Relevance. Communication and Cognition* (Oxford, 1986)

Spufford, Margaret, 'First steps in literacy: the reading and writing experiences of the humblest seventeenth-century autobiographers', *Social History*, 4 (1979), pp 407–35

Spufford, Margaret, *Small Books and Pleasant Histories. Popular Fiction and its Readership in Seventeenth-Century England* (Cambridge, 1981)

Square Caps Turned Into Roundheads, Or the Bishops Vindication, And the Brownists Conviction. Being a Dialogue between Time, and Opinion (1642), BL E. 149.1

Statutes of the Realm 1 Eliz.c.5, 6. A.D. 1558–59.

Steele, R., *Bibliotheca Lindesiana. A Bibliography of Royal Proclamations of the Tudor and Stuart Sovereigns* (Oxford, 1910)

Stempel, W.-D., 'Fiktion in Konversationellen Erzählungen', in *Funktionen des Fiktiven*, Poetik und Hermeneutik, 10, ed. D. Henrich and Wolfgang Iser (Munich, 1983), pp 331–56

Stephen, James F., *A History of the Criminal Law of England*, 3 vols. (London, 1883)

Stevenson, John, '"Moral Economy" of the English Crowd: Myth and Reality', in *Order and Disorder in Early Modern England*, ed. Anthony Fletcher and John Stevenson (Cambridge, 1985), pp 218–38

Stone, Lawrence, *The Crisis of the Aristocracy* (Oxford, 1965)

Stuart Royal Proclamations, 2 vols., (Oxford, 1973), ed. James F. Larkin and P. L. Hughes

Swan, B.F., *Gregory Dexter of London and New England 1610-1700* (New York, 1947)

Taylor, John, 'A Ribble-Rabble of Gossips. Wit and Mirth. Chargeably Collected out of Taverns, Ordinaries, Innes, Bowling-Greenes and Allyes, in *Shakespeare Jest-Books*, ed. William C. Hazlitt, 3 vols. (London, 1864)

Taylor, John, *A Delicate, Dainty, Damnable Dialogue Between the Devill and a Jesuite* (1642), BL E.142.8

Taylor, John, *A Tale in a Tub; or, A Tub Lecture, as it was delivered by Me-heele*

Mendsoale, an inspired Brownist, in a meeting house near Bedlam (1641), BL E.138.27

Taylor, John, *Religion's Enemies* (1641), BL E.176.7

Taylor, John, *The Carriers Cosmographie* (1637)

Tel-troth, Thomas, alias J. Swetnam, *Arraignment of Lewd, idle, forward and unconstant women* (London, 1615)

Thanks to the Parliament, repr. in Rollins, *Cavalier*, pp 139–43

The Actors Remonstrance Or Complaint (1643), B.L. E.86.8

The Adamites Sermon (1641)

The Anatomy of a woman's Tongue, divided in five parts: A Medicine, a Poison, a Serpent, Fire, and Thunder. Harleian Misc., ed. T. Parker, 12 vols. (London, 1808–1811).

The Bishop's Potion, or, A Dialogue betweene the Bishop of Canterbury and his phisitian (1641), BL E.165.1

The Bishops Last Good Night (1641), BL 669.f.4.61

The Bishops Potion (1641), BL E.165.1

The Black Box of Rome opened (1641), BL E.206.1

The Brothers on the Separation; or, a relation of a company of Brownists (1641), BL E.172.11

The Brownists Conventicle (1641), BL E.164.13

The Case of the Undertakers For reducing Postage of inland Letters to just and moderate rates, Stated. And therein, the Liberty of a Commonwealth ... and the birthright of every free-man vindicated from Monopolizing restraints, and mercenary Farming of Publicke Offices [1646]. Harl. MS 5954.6/7

The Cavaliers Bible, A Squadron of xxxvi Severall Religions by them held and maintained (1644), BL E 4/24

The Cities Warning-Peece, in the Malignants description and Conversion (1642), BL E.246.28

The Concise Oxford Dictionary of English Etymology, ed. T. F. Hoad (Oxford, 1991)

The Constitutional Documents of the Puritan Revolution 1625–1660, ed. Samuel R. Gardiner (Oxford, 1979)

The Copie of a Letter sent from the Roamy Boyes in Elizium (1641), BL E.156.8

The Courtiers Health, Firth b.19 (4), undated, probably about the mid-1640s

The Criers and Hawkers of London. Engravings and Drawings by Marcellus Laroon, ed. with an introduction and commentary by Sean Shesgreen (Aldershot, 1990)

The Decoy Duck: Together with the Discovery of the Knot in the Dragon's Tayle called etc. (1641), BL E.132.135

The Devills White Boyes Or, A mixture of malicious Malignants with their much evill and manifold practices against the Kingdome and Parliament (1644), BL E.14.11BM Parthey's Wenceslaus Hollar, No. 483 (1641)

The Diary of John Rous, ed. Mary A. Everett Green (Camden Society, 1861)

The Discovery of a Swarme of Separatists, Or A Leatherseller Sermon Being a most true and exact Relation of the tumultous combustion in Fleet-street last Sabbath day being the 29 Dec (1641), BL E.180/25

The Divisions of the church of England crept in At XV Several Doores (1642), BL
E.180.10

The dolefull Lamentation of Cheapside-Crosse: Or old England sick of the Staggers
(1641), BL E.134.9

*The Downfall of Temporizing Poets, unlicenst Printers, upstart Booksellers, trotting
Mercuries, and bawling Hawkers* (1641), BL E.165.5

*The English Drama and Stage under the Tudor and Stuart Princes 1543–1664. Illus-
trated by a Series of Documents, Treatises and Poems*, ed. William C. Hazlitt (London, 1869)

The Full View of Canterburies fall (1645), BL E.26.1

*The great Eclipse of the Sun, or, Charles his Wane Over-clouded By the evil Influences
of the Moon* (1644), BL E.7.30

The humble petition and information of Joseph Hunscot, stationer (1646), BL E.340.15.

The Just Reward of Rebels, or the life and death of Iack Straw and Wat Tyler (1642),
BL E.136.1

*The King's Cabinet opened: Or certain Pacquets of secret Letters and papers. Written
with the King's own Hand, and taken in his Cabinet at Naseby Field, June 14,
1645, by victorious Sir Thomas Fairfax*, repr. in *Harleian Miscellany*, ed. T. Parker,
12 vols. (London, 1808–1811), vii, pp 544–77

The Kingdomes Monster uncloaked from Heaven (1643), BL 669.f.8.24

'The King's Crown is the Whore of Babylon: Politics, Gender and Communication
in Mid-Seventeenth-Century England', in 'Presentations of the Self in Early
Modern England', *Gender and History*, Special Issue, 7/3, ed. Amy L. Erickson
and Ross Balzaretti (November, 1995), pp 457–81

The Last Advice of William Laud, late Archbishop, to his Episcopall Brethren (1645),
BL E.269.10

The Last Advice. Rainer Pineas, *Anti-Catholic Drama*, Bibliotheca Humanistica and
Reformatorica (New York, 1972)

The Laudians and the Church of Rome c.1625–1640 (PhD dissertation, University
of Cambridge, 1989), pp 128–31

The Leveller Tracts 1647–1653, ed. William Haller and Godfrey Davies (Glouces-
ter/Mass., 1964)

The Levellers in the English Revolution, ed. Gerald E. Aylmer (London, 1975)

The Liar (1641), BL E.169.8

*The Life and Death of Jacke Straw, A notable Rebell in England: who was kild in
Smithfield by the Lord Maior of London*, repr. in *The Tudor Facsimile Texts* under
the supervision and editorship of J. S. Farmer (New York)

The Lineage of Locusts or the Popes Pedegre (undated), BL 669.f.4.21

The Lofty Bishop (1640), BL 669.f.8.32

The Malignant's Conventicle (1643), BL E.80.5

The Malignants Conventicle (1643), BL E.245.24

The Malignants trecherous and Bloody Plot (1643), BL 669.f.8.22

The Organs Eccho (1641), BL 669.f.4.32

The Parliamentary or Constitutional History of England (London, 1762)

The Petition of Alderman Wollaston and other citizens of London. LJ IV.651–52, LJ
      V.78 and LJ V.151
The Poet's Blind mans bough (1641), BL E.172.6
The Poets' Knavery Discovered, in all their lying Pamphlets. Written by J. B. [1641?],
      reprinted in *Harleian Miscellany*, 12 vols. (London, 1808–1811), ed. Thomas
      Parker
The Pope's Benediction (1641), BL E.158.15
The Ranters Declaration with Their new Oath and Protestation (1650), BL E.620.2
The Ranters Ranting (1650), BL E.618.8
The Rebellious Life and Death of Wat Tyler and Jack Straw (1642), BL E.136.1 (1642)
The Resolution of the Women of London to the Parliament (1642), BL E.114.14
The Routing of the Ranters (1650), BL E.616.9
The Sermon and Prophecie of Mr James Hunt of Kent (1641), BL E.172.26
The seven Women Confessors (1642), BL E.134.15
The Sheperds Oracles (1645), BL E.310.20
The Staple of News (1625), ed. Anthony Parr (Manchester and New York, 1988)
The *Stationers' Company Apprentices 1641–1700*, ed. Don F. McKenzie, The Biblio-
      graphical Society (Oxford, 1974)
The Sussex Picture, or, An Answer to the SEA-GULL (1644), BL E.3.21
The Triumph of the Roundheads, Ashm Ms 36.81v., repr. in Rollins, *Cavalier*
The World Is Turned Upside Down (London, 1646)
*The Wrens Nest Defild or Bishop Wren Anatomized, His Life and Actions Dissected
      and laid open* (1641), BL E.165.14
The Young-Mans Second Warning-peece (1643), BL E.78.7
Thomas, Keith, 'Cases of Conscience in Seventeenth-Century England', in *Public
      Duty*, ed. Morrill et al, pp 29–56
Thomas, Keith, 'The meaning of literacy in early modern England', in Gerd Baumann
      (ed.), *The written word. Literacy in transition*, Wolfson College Lectures 1985
      (Oxford, 1986)
Three Figures Ecclesiastical described as Sound-head, Rattle-head and Round-head
      (1642), BL 669.f.6.94
*Three Figures Ecclesiastical, Heads of all Fashions. Being a Plaine Desection or Defi-
      nition of diverse, and sundry sorts of heads, Busting, Jetting, or pointing out vulgar
      opinion*, with a woodcut (1642), BL E.145.17
Three Speeches, Being such Speeches as the like were never spoken in the City (1642),
      BL E.240.31
*Times Alterations or A Dialogue betweene my Lord Finch and Secretary Windebancke;
      at their meeting in France, the eight of January 1641.* BL 669.f.4.5
Tolmie, Murray, *The Triumph of the Saints. The separate churches of London 1616–
      1649* (Cambridge, 1977)
Trevor-Roper, Hugh, *Archbishop Laud 1573–1645* (London, 1940)
Underdown, David E., 'The Taming of the Scold: the Enforcement of Patriarchal
      Authority in Early Modern England', in *Order and Disorder*, ed. Fletcher and
      Stevenson, pp 116–36

Underdown, David, *Revel, Riot and Rebellion. Popular Politics and Culture in England 1603–1660* (Oxford, 1985, pb. 1987)

Untitled broadside (1645), BL 669.f.10.18

Upon the valiant Colonel Alder[...] (1642), Ms, SP 16/490.51

Walker, Henry, *Taylors Physicke has Purged the Divel* (1641), BL E. 163.9

Walter, John, 'Grain Riots and Popular Attitudes to the Law: Maldon and the Crisis of 1629' in *An Ungovernable People*, ed. John Brewer and John Styles (London, 1980), pp 47–84

Walter, John, 'Grain riots and popular attitudes to the law: Maldon and the crisis of 1629', in *An ungovernable People. The English and their law in 17th c. and 18th c.*, ed. John Brewer and J. Styles (London, 1980), pp 47–84

Watt, Tessa 'Piety in the pedlar's pack: continuity and change, 1578–1630', in *The world of rural dissenters, 1520-1725*, ed. Margaret Spufford (Cambridge, 1995), pp 235–72

Watt, Tessa, *Cheap Print and Popular Piety* (Cambridge, 1991, pb. 1994)

Webster, John, *The White Devil*, (1624), ed. John A. Symonds (London, 1959)

Wenzel, Horst, *Hören und Sehen. Schrift und Bild. Kultur und Gedächtnis im Mittelalter* (Munich, 1995)

Whately, W., A *Bride-Bush, or Wedding Sermon: compendiously describing the duties of married persons*, (London, 1624)

Whiting, J. R. S., *A Handful of History* (Gloucester, 1978)

Wickham, Chris, and James Fentress, *Social Memory* (Oxford, 1992)

Wiener, Carol Z., 'The Beleaguered Isle. A study of Eizabethan and early Jacobean Anti-Catholicism', *Past and Present*, 51 (1971), pp 26–62

Wilke, J., 'Geschichte als Kommunikationsereignis. Der Beitrag der Massenkommunikation beim Zustandekommen historischer Ereignisse', in *Massenkommunikation. Theorien, Methoden, Befunde*, Kölner Zeitschrift für Soziologie und Sozialpsychologie, ed. M. Kaase and W. Schulz (Opladen, 1989), pp 57–71

Wilkins, William Walker, *Political Ballads of the Seventeenth and Eighteenth Centuries*, 2 vols. (London, 1860)

Williams, Tamsyn, '"Magnetic Figures": Polemical Prints of the English Revolution', in *Renaissance Bodies. The Human Figure in English Culture c.1540–1660*, ed. Lucy Gent and Nigel Llewellyn (London, 1990), pp 86–110

Winter, Jay, *Sites of Memory, Sites of Mourning: The Great War in European Cultural History* (Cambridge, 1995)

Wiseman, Susan, '"Adam, the Father of all Flesh": Political Rhetoric and Political Theory in and after the English Civil War', in *Pamphlet Wars*, ed. Holstun, pp 134–57

Wohlfeil, Rainer, 'Reformatorische Öffentlichkeit', in *Literatur und Laienbildung im Spätmittelalter und in der Frühen Neuzeit*, Symposium Wolfenbüttel 1981, Germanistische-Symposien Berichtsbände, 5, ed. Ludger Grenzmann and Karl Stackmann (Stuttgart, 1984), pp 41–52

Women and the Literature of the Seventeenth Century, An annotated Bibliography based on Wing's *Short-title Catalogue,* ed. Hilda L. Smith and Susan Cardinale, (New York and London, 1990)

Woodfield, Dennis, *Surreptitious Printing in England, 1550-1690* (New York, 1973)

Woodward, H., *Light to Grammar and all other Arts and Sciences. With a Gate to Sciences opened by a Natural Key,* (1641)

Wrens Anatomy. Discovering his notorious Pranks and Shameful Wickedness with some of his most Llewd Facts and Infamous Deeds (1641), BL E.166.7

Wrens Anatomy. Discovering his Notorious Pranks and Shameful Wickednesse (1641), BL E.166.7

Wright, Thomas, *Political Ballads published in England during the Commonwealth* (London, 1841)

Würgler, Andreas, *Unruhen und Öffentlichkeit. Städtische und ländliche Protestbewegungen im 18. Jahrhundert,* Frühneuzeitforschungen, 1 (Tübingen, 1995)

Würzbach, Natascha, *Die englische Straßenballade 1550–1650: Schaustellerische Literatur, Frühform eines journalistischen Mediums, populäre Erbauung, Belehrung und Unterhaltung* (Munich, 1981)

Yates, Frances, *The Art of Memory* (London, 1966)

Young Kunze, Bonnelyn, *Margaret Fell and the Rise of Quakerism* (London, 1994)

Your Brethren Strange and Lusty, Ashm Ms 36.76r-77r., repr. in Rollins, *Cavalier*

Zemon Davis, Natalie, 'Printing and the People', in ead., *Society and Culture in Early Modern France* (Stanford, 1975), pp 189–226

Index

A

Abell, William, Alderman of London 123
Achinstein, Sharon 2 10 11 17
actors 9
Adamites 86 128 141 172
Aldermen 117
Aldersgate 192
Aldersgate Street 105
Aldgate 142 179
Alsop, Bernard 104 105 106 107
Amsterdam 90
Anabaptists 192 254 272 289 293
Apocalypse, imagery 143 144 173 191 245
Archy, jester at the court of Charles I 32 33 224

B

Bacon, Sir Francis (1561–1626) 185
Bale, John (1495–1563), theologian and reformator 144
ballads 6 16 20 45 86 93 127 129 147 150 163 195 198 200 201 207 240 244 248 249 254 255 257 258 259 260 283 301 302 304
    Bishops' War 257
    burning of 45
    manuscript 149 151 153 158 163

Barebone, Praisegod (c. 1596–1679), leatherseller, separatist 141 173
Barker, Robert (d. 1645), King's printer 66 70 261
Bartlett, John 45
Bastwick, John (1593–1654), physician and clerical pamphleteer 32 34 59 64 143 168
Bates, Thomas 105 107 118 119 120 201 248
Beaumont, Francis (1584–1616), dramatist 251
Bedlam Hospital 96
Bell, Maureen 78 90 95
Bellany, Alastair 129 199
Berghaus, Günter 16
Berkenhead, Sir John (1616–1679), author of Mercurius Aulicus 148
Bill, Edward, servant 109
bishop 3
Bishopsgate 100 142
Bishopsgate Street 99 116
Black, Barbara, widow 255 256 258 259 295
Black Book 97
Bloomesbury 103
Bond, John 6 46 65 84 106 107